Britons in the
Ottoman Empire
1642–1660

PUBLICATIONS ON THE NEAR EAST

*Poetry's Voice, Society's Song:
Ottoman Lyric Poetry*
Walter G. Andrews

*The Remaking of Istanbul: Portrait of an
Ottoman City in the Nineteenth Century*
Zeynep Çelik

*The Tragedy of Sohráb and Rostám from the Persian
National Epic, the Shahname of Abol-Qasem Ferdowsi*
Translated by Jerome W. Clinton

The Jews in Modern Egypt, 1914–1952
Gudrun Krämer

Izmir and the Levantine World, 1550–1650
Daniel Goffman

*Medieval Agriculture and Islamic Science:
The Almanac of a Yemeni Sultan*
Daniel Martin Varisco

*Rethinking Modernity and
National Identity in Turkey*
Edited by Sibel Bozdoğan and Reşat Kasaba

*Slavery and Abolition
in the Ottoman Middle East*
Ehud R. Toledano

Britons in the Ottoman Empire, 1642–1660
Daniel Goffman

Britons in the Ottoman Empire 1642–1660

DANIEL GOFFMAN

University of Washington Press
SEATTLE AND LONDON

Copyright © 1998 by the University of Washington Press
Printed in the United States of America

All rights reserved. No part of this publication may be reproduced or transmitted in any form or by any means, electronic or mechanical, including photocopy, recording, or any information storage or retrieval system, without permission in writing from the publisher.

Library of Congress Cataloging-in-Publication Data
Goffman, Daniel, 1954–
    Britons in the Ottoman Empire, 1642–1660 / Daniel Goffman.
       p.   cm. — (Publications on the Near East)
    Includes bibliographical references (p.   ) and index
    ISBN 0-295-97668-3 (alk. paper)
      1. British—Turkey—History—17th century. 2. Turkey—Relations—Great Britain. 3. Great Britain—Relations—Turkey. I. Title. II. Series: Publications on the Near East, University of Washington.
DR435.B74G64   1998   97-25422
956.1'00421—dc21   CIP

The paper used in this publication meets the minimum requirements of American National Standard for Information Sciences—Permanence of Paper for Printed Library Materials, ANSI Z39.48–1984. ∞

for
Eve and Casper Goffman
and
Louise and Richard McCue

Contents

Preface ix

Acknowledgments xi

Note on Usage xiv

1 / The Proto-Imperialist 3

2 / The Englishman and the Ottoman Other 13

3 / Three English Settlements 29

4 / English Traders on the Ottoman Frontier 45

5 / The Ambassador's Gambit 68

6 / Parliament or King? 88

7 / Pretenders to the Ambassadorship 98

8 / Adapting to the Ottoman Commercial World 125

9 / The Sublime Porte, the Ambassador, and the Provinces 146

10 / An Ambassador Besieged 158

11 / The Commonwealth and the Levant 177

12 / Uniformity Restored 194

13 / Domestic Politics and Worlds Overseas 212

Notes 222

Glossary 268

Bibliography 271

Index 290

Maps

Ottoman Empire, 17th Century   2

Istanbul   32

Izmir   36

Route of Sir Thomas Bendysh   100

Preface

Research and writing in cross-cultural history generate the particular obstacle of mastering the pasts and records of at least two distinct civilizations. The outcome is typically imbalanced, with one civilization becoming remarkable and the others obscure. This predicament usually manifests itself when those trained in European history write about Western encounters with other regions of the world. Because of those cultural assumptions labeled "orientalism" by Edward Said and because of unfamiliarity with the languages and histories of "engendered" civilizations, such writings too often deceptively portray the non-European as indistinct and powerless.

Works on Anglo-Ottoman relations certainly present such skewed portrayals. Historians of the Ottoman Empire and England rely on vastly different methodologies. Simply put, the specialist in English history usually must explore a vast historiographic corpus in order to find lodging in that society's elaborate and sophisticated historical mansion, whereas the Ottoman specialist, struggling with a complex language and a rich yet little explored civilization, faces a virtual tabula rasa and often acts more like a philologist than a historian. It is difficult to combine such disparate disciplines and give each its due. Most attempts to do so have come from English specialists and have resulted in lopsided narratives in which a dynamic and dominant English civilization seems able to act with impunity upon a torpid and waning Ottoman body politic.

As a specialist in Ottoman history, my difficulty has been the reverse: how to master English history and historiography well enough to balance it with an Ottoman world on behalf of which I am shamelessly zealous. I have attempted to do so through the fruitful device of collaboration. In 1987, Mark Charles Fissel, a colleague of mine at Ball State University who specializes in Tudor-Stuart English history, and I decided to combine our skills to investigate the circumstances that led in 1651 to the execution on the scaffold in London of Sir Henry Hyde, a spirited wanderer who drifted between the Ottoman and English worlds during the English civil wars and early commonwealth. This modest beginning plunged us into a four-year labor that not only yielded an article but also taught us enough about each other's fields that we each are now writing Anglo-Ottoman studies of our own. Professor Fissel's enthusiasm for my work, as well as what he has taught me about Stuart England, gave me the confidence to embark upon this intercultural exploration into Ottoman and English civilizations.

This book is not a mere spin-off from our collaboration, however. It derives most essentially from my earlier work on the Ottoman city of Izmir, which in the seventeenth century freed itself economically from Istanbul's control and became a principal conduit for western Europeans into Ottoman domains. This transcultural port city was a caldron of diverse peoples who routinely lived with and accommodated each other's cultures and religions. Studying that town led me to ponder how Ottoman Christians, Muslims, and Jews and their Dutch, English, French, and Venetian interlocutors must have imagined, collided with, and refashioned each other on the cultural borderlands of the eastern Mediterranean Sea. *Britons in the Ottoman Empire* is one outcome of that inquiry.

Acknowledgments

This book has been a decade in the making. It is a pleasant duty to acknowledge some of the people and organizations who facilitated its research and composition.

I have inhabited two history departments during the past several years, one at Ball State University and a second at the Bosphorus University. Individuals at these institutions have each nurtured this project, if in different ways. My talented and rigorous colleagues at Ball State, chiefly Andrew Cayton (now at Miami University of Ohio) and Mark Fissel, helped me conceptualize my ideas in terms of other fields and disciplines and draw upon the sophisticated models of U.S. and British history. Those at Bosphorus, especially Selim Deringil, Edhem Eldem, and Selçuk Esenbel, constitute a supremely gifted, stimulating, and supportive group of Ottoman historians. Becoming a part of that intellectual community in 1993–94 propelled me through the final stages of this project.

The research upon which this book is based demanded long stays in Turkey and England (about three years altogether). Of the many who befriended me during that period, I would like to single out Marise Hepworth and Zara Woolf in London and Belinda and Civan Bakırgil, Mary Berkmen, and Sedef Eldem in Istanbul, who, particularly when my family could not join me, routed my sense of isolation and provided homes away from home.

Oral presentations constitute one of the best ways to test hypotheses and get ideas, and I particularly would like to thank the participants in two seminars for their counsel. One was Conrad Russell's Tudor-Stuart seminar at the Institute for Historical Research in London, where in 1993 I released a trial balloon of chapter five. The other was the Sarıca

Forum in Istanbul, where in 1994 I did the same with chapter four. Presenting my findings in these two cutting-edge arenas, one focusing on English history and the other on Ottoman studies, proved vastly stimulating and heartening.

A number of organizations have supported my research on this book. The Ford Foundation and the National Endowment for the Humanities as administered by the Near and Middle East division of the Social Science Research Council, and the Institute of Turkish Studies, Inc., were the generous sponsors of a nine-month residency in Istanbul in 1986, during which I undertook most of the Ottoman portion of my research. A grant from the American Research Institute in Turkey allowed me to return for three months in 1989 to complete the arduous task of sifting through hundreds of catalogues and thousands of documents. For the English segment, a Ball State University–Westminster College faculty exchange gave me several well-spent months in Oxford in 1991, and the Summer Stipend Division of the National Endowment for the Humanities afforded me another three months in London. Such awards constitute the necessary underpinning of academic research, and I greatly appreciate not only the grants themselves but also these organizations' patience during the several years required to complete the project. Throughout this period, the Office of the Dean of Sciences and Humanities, the Office of the Provost, the Department of History, and the Office of Research at Ball State University supported me with matching and summer research money. Connie McOmber, Ball State's cartographer, skillfully prepared the maps. Such institutional support is rare in this era of slashed budgets and rerouted resources, and I thank my administration and my department for so generously backing my research and writing.

These organizations provided the funding that made this book possible. Others furnished the materials. In Istanbul the personnel of the Başbakanlık Osmanlı Arşivi, in which are housed most documents generated by the Ottoman bureaucracy, courteously responded to my many requests and helped me through that facility's tortuous catalogues. In Oxford and London the professional staffs of the Bodleian Library, the Public Record Office, the British Library, and the Library of the School of Oriental and African Studies assisted me professionally and graciously, as did the staff of the Library of Congress in Washington, D.C., particularly Dr. Christopher Murphy.

Acknowledgments

At every stage in its development, a book is a collaboration. Its final stages call for cooperation between an author and a publisher, in this case the University of Washington Press. Several readers—Virginia Aksan, James Alsop, Carolyn Goffman, and two anonymous readers for the press—rigorously critiqued this manuscript in its penultimate form and delivered it from some serious factual and structural errors and failures of interpretation. The University of Washington Press assigned a copy editor, Jane Kepp, who not only smoothed my prose but also caught many textual inconsistencies. I of course bear sole responsibility for any remaining errors in form or content.

Finally, I wish to thank my family, who have lived this project for several years. When I began it, Laura had not yet been born, and Sam was too young to know much more than that daddy was busy (and too often grumpy) because of his work. They relocated several times—to Istanbul or London or Oxford—because of their dad's job. Only slowly have they begun to comprehend what that work is and why I am doing it. What a pleasure it has been for me to see their own intellects grow as they embark on their own creative endeavors.

Even though Carolyn understood what I was up to from the beginning, my debt to her has grown ever larger, ever more intellectual. Not only has she been my comrade throughout this book's development, but much of whatever is cross-disciplinary about it derives from conversations with her and my readings of her writings in postcolonial literature. The rest I obtained from my American and Turkish students during a well-spent decade of conversation in my symposia in global studies.

Britons in the Ottoman Empire is dedicated to my parents and my wife's parents for their sustained support, both emotional and financial, and for their broad-mindedness.

Note on Usage

Constructing and maintaining a "scientific" procedure of transliteration in a book concerned with cross-cultural history seems not only frightfully complicated and unnecessarily pedantic but also a perversion of the historical realities of a world that was essentially polyglot. Such is particularly the case in regard to the many persons in this narrative who inhabited several linguistic worlds simultaneously (for example, does one employ Abraham, Avraham, Avram, or İbrahim?). Consequently, I have remained as much as possible true to the documents upon which this book is based. Some decisions have unavoidably been made, however. Seventeenth-century orthography, even within a particular language and even of names, was variable. For example, the English ambassador in Istanbul in the 1650s signed his own name capriciously as Bendysh, Bendyshe, Bendish, or Bendishe. I have chosen in this and other cases the spelling that seemed commonest.

Transliteration of terms recorded in the Arabic script is a second area in which one must make decisions about spelling. For the sake of simplicity, in these cases I have adopted modern Turkish orthography (except for words that have found their way into the English language, such as kadi or pasha). Several simple rules will allow the reader to pronounce these words with some accuracy:

c sounds like the English *j*
ç sounds like the English *ch*
ğ is silent but lengthens any preceding vowel
ı sounds like the *a* in *serial*
j sounds like the French *j*
ö sounds like the French *eu* in *peu*

ş sounds like the English *sh*
ü sounds like the French *u* in *lune*

Vocalization that stresses no syllable generally is the most faithful. Ottoman terms are contextually defined in the glossary and can be found with their Ottoman-Turkish spellings in *The New Redhouse Turkish-English Dictionary* (Istanbul: Redhouse Press, 1968).

Britons in the
Ottoman Empire
1642–1660

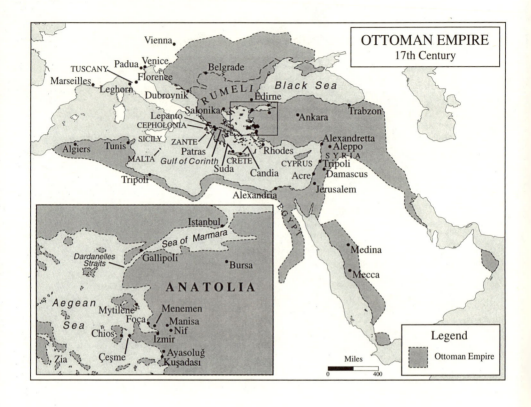

1 / The Proto-Imperialist

> We call ourselves insular, but the truth is that we are the only race on earth that can produce men capable of getting inside the skin of remote peoples. Perhaps the Scots are better than the English, but we're all a thousand per cent better than anybody else.
> —John Buchan, *Greenmantle*, 1916

The Englishman overseas is often viewed as the imperialist incarnate. We recall how he exercised, through his sense of religious, cultural, and racial superiority, an unparalleled conceit which helped bring England vast colonies in America, Asia, and Africa. We recollect that he also encouraged the English government to rationalize a mistreatment of peoples and their cultures which horrifies our postmodern sensibilities. The English colonial, with an overweening, almost mystical sense of mission, seems to have forced his politics, language, and culture upon ostensibly passive and unsuspecting colonies around the world.

This image of a mature, even sanguine, Englishman abroad is perhaps not so far from certain nineteenth-century realities. Yet students of the sixteenth through the eighteenth centuries have sometimes succumbed to the temptation to transfer this haughty imperialist, unaltered, to their own periods when investigating English diplomats, travelers, and settlements.[1] The Indian-American novelist Bharati Mukherjee recently wrote of a late-seventeenth-century English merchant in India, with some irony, to be sure, that "it was unthinkable that a noble Englishman, the fairest of God's creatures on earth, should be stripped and flogged by men under a distant authority." Mukherjee, writing in her sweeping historical novel *The Holder of the World*, whose English colonial and modern American heroines inhabit three continents and are informed by the cultures of both American and Asian Indians, further related that this "first condemned Surat factor, white skinned, blue veined, suety from long hours in some local punch house, had died of apoplexy when the flogger raised his arm."[2] While it is perhaps imaginable that Buchan's early-twentieth-century Englishman might have died from such an outrage, it is doubtful that a seventeenth-century Englishman, perched precariously on the edge of the mighty Mughal Empire almost two centuries before the establishment of the British Raj, would have responded so self-destructively to a humiliation.

In an Eastern setting at least, such depictions reek of ahistoricality. Given the relative insecurity of his position in the East, it seems more likely that the seventeenth-century Englishman, in his guises as merchant, diplomat, and even missionary (the three types who usually ventured to Asia), was more accommodating, sensitive, and respectful toward his powerful hosts than were his more intransigent, acerbic, and contemptuous nineteenth-century progeny. In short, the Englishman's imperialism is not innate, and his image as an imperialist is a transfigured one created by the changing relationship between the growing power and prestige of his own state, on one hand, and, on the other, the receding abilities of the societies he sought to enter and exploit to resist the importunities of the powerful second British Empire. Perhaps the nineteenth-century Briton could get under the skin of the colonial; in the seventeenth-century Mughal and Ottoman empires, it was more likely the Englishman whose shell would be pierced.

Nevertheless, the power and splendor of the great Muslim empires of the early modern world did not invariably compel English compliance. Drawing perhaps on that sense of religious superiority which characterizes the civilizations of both Christianity and Islam, individual Britons aggressively pursued both their state's and their own interests, even in the face of overwhelming demographic, geographic, political, and military might. Particularly during the 1640s and 1650s, when the internal turmoil of the English civil wars and interregnum seemed about to bring down their own state and society, English diplomats, merchants, and divines marched, often boldly and effectively, across the Ottoman commercial, political, and ideological terrain.

In the pages that follow, I seek not only to reconstruct the middle ground between the civilizations of the Ottoman and British empires in the mid-seventeenth century but also to re-create the lives of some of the people who inhabited that territory. Henry Hyde, a royalist adventurer, in the early 1640s simultaneously held influential posts in the administrations of the Ottoman Empire (as *voyvoda* of Patras) and the English Levant Company (as consul of the Morea, or Peloponnesus). Under commission from the exiled Charles II in 1649–50, Hyde subsequently tried to wrest first the consulship of Izmir and then the ambassadorship itself from company control, and in 1651 lost his head as a traitor to England at the scaffold in London.

In 1646, an obscure career diplomat stationed in Venice sold to the impecunious Charles I a desperate scheme to grab the wares of English merchants living in the Levant in order to help finance the king's war against parliament. Sir Sackvile Crow, as Charles's ambassador in Istanbul, disastrously turned to the Ottoman government for aid in his attempt to implement this design. As we will see, it was other Englishmen—most of them members of the English communities in Istanbul and Izmir—who colluded with Ottoman officials in order to thwart this internecine conspiracy and deport first Crow and then Hyde to commonwealth England. Thus was the crisis in England mirrored in the Levant by way of company, parliamentary, and royalist sympathizers. In the name of loyalty and ideology, Englishmen battled in the streets and markets of Istanbul, Izmir, and Aleppo for control of the company's men and assets.

Great compromisers as well as fervent royalists and parliamentarians also inhabited this exilic world. Indeed, one might anachronistically label Crow's successor to the ambassadorship, Sir Thomas Bendysh, a Teflon diplomat. No one ever quite fathomed his political sympathies; he seemed equally relaxed with company and parliament, with Charles I and Cromwell, with royalist and roundhead. Bendysh guided the Levantine English community effectively through the crises that plagued both the English and Ottoman states and societies—and all of absolutist Europe—during the mid-seventeenth century. This book is about this community of expatriate eccentrics and the eastern Mediterranean borderlands they inhabited and helped recast into a shape more responsive to English and eventually British aspirations.

The British Empire collapsed after World War II, and even though England has preserved its cultural influence by means of its language and its neocolonies in the Americas and Oceania, the English state's political and economic power has withered. Despite this breakdown, the brazenness embodied by Buchan and other late imperial authors still distinguishes many English travelers in the postimperial world. A Turkish friend who speaks perfect British English, for example, tells the story of his chat with an English businessman in the departure terminal of the Atatürk International Airport in Istanbul. As the Englishman picked up his bags to board his plane, never having fathomed that he was speaking to a native, he departed with the guilelessly stinging remark: "Lovely country. Pity about the inhabitants."

Oliver Cromwell might have uttered a similar comment as he surveyed his Irish conquests in 1650. The tossed-off phrase reflects, if tritely, one archetypal image of the English wayfarer's attitude toward the rest of the world. An assumption of this image's innate accuracy in regard to all Englishmen permeates even the most sophisticated historical scholarship. Speaking of "English encounters with alien peoples," for example, the American historians Bailyn and Morgan note the "pervasive trait" of "English hostility to, or at least disdain for, the people they encountered and engendered."[3] Such an assertion, which tends to caricature and demonize an entire nation, flies in the face of the authors' laudable intent (characteristic of late-twentieth-century scholarship) to depict a first British Empire that was multicultural and diverse and whose boundaries and very definition were ever-shifting.

Bailyn and Morgan join other scholars in efforts to compensate for the excessive chauvinism that typifies much of English historiography. Even the most recent works on the English civil wars and interregnum have hardly begun to consider the broader British dimension—that is, the three very different political crises involving England, Scotland, and Ireland which brought about that conflict—much less worlds overseas. Hirst, in an article on the meaning of "Britain," considers almost exclusively Irish and Scottish policies in the English republic and concludes that although the Cromwellian regime may have been "shaped by its British subjects," this early exercise in imperialism nevertheless affirmed and intensified a deep-seated English chauvinism.[4] Ashton's comprehensive work on the causes and events of the second civil war (1646–48) makes not the slightest reference to Charles I's lunge for Mediterranean money and manpower and consequently misses a vital (even though non-British) dimension of the royalist struggle during those years.[5] Perhaps most striking is an article by Pincus that surveys English relations with the "world" during the 1650s. The author projects his investigation no further than the Catholic-Protestant rivalry as reflected in English relations with the Netherlands and Spain.[6]

In 1975, in a prescient article, Pocock argued for the inclusion of the conquered in imperial history, adding how difficult it would be to give these people existence, for the conqueror "sets the rules of the game; he determines, in proportion to the extent to which his domination becomes effective, what people shall do, how they shall think, and what they shall remember."[7] The author's reasoning, summarized in his assertion that "the fact of a hegemony does not alter the fact of a plurality, any more than the history of a frontier amounts to denial that there is history beyond the advancing frontier,"[8] focuses steadily upon the British case. His logic can be applied to other domains as well. What of the frontier *between* two hegemons, for example? Does not one also find a pluralistic and plastic boundary between two empires such as the Ottoman and the British?[9] Does not the plurality of such a borderland inspire its inhabitants just as surely as does the advancing frontier of aggressive imperialism?

In light of Pocock's summons, Bailyn and Morgan's incorporation of the British colonies into their imperial framework is a radical and welcome departure from the hidebound historiography championed especially by the "Little England" school.[10] In their bid to correct the dominant image in English historical writing that focuses almost exclusively upon the English in studies of British imperialism, they imagine and seek to construct a new historiography that will accelerate the process of integrating non-English peoples into that momentous story. The new historiography's vision is not revolutionary enough, however; Bailyn, Morgan, and their collaborators derive their proofs exclusively from the island's early modern triumphs. Their approach fails to appraise the concurrent English contacts with non-British civilizations and the way those civilizations might have influenced the Briton.

Consistent with Bailyn and Morgan's notions, their collection of essays considers Scotland, Ireland, colonial America, Africans in the Americas, the West Indies, and Canada. Although a diversity of peoples and their comminglings forged and helped make unique these frontier societies in the seventeenth and eighteenth centuries, in each case the English ultimately dominated and largely defined the terms of the mix. Despite an intent to scrutinize non-English peoples, each author in the resulting anthology determined (in most cases quite rightly) that ultimately none of their English protagonists confronted a people, a culture, or a state that might have defeated them. The result is a framework of British supremacy that remains teleological and, I believe, illusive. In short, the very model that the editors selected (which by definition neglects early English encounters with the peoples of future colonies such as India or Malaya) determined the misleading conclusion of an inevitable English triumph and a ubiquitous English haughtiness during the period of the first British Empire.

Correctives to such perceptions are not hard to find, for the English triumph was *not* universal. Indeed, even in the West, some settlements and colonies failed abjectly, in some measure from Native American resistance, and all their destinies diverged markedly.[11] In the East, where the early imperialists encountered peoples they could not swiftly and easily "engender" (or, preferably, refashion or exploit), it took centuries for them to advance much beyond "trade and plunder."[12] In seventeenth-century south and southeast Asia, for example, the initial encounters were at best a stalemate and sometimes produced serious reversals for the English. In the Ottoman Middle East—in the port towns where Englishmen resided long before the imperialistic seventeenth century dawned—it was they and not their alien associates who had to conform. Whereas there is little evidence that British culture much influenced Ottoman society during this period, many of the individual Britons who resided in seventeenth-century Ottoman settlements such as Aleppo, Istanbul, Izmir, and Patras found themselves conforming to their environments. They changed their behaviors and sometimes even their convictions about the world and England's place in it.[13]

The historian of British empires may protest that to compare intra- and interimperial encounters is to measure apples against oranges, and it is true that whereas one confrontation undeniably involved a massive military, material, and organizational imbalance, the second occurred between well-matched (if fundamentally dissimilar) realms. But this is to consider only consequent trajectories. One should not forget that initially it was the same English worm that confronted both the permeable colonial apple (the Americas) and the solid imperial orange (the Ottomans, Mughals, and Manchus). In any case, historians lately have begun to emphasize that even within his own empire the English sojourner (and how much more the colonist!) encountered a great diversity of peoples who were not always easily broken and who changed him in manifold ways.[14]

Scholars have not often acknowledged, or even conjectured about, how much an Ottoman sojourn could influence individual Englishmen.

Despite its increasing sophistication, even more than the historiography of cultural boundaries between peoples within the first British Empire, English scholarship dealing with the cultural margins of the empire itself has continued to be smothered by its insularity and anglocentrism. Despite methodological refinement, the documentary underpinning of recent research upon the English Levant Company and its representatives has not moved much beyond that of the early-twentieth-century formative works of craftsmen such as Chew and Wood.[15] Wood considered the 1640s and 1650s disastrous for English trade everywhere, especially in the Levant. As he argued, "in such circumstances it was natural that a body like the Levant Company ... should suffer from the effects of the [English civil] war, and such evidence as is available shows that its trade was adversely affected."[16]

Vaughan, writing some twenty-five years later but carrying similar assumptions and employing virtually the same data base, did not question Wood's judgment but ascribed the failings to personality rather than political circumstances. She declared that the successors to Sir Thomas Roe, ambassador in the 1620s, "were less able men, and the Civil War and Commonwealth produced the spectacle of two rival English envoys at the Porte [the grand vizier's chambers in Istanbul]. It was not until England's military and naval reputation had been built up afresh by Cromwell and Blake that she carried much weight in the sultan's neighborhood."[17]

Even though such sweeping assessments thoroughly confuse the circumstances with the persons, they remain unchallenged in even the most recent scholarship. Andrews, despite a brilliant discourse upon plunder and trade and an admirable integration of domestic and international concerns into his analysis of early English expansion, could still proclaim that "ambassadors, consuls and factors in the Levant ... generally failed to bridge the cultural gap between Turkey and England or to develop meaningful contact with the Turkish people."[18] Anderson, in her exhaustive and multilayered biography of Paul Rycaut, a shrewd English diplomat and penetrating scholar who spent most of his adult life in Istanbul and Izmir,[19] seems baffled by his subsequent discontent in the quiet and predictable England of the Glorious Revolution.[20] Brenner, in his massive and thorough analysis of commerce during the late sixteenth and early seventeenth centuries, mentions neither Crow nor Bendysh (the English ambassadors in Istanbul during the 1640s and 1650s) and seems oblivious to anything happening outside the City of London, much less England (a slight widening of the angle of his vision would quickly have brought down his thesis concerning a royalist and reactionary English Levant Company).[21] Each of these authors largely neglects even the substantial English-language scholarship on Ottoman social and economic history, probably because it seems irrelevant in terms of some anachronistic assumptions about the structure of the British Empire.

It is both fascinating and puzzling that in our age of unprecedented sensitivity to multiculturalism and diversity, these and other analyses of early English probes into the eastern Mediterranean still depict the Islamic Ottoman Empire as an immobile and almost irrelevant backdrop for English ventures. They seem unable to do much better than allude to that complex and subtle realm—which was, after all, England's primary communicant in the region—as "Turkey" or "the Turkish state," or even more absurdly to personalize this largest state in the world as "the sultan." Such phrases comprise banal and crude reductions of the Ottomans and their varied civilization. The culturally—even racially—arrogant subtext of this neglect probably is in part a reflection of England's second rather than its first empire and in part an expression of a national hubris that seems dismally pervasive in the late-twentieth-century world.[22]

The investigator into any empire has the daunting task of fighting through the master's vision of the past in order to uncover (or at least imagine) a likeness of the vanquished. In the British empires beyond the Atlantic archipelago (and perhaps in some parts of those islands as well), the challenge is sharpened because, through a deconstruction and reinterpretation of the conqueror's sources, the historian must often try to reconstruct an encounter between one people who had written records and a second who did not. This assignment is formidable. Indeed, it may be that the venture to decode and reconstitute the illiterate society's transformed past sometimes is in vain, and that such worlds must remain imagined.

At first glance, an examination of the confrontation between the Ottomans and the English seems not to share this formidable obstacle, because both the British and Ottoman civilizations were richly literate and left many accessible depositories of seventeenth-century texts and documents. The undertaking has corresponding obstacles, however, for the distinct organizations of the two states and societies generated vastly different sorts of paperwork. Thus, one of the foremost problems for a researcher into Anglo-Ottoman connections is the troubling dissimilarity between the two sets of sources, which yield few instances of topical overlap. Whereas extant English writings are often personal, anecdotal, and psychologically revealing, Ottoman sources—despite an occasional splendid narrative—tend to be administrative, dry, and oblivious to often historically significant, sometimes farcical, and always revealing intercultural encounters.

This difference may be caused partly by the Ottoman failure to establish commercial organizations such as the English companies that produced rich and plentiful personal correspondence. Or it may derive from the practices of a civilization that, despite a vast accumulation of written materials, preserved a strong oral tradition even at the highest administrative levels. It seems likely, for example, that the messengers (*çavuşes*) who helped project imperial authority into the Ottoman provinces possessed more detailed instructions about, and more profound understandings of, their particular problems than is represented in the rather summary rescripts that empowered them. Arbel has proved—on the basis of Venetian rather than Ottoman sources—the critical role of such pursuivants in late-sixteenth-century Veneto-Ottoman relations,[23] and English manuscripts counsel that several mid-seventeenth-century Anglo-Ottoman affairs engrossed such Ottoman agents far more thoroughly than Ottoman sources suggest.

One objective for the historian who wants to explore Anglo-Ottoman contacts, therefore, must be to give the Ottomans a voice. A related and even more troubling dilemma is that of deciphering, or deconstructing, the Ottoman materials from which such a voice must be fashioned. Most historians, even those who are citizens of Ottoman successor states, feel more comfortable with western European than with Ottoman sources because they are trained in Western techniques, models, and thought processes, which developed out of a European rather than an Ottoman or other corpus of sources. This is a form of orientalism to which postcolonial intellectuals also fall victim and which it is difficult to imagine how to counteract. Whatever the root of the problem in dealing with two sets of sources, the two collections of Ottoman and English documents stubbornly resist fusion into a fluid historical narrative.

One example may serve to illustrate the point. This book sets out to examine those marginalized Britons who populated the cultural and commercial overlays between the British and Ottoman worlds during the mid-seventeenth century. The British Library, the Public Record Office, the Bodleian Library, and other English depositories are rich with details about these adventurous characters. Yet in the thousands of Ottoman documents and narratives through which I have combed, only Thomas Bendysh (a prominent character in the narrative to follow) is referred to by name—twice.[24] Although men such as Robert Bargrave, Henry Hyde, and Sackvile Crow enlivened the Ottoman and English worlds as well as this book, we still know frustratingly little of their Ottoman peers, much less of specific encounters between representatives of the two civilizations.

Unfortunately, in the current state of Ottoman studies we can do little more than sketch the Ottoman context without really fleshing out the personalities who inhabited it. Perhaps we can contextually conceive of how they must have lived and what they might have thought. Nevertheless, few historians are yet willing to resort to such slippery methods in order to fill, imaginatively, the enormous gaps in our knowledge.[25] Until we are ready to do so, or until a new type of Ottoman source appears, or until we make more thorough and creative use of available materials,[26] cross-cultural Anglo-Ottoman narratives, such as this one, must continue to utilize Ottoman sources for context and English ones for chronology and narrative integrity.

2 / The Englishman and the Ottoman Other

One of the first non-Christian environments in which Englishmen established a presence was the Islamic Ottoman Empire. In the late sixteenth and the seventeenth centuries, Dutch and English innovations in commercial techniques propelled these two states into competition with their European rivals and generated dramatic changes in commercial relations between Christian Europe and the Muslim Middle East.[1] Representatives of these Atlantic seaboard states introduced myriad technological and administrative alterations to commercial undertakings in the eastern Mediterranean and elsewhere.

ENGLISH ADMINISTRATION

The most striking novelty lay with the ships that carried the Dutch and English to the Levant. Whereas the Venetians, Genoese, and Ottomans had developed their vessels to meet the requirements of contiguous Mediterranean waters, merchants from these two western European states had to cut first through the turbulent and unpredictable Atlantic before venturing into the relatively placid Mediterranean. Accordingly, by absorbing and adapting Iberian models, they built wind-driven rather than oar-driven ships that were smaller, stronger, better armed, and more maneuverable than those fashioned by their Mediterranean competitors. These unconventional craft proved particularly formidable within the Straits of Gibraltar, not only in legitimate commerce but also in preying upon and plundering galleys, galleons, and other vulnerable vessels.[2]

Although such ships had begun roaming the Mediterranean before the 1580s, those who fully exploited their potential were the joint-stock establishments (the English and Dutch Levant companies) these western European states subsequently established. Rather than gamble great fortunes on large but relatively secure ventures or invest small amounts in several riskier projects, these organizations could use the relatively small contributions of many investors to outfit and dispatch large, chancy, and potentially lucrative commercial undertakings. And because their governments granted them regional monopolies and occasionally even furnished them navies, such companies of merchants could establish unprecedented commercial and even political networks and presences across the Levantine world. In other words, they could, and eventually did, command more resources, act more patiently, punish more certainly, and plan more thoroughly than did or could the individual merchants or even the communal trading diasporas that until the 1580s had dominated Mediterranean commerce.

For the English, the center of this commercial web was London, where the company's principal merchants resided. From this nucleus, company members dispatched representatives, whom they termed "factors," to the Ottoman domains and elsewhere to manage the company's transactions. By the early seventeenth century, several dozen of these factors residing in Istanbul, Izmir, Aleppo, and other Ottoman cities had organized themselves into communities, designated "factories," complete with appointed consuls, treasurers, and ministers. At the head of this organization stood an envoy—soon to be labeled ambassador—who resided in Galata, just across the Golden Horn from Istanbul proper.

Until after the Stuart restoration of 1660, this representative was not, strictly speaking, an ambassador, for it was the company rather than the monarch or parliament who picked him. From the very beginning, however, the state claimed a stake in this selection, and the gnarled issue of whether the ambassador's first allegiance was to monarch or company clouded the first century of Anglo-Ottoman relations, as did the matter of the English consuls. The company, the ambassador, and the consuls' respective factories each wanted to choose, supervise, and contain consular representatives. The company attempted to do so by making the position salaried, which acted also to make the English consuls freer than their French and Venetian rivals from the intrigues and discords of the cutthroat marketplaces of the Levantine world. These English ambassadors, consuls, and factors who inhabited Ottoman frontier cities had to deal with each other, their company, and their home government as well as with their Dutch, French, and Venetian rivals.

It soon became clear that the advantages the English held over their commercial rivals were notable. As the English Levant Company found in Istanbul a market for domestic broadcloth and other textiles, the Ottoman government developed a dependency upon English gunpowder and tin. The rugged sailing vessels that carried English merchants and goods not only let licensed English craft roam Levantine waters with relative impunity but also permitted English renegades to engage in profitable marauding and smuggling. Indeed, the Venetian and Ottoman governments soon began soliciting English aid in their recurring and crippling wars.

Although the struggles between these two states occasionally imperiled Englishmen residing in Mediterranean port cities, more often the menace of English sea power, or the offer to supply it, provided political and commercial leverage for English diplomats and merchants. Furthermore, the monopolistic pretensions and relative autonomy of the English Levant Company both centralized and depoliticized its policy decisions. The company's ability to appoint and its willingness to provide salaries for its servants furnished its ambassadors and consuls with unrivaled competence, loyalty, and longevity.[3]

Owing principally to such advantages, the English soon challenged the French as the dominant foreign factory in Istanbul. The capitulations that Ambassador Henry Lello was able to wring out of the Ottomans in 1601 certified English prominence.[4] Yet this success did not mean that an English ambassador could simply settle in and pilot a well-oiled machine of British diplomacy, commerce, and imperialism. A disparate and seemingly endless array of crises confronted ambassadors Wyche in the 1630s, Crow in the 1640s, and Bendysh in the 1650s.

Changing fortune produced some of these difficulties. When the English Levant Company was fledgling and weak, the queen or king of England paid it little heed. Elizabeth I, who first incorporated it, granted the company generous entitlements to appoint consuls and envoys and to collect consulage and other duties. Her heirs were less magnanimous. As commerce between England and the eastern Mediterranean flourished in the early seventeenth century, first James I and then Charles I, immured in fiscal emergencies, coveted and attempted to seize some of the company's profits.[5] They also sought to appropriate ambassadorial appointments. The English civil wars of the 1640s only sharpened and made ideological a struggle that even before 1642 had already drawn in and divided the English "nation," or community of Britons, in the Levant, even as the desperate conflict hardened English representatives overseas.[6]

Company achievements drew envy from other quarters, too, particularly from the established trading states of the Mediterranean world. For centuries, Venice had cultivated the commerce of the Levant.[7] The city-state had only recently driven its Italian rivals from the sea, and it enjoyed a near monopoly along its eastern commercial corridors. It did not welcome new rivals. Nor did the French, whom the Dutch and English had virtually thrust out of the Atlantic and who, since the 1530s, had been building their own Mediterranean commerce through the trading city of Marseilles. Both the Venetians and the French fought bitterly against English and Dutch incursions into the Mediterranean economy. Their understanding of Ottoman procedures helped force Dutch and English representatives to master them as well, and to push the newcomers deep into the morass of Ottoman politics.

OTTOMAN ADMINISTRATION

The English faced many challenges in what was to them the profoundly novel Ottoman civilization. Simple translation—of both language and culture—was the most immediate obstacle to Anglo-Ottoman communications. Dragomans (who were more often indispensable interpreters than mere translators) helped surmount this barrier. These intermediaries, usually polyglot Armenian, Jewish, or Greek Orthodox Ottoman subjects, served as salaried retainers to English ambassadors and consuls, who depended utterly upon their presence in dialogues with Ottoman officials and many other subjects. Indeed, dragomans probably never translated negotiations verbatim; to do so would have been rash, dangerous, even life-threatening, because of misreadings of words, intonations, and gestures. Their task was more to convey content—to decode signals transculturally—than literally to render text, and their abilities to interpret and even "touch up" statements engendered power. Fluency, therefore, was not the only required skill. Even more valuable were savoir-faire and discretion.[8]

Britons made use of these dragomans in negotiations with myriad Ottoman officials and subjects. They included viziers, pashas, kadis, *yasakçı*s, *çavuş*es, and *emin*s, all of whom were important figures in the Ottoman elite. Although none of these officials is easily defined or described, English agents and their dragomans had to deal with all of them occasionally and some every day.

Viziers, who sat on the imperial divan and acted as the Ottoman sultan's public voice, stood at the apex of the Ottoman administration. The most visible part of the English ambassador's job was to negotiate with the grand and other viziers for privileges and petition them with complaints. For the consul (in Aleppo at least), a pasha, who represented Ottoman military power in many provincial centers and in the field, served a similar function. Some of the most dramatic and revealing cross-cultural encounters between Ottomans and Britons occurred in audiences Englishmen had with grand viziers and pashas. Such volatile moments stretched the interpretive talents of dragomans to their fullest.

Viziers and pashas were not the most influential Ottomans in English lives, however. *Yasakçı*s, janissary gendarmes appointed to serve and protect foreigners, were in daily and often intimate contact with English diplomats and traders. *Çavuş*es, who conveyed decrees and communications from the sultan and his viziers to the Ottoman provinces as well as other states, sometimes traveled and worked closely with Englishmen over extended periods. Muslims invariably retained all of these appointments.

Such was not the case with *emin*s, or stewards, who tended to be either Armenian or Jewish and with whom many English merchants held particularly acrimonious relations. A certain type of *emin* purchased licenses from the state to gather customs in the ports and cities of the Ottoman Empire. Each time a factor conveyed wares into or out of the empire, he had to pay a percentage to this official; each time such a trader attempted to smuggle merchandise, his purpose was to evade the *emin*. In short, the English factor's business was to avoid customs, and the *emin*'s duty was to collect tariffs. These clashing agendas induced enmity and produced periodic complaints and lawsuits.

In Istanbul, the ambassador could air such grievances in the imperial divan; elsewhere, English factors and their representatives usually went first to the kadi's court. The kadi was the chief magistrate in an Ottoman city, where his judgments were meant to rest upon first Islamic, then sultanic, and then, as a last resort, customary law. The state also called upon him to execute sultanic decrees (particularly in a city such as Izmir, where no pasha resided). A *çavuş,* for example, before carrying out a vizier's orders, might first confer with the town magistrate. Although this judicial system was sophisticated and relatively fair, to English factors it seemed alien and arbitrary. Consequently, Britons turned to the Ottoman courts only as a last resort.

Circumstances, nonetheless, forced foreigners to employ the Ottoman judiciary with some regularity. The diversity of Ottoman society also spawned autonomous Greek Orthodox, Armenian, and Jewish legal edifices. One consequence of this heterogeneity was a profusion of cross-communal lawsuits, in which most litigants favored the relative impartiality of the Islamic court over the perceived capriciousness of communal tribunals. Normally, the kadi himself would make a judgment. In exceptional circumstances, a suit might find its way to Istanbul, accompanied by an *arz,* or petition, from the magistrate. The Briton in the Ottoman Empire found himself enmeshed in a most complex and unsettling world.

OTTOMAN RELIGION AND ETHNICITY

To visitors from the Atlantic seaboard, Ottoman society seemed no less alien than did Ottoman administration. The realm in which these Englishmen had now to operate differed radically from their own, a land that was both distant from Mediterranean loci of power and commercially rather feeble—not yet the nucleus of a vast empire. The most fundamental contrast probably lay in the attitudes of England and the Ottoman Empire toward religious and cultural diversity. England, on the one hand, shared with the rest of Christian Europe a demand for uniformity. The English had achieved relative homogeneity by either banishing or forcing public conformity upon those subjects who seemed too remote from English mores. Although the crown at times could license certain "foreign" religious practices, English society was essentially intolerant and cast out both Catholics and those who espoused religions other than Christianity. Furthermore, although there were some corporate divisions within England, it utilized a ponderous system of customary laws in order to construct a civic impartiality for those whom it defined as English (in religion, in language, in culture), even as it excluded those who did not fit this definition.

In contrast, Ottoman society pretended no such exclusive equality. The Ottoman state did not deal with the "other" (apart from the zealous heretic) by either expulsion or an imposed uniformity but by encompassing differences within the empire's political structure and religious ideology. In particular, the Islamic state did not require Christians and Jews to convert or be driven into exile but allowed them religious and even political and cultural—that is, corporate—autonomy in return for special taxes and certain other actual as well as symbolic liabilities (an ordering of society often called the "millet" system).[9] This social construct was eclectic, varied, and bafflingly enigmatic to the seventeenth-century Englishman (our late-twentieth-century grasp of it is not much better, even—or perhaps particularly—among citizens of Ottoman successor states).

Historians of the Ottoman Empire have long considered the millet, denoting the fundamentally religious structure through which the Ottoman state administered and taxed its religiously, ethnically, and linguistically diverse non-Muslim subjects, to be one of the fundamental building blocks of Ottoman society. The rationale for this assumption has been that, just as the fundamental legitimacy for Ottoman rule lay in Islamic religious law (the Shariah), so was the state's governance of its many Christian and Jewish religions and sects couched in the pronouncements of the Koran and the actions of the prophet Muhammed. Since non-Muslim "people of the book"—Ottoman Armenian, Greek Orthodox, Roman Catholic, and Jewish communities—retained relative autonomy in most spheres, or so scholars usually contend, it is proper to study the empire's administrative, social, and even economic structure through its distinct ethnoreligious components. Those interested in specific segments of Ottoman society argue, at least implicitly, the validity of isolating these communities from their immediate milieus.[10]

The assumption that there was a sweeping, pristine, and somehow organic Ottoman millet system overlooks the way each of these communities constituted an inseparable part of an ever-changing Ottoman whole.[11] The Western-influenced and highly bureaucratized millet system of the nineteenth century differed immensely from the structure that existed four centuries earlier, which may have been largely inchoate. Similarly, the system that predated the conquest of Constantinople (1453) differed dramatically from the one that followed, and the one organized after the Ottoman conquest of Syria and Egypt in 1516–17 differed from the one induced by the Treaty of Karlowitz (1699).

Indeed, the very plasticity of the millet system constituted its genius, and foreigners daily had to confront and cope with this unsettling flux. Even during a single era, the realities of intercommunal relations differed dramatically in various parts of the far-flung and diverse Ottoman realm. For example, one Ottoman firman, issued on 24 August 1614, answered a Venetian grievance against members of Greek and Armenian millets living in Jerusalem who impeded a Greek Orthodox congregant from attending Latin services. Another sequence of Ottoman decrees issued in the 1630s and 1640s reacted to "priests, bishops, and archbishops of the Serbian millet" who ventured to prevent Latin monks from wandering through the Ottoman Balkans offering comfort and prayers to Ottoman subjects of the "Latin millet."[12] Such proclamations verify that rather than actively oppressing Christianity in the empire, the government in Istanbul often acted as referee between rival Christian faiths, and at least in the early seventeenth century, Ottoman bureaucrats occasionally used and interpreted the concept of "millet" inconsistently.[13]

Discerning such an essentially semantic issue is important because millet consciousness affected communication between the various segments of Ottoman society and between those elements and the outside world. Such a system linked components of Ottoman society and economy that might seem to us, in an era dominated by national polities, irreconcilably hostile. In short, although early modern Ottoman society rested upon a theory of basic inequality among the members of its body politic, it was in fact far more inclusive—or pluralistic—than was England or other rigidly Christian European states. This social order delivered Britons into daily contact with a mélange of peoples.

THE FOREIGNER IN OTTOMAN SOCIETY

It should be obvious, then, that this empire was no monolith. The Ottoman world was remarkably disparate and contradictory. It was not sufficient for Englishmen embarking upon careers in the Ottoman milieu to acquire a cursory understanding of Islam and Ottoman civilization; they also had to learn the peculiarities of whichever Ottoman city, usually Istanbul, Izmir, or Aleppo, they chose to inhabit. Istanbul was the Ottoman capital, home to the empire's government (the Sublime Porte) and thus a political as well as a commercial center. There, the English ambassador and merchants coped with astute and long-sojourning French, Venetian, Genoese, and Dutch representatives as well as a cluster of Ottoman—that is, Muslim, Jewish, Orthodox, and Armenian Christian—politicians, officials, merchants, and shopkeepers.

Whereas the Englishman in mid-seventeenth-century Istanbul had to bargain with both Ottoman and English central authorities, his compatriot in Izmir could pretty much ignore them. Izmir, which had scarcely existed forty years earlier, was a product of the very transformations that allowed Englishmen to perform so notably in the Ottoman milieu. An ever-changing roster of local dignitaries, some of them English, dominated trade there. English consuls in Izmir often could employ local political and economic networks to shield their factory from the bloody Ottoman intrigues of the 1650s, as well as from the vicissitudes of English civil war, interregnum, and restoration politics.

The lines of Ottoman and English authority were even more tenuous and thus more fluid in Aleppo. First, the city was not a port. Because it was landlocked, its merchants had to employ caravans to transport silks and spices from the east and deliver them to the coastal towns of Alexandretta and Syrian Tripoli. At each of these sites, merchants negotiated with provincial Ottoman officials (as well as with chieftains) who regularly interpreted imperial directives according to local conditions or to serve personal ends, and did so with impunity. Customs collectors (*gümrük eminleri*) were especially well placed to exploit constantly shifting lines of authority. These men often were both government officials—who increasingly purchased their rights to collect dues—and influential notables—who carefully maintained links with coreligionists and other local power brokers. They had, in the eyes of Western merchants, a reputation for avarice, but they probably achieved it not because they were more corrupt than other officials but because consuls and merchants grew frustrated at their inability to use the authority of the Sublime Porte in order to defeat the *emins*' stratagems. Compatriots of these Aleppine factors who lived in Istanbul or even Izmir were much more effective at summoning to their aid the power of the central government.

The Dutch, English, French, and Venetians residing in Levantine port cities had to integrate themselves into this rich cultural and geographic pluralism. Initially, the Ottoman state defined such alien communities according to Islamic law. That is, they legally became *müste'min*—communities of foreigners who were granted temporary rights of residence in the Ottoman dominion. The practice of functioning as a part of, rather than parallel to, the remarkably flexible Ottoman society followed accordingly. Although categorizing foreign merchants as *müste'min,* through the vehicle of the *ahdname* (the so-called capitulations), granted their communities special privileges and obligations, it did not mean their factories could function according to "Western" judicial traditions.[14]

Indeed, the factories had to be constantly vigilant in order to avoid absorption into Ottoman society. Incursions into communal autonomy could occur at several levels, as the Venetian community of Galata discovered in 1605–6. On one front, janissary watchmen, candle makers, and customs collectors tried to assess taxes on meat and suet bought and butchered for the Venetian community, as if it were a millet. On a second front, Ottoman administrators ventured to collect a head tax (*cizye*) from dragomans and doormen serving the Venetians, as if they were unprotected non-Muslim Ottoman subjects. And on a third front, tax collectors and janissaries attempted to categorize as non-Muslim subjects Venetian merchants who leased shops in the bazaars of the city.[15] Several decades later, the problem had intensified; in 1646 and again in 1651, the French ambassador denounced the attempt of the government's agent (*voyvoda*) to gather a head tax from Frenchmen living in Galata.[16]

These incidents illustrate the precariousness of foreign autonomy in the Ottoman Empire, and it cannot be too strongly emphasized that both the term *müste'min* and the ideas behind it developed out of the Ottoman and Islamic world rather than out of the English, French, or even Christian or Enlightenment ones. Only as the Ottoman Empire's relationship with other European powers changed, especially in the eighteenth and nineteenth centuries, was the West able to pluck these merchant groups from the Ottoman body politic and impose its own principles over them.[17] For earlier periods, it makes more sense to view these communities as part of the Ottoman social structure than to view them as superimposed yet separate entities.

Imagine how unprepared the Englishman who confronted such a society must have been! England, it should be remembered, had for several centuries kept itself free of Jews, Muslims, and Armenian and Greek Orthodox Christians. In truth, before the English traveler met such people in the eastern Mediterranean, they constituted only abstractions to him. Yet such groups resided and even thrived in the Ottoman Empire. They also had carved out distinct economic spheres there. The resultant socioeconomic structure, so different from England's, meant that English merchants, diplomats, and pilgrims had to exhibit not only enormous flexibility in their business practices and travels but also a tolerance, even if feigned, for which their English culture could not have prepared them.

An English diplomat disembarking in Istanbul in the middle of the seventeenth century was unable to communicate directly with high Ottoman officials; his go-between often was a Jew. The Englishman consequently was forced into professional reliance upon an utterly unfamiliar sort of person, one whom English society had marked as naturally mendacious and even demonic. An English merchant arriving in Izmir might be tempted to engage an Armenian or Greek broker in order to penetrate the commercial culture of that port town, even though members of these communities were barred from residence in his native England because of their heretical forms of Christianity. An English pilgrim entering Aleppo en route to Jerusalem might have had to hire several Muslim janissaries—fearsome types, according to his English education—and remain under their protection throughout his Syrian trek. In short, in order to survive in the Ottoman Empire, the English sojourner had to adapt quickly and competently to his new environment.

A CULTURAL BORDERLANDS

At most times such cultural chameleons are rare. In the 1640s and 1650s, however, England experienced a political and social disorder that thoroughly jolted long-held suppositions about the body politic.[18] Nonconformists, preaching fantastic theosophies and theologies that assailed the very bases of Christian dogma, roamed the streets of

London. Some even demanded the readmittance of Jews or Christian dissenters into England, or questioned the authority of the House of Stuart. The English diplomat, trader, or divine who traveled at that time embarked from a tumultuous island that was, however briefly, deviating from relative uniformity and becoming a society that could better appreciate (even if it could never truly condone) the type of inclusive pluralism that characterized Ottoman society.

This dramatic shift in English politics and society combined with new phenomena within the Ottoman Empire to ease the maneuverings of the English there. The alterations simultaneously disrupted the commercial endeavors of others, particularly the Venetians, whose traditions and outlook fastened them to a commercial structure that was quickly becoming obsolete.[19] By the middle of the seventeenth century, English factors, consuls, and ambassadors had proved particularly effective at combining their cultural knowledge of the Ottoman world with English commercial institutions, individual acumen, and their experiences in England, which was itself unraveling both socially and politically. This blend was critical to English economic expansion into a foreign, mercurial, and sometimes hostile world. These people were a far cry from the stereotypical English imperialists of a later time, who carried England with them. Men with such attitudes could not have survived in the still vigorous and confident Ottoman realm. Rather, they were more nearly marginal men, even cultural hybrids, who prospered by learning to live with, rather than by trying to recast, the civilization with which they had to treat. These Britons attempted to use their knowledge of that world; they did not and dared not either openly condemn or attempt to transform it.

English merchants and diplomats throughout the empire had to get along with Ottomans (Muslim as well as Armenian, Greek Orthodox, and Jewish), and English accomplishments in Aleppo, Izmir, and Istanbul depended upon a continuous cross-cultural dialogue. Younger people usually adjusted most easily, for the Ottoman way of life charmed, mesmerized, and often seduced young Englishmen who sought fame and fortune in the empire in the mid-seventeenth century. Robert Bargrave, for one, in 1647 accompanied Sir Thomas Bendysh to his post as English ambassador in Istanbul. They landed first at Izmir, where the youth described with enthusiasm his introduction to the easygoing opulence of foreign life in the Ottoman realm:

> [W]e were at length invited by the Nation to a Generall Enterteinment, in a wood about :6: miles distant from the Toune: where they treated us Alla Turchesca to the height: Holes were dugg in the Earth for Chimneys, our Spitts were made of Sticks, our burning wood chopt as it grew; our Carpetts spread und'r a Shady tree, beside a Fountaine of delicat water; & we all feeding on the ground a cross legg: but the Complement of our Entertein the wood it Selfe produc'd, in great varieties of curious Fruits, to say Grapes, Pomegranads, Wallnutts, Chestnuts, small nutts, aples, Figgs & Plummes.[20]

Such an introduction to the food, the weather, the company, the rich tradition, and the vistas of the Anatolian coast must have impressed men like Bargrave, who often threw themselves into their new environs wholeheartedly and soon excelled at communicating with the fearsome "orientals" among whom they lived.

The routine into which Bargrave inevitably settled once established in Istanbul did not much dampen his enthusiasm. Although he resided in the congested quarter of Pera, he spent a good deal of time "in a fair Country palace, about :6: miles distant from the City, where we had many pleasing divertisements, & sundry Priveledges graunted us by our noble Patron."[21] The English factory's Ottoman patron in Istanbul was Mahmut Efendi, a member of the religious elite (*ulema*) who served as chief religious magistrate (*kadiasker*) for both Anatolia and Rumeli, and with whom Ambassador Bendysh enjoyed a warm friendship. He, Bargrave, and others of his nation frequented Mahmut Efendi's estate, which

> was situat on the side of a litle Hill, over a pleasant narrow Dale, which was embrac'd by a Rivolett in two Branches, & fenc'd with woods almost round it: such as afforded a various & a pleasant chace of wild Boars, of woolves, of Jackalls, & of wild Deere: so that we seldome wanted Venison of sundry sorts, besides Phasant, Partridge, & wild=foule in cheap Plenty.[22]

Thus, Bargrave's initial conception of an Ottoman cornucopia was not disappointed.

Nor was more titillating diversion lacking. The factor described Ottoman households who visited the estate and shared with the English its spacious quarters and grounds. Oftentimes, Bargrave reported, "came theyr great Families of Concubines to recreat themselves, attended only by theyr Eunuchs, not contented unless they saw the Franks Chambers ... & there enterteining themselves & us, with Dauncing, Leaping, & roaring like wild persons let out of a Prison." Such tantalizing depictions of the female occupants of harems circulating among foreigners may represent wishful thinking, or they may have been meant to play to English desires and expectations.[23] Nevertheless, they present a startling portrait of eminent Ottoman women, a group that, although known to have had some indirect access to power through their husbands and masters,[24] usually is assumed to have been notoriously isolated.

ENGLISH LIFE WITH THE OTTOMANS

We often imagine a factor of the English Levant Company to have been an impoverished younger son who made his fortune as quickly as possible and then hastened back to the familiarity, serenity, and civility of England. Such was sometimes the case. Richard Lake, a factor in Aleppo during the late 1650s and early 1660s, wrote dozens of frantic letters home to his mother, sister, mistress, principals, and close friends, pleading for commissions so that he could make his fortune quickly and return to England. He lived and breathed for the arrival of caravans from Alexandretta, not for the goods they transported but for the mail they too infrequently delivered.[25]

Homesickness sometimes vanished with time (Lake's letters gradually lose their sense of desperation), and certainly it was not universal. John Erisey, for example, arrived in Istanbul in 1645 or even earlier and died there some twelve years later. His extensive estate suggests an established and contented existence.[26] His abode in Pera was richly appointed with carpets, books, and dozens of chairs, tables, and other furnishings, and he had also organized a second home in Belgrade.

The list of Erisey's creditors and debtors suggests a career firmly embedded in Istanbul's diverse commercial world. Among his professional associates were the Greek Giorgiachee, the "Morish Frank" Herkim Ogli, and the Jews Joseph Cario, Signior Gallipoleet, Nesim and Rosalles Pardo, Abraham, Jacob Habshim, Joseph Capoano, Exeno, and Jacob son of Nephtali. Some of these non-Christian businessmen had secured important accounts with Erisey, and their names occur frequently in the inventory of his estate.[27] The prominence of "renegade"

Christians and Jews among them declare how thoroughly Erisey had adapted to a society that boasted a multiplicity of beliefs.

There is much additional evidence of such cordial, even intimate, relations between Englishman and Ottoman. In 1670, John Covel recorded effusively the English community's attendance at a Muslim circumcision. Several years earlier, one of Ambassador John Finch's closest friends was an Ottoman customs collector. At about the same time, Consul Paul Rycaut regularly frequented the homes of Ottoman officials and viziers, and in the 1650s, the English merchant Edwards often hosted lavish parties at which hobnobbed Ottoman Muslims, Greeks, and representatives from the various nations of western Europe. The Chevalier d'Arvieux described these gatherings:

> I was one of those who used to assemble on most evenings at the house of M. Edouard, a well-known English merchant.... [His wife] was young and beautiful, and had waiting on her four Demoiselles, who were not inferior to herself in youth and beauty and who made many of us youngsters sigh.... Often there was a dance, and afterwards supper. Greek ladies were invited ... came, and enjoyed it.... Turkish guests, who were at first greatly shocked at these goings on, became accustomed to them.[28]

Such social relations were a concrete and continuing affirmation of English and Ottoman explorations into each other's civilizations.

The crossing of the cultural barrier was not only social, however. English ambassadors (most notoriously Sir Sackvile Crow) and consuls employed Ottoman authorities to strong-arm their own compatriots. English ship captains negotiated and renegotiated port charges and anchorage dues with customs officials, and English merchants often negotiated with native Christians, Jews, and Muslims and confronted them in Ottoman law courts. They could not shrug off or dominate these encounters as their nineteenth-century successors did. Rather, such meetings powerfully influenced these men and the commerce they directed. They were not yet imperious Englishmen overseas, personifying empire wherever they strode. They often developed an acute understanding of, and even sympathy for, the diverse peoples and cultures among whom they lived. They punctured, however tentatively, the hard boundaries defined by the English nation, its culture, and its language. After long separations from their homeland, many became professional expatriates who were restless in and discontented with the monotonous homogeneity of England during the late interregnum and restoration, and who were effective only while overseas in Istanbul, Izmir, or Aleppo. The immediate result of these early encounters was often a reluctant respect for (and occasionally open adulation of) the society which the Englishman was visiting. It is unfortunate, but fascinating and perhaps symptomatic of Western civilization, that these men's achievements ultimately begot self-congratulatory disdain toward the societies over which England came to reign.

3 / Three English Settlements

Although English vessels had prowled the eastern Mediterranean much earlier, official relations between England and the Ottoman Empire began in the 1580s with the establishment of the English Levant Company and that organization's decision to send a representative, soon designated ambassador, to the Ottoman capital city of Istanbul.[1] The company quickly expanded its activities, organizing consulates at Aleppo, at Patras (Patrai) in the Morea, on the Aegean island of Chios, at Syrian Tripoli, at Alexandria, and at Algiers. It also attempted, less successfully, to found communities of English merchants at Ankara and Trabzon. By the 1620s, the three cities of Istanbul, Izmir, and Aleppo had emerged as the principal "factories" of the English "nation" in the Levantine world.

A REMOTE ENTREPÔT

In the seventeenth century, each of these cities boasted a thriving English colony. Nevertheless, only Istanbul and Izmir thoroughly participated in the events with which this book is concerned; Aleppo was undoubtedly marginal. This asymmetry developed in part because the sea road between London and Istanbul bypassed Aleppo and in part because, as an outcome of Izmir's sudden commercial and political emergence in the early seventeenth century, the English nations in Istanbul and Izmir acted almost as antipodes during the years of the English civil wars and interregnum. English factors in Aleppo often had almost no influence over and relatively little knowledge of the ideological and corporate battles then raging in the English factories in the other two Ottoman cities.

The English factory of seventeenth-century Aleppo was more distant and isolated than Istanbul's or Izmir's, at least in its Ottoman context.[2] This divergence was perhaps not seen from the perspective of London, where the English factory of Aleppo seemed as prominent and powerful as those of its rival Ottoman cities. When viewed from Istanbul or Izmir, however, Aleppo seemed a political and economic backwater, and its factory played relatively little part in the intracommunal turmoil that riddled the other two sites.

Just as important as geopolitics and the logistics of communicating from and regulating a city so distant from Istanbul was Aleppo's historical role in the Ottoman world. The Ottomans had conquered Aleppo relatively late in the history of their state. By the time their armies marched into the city in 1516, they already were a mighty empire, committed to their capital in Istanbul and firmly entrenched in both the Balkans and Anatolia. At the same time, the Ottomans, as an Islamic state, could not simply ignore the historical relevance of Aleppo. Although not as sacred as Mecca, Medina, Jerusalem, or even Damascus, as a chief city of the Arab world Aleppo enjoyed a particular, almost sacrosanct, status in the Ottoman mind. Consequently, the state hesitated from imposing on the city the same economic, military, and land-tenure systems that it had devised for its earlier conquests, achieved mainly at the expense of Christians.[3] Instead, the Ottomans accommodated themselves to the institutions, the notables, and even the language (which, after all, was that of the Koran and the Prophet) of Aleppo and other Arab lands.[4]

This inordinate sensitivity to regional custom had notable ramifications for merchants from England and other Christian European states. Most strikingly, Venetian, French, English, and Dutch colonies could not simply mold the commercial landscape to their liking, as they sought to do in Izmir with some success. Instead, they had to fit themselves into preexisting regional and international networks long controlled by well-established organizations and individuals. This environment gave not only indigenes but also the ensconced Venetians and French an edge over English and Dutch interlopers.

Furthermore, none of these alien merchants could much rely on their representatives in Istanbul to deliver them from rivals and abuses or to execute their demands. Aleppo was simply too distant from the Ottoman capital for effective enforcement, and the Sublime Porte's power there was typically indirect, dispersed, and difficult to identify. Of course, Ottoman decentralization in the seventeenth century affected Syria as well as western Anatolia.[5] Nevertheless, the effects of military and fiscal reorganization at the political core reverberated differently in the two territories. Whereas the English merchant in seventeenth-century Izmir confronted local authorities who themselves tended to be recent creations, those in Aleppo usually arose out of existing networks. In the former case, all parties, including those based in Istanbul, had to explore a commercial and political frontier together; in the latter, it was more a case of rediscovering and recasting long-present commercial and political organizations and traditions. The advantages that novelty brought to the frontiers of western Anatolia could become drawbacks in the more ossified commercial terrain of northern Syria.

In general, the factor living in distant Aleppo was less concerned with Istanbul than was his compatriot in the more accessible Izmir, and the English official in Istanbul tended to be more responsive to the demands of the English factory in Izmir than to those of its counterpart in Aleppo. Consequently, Aleppo's commercial and even administrative tendrils stretched out to the east and the west, rather than to the north, and the English factory there lived in a separate world, far removed from Istanbul, the hub of Ottoman and English power in the eastern Mediterranean.[6]

ISTANBUL

In the decades before 1453, the Ottomans had pushed far into southeastern Europe. Beginning with their beachhead in the Gallipoli peninsula in 1354 or thereabouts,[7] Ottoman armies thrust northward and eastward up the tributary river valleys of the Danube, relentlessly consuming Byzantine, Latin, and other Christian territories in southeastern Europe. The Byzantine state, which already had lost its Anatolian lands to these and other Islamic conquerors, now faced encirclement. Although it took time for the Ottomans to smash through the walls of Constantinople, the heart of the eastern Roman Empire, when they finally did so in 1453 it spelled the end of Byzantium.[8] The conquest also was a new beginning, for it reunited the two halves of a water-linked empire, and Istanbul soon resurfaced as the center of the eastern Mediterranean world.

ISTANBUL

The city revived both economically and politically. Merchants constructed a network of international commerce with Istanbul as its hub. Its threads reached out via Crimean ports to Russia, via Zagreb and other Balkan cities to the Habsburg Empire and Poland, via Salonica, Dubrovnik, and the Aegean islands (as they fell one by one under Ottoman control) to Italy and the western Mediterranean, via Bursa and Trabzon to Persia, and via Aleppo and Alexandria (after 1516–17) to the Indian Ocean and the east. These routes brought bullion, woolens, leathers, furs, silks, and spices into and out of the Ottoman Empire. Several communities shared in profits from these trades. Armenians, Jews, and Muslims dominated the commerce in silk; Italians, Jews, and Muslims controlled East Indian spices; Italians exchanged textiles; and Greeks and Jews monopolized wines.[9]

The montage of peoples who made up the Ottoman polity and the empire's intricate socioreligious organization of them energized this elaborate commercial network. After some vacillating, the Ottoman conqueror of Constantinople, Mehmed II, chose to transfer his capital from Edirne (Adrianople) to the substantially depopulated capital of Byzantium. Once the decision had been made, he acted forcefully to repopulate and reinvigorate the city.[10] Its reduced inhabitants were encouraged to remain, and Turks were urged to settle there. Greeks who had fled before or had been swallowed by the Ottoman advance were persuaded to return. Armenian merchants and shopkeepers were urged (and sometimes compelled) to follow suit, and most of the Jews of the Ottoman Balkans and Anatolia were resettled, sometimes by coercion, in Istanbul.[11] The sultan granted each of these communities considerable religious and even legal autonomy and subsidized their relocations with substantial tax breaks.

The new rulers of Istanbul also utilized the Genoese colony of Galata, across the Golden Horn from Istanbul, in order to help integrate their city into the seaborne commercial corridors linking the Mediterranean and Black Seas. Mehmed negotiated commercial agreements (capitulations) with the Genoese, as well as with Venetian representatives who hurried to his presence as soon as news reached the Italian port city that Constantinople had fallen. These agreements imitated previous ones between Latin trading states and Levantine powers, and they contributed to relative stability and continuity in the eastern Mediterranean world of commerce, despite the region's sudden and violent ideological and geopolitical metamorphosis.

By the time Mehmed II died, in 1481, Istanbul was the largest city in his empire. Indeed, the site's natural advantages, joined with the Ottoman Empire's ability to accommodate, even as it devoured, a kaleidoscope of religions, peoples, and states, soon made it the largest and liveliest metropolis in the Mediterranean world. As the commercial, political, and military nucleus of a vast and expanding empire, it also became massively complex and notoriously difficult to manage, boasting an enormous imperial household, a vast revenue-collecting bureaucracy, a growing military establishment, and a complex and eclectic industrial and commercial sphere.

A bewildering tapestry of peoples—Armenian, Greek, Jewish, and Muslim—drove Istanbul's economy, attracted to the city by both its natural advantages and the receptiveness of Mehmed II and his heirs to immigrants and non-Muslims. The city soon became renowned for its consumerism. As the political, military, and commercial center of an immense empire, it sucked in the best provisions, the most luxurious goods, and the most talented people. Few commodities or people ever escaped.[12] Like old-regime Paris, Istanbul became infamously parasitic.

By the time the English Levant Company arrived some one hundred thirty years after the city's conquest by the Ottomans, Istanbul stood at the core of the largest state in Europe and the Middle East. It was the focus of a highly ritualized system of government and a bewilderingly elaborate and voracious military and commercial complex. The city, in fact, had become three cities (which together retained the name Constantinople), each with its own character and distinct function. The finger of land that had constituted Christian Constantinople remained the administrative and political capital of the Ottoman Empire. The Ottomans called this district of the city "Istanbul." Within its Byzantine walls were the empire's principal mosque complexes (including Mehmed's, Süleyman's, and Ahmed's), the sultan's sprawling palace, and a host of crowded Armenian, Greek, Jewish, and Muslim quarters.

Just across the channel that divides Europe from Asia, at the point where the Bosphorus debouches into the Sea of Marmara, Üsküdar developed. This predominantly Muslim suburb became the chief Asian colony of the capital city, functioning as a conduit for peoples and goods en route to and from Istanbul. A large fleet of small boats (*kayıks*) continuously plowed through the waters of the strait, linking Üsküdar, as well as settlements across the Golden Horn, to the city's heart and soul.[13]

Galata completed the tripartite Ottoman capital. Located just across the Golden Horn from Istanbul, this town had for centuries served as a residence for Latin merchants. In the sixteenth century, western Europeans joined their southern associates and helped transform the site into a hub for international trade, politics, and intrigue. Its development drove the colony physically upward on the landscape, and by the early seventeenth century the fashionable quarter of Pera had materialized on the hillside above Galata. It was there that ambassadors and other foreigners built their lodgings, there that they lived and entertained, and from there that they periodically plunged down to the Golden Horn and embarked in *kayıks* for visits to the imperial palace or occasionally explosive meetings with high Ottoman officials.

From the Ottoman perspective, Pera became notorious as a stronghold for foreign and often idiosyncratic peoples, behaviors, beliefs, and infamies. All the foreign nations residing there enjoyed various exemptions from Ottoman sumptuary laws, most infamously those governing dress and the production and consumption of wine. Ambassadors and wealthy factors took particular delight in their well-stocked cellars, perhaps envisioning them as indispensable perquisites of a daunting post. They dreaded and vehemently resisted the periodic Ottoman crackdowns on the vending and consumption of alcohol, usually incited by popular riots protesting such ungodliness.[14] The government occasionally intervened on its own initiative, as it did in 1647 when, after a fire had engulfed several taverns in Galata, a non-Muslim Ottoman subject requested permission to rebuild them. The Sublime Porte refused because of an adjacent mosque.[15] Usually, however, the wine flowed freely in private residences as well as in public taverns along the boulevards and back alleys of the quarter, advancing Pera's reputation for foreign irreligiosity.

Not that Galata and Pera entirely deserved their disrepute. In fact, the communities were far less "Western" or "Christian" than is frequently supposed, and demographically at least, they remained overwhelmingly Ottoman and even Muslim (although probably a majority of these subjects served foreign masters as servants, dragomans, brokers, and shopkeepers). Nevertheless, in the popular imagination Galata remained the prototypical alien implant and became the model for similar "infidel" settlements in Aleppo, Izmir, and elsewhere.

The physical and functional segregation of the three districts—Istanbul, Üsküdar, and Galata—each espousing distinct roles and personas, perhaps made a complex city more manageable. Still, the metropolis's rich yet hidebound traditions, replete with religious, military, political, bureaucratic, economic, and commercial overlays, must have seemed baffling, particularly for someone arriving from a land as rigorously uniform as England. Wading through the alien mélange demanded experience and acumen, a polyglot's talent for language, and uncommon pluck. The English diplomats and merchants who arrived in Istanbul from their small and relatively backward island not only had to learn to compete against Venetian, Jewish, Armenian, and other seasoned rivals (as well as other newcomers such as the French and the Dutch) in this perplexing and protean world but also had to resolve the stunning contradiction between their deep sense of religious and cultural superiority and the facts of Ottoman domination, competence, and refinement.

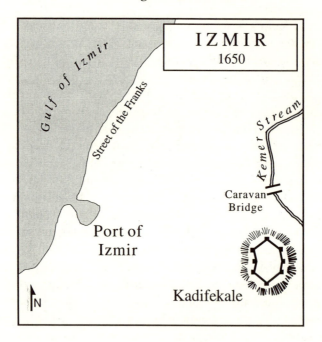

IZMIR

Whereas Istanbul was already an established political and commercial capital when the Ottomans conquered it in 1453, in the classical Ottoman Empire Izmir (Smyrna) was a town of little political and economic consequence.[16] Under Roman and Byzantine rule the port had enjoyed periods of vigor, most recently during the Byzantine interregnum of 1204–61, when the emperor founded a capital-in-exile at Nicaea and utilized Smyrna as his principal port. It also had enjoyed a brief resurgence in the fourteenth century under the Turkoman emirate of the Aydınoğlus.[17] Generally, however, the port had languished before the definitive establishment of Ottoman rule in western Anatolia during the 1420s. Its troubles had derived in part from the Byzantine Empire's fixation on its European territories, in part from the proximity and success of alternative port cities such as Foça (Phocaea) and Ayasoluğ, and in part from the presence, until 1402, of a band of Christian crusaders who stubbornly clung to Izmir's lower castle, turning the town into an ideological frontier and acting to extinguish commerce there.

The reconsolidation of Ottoman rule in western Anatolia after the interregnum of 1402–13 did not much improve Izmir's condition. It is true that Manisa, whose natural harbor Izmir was, became a principal training ground for Ottoman princes such as the future Murad II and Mehmed II. Nevertheless, so long as Constantinople existed, both Latin traders and the Ottoman sultan remained fixated on that imperial capital. Genoese and Venetian traders continued to build their Black Sea and Aegean empires around Constantinople; Murad II and Mehmed II continued to focus their power and energy upon its Balkan hinterlands.

After 1453, the enthrallment of western Anatolia and Izmir to the new Ottoman capital only deepened the region's provincialism. Its dependence derived in part from the sultan's inability to capture control of the Aegean; as late as 1472, a Venetian fleet penetrated Izmir's gulf and pillaged and torched the town. More important in Izmir's inability to develop were the reemergence of Istanbul as a parasitic city and the Ottoman vision of western Anatolia as one of its hosts. In the late fifteenth and the sixteenth centuries, the region served as the new capital's chief supplier of fruits. Sultanas from Manisa and Marmara, figs from Izmir, and raisins from Izmir, Menemen, and Nif dominated the markets of the capital city. Izmir, as a potential urban concentration in western Anatolia (that is, as a dormant parasite), could pose a threat to this provisioning network. With their strictly centrist view of their realm, Ottoman authorities in Istanbul strenuously resisted the progress of such a rival.

Izmir thus remained little more than an agricultural town until the early seventeenth century. When it finally began to flourish commercially, it did so despite Ottoman opposition. The impetus behind Izmir's success was the same global realignment in commerce that contributed to English expansion into the Levant.[18] Before about 1620, Bursa, Aleppo, and Alexandria had retained their positions as middle cities in the ancient spice trade that dominated global commerce. After that date, pepper, cinnamon, and even silks and porcelains became less central to international commerce in the Middle East as bulkier goods such as woolens, cottons, and dried fruits began to displace them. Izmir's location on the seaboard of a rich western-Anatolian hinterland attracted merchants seeking these products.[19] Several decades later, Persian silks also began to find their way to the port town. Consequently, during the very period that historians often oversimplify as the beginning of Ottoman decline, the town embarked upon dramatic economic and demographic growth.

Indeed, the very failures of the central government quickened Izmir's affluence. In the late sixteenth and early seventeenth centuries, the Sublime Porte's control over western Anatolia loosened, the lines of authority became fragmented and localized, and the Ottoman provisioning network weakened. At the same time, new trading states—principally England and the Netherlands—in search of new commercial opportunities used innovative techniques to exploit such indigenous changes. From about 1610 to 1630, Dutch and English merchants, and then their French and Venetian counterparts, ignored or repudiated Istanbul's commands, dealt independently with local brigands and notables, probed the Anatolian hinterlands, and carved out superimposed and largely autonomous trading networks.[20] They strove, quite successfully, to reconfigure trade in western Anatolia. The world of Anatolian commerce no longer revolved almost exclusively around Istanbul. Izmir's fate depended increasingly upon policies, even attitudes, formulated locally and, ultimately, in London, Paris, and Amsterdam.

A concurrent settlement in Izmir of Armenians, Greeks, Jews, and Muslims reflected these global transformations. The proprietors of the consulates and homes that sprang up along the Street of the Franks, stretching along the town's seafront, demanded servants, brokers, money changers, customs collectors, and tavern keepers. Representatives of every ethnoreligious group filled these positions. Many flooded into the town to profit from the commercial network that was insinuating itself into the valleys of western Anatolia. The creators of the system eagerly exploited their assorted skills.

The Armenians are a good example of this movement of peoples. Although Izmir's initial growth derived from demands for bulky commodities, by the 1640s silk dominated commerce in the port town. This redirection of the silk trade from Bursa and Aleppo was an opportunity for Armenian merchants whose commercial diaspora already stretched across much of the Middle East and Europe.[21] They helped construct a caravan network that linked Izmir to silk-producing regions in Persia. The demographic result was that whereas in 1600 virtually no Armenians lived in Izmir, by the 1650s a community of several thousand had settled there.

The town also drew large numbers of the Greek Orthodox from nearby Ottoman villages and towns. The most dramatic such relocation came from the island of Chios, which juts up out of the Aegean near Izmir's gulf. Throughout the 1500s, the island, under indirect Genoese control until 1566, had served as an important nexus for trade between the Christian and Islamic worlds. By the early 1600s, Izmir had displaced it, with the consequence that many of the Greek (and Jewish) merchants who had lived and worked there moved to the mainland port.[22] Greeks from Kuşadası, Foça, Çeşme, and other regional centers joined them, and by 1650 several thousand Greeks worshiped in rebuilt churches in Izmir and operated the numerous shops, fisheries, taverns, and other businesses that opened in the bustling town.

The story of Izmir's Jews is similar. Jews had long been prominent as governmental representatives in Istanbul, Aleppo, Alexandria, and elsewhere; some of them naturally sought similar posts in the new city. Between 1610 and 1650, most collectors of customs (*emin*s) in Izmir were Jewish,[23] and Dutch, English, and French merchants felt compelled to surround themselves with the coreligionists of these officials if they hoped to negotiate effectively with the Ottoman government and bureaucracy. Ottoman titles of appointment (*berat*s) from that period reflect this Jewish dominance. For instance, in 1638 "some people" demanded the removal of a Jew named Isaac from his position as dragoman of the merchants of Antalya. The French community resisted this pressure and secured a command confirming him in his post.[24] Two years later, the French ambassador vigorously campaigned in the Sublime Porte for the appointment of the Jew Avraham veled-i Yusef as dragoman to the French consul in Izmir.[25]

Muslims (most of whom must have been of Turkic descent) are less visible in the commerce of seventeenth-century Izmir than are non-Muslim Ottomans. Their role is veiled partly because of the nature of our sources, which are overwhelmingly either administrative or foreign. It is likely, though, that the silence of such documents reflects a certain reality. Unlike their counterparts in either Istanbul or Aleppo, the principal founders of commercial Izmir were western Europeans who, both linguistically and culturally, communicated more easily with Christians and even Jews than they did with Muslims. Although this obstacle, which barred the admission of most Muslims into the core of Izmir's commercial life, was surmounted more frequently than is often supposed, its presence did mean that the Muslim role in Izmir's commerce was relatively slight. With time, it was to recede even further.

The central place of non-Ottomans in Izmir's development did not preclude Turko-Muslim involvement, however. Certainly Turks dominated demographically, probably never dropping below an absolute majority of the city's population. They were active in the site's markets and bazaars and almost singlehandedly provisioned its people. More importantly from the English point of view, they constituted the *ayan,* the notable persons, of Izmir and its surroundings, and they could, and often did, serve as foils against both the Ottoman administration and merchant competitors.[26]

Most germane for the English and other foreigners was the certainty that every Ottoman military man and high administrator was a Muslim and probably a Turk. This reality was particularly prominent in Izmir, over which no Ottoman governor (*beylerbeyi*) enjoyed a jurisdiction. It is true that the Ottomans placed the district of Izmir within the bailiwick of their admiral (*kapudanpaşa*) and that in the seventeenth and eighteenth centuries his ships and mariners notoriously anchored in the Gulf of Izmir and preyed upon the city's inhabitants. Nevertheless, the naval commander's concerns were more strategic than administrative, and he interfered little with the daily operation of the town. Thus, no countervailing force limited the authority of the city magistrate (kadi), who consequently could be (and at several moments of crisis in the 1640s and 1650s was) dragged into the affairs of foreign merchants. Not that the English were always pleased with his judgments. Indeed, English as well as Dutch, French, and Venetian protests against the kadi and other Ottoman officials often drew the Ottoman central government into local disputes and sometimes obliged the state to dispatch *çavuş*es to attempt to settle them.[27]

The most concrete sign of foreign autonomy in Izmir was the raising in these very years of *gavur* Izmir, or the Street of the Franks, along the city's shoreline. This district sometimes is unjustly portrayed as a pale imitation of the Pera prototype, which in fact it far outstripped as a bastion for European peoples and culture. Unlike the case in Pera, there was no Ottoman majority living on the Street of the Franks. Nor was there in Izmir as swollen and zealous a bureaucracy eager to intrude, or as massive and exposed a citizenry that might hold the wealthy foreign diplomats and merchants accountable for scarcities of food and other goods. In short, whereas in the capital city the foreign community was one of the most vulnerable among a vast array of political and economic clusters, in Izmir it quickly became preeminent. In such a constellation, the principal challenge to English autonomy and trade came not from Ottomans but from representatives of other foreign nations or, even more ominously, from fellow countrymen.

Comparison with the physical design of Aleppo's foreign settlement further dramatizes the singularity of Izmir's Street of the Franks. If the foreign quarter in Izmir was a Europeanized variant of Pera in greater Istanbul, then the foreign factories of Aleppo formed an Islamic rendition of that norm. Merchants in Aleppo rarely had private residences. Instead, they lived together in *khan*s, often fortified more against the crowd than against the army and always shared with merchandise and beasts of burden. Nor were they the directing agents of commerce in Aleppo as they were to become in Izmir. Indigenous actors continued to dominate Aleppo's economy long beyond the mid-seventeenth century. Even non-Muslim worship was more restricted in the Arab city. Whereas several new churches went up in seventeenth-century Izmir and the sound of worship and Sunday psalms regularly drifted across the city,[28] in Aleppo even the renovation of ancient churches (much less the construction of new ones) was problematical, and frequent Muslim objections to the insulting clamor of infidel ceremony helped silence Christian hymn and Jewish chant.

In addition, Aleppo, unlike Izmir, was not a port city. The hard-pressed English consul or merchant residing in Izmir could simply slip out his back door and into a *kayık* that would transport him to the safety of a fortified vessel.[29] From there, he could sail away, negotiate, land a party of mariners in the city, or even lob cannon balls at it. The Aleppine merchant had no option but to negotiate. The city's interior location also demanded an extra transfer of goods from one caravan to another. Each such transfer brought an additional expenditure of time and labor which mightily displeased the foreign factors and their sponsors in London.

Nor did Izmir have to contend with the physical division of merchants from mariners that Aleppo's interior location demanded. Whereas roughneck seamen, aching for diversions after weeks of disciplined confinement aboard a small vessel, could satisfy their desires in the streets of Izmir, they had few outlets in Alexandretta, and few compatriots to police them. Furthermore, it was difficult for the company to find competent officials to fill the isolated, troublesome, and unprestigious post of vice-consul. Consequently, whereas Aleppo became notorious for strife between foreign factors, Ottoman officials, and indigenes, it was in Alexandretta that most embarrassing and sometimes expensive rowdiness and interfactory confrontations occurred.

The decentralized political and administrative edifice that distinguished the Ottoman Empire in the mid-seventeenth century left each English nation to operate within its own particular matrix. This system both complicated the commercial activities of English factors in Aleppo and made it easier for their countrymen to encourage and direct the development of commerce in Izmir.[30] During the 1640s and 1650s, the English and other European nations of Izmir effectively challenged the authority of both the central government and their own representatives in Istanbul. In order to succeed, the English consul in Izmir and the ambassador in Istanbul needed to understand this peculiar relationship, particularly characteristic of the mid-seventeenth- and much of the eighteenth-century empire, between the capital city and its provinces.

The English ambassador in Istanbul during the 1630s, Sir Peter Wyche, got a taste of the leverage wielded by individuals stationed in the Ottoman provinces (in this case, his own consul) in his effort to appropriate for his king the revenue from an important surcharge called the strangers' consulage.[31] On 20 August 1636, he reported that the English consul in Izmir had

> put me to use the utmost force I could, nay he would wrest that to Turkish justice, and had spent some monies that way to make that good against me which I could not in honor of his Majesty's justice brook or give way unto; Therefore I took out more forceful commands and sent them down by my Druggerman [dragoman] the second time, which the justice of the place dare not withstand, and then the consul gave way.[32]

Suggested here is that the English factory in Izmir, having solicited support from the kadi of Izmir in order to defy the ambassador's right to collect the strangers' consulage, had succumbed only to the full weight of both ambassador and sultan, whose authority was embodied in the person of Wyche's personal dragoman.

As the entrepôt of Izmir became increasingly influential in the succeeding decades, ambassadors found the English factory there even more obstreperous and demanding. On the one hand, as we will see, Sir Sackvile Crow, the ambassador during much of the 1640s, lost his post and his freedom partly because he failed to secure backing from the English factory in Izmir. On the other hand, his successor, Sir Thomas Bendysh, retained his station throughout the difficult years of the second civil war in England, the executions of the sultan İbrahim and the king Charles I, and the deep turmoil that distinguished imperial politics in Istanbul and commonwealth politics in London during the early 1650s. Bendysh succeeded in part because he cultivated the patronage of the English factories both of the Street of the Franks in Izmir and of Pera in Istanbul. In each case, success and failure were predicated upon appreciation of the elaborate political and economic bonds within and between the two cities, as well as upon an understanding of the English nation itself.

AN ENGLISH COMMERCIAL LATTICE

The successful official, merchant, or community of traders operating in the eastern Mediterranean appreciated that in the seventeenth-century Ottoman Empire it did not suffice to negotiate exclusively with the central authorities. Power and authority were diffused over a vast and diverse realm, and forces outside the control of the central government often stimulated change, particularly economic innovations. On the one hand, a penetrating grasp of imperial Ottoman politics offered little help in comprehending the localized commercial patterns radiating out of Aleppo or Izmir; on the other, an understanding of provincial politics probably was of little use in the capital city. These divergences meant that the foreigner had either to exhibit exceptional plasticity as he roamed between Ottoman commercial nodes, remain anchored to one locality, or acquire a network of loyal servants and colleagues.

It was such a network that Britons built in the seventeenth century. In intriguing ways it resembled the classic "trading diasporas" that Curtin and others have identified and portrayed.[33] For example, the English factors carved administrative and cultural islands—that is, trade settlements—out of the landscapes of Istanbul, Izmir, and Aleppo. They concentrated on a specific economic endeavor which the community of

Ottoman subjects was unable (or unwilling) to perform. Furthermore, many Englishmen—at least in the early decades of their presence in the Ottoman realm—were simultaneously "members of an urban society" and of "a plural society, where two or more cultures existed side by side,"[34] a difficult middle ground that characterized trading diasporas and that the Britons conserved by means of a thicket of regulations and fines raised to sustain their cultural distinctiveness as well as their economic autonomy. They employed these methods and organizations, all trademarks of trading diasporas, to weather the ideological and political storms that swept through the mid-seventeenth-century Mediterranean and European worlds.

4 / English Traders on the Ottoman Frontier

In the mid-seventeenth century, a complicated latticework of political power and economic control enmeshed the cities of Istanbul, Izmir, and Aleppo. Indigenous and foreign merchants settling in these cities and elsewhere in the Ottoman Empire sought to manipulate the networks in their particular surroundings even as they bargained with, swindled, and conspired against each other. Their acumen and the strengths, capacities, and attitudes of the authorities upon whom they depended decided their fates. Among these operators were English ambassadors, consuls, and merchants, who strove, with varying effectiveness, to "work" the changes in state legitimacy and the societal disarray that typified Ottoman political and economic structures during the period. The situation was even more complicated than this, however. Englishmen also had to contend with domestic strife as their island kingdom lurched through the crises of civil war, commonwealth, and restoration. Scheming was an everyday constant of the merchants' lives in the Levant. Although their conniving sometimes produced fortunes, at other times it exploded in their faces.

INTRACOMMUNAL DISPUTES

Complicated commercial dealings tested the capacities of these men. An English factor whom London merchants sent to Aleppo typically dealt on his own behalf as well as his principals' in bullion, silk, cotton, broadcloth, spices, and sundry other commodities. He might hire an Armenian broker for his silks, have extensive dealings with an Arab partner for produce of local provenance, exchange specie with a Jewish money changer, negotiate with local officials for favors and exemptions, seek to protect his interests through his consul and ambassador, and strive to outguess his competitors on when to buy, sell, hold, and ship goods. Such arrangements, normal in a busy marketplace, must have occurred many times daily in the commercial centers of the Ottoman Empire.

Usually the system worked well and quietly and left virtually no trail for the historian to follow. Bitter disputes were disastrous; they meant loss and sometimes ruin for individual merchants and even entire commercial nations in the Levant. Yet they did sometimes occur, and it is such extraordinary conflicts that help us discern the mechanisms of commerce in the eastern Mediterranean world.

Such a breakdown struck the English nation of Izmir in 1639.[1] In that year, the recently arrived English ambassador in Istanbul, Sir Sackvile Crow, and the new English consul in Izmir, Edward Stringer, had to resolve a bitter dispute between two factors of Izmir, Richard Lawrence and Frances (*sic*) Reade. In doing so, they not only uncovered the workings of the English political hierarchy but also recorded the considerable involvement of Ottoman Jews, Muslims, and Armenians in this vitriolic clash.

Two or three years earlier, it seems, three of Reade's principals in England—Sir Morris Abbott, Mr. Edward Abbott, and Mr. Lewise Roberts—had become suspicious of his ventures on their behalf. Within the structure of Levantine trade, the factor's primary task was to serve as agent to his principals. The more trustworthy and profitable a factor's performance, the greater would be his commissions and the more quickly could he move up the administrative ladder in the Levant or engineer a return to England. Should a principal become distrustful of a factor, he might transfer his goods and money to another and also dissuade his associates in London from engaging the man's services. In other words, a factor could easily be blacklisted and thus financially ruined.[2]

The letter-book of a later factor, Richard Lake, for example, reveals that this was exactly his fate in Aleppo during the late 1650s and 1660s. Lake arrived there after a seven-year apprenticeship in London under a certain Tho: Rich, who should have become the young factor's most indispensable principal. Such was not the poor man's lot. Instead, the master worked hard to ruin his protégé's career, and one of Lake's several urgent letters to Rich's wife, Mary, suggests why:

> I will ... freely confesse that I was a very lewd, debaucht and vitious person; and what other Enormities man may bee guilty off, my green yeares, had quickly and too Early Entertaned. ... My greatest crime, I doe believe, when shall have the happiness to know itt from you—was my too much love of wine and Company.[3]

Other letters mention an outstanding debt to his master and even imply a dalliance with Mrs. Rich. In dozens of frantic epistles to relatives, friends, and other merchants, Lake pleaded for commissions, unavailingly, it seems.[4] Rich chose to engage other Aleppine agents and urged his colleagues in London to do likewise. Without such contracts, the lonely factor's prospects of returning to England were bleak.

Fierce competition among factors for commissions characterized each English factory. Whereas Lake's dissolute youth in London sabotaged his business in Aleppo, Reade feared for his honor in the Levantine world. An important function of the English consuls and ambassadors was to keep the commercial playing field as level as possible by safeguarding their merchants against slander and other defamations. The quarrel between factors Reade and Lawrence severely tasked Levant Company appointees in this regard.

Lewise Roberts asked Lawrence (who had previously acted as English consul in Izmir) to investigate his misgivings about Reade, and the consul soon reported back that Reade had lost 20 percent of his principal's money on poor investments in pepper and on exorbitant freighting costs. Faced with the choice of ruin or wronging his principals, Reade seemingly had decided on the latter course and sold Roberts's textiles at seventy-three lion dollars per cloth while reporting that he had received only sixty-six dollars. Lawrence also detailed an unlawful deal for indigo from Lahore, in which, the consul charged, Reade had taken a bribe of two thousand lion dollars from an Armenian merchant, Hoggia Toma, and also connived with the man who had brokered the deal, a Jew named Simsson Cress.[5] Cress ostensibly confirmed Reade's treachery before some rabbis and two Jewish witnesses—Mosse Morell and Joseph Morian, whose testimony Lawrence secretly forwarded to London. The alleged conspiracy thus ranged across several Ottoman communities, for Cress was said to have been in partnership not only with another Jew, Mayer Bevenias, but also with two Armenians—the previously mentioned Hoggia Toma and a Hoggia Murat—and with a Muslim, Hoggia Achmett. The scheme having fallen through, Toma, Lawrence contended, now demanded his money back from Reade.

On 10 September 1639, Reade complained to Ambassador Crow that these allegations, which Lawrence had recorded and forwarded to Reade's principals without consulting either the accused or the English nation of Izmir, were slanders that severely damaged his reputation, made it difficult for him to find patrons, and had cost him at least twelve thousand lion dollars. On 4 November, the merchants of Izmir confirmed Reade's contentions, a charge to which Lawrence responded by accusing the entire English factory of Izmir of raising false witnesses against him and illegally entering his home and seizing papers. Crow next ordered Stringer, the consul in Izmir, to convene twelve of the "chief of the nation" there to investigate the case and appoint four "indifferent" men to decide it.

The English nation of Izmir verified Reade's account and pronounced Lawrence guilty of libel. Stringer and the four supposedly impartial men (George Juatt, John Lancelot, Thomas Milward, and William Vuedall) concluded that Reade, although he had invested Roberts's money poorly, had recovered his patron's losses through other savvy bargains. They also interviewed Simsson Cress about the indigo. The Jewish trader denied having denounced Reade and insisted that Morell and Morian, supposedly his witnesses, were in fact his commercial adversaries and thus were determined to testify against him. The two men, Stringer informed Crow,

> are in repute in their own Nation, as honest men as [Cress] who indeed is not a man of the best fame, & it appears by all probabilities grounded his speeches on some idle reports not that he had any certain knowledge of that bargain, whereof he makes his relation, being not broker in the same, but only thought to gratify Mr. Lawrence & thereby to advance some profit onto himself.[6]

Stringer and his merchants conjectured that Cress had tried to ingratiate himself with Lawrence in order to drum up business at the expense of his coreligionists. As Crow concluded after reading their account: "Richard Lawrence had inveigled ... Simsson Cress a Jewish broker by fair promises of his business to deliver testimony against Frances Reade."[7]

The English nation of Izmir's investigation of the Armenian Toma proved equally absolving for Reade. Toma now denied the claim that Reade had received a bribe in a deal for indigo. Even the breaking into Lawrence's home had been undertaken legally, so the nation insisted, by the consul's dragoman under the supervision of six honest merchants. They had removed from the premises only an incriminating letter-book, which the dragoman had properly sealed before witnesses. This volume was fully intact and waiting at the consul's home for Lawrence to reclaim upon his return from Candia (modern Iraklion, Crete) to Izmir.

Crow's ostensible task was a simple judgment in a conflict between two factors. Izmir's overwhelming support for Reade, however, made his job extremely difficult, for Crow must have guessed, or even known, that the English nation of Izmir had driven the ineffectual and perhaps rapacious Lawrence from the consulship. Furthermore, an ambassador could ill afford to antagonize the consul and merchants of Izmir, from whom he ultimately derived much of his authority and, equally important, his income. The reports from Izmir made the case against Lawrence seem strong, and Crow concurred with them. He acted immediately to "sequester & suspend the said Lawrence from all assemblies of the courts of the Nation during his residency in Turkey."[8] This severe action constituted a ban against Lawrence's commercial dealings in the Levant. Although this response was politically astute and certainly secured for Crow the support of the chief English factors of Izmir, it is less clear that the judgment was fair. Indeed, the case festered for a decade and would be reopened by Crow's ambassadorial successor.

AN ENIGMATIC SOCIETY

Most of us suppose that the actuality of seventeenth-century Ottoman port cities reflected the theoretical ideal. Many of our sources suggest that such towns were built of discrete social and economic units. Myriad quarters (*mahalle*s) containing distinct ethnoreligious communities (millets) possessed considerable religious, legal, and even political autonomy. One might study the capitulations that defined the legal context for interstate relations in the Ottoman Empire, as well as the correspondence between traders and officials, and conclude that foreign settlements emulated this urban organization. Western European states and companies established the *khan*s in Aleppo, the Street of the Franks in Izmir, and Pera in Istanbul, within which nations sought to govern themselves according to the laws and regulations of their own states and trading companies just as Ottoman Armenians, Greeks, Jews, and Muslims abided by their own religious and legal traditions within discrete, segregated social and economic sectors.

The case of Reade versus Lawrence suggests that relations between groups were in fact many-sided and muddled. Intricate economic and social links bound together the various socioreligious communities in an Ottoman commercial center, and the religiocommunal lines often said to define Ottoman society blurred together in a multitude of ways. Armenians, Jews, Muslims, and Greeks broke their autonomies in combinations against Dutch, English, French, and Venetian merchants. The governors of foreign nations sought to counter such alliances by demanding that their compatriots live and work together and keep each other abreast of their commercial activities. The authorities constructed a gamut of religious and linguistic loyalties, a hierarchy of administrative officials, and penalties such as the "battulation," or boycott, in order to maintain communal integrity and autonomy.

The conflict between Lawrence and Reade suggests how easily the petty jealousies and greed that perhaps inevitably seep into even (or especially) the closest social and commercial associations could tear down these communal ramparts. If we tentatively accept the admittedly suspect findings of the English nation in Izmir, we can conclude that the Jewish merchant Cress chose to break with his coreligionists and perhaps even perjure himself before his own rabbis in order to exploit the English network of trade. Apparently the Armenian Toma resorted to perjury or perhaps even blackmail to settle some bargain involving indigo from Lahore, and the Englishman Lawrence broke several rules governing proper behavior in the English nation, exhibiting even a willingness to shatter the integrity of English trade in Izmir in order to undercut Reade, his fellow countryman and rival. It is possible of course, that the principal English factors in Izmir resented Lawrence for malfeasances committed during his term as consul and thus orchestrated or even concocted the entire episode in retaliation. Fault is not the issue, however; in either case, communal solidarity proved elusive. Each man went to great lengths to destroy his compatriot rival.

Although neither Reade nor Lawrence appears to have used it, recourse to Ottoman legal and political authorities was among the choices open to these merchants, whether Ottoman subjects or outsiders. It is true that all foreigners considered appeal to this legal and religious heritage dangerous, perhaps because they judged the Ottoman system untrustworthy and arbitrary, or perhaps because of its unfamiliarity. Hence, both subject communities and foreign nations constructed a thicket of ordinances and penalties to forestall recourse to Ottoman courts. Yet the very existence of these regulations and the frequency with which they were reiterated suggest how often they must have been defied.

Indeed, they offered several loopholes. Even though both the French and English capitulations then in place proscribed foreign merchants from turning to Ottoman courts in lawsuits against each other, the agreements did not yet provide foreigners with much protection against Ottoman subjects—particularly Muslim but also Christian or Jewish—who chose Islamic, patriarchal, or rabbinic justice.[9] Extraterritoriality was only one among many legal conventions flourishing in the Ottoman realm, and the foreign consul caught in a quarrel with an Ottoman subject might find himself lost in a morass of sometimes conflicting and always bewildering legal conventions and mores. He could not always escape to the protection of the capitulatory regime.

EXPLOITING THE OTTOMAN BORDERLANDS

The intimacy of intercommunal arrangements occasionally drove foreigners into Ottoman law courts and often compelled ambassadors and consuls to call Ottoman witnesses in internal feuding. Shortly after Crow ruled on the Lawrence-Reade case, for example, he was asked to decide a complicated dispute between two ambitious and short-tempered Englishmen—Gyles Ball and Henry Hyde—over control of the consulship of the Morea (the Greek Peloponnesus).[10] The ambassador soon found himself hearing testimony from members of virtually every nation and community residing in the Ottoman Empire, for in the preceding year the two men's stratagems had drawn into their feud not only many English merchants and mariners but also Jews, Muslims, Greeks, and Frenchmen. They also had appealed against each other to the Ottoman kadi, *kaymakam,* and pasha residing in the Morean port town of Patras.

English traders had long coveted the consulate of the Morea, the station for which was at Patras, just across the straits of the Gulf of Corinth from Lepanto, site of a historic sea battle in 1571. It lay at the western reaches of the Ottoman Empire, near the border between the Ottoman and Venetian domains. Thus, it was rather distant from Istanbul, the center of both Ottoman and English power in the Levant. At the same time, it lay on the frontier between the two most powerful, and often antagonistic, Mediterranean maritime powers, and the English consul at Patras was often in a position to mediate between, play off, and spy upon the Venetian and Ottoman states. There are several indications that he did so, such as in 1649 when a Venetian official on the island of Zante (Zakinthos) reported with satisfaction to the Senate that the English consul, "who lives near here on the mainland," regularly provided information about Ottoman military movements.[11] In short, the English consul of the Morea resided at one of the hubs of Mediterranean trade and politics.

The position existed for economic reasons. An English passion for the currants of the Venetian islands of Cephalonia and Zante, available also from western Anatolia and the Ottoman Morea, constituted in its early existence the backbone of the Levant Company's prosperity. The consul's principal responsibility was securing an ample and economical supply of these small dried fruits for his insatiable countrymen. Normally, the assignment amounted almost to a sinecure; his 2- or 3-percent consulage from this commerce could allow him to reside most regally in the Peloponnesus.

Henry Hyde, the consul of the Morea in the late 1630s and early 1640s, took full advantage of his position not only to live well but also to carve out a base of considerable influence in both the English and Ottoman spheres. Currants provided the fiscal underpinning for this political and social leverage, particularly after 1642, when an English boycott of Venetian currants suddenly increased the demand for those produced in the Morea and western Anatolia.[12]

Even as Hyde served the English as consul, he also had the perspicacity to implant himself in the Ottoman political and economic administration by purchasing a *voyvodalık* in the region surrounding Patras, a position that granted him virtually the authority of an Ottoman pasha. He also bought a *bacdarlık,* which transformed him into an Ottoman customs collector.[13] Hyde thus was able to establish what amounted to a small fiefdom. He built an impressive house and chapel at an estate called Holmuch that lay west of Patras and overlooked the island of Zante.[14] He also seems to have invested in shipping and owned at least one vessel, fittingly named the *Spahee*.[15] The currant trade gave Hyde the funds for these exploits and investments; the peculiarities of Ottoman rule granted him the authority to pursue them.

UPROOTING AN ENGLISH DESPOT

Hyde's successful maneuvering does seem to have cost him a great deal of money and made it difficult for him to maintain his principal obligation to supply the Levant Company with dried fruits. In March 1641, he received a reprimand for negligence, having kept company money in his own hands, presumably to cover the expenses of buying Ottoman positions and keeping up an estate rather than purchasing and shipping currants and figs.[16] The power and autonomy of his various posts also seem to have gone to his head, for the consul responded aggressively, writing to the company that he would begin charging one-half dollar per sack of currants to cover his and Ambassador Crow's expenses.[17]

The company responded to this news decisively. On 2 February 1643, the directors stripped Hyde of his consulship and appointed Gyles Ball to replace him.[18] They also granted Ball the authority "to require of Henry Hyde the late consul there the surrendering of all Magazines or whatever else belongs to the Company & the Law to be restored into his Custody & possession for the Company's use."[19] The directors knew that this commission threatened Hyde's position. They also seem to have realized that the civil war in England, which had commenced only months earlier but already had begun to dismantle English government and society, would give Hyde and other appointees the opportunity to question the company's authority. Three months later, on 29 April 1643, the directors ordered Ball to procure a letter from the king to Crow appointing him consul "in case Mr. Hyde should anyways oppose him."[20]

Hyde contested this company initiative bitterly and hard. In letters that the directors received in October 1643 and March 1644, the consul claimed, in a manner deemed "very peremptory and snappish ... much unbeseeming a Minister to a Society by whom he was employed,"[21] that they owed him 12,033 lion dollars, which they had refused to acknowledge. In a third letter, received in April 1644, Hyde linked reimbursement for this debt to his willingness to relinquish his post, declaring that he would not surrender the consul's magazine to his successor until the company had settled it.[22]

The directors of the company systematically repudiated Hyde's claims in a lengthy letter dated 22 December 1644. They insisted that others had financed the 6,386 lion dollars Hyde claimed to have paid "the Turks at Petras" for a debt contracted by a Master Bunington of the *Resolution*. They pointed out that the company and owners of the ship *Unicorn* already had provided the monies Hyde claimed for settling a mysterious case of manslaughter, and they disavowed a succession of alleged charges for dragomans, janissaries, gifts, payoffs, and redemptions of slaves.[23] Not that Hyde found the company's denials convincing. Indeed, its refusal to acknowledge these debts turned him into an implacable foe. With obdurate steadfastness he continued to demand reimbursement up to his last breath in March 1651.[24]

Despite these troubles, Hyde in 1644 still served as the company's agent in the Morea and accepted its orders for currants. On 25 June, Governor Isaac Pennington, Deputy Governor William Cokayne, Henry Hunt (an officer known as the husband), and other directors of the Levant Company instructed him to gather currants for lading aboard the *Goulden Faulcon,* then en route from London for Patras.[25] Hyde, in Istanbul at the time, duly dispatched Thomas Colman, a member of the English nation in the Morea, across the straits to Lepanto in order to purchase fruits. Pennington later issued instructions to Mr. Goodlade, the master of the *Unicorn,* ordering him to prevent "meddling with the currants or disturbing Mr. Hyde therein, wherewith if you find the said Mr. Ball willing to comply and that he do accordingly forbear to perplex our business, or molest Mr. Hyde, you may then promise to see him satisfied the consulage upon the said currants."[26] The company directors, it seems, appreciated on the one hand that they would not secure shipment of their precious currants without Hyde's assistance, and on the other that Ball's appointment was meaningless without control over this commodity. Their instructions amounted to a clumsy and, as it turned out, spurned venture to buy off their new consul.

Gyles Ball, traveling aboard the *Defence* (soon thereafter anchored in Patras Road) to assume his new posting as consul, apparently heard that the standing English consul was filling a large order for currants. Disembarking at Lepanto, he met Hyde's agent, Colman, with whom Ball began to feud rather than cooperate in company business. Colman, it seems, had signed agreements with several Muslim merchants for a considerable quantity of currants, contracts that Ball scorned. Colman and seven compatriots later petitioned Ambassador Crow in Istanbul that Ball had

> by extraordinary presents to Turks at Lepanto raised the price of those currants to about $4 per sack (whereas Mr. Hyde's usual price is not above 1\frac{3}{4}$ first cost) and did moreover cause a boat of Lepanto which was laden with currants & ordered to discharge at Patras in the said Mr. Hyde his magazine, for the Company's account, to go directly aboard his ship Defence in Patras Road, & there discharge his currants without the license of the customs, caddie or Badshaw's officers, to the prejudice of the Company & unavoidable danger of Avanias from those Turks on the Nation their estates in the country.[27]

This petition (as well as a second one to London a month later) suggests that Ball began his tenure as consul with several surprising errors in judgment.[28] His intent, no doubt, was quickly and decisively to assert authority against the deposed consul, a man he knew to be ambitious, resourceful, and vengeful. Nevertheless, the consul's principal duty in the Morea was to furnish the company with currants at reasonable cost, and the last thing either the directors or the resident factors wanted was a bidding war, particularly one between compatriots. A commercial dispute could only weaken English autonomy and the nation's ability to compete in the bitter fight for Levantine wares.

Ambassador Crow was well aware of the dangers of a squabble between two pretenders to the consulship of the Morea. On 28 August 1644, he ordered Ball (futilely, it seems) to stop interfering in Hyde's collection of currants.[29] He also instructed the new consul to protect his predecessor from the unjust claims of malicious persons. Indeed, Crow insisted that Ball ensure that "neither the person nor estate of the said Mr. Hyde ... be molested, hindered or impeached without first advising us thereof, with the cause, matter, & pose against him." The ambassador, in effect, was making it legally problematic for Ball to strike at Hyde's assertions.[30]

Yet a confrontation is exactly what Ball initiated. As the previously quoted passage states, he apparently went directly to two powerful Muslim merchants, Abisutt Effendi and Mehemet Agra, and offered them several dollars more per sack than Hyde's agent, Colman, had earlier negotiated. Ball also defied both Hyde's and local Ottoman authority (perhaps one and the same) by seizing a coastal vessel laden with currants and bound for Hyde's storehouse at Patras. This maneuver particularly troubled the English community in Patras, for it feared that the Ottoman customs collectors, kadi, and military officers would retaliate with an irregular and possibly crippling levy (*avania*) against it. Finally, Ball had Hyde dragged into the presence of Mahmud, the kadi of Patras, where he ostensibly proclaimed that "all such imperial commands as your Lordship [Crow] had given Mr. Hyde, were false."[31] The consul-designate produced no proof for this charge, however, and the Ottoman official refused to act upon it.

Even after the *Goulden Faulcon,* accompanied by the *Tallent,* had docked at Patras on 20 November 1644 and its commander, Lambert Pitches, had presented an order confirming that Hyde should supervise the lading of the vessel, Ball continued to intrude. On 24 November (a Sunday, as Hyde priggishly observed), four days after the arrival of the ships, Ball again brought Hyde before "Turkish justice" and again failed to convince the local authorities to act against someone who "is beloved and bears rule in the country." Frustrated by these repeated setbacks, Ball next urged Pitches and Captain Thomas Harman of the *Goulden Faulcon* "that if they could get the said Mr. Hyde aboard either of their said ships to carry him perforce to England,"[32] he could gain the warehouses, casks, and other material required for his job.

THE POWER OF THE CULTURAL CHAMELEON

Perhaps unwittingly, Ball had plunged himself into an unwinnable contest. His rival, who had lived in the Morea for several years, enjoyed not only support from English merchants but also rank as an Ottoman official and patronage from powerful native merchants and bureaucrats. Ball found Hyde's position virtually unassailable in the Morea, so he looked to England for assistance. When letters from the company and the king proved insufficient, he solicited help in physically removing

Hyde to his homeland. This maneuver failed, too, and Ball was left to implore his ambassador in Istanbul for assistance.

The consul-designate had visited Crow on his voyage to the Morea in the late summer of 1644 (indeed, in mid-August, both he and Hyde wrote letters to the company from Istanbul),[33] and he had been well received. He had departed for the Morea in mid-September.[34] On 22 December 1644, he wrote to the ambassador to explain his actions during the previous few months and to tender his grievances formally against Hyde. His words convey his fury. Ball first reported that despite letters from company, king, and ambassador, Hyde had refused either to resign his office or to deliver over the capitulations that defined and legitimized his authority. He then exclaimed:

> The rising of this little cloud presaged some approaching storm of unquietness which since, succeeded to the full extent of his power, & malice, & that truth might not want his justifiers. I shal now present you with a cloud of witnesses of all proceedings. And among others for your more clear satisfaction, the Druggerman & Janissary spectated all of the passages detailed necessarily & purposely to represent faithfully unto your Lordship Mr. Hyde's regardlessness of your directions, & his undue carriage & gross incivilities expressed towards me, in word, in act, to the impeachment of the consular office.[35]

Ball's willingness to express himself with such passion to an official whom he hardly knew displays the rage of frustration and personal animosity. One discerns even in these words, however, the tenuousness of his position: his key witnesses were not even Englishmen, but Greek and Muslim Ottoman subjects.

A harsh and rambling condemnation followed this outburst. Ball maintained that Hyde used his authority as *voyvoda* and *bacdar* to disrupt Ball's commerce, forcing him "to visit the Caddee, once or twice a day & my Druggerman half a score times a day," and that Hyde followed Ball around with five janissaries and a regiment of "Sbandnditoes" (bandits) in order to harass him, abuse his servants, and underbid him in all his dealings.[36] Among many other sinister ventures, Hyde also sent a boatload of janissaries aboard Ball's vessel, the *Defence,* one night, endangering lives and inviting an Ottoman fine. He pillaged a boat filled with currants and Ball's correspondence, and he used his residency at Holmuch,[37] which lay along the westerly mail route, to intercept Ball's letters. The alleged victim asserted that it was time "to check his wild career, to indicate all these misdemeanors, to seize his person." He pointed out that although he could not contain Hyde alone, "the Caddee can but will not without commands, the common people would but dare not, without the Caddee's warrant, & to attempt ought of force by the hands of soldiers ... with the apparent danger of shedding of blood ... I rather am content to bear the weight of this heavy burden awhile."[38]

Ball's tone of bitter resignation was partially ruse, for at exactly the time he conveyed to Crow his resolve to delay action and leave his fate in the ambassador's hands, he also proceeded against Hyde by way of Ottoman subjects and provincial authorities. He obtained two petitions criticizing Hyde's misconduct, one from forty-three persons "of the community of Patras" and the other from twenty-seven "Turks" in the port town. The first of these documents, addressed to the Sublime Porte, was a vague blanket condemnation. The second was written for the English ambassador and more specifically argued a contrast between the personable, sincere, and beneficent Ball and his evil and false rival, whose illegal actions much damaged the merchant and Muslim communities of Patras.[39] Ball also secured two *arz*es (petitions to the Ottoman government) from the kadis of Patras and Lepanto, dated 20 and 30 December 1644.[40] These objected to Hyde's procurement of imperial commands countermanding the *berat* that had appointed Ball consul. Ball presented to Crow copies of all these appeals.

It is ironic that Ball bothered to obtain these petitions from Ottoman subjects who, if they had any interest at all in the squabble between the Britons, were probably more sympathetic to Hyde's position. Ball himself knew of and denounced the friendship (or at least close association) between his rival and the kadi of Patras. Perhaps he grew frustrated at Hyde's ability to outmaneuver him and decided to try his hand at playing the Ottoman administration, or perhaps he had some faith that the wheels of Ottoman justice would turn efficiently and impartially. Whatever the case, there is no evidence that Ball's appeals to Ottoman justice achieved any result.

Although Ball claimed to have left in Crow's hands the matter of procuring the requisite decrees from the grand vizier directing the pasha and kadis to assist Ball in ousting and imprisoning his rival, he clearly distrusted the ambassador and took such initiative himself. Indeed, he further complained directly to Crow that Hyde's *berat* had appointed him consul of the Morea and Romelia, whereas his own, secured by Crow, spoke only of the Morea. Thus, rather than replace Hyde, the Ottoman documents seem to have devised a dual consulate, to be administered jointly by the rivals. Ball advised (or rather threatened) his ambassador that he intended to notify both the king and parliament, as well as the pasha of the Morea, just returned from Istanbul, about the situation. After a discursion into Hyde's foot dragging in the collection of currants for the company, Ball ended his long petition to Crow curiously:

> Besides Mr. Hyde's personal Abuses, he abetted Mamut Basha, the serdar of the janissaries ... who threatened my servants & offered them Abuses at Marine, & since, I being at the Justice seat, & there complaining in a full assembly of this serdar, he thereupon took occasion to revile me ... and called me Ghour ... whereupon I instantly took witness, & caused it to be siggil'd.[41]

Ball's public confrontation with the leader of Patras's garrison of janissaries was a serious mistake. For one thing, Hyde, who apparently was Mahmut Pasha's friend, had engaged a company of the *serdar*'s troops and operated under his protection and as his Ottoman colleague. Furthermore, as was usual in an Ottoman town, the commander's authority was military and thus distinct from the kadi's. It did Ball little good to complain against him in the religious court of Patras; punishment for his abuses had to come from the pasha or directly from the Sublime Porte. Ball realized his error too late, however. He asked Crow "to move pressingly for justice on my behalf, that [Hyde] may be Maasool'd [dismissed], & by a command sent for to the Porte," and in a postscript confessed that the kadi had refused to give him an *arz* against the janissary captain.[42] Finally, Ball stumbled into the faux pas of permitting an important Ottoman official to call him a *gavur* (a godless heathen) in an open Muslim court. The tale of this dramatic encounter would have circulated quickly through the town, and the insulting label could only have subverted the consul-designate's ability to function effectively on behalf of his nation and company.

Somewhat over two months later, on 8 March 1645, Ball wrote a second, more despairing, letter to Crow.[43] The correspondent was aware that Hyde had written to the ambassador and feared that his "implacable adversary, whose malice rests not" would "take advantage of the distance of place" to defame Ball's character and whisper falsehoods into Crow's ear. Ball again defended his decision to collect currants, although his repeated phrases, such as "they all refused to satisfy me," "I had just cause to believe their design also," and "was for particular accounts" (rather than for the company's), convey a markedly defensive tone. Indeed, Ball had no persuasive rejoinders to Hyde's accusations that he had damaged the company's commerce by forcing a dramatic rise in the price of currants, had perilously sought to evade the kadi and customer by smuggling currants aboard the *Defence,* and had declared in the kadi's presence that all of Hyde's imperial commands were forgeries. He could only protest his innocence, an approach that seemed particularly hollow in light of Hyde's receipt of a recent letter from the husband of the company in London, again instructing him to prepare casks for an order of Morea currants.[44]

CENTER AND PERIPHERY IN A FOREIGN LAND

Sir Sackvile Crow spent much of the summer of 1645 hearing testimony on, taking affidavits about, and trying to sort out the Ball-Hyde intrigue. On 14 June, Hyde submitted to him a petition and articles of complaint against his opponent.[45] Most of the details merely elaborated what Crow already knew: that Ball had spoiled Hyde's bargain for currants; that he had, impatiently and potentially ruinously for the English nation, presented himself before the kadi of Patras without proper documentation; that he had humiliated Hyde before "Turkish justice" by kicking aside the stool that the kadi had provided him; that he had condemned the old consul's imperial commands as false; and that he had attempted to commission English ships in a plot to entrap Hyde and dispatch him for England.

The petition also presented some new intelligence. Hyde described an episode in which an English vessel, the *Edward,* anchored off Patras in order to load oils, had to withdraw after two months because of Ball's deceitful declaration before the kadi of Patras that its captain meant to transport wheat, the export of which the Sublime Porte had recently banned because of war with Venice.[46] Whether or not Ball had, in fact, made such a declaration, Crow, who was struggling to convince the Ottomans that only renegade English vessels were running the Ottoman blockade against Venetian troops in Candia, would have found such contradictory evidence particularly dismaying.

Hyde also supplied an outline of Ball's activities since his failure to hustle his rival off for England. According to him, Ball had next

> applied himself to the Caddie, to cause him to render me into his hands, & finding that would take no effect, he addressed himself to the Bashaw of the place, seeking by his means to reduce me to his power & work my ruin. This being refused him likewise of the Bashaw, he hired Turks & others of Patras, Lepanto &c. to make Arz and Maxarz to be delivered to the Vizier & Tefterdare, in such a dangerous way, as if not prevented by your Lordship, might very well have rendered my life & estate liable to the Turkish Law.[47]

This short passage not only reveals the passion of the contest between the two pretenders to the consulship but also demonstrates their (particularly Hyde's) mastery over Ottoman provincial administration. Unable to turn either the kadi or the pasha of the place to his purpose, Ball attempted to go over their heads by appealing to various Ottoman subjects, both Muslim and non-Muslim, in the local port towns to petition Istanbul against Hyde. In fact, only Crow's intercession prevented the wholesale removal of their dispute from English to Ottoman justice. According to Hyde, Ball's paramount purpose in these bold strokes was to seize his properties in the Morea. He asked the ambassador for twenty thousand dollars in compensation for Ball's "violent & unwarranted proceedings."[48]

It was Sir Sackvile Crow's responsibility to decide the case (although, considering its tortuous course, he may have wished it upon the Ottomans). Ball's tale of the events, which the ambassador received on 18 June 1645, contradicted virtually all of Hyde's contentions.[49] Ball condemned his foe for withholding the capitulations and other commands from him, for exporting goods without paying consulage, for diverting commerce from the usual scale, for threatening to have the mariners of the *Defence* (the vessel that had brought Ball to Patras) enslaved, for dangerously sending "a boatful of janissaries and other Turks aboard the

Defence" under cover of darkness, for abusive language, for ordering his company of janissaries to plunder a dinghy dispatched to the *Defence,* then riding anchor on Nathalico Road, for intercepting his letters at Holmuch, and for allowing the *serdar* of the janissaries, then Hyde's "hired servant," to revile him. In short, Ball insisted that Hyde "embroils himself in the Turks' affairs in Morea, laboring (merely out of humor) to supplant, and Mazull [dismiss] general Officers, though of most approved integrity & merit, a practice in sundry respects of ill and dangerous consequence, to the whole Nation."[50]

Although the Sublime Porte did not involve itself directly in the dispute, it did allow the ambassador to summon to Istanbul a diverse array of participants and witnesses whose testimony he desired.[51] Their statements consumed the second half of June and early July 1645. Moise Levi, Ball's Jewish dragoman, attested that the actions of his employer had inflated the price of currants in both Patras and Lepanto, a judgment that Saphiere Philorito, a Greek commissioner of the town of Patras, confirmed. Nicolo Villeroy, the French consul of the Morea, then stated that the previous September, Hyde's servant Coleman, accompanied by a Jew named Salla, had concluded bargains for currants at Vestizza, Lepanto, and Patras and that one of Hyde's warehouses was already filled with such currants. Ball had arrived the following month and advanced a higher offer for the same currants. According to Villeroy, this competition had sparked the rivalry between the two men.

The French consul also contended that Hyde had asked him to intercede with the chief owners and dealers in currants, Abisutt Effendi and Mehemet Agra, in order to persuade them not to renege on their bargains. Rather than consent, the astute businessmen had invited a bidding war between the Englishmen. Mehemet first proposed that Hyde raise his offer to meet Ball's and also provide him with two or three vests, whereupon he would gladly sell him the currants. Abisutt then extended a similar proposal but suggested in addition a gratuity of two hundred seventy lion dollars. Villeroy remarked that Hyde had rejected both offers.

Written testimonies soon arrived that confirmed the statements of Levi, Philorito, and Villeroy.[52] Three of these were affidavits from Thomas Day, Robert Corbin, and Jeremy Fisher, respectively the commander, chief mate, and boatswain of the *Edward,* the vessel that had waited for two months in Nathalico Road before fleeing as a result of

Ball's allegations. From Patras, the *Edward* had sailed for Izmir, whence the three men wrote to Crow. Their words demolished Ball's claims. They testified that their vessel had been consigned to Hyde. When the captain and two of his men came ashore to confer with Hyde about loading his casks, they were so bullied by two of Ball's servants that they hastily retreated to their ship. Two days later, hearing that Ball had gone to the kadi's court in order to denounce the *Edward* as a "Maltezi"—a Christian privateer out of Malta—disguised as an English vessel and thus liable to attack and enslavement, Day weighed anchor and fled the port. Several weeks later, frustrated by the long delay, he decided to abandon the Morea entirely and set sail for Izmir.

Confronted with condemnatory testimony from Greek, Jewish, French, and English witnesses, Crow was inclined to rule against Ball. As the ambassador himself pronounced, "it was not proved by the said Ball how or wherein the said Hyde had encroached on any of the privileges proper to his office of consul."[53] Of the host of witnesses, Crow observed, only Ball's servant (and presumed kinsman), Nicholas Ball, confirmed that Hyde had shipped goods without paying consulage. Hyde's only offense seems to have been to take too seriously his duties as *voyvoda* by detaining for two or three days a few of Ball's casks, currants, and cloth because of his refusal to pay a surcharge to an Ottoman official.

Crow recorded how Hyde and his defenders were able to discredit each of Ball's accusations. He noted that there had been no witnesses to Hyde's alleged threat to enslave English sailors. Hyde also answered the more serious grievance concerning the nighttime janissary boarding of the *Defence* by insisting that it had not been his idea. Rather, the kadi, the customs collector, and other officials in Patras had suspected the ship's crew of smuggling goods; Hyde merely had wielded his position as *voyvoda* to send along his personal janissary in order "to prevent mischief by the others."[54]

Hyde also adroitly answered Ball's objection that an official of the English Levant Company should not simultaneously act as administrator (*voyvoda*) and customs collector (*bacdar*) for an opposing government. The consul's rather disingenuous response was that

> for his better ease in the way of trade and security from such insolences and injuries as might be offered him he found it convenient (though at some loss & charge by the year) to buy the power of the voyvodelik of

Patras of the Bashaw of the place, with liberty to exercise it by a subject of the Grand Signor, & so likewise the Basdarlik the last year . . . and where it was said that the said Hyde's taking those Offices was disliked by the country, no such thing appeared . . . nor was it manifested how his taking upon him those offices, behaving himself as became an honest man . . . that the Company should anyways in probability be prejudiced thereby, the said Hyde having house & lands in the country valuable to answer far more than the rent.[55]

Hyde was here discussing positions of great influence. Not only did he possess extensive lands, but the consulship also granted him authority over English commerce and merchants in the Morea. The *voyvodalık* of the pasha provided him a contingent of janissaries as well as considerable prestige among Ottoman subjects in and around Patras (indeed, Ball declared that Hyde had threatened to exercise the privileges of that office to seize his entire estate). And the *bacdarlık* sanctioned his duty-free commerce and his imposition of levies upon commodities that the English and other foreigners bought and sold. The blending of these three posts helped Hyde amass a fortune and permitted him to stymie Ball's every action. Even though he insisted that he had exercised this considerable power only for the welfare of his company and nation (and Crow accepted him at his word!), Hyde nevertheless pledged to relinquish the Ottoman offices as soon as Crow freed him from Ball's oppression.

Hyde was even able to explain away the alleged seizures of Ball's correspondence. In the case of the dinghy boarded on its way to the *Defence,* Hyde maintained that an overzealous Ottoman deputy had suspected the trafficking of unlicensed currants; as *voyvoda,* it was his duty to investigate the report. In the scuffle that followed, Hyde imagined, Ball's letters must have been lost. In the case of the mail supposedly intercepted at Holmuch, an English minister, Thomas Prichett, claimed to have received them at Modon and simply forgotten to forward them to their addressee. Prichett was an impeccable witness: he "made a solemn protestation as he was a priest & hoped for salvation that he did not detain those letters from the said Ball of design to his prejudice, or by the direction or order of the said Hyde."[56]

On 30 August 1645, Sackvile Crow finally concluded his long deliberations with a condemnation of Ball's treatment of Hyde.[57] He declared that the consul-designate should not have "called the said Hyde before the Caddie to stand to the Judgment of the Turkish Law" and that their public quarrel had endangered the English nation in Patras. He censured Ball's plot "to apprehend & carry" Hyde to England, his complaint to the pasha, his procurement of petitions against his rival, and the manner in which he had driven the *Edward,* unladen, from the Morea. Because of Ball's blunders, Crow decided to initiate proceedings to remove him from his consulship.[58]

By the end of August, the ambassador must have known that the company already had reached and acted upon the same decision. A letter he had dispatched on 25 January about the dispute had been read at a general court on 17 April, and the resolution was immediately made not only to recall Ball but also to return the pending order for currants into Hyde's hands.[59] This decision was confirmed on 8 May and again on 12 June, when the company rather cryptically explained that "Mr. Giles Ball, who is to be informed of the reasons moving the Company herein," was to be "ordered not to interrupt Mr. Hyde."[60]

Even more insulting to Ball than his removal from office was that the ambassador charged him the expense of dispatching a *çavuş* to fetch the two pretenders to Istanbul, assessed him one thousand dollars for Hyde's travel expenses, and left "the said Hyde still at liberty to pursue his farther demands & pretenses at Law before his Majesty or any of his Courts of Justice as to him shall seem good."[61] Crow undertook these punitive rulings without consultation with king, parliament, or company.

ROYALISM INTRUDES

At first glance, Crow's verdict seems just. Nonetheless, Ball's letters express a righteous and persuasive indignation that seems no pretense. Although Sir Sackvile claimed that his ruling against Gyles Ball was based on overwhelming evidence, the ambassador's true motives were more convoluted and conspiratorial. First, Hyde had always administered the Morea well, or at least quietly; Crow may have been irritated that only after Ball's arrival was he distracted by that region and its currants. The ambassador was not so dense, however, as to have misread Hyde's machinations. Although he may not have acted criminally in his clash with Ball, it is clear that Hyde worked hard to impede the new consul, whom he should have aided in every way. Hyde could not have realized his various achievements in the Morea without cleverness and mettle. Ball's angry frustration suggests that the sitting consul effectively employed these same qualities in their battle over the consulship.

Second, although the ambassador was aware of Hyde's simmering feud with the company, Crow did not consider it a sufficient motive for Hyde's resentment against his replacement. We know, however, that Hyde was so incensed at the directors' decision to supplant him that he spent the next six years in an obsessive campaign to undermine the English Levant Company's commerce. One of his first assaults against the company in his quest for compensation was a petition to Charles I, to which the king, already under siege at Oxford, responded favorably.[62] A second petition futilely demanded a "leviation"—a special tariff that an ambassador had the right to impose—from the English factory at Izmir.[63] Hyde probably wrote it in late 1647, by which time he and Crow were on a vessel en route to London—where Crow would spend almost ten years imprisoned in the Tower—and the first civil war had ended with the king's defeat.

Nor do contemporary observers of Henry Hyde's demeanor absolve him. Several acquaintances later wrote assessments of his actions during his consulship of the Morea. Most are disapproving, and some make him seem utterly reprehensible. Ambassador Sir Thomas Bendysh, with whom both Crow and Hyde were later to clash, condemned him harshly and, after a desperate if sporadic struggle upon Hyde's return to the Levant, sent him to his death in 1651. Robert Bargrave, an admittedly partisan writer, contended in 1652 that "Sr. Hen: Hide . . . had a Fame sadly foule in matters of greatest moment (vizt. of having pois'ned diverse merchants und^r him in the Morea, & made use of theyr Estates. Too true it was, they died neer at the same time; & being dead, he seiz'd what was left in theyr hands."[64] Although Bargrave stopped just short of charging Hyde with murder, he certainly objected harshly to his performance in the Morea.

Crow disregarded this infamy, and the principal reason for his apparent obtuseness related to happenings in England. By 1645 the civil war had been raging for three years, and its fury had boiled over onto the English nation of the Levant. As early as 1643, Crow had revealed his colors. In that year, the English factory in Izmir was fiercely divided over the clash between king and parliament, and one party reported to Crow that a certain Walter Elford "had concealed a licentious discourse or dispute had between two English men at his table, concerning the Parliament, and the ... king."[65] The ambassador, guided by these defamations, allegedly had Elford, together with a surgeon named John Bond, imprisoned for thirty months, despite the company's having ordered his release,[66] "till news came of the Parliaments victorious successes." As an appointee of the crown and a militant royalist, Crow was as avid a protagonist in the dispute between Ball and Hyde as he had been in the case against Elford. As almost every packet of mail conveyed more distressing tidings about Charles's prospects, he simply found it impossible to arbitrate impartially between Henry Hyde, an appointee of the king and a committed royalist, and Gyles Ball, a Levant Company man whom Crow suspected of parliamentarian sympathies and whose letter of appointment had perhaps been forced out of an embattled monarch.

By 1645, Crow himself wished to join the fray and turn the power of his ambassadorship to the king's cause, but he was unsure how to do so. Obviously, he could not rely upon his direct superiors, the directors of the company, who had opposed his appointment a decade earlier, who had long vied with him for the strangers' consulage and other revenues, and many of whom now sympathized with or even actively supported parliament. Although as ambassador, Crow was well placed to exploit the Ottoman political and administrative system, he nevertheless lacked the experience and expertise to match his desire, and he saw in Hyde a cunning royalist who could help him turn the Ottomans to his cause.

Through his training in the Morea, Hyde had shown a facility far exceeding that of compatriots such as Richard Lawrence or Frances Reade to fathom and blend into the richly diverse Ottoman realm. Not only had he fashioned alliances with Greek Orthodox, Jewish, and Muslim Ottoman subjects, but he had also mastered the mechanics of Ottoman administration and penetrated it. He was a superb manipulator of English Levant Company regulations and also seemed able to move easily through the tangle of Ottoman judicial and military jurisdictions—even befriending the kadi and pasha of Patras. Considering Hyde's loyalties and credentials, then, Crow's judgment against Ball was eminently expedient and pragmatic. It set the stage for a lengthy alliance between Crow and Hyde that would end only with Crow's incarceration in the Tower of London and Hyde's beheading.[67]

5 / The Ambassador's Gambit

By 1645, the royalist position was desperate, both financially and militarily. Charles had met repeated defeat on the battlefield. He was bottled up in Oxford with a small retinue, little food, and dwindling hope for outside support. The rich City of London had embraced the parliamentarians. The monarch's negotiations with parliament, the Scottish Covenanters, his fellow princes of western Europe, and the governments of the Netherlands and Venice had proved futile.[1] He was, in short, near the end, and was prepared to try almost any measure that might help his cause and preserve his throne as he conceived it.

A SUPPLICATION TO THE EAST

It was in these hostile surroundings that the English chargé d'affaires in Venice, George Talbot, handed Charles the idea of appealing to the Ottomans for assistance. To Charles's advisors, the suggestion must have seemed mad. Even though the mid-seventeenth-century Ottoman Empire was no longer the terror it had been, it still was a dangerous and implacable enemy of Christian Europe. Although Charles's potential allies on the continent had offered little help against his rebels, and intolerant religiosity may have been in disrepute as the Thirty Years War wound down, a compact between Charles and an Islamic empire, particularly a conquering one, would certainly have made his kingdom a pariah within the fractured Christian ecumen.[2] Furthermore, an infidel presence (even if indirect) in an England already shattered by religious dissent could only have deepened already widespread apocalyptic hysteria. Nor were the benefits to Charles readily apparent. The Ottoman Empire's treasury in the 1640s was notoriously depleted, its military disordered, and its government unpredictable. Altogether, the distant state's monetary and even military significance in the English civil war could have been no more than trivial.

Despite these many objections, a supplication for financial assistance was made to the sultan—after an abortive attempt to seek aid first from Venice—at the suggestion (if one can believe his own account) of Sir George Talbot. In 1638, Talbot had been appointed chargé d'affaires in Venice, a post he still held when the civil war began four years later. In a short memoir written in 1680, he contended that during the three years after the fighting began (1642–45), the Venetian ambassador in London had unjustly favored the parliamentarians against the king in his reports to the doge (Francisco Erizzo) and Senate, and that he, Mr. Talbot (he was not knighted until 1645), had effectively neutralized such reports.[3] Venice became so sympathetic to the king's predicament that upon hearing of the royalist disaster at Marston Moor in the summer of 1644, the Venetian government had offered "men, money, Arms, or Ammunition" to assist him. In his memoir, Talbot insisted that he had forwarded this Venetian proposal to Edward Nicholas, Charles's secretary at Oxford. He had received no reply, however, and finally had set out for England himself early in 1645. He found Charles in Oxford

> in great want: and the Lord Cottington, Secretary Nicholas, Chancellour Hyde, and Mr Jo. Ashburneham were in consultation which way to procure a subsistance for the Houshold, which for some weeks had been supported by the Sundays offerings. I had at that time occasion to speak with Sr Ed. Hyde, and sent my name in to him, he called for me in, and said to the rest in his merry way, possibly this Forreign Minister may acquaint us with some Foreign Project to get money when we want, and desired me to impart my skill. I told him he not ill addressed to me, For I had been a long practitioner in that Art, yet I knew but one way, which was, when we have not of our own, we must borrow of our Friends. He replyed, my invention was dull, for they had tryed all their Friends already. I asked Leave to differ from him in Opinion, For I was well assured, they had not tryed the Venetians. It is, said he, because we do not take them to be so much our Friends as to lend us money. That is your own fault said I, Sr Edw. Nicholas can give you a better Character of them; No, believe me said he, not I, Do you keep my Copies of dispatches by you, said I? Yes replied he, I desired him to examine my Letters of

such a Month. He went to his Office, and immediately returned with the Original Order of the Senate.

They all cryed out upon him; and he defended himself by the Hurry and confusion of Marches which caused his forgetfulness.

Away ran Mr. Ashburneham to the King with this matter; and I was immediately sent for, His Matie askt me why he was not made acquainted with this Affair sooner? I answered, I presumed it had been imparted to him when I transmitted it at first, to his Secretary.

Talbot's tone throughout his memoir (which he wrote in his seventies, some thirty-five years after the event) is perhaps overconfident, even self-congratulatory. Nevertheless, it is clear that he found Charles's party despairing of success and eager to solicit Venetian succor. Charles appointed Talbot "envoy extraordinary," knighted him on the spot, and hurried him back to Venice to negotiate for aid.

Talbot, barely avoiding Edward Massey's cavalry, sped back to Venice, only to discover that tensions between that city-state and the Ottoman Empire were high and warfare seemed imminent. Under such circumstances, it seemed unlikely that Venice could offer Charles substantive help. Thus, rather than ask the doge for assistance, he instead suggested that the king's ambassador in Istanbul (Sir Sackvile Crow) might mediate between the Mediterranean powers, no doubt hoping that a grateful republic later would aid his king. Talbot also claimed at that time to have first considered the notion that the Ottomans might assist Charles, and he wrote to Crow "both to acquaint him with the Miscarriage of my bussiness; and to advise him to try whether the Grand Signior might not be prevailed with, to espouse his Maties cause against his Rebels." He then set out again for England.

Before Talbot could reach the king, however, a commission from the Prince of Wales made him governor of Tiverton, where he first repulsed an assault by Massey, then was captured by Thomas Fairfax, and finally was exchanged into the hands of the king in Oxford. There he soon received a reply from the ambassador in Istanbul, who offered to negotiate with the sultan in the king's name. In response to this, Talbot reported, Charles had

> immediately sent away full power to Sr. Sackville Crow to pursue the Proposal, which was, that [because] the English Rebels had got the

possession of all the Revenues of the Crown into their hands, the Grand Signior would give Leave to the Embassadour to confiscate and seize all the English Merchants effects throughout his Dominions for his Ma^(ties) Service, whereunto the Grand Signior condescended.

Talbot insisted in his memoir that he had disliked this command, fearing that the merchants would "outbribe" the English ambassador. He had suggested instead that "his Ma^(tie) should borrow a considerable sum of that Emperour and impawne his Subjects Effects for reimboursement." The advantage of this procedure would have been the requirement that the sultan collect his own debts. Talbot concluded his short memoir with the sweeping appraisal that Charles had ignored his advice, squandered his chance to borrow vast sums from the Ottoman sultan, and thus lost his kingdom and his head.

MONARCHICAL CONSPIRINGS

This tale certainly benefits from the hindsight of Talbot's comfortable retirement in restoration England, and indeed, much of its detail may be fanciful. The gist was authentic enough, however, for on 21 March 1646, the very day he lost what remained of his tattered army at Stow-on-the-Wold, Charles did send to Sir Sackvile Crow, his ambassador in Istanbul, a commission and instructions in which he ordered Crow to undertake exactly the course that Talbot claimed to have urged.[4] The commission directed that

> Whereas diverse Merchants inhabitants of our City of London, and other parts of this our kingdom, now or lately trading at Constantinople or elsewhere in Turkey, are actually in arms against us or aiding assisting or abetting to the present Rebellion, whereby, by the known Laws of this Kingdom, their persons are guilty of high treason, & all their Goods, Merchandizes, & Estates, in what part soever are forfeited & confiscated unto us; our Will & pleasure is, that you represent the same from us to the Grand Signior, desiring him to give you authority to seize & to take into your custody, the merchandizes, goods, specialties, & estates of all such merchants in Rebellion against us & trading in his Dominions, & that he will permit you to dispose of all such merchandizes, goods, & estates, to & for our use, according to such orders as you shall herewith or hereafter

receive from us; And for the better discovery of such merchandises, goods & estates that he will likewise give you authority to apprehend and imprison the persons of such Merchants in Rebellion against us, together with their factors, agents, & ministers or other wise so to proceed against them.

Although this commission condemned as treasonous Levant merchants residing in London, it was directed primarily against the persons and goods of English factors posted in the Ottoman Empire. The accompanying instructions charged Crow to advise the sultan, İbrahim, that the English rebellion constituted a dire threat to monarchical legitimacy everywhere and to entreat the grand vizier and other Ottoman principals to facilitate the seizure of English goods and persons. The king also directed Crow to return bills of exchange not to Oxford (he doubtless feared their interception—this was, after all, a time when royalist couriers carried messages inside hollowed-out bullets which they were to swallow if apprehended) but to Richard Forster in Paris.

The first English emissaries to Istanbul—William Harborne, Edward Barton, and Henry Lello—had represented the English Levant Company more than the monarch, who had yielded much control over Levantine appointments to company stockholders. Diplomatic representation in the Ottoman Empire, however, grew more important and prominent in the early decades of the seventeenth century. This influence, combined with the company's growing prosperity, had led the monarchy to press for more control over the ambassadorial selection.

Throughout the 1620s and 1630s, the same Charles who was so reduced in 1646 had conducted a long campaign against the company not only for dominion over the company's strangers' consulage and other sources of revenue but also for the right to appoint company officials overseas.[5] Crow's predecessor, Peter Wyche, who, during his long tenure, had secured the consulage for himself in the name of the king, had to answer to both the king and the company in 1640 when he finally returned from his Istanbul posting. The company directors accused him of seizing the consulage for his own use, at which the king, desperate for funding to advance his wars against the Scots, proclaimed the consulage his and ordered both Wyche and the company "forthwith to bring ... a true account of all the Strangers Consulage received in Turky from the first."[6] Charles thus astutely played the ambassador and the company against each other in order to proclaim jurisdiction over this important resource.

The king in fact had won the struggle over consulage when the company assented to Charles's nomination of Crow in 1634, although neither the company, the Venetian envoy in Istanbul (the *bailo*), nor the French ambassador ever admitted that Crow was an ambassador rather than an agent, and he did not arrive in Istanbul until 1638. Even after his appearance in Istanbul, Crow did not immediately obtain the strangers' consulage, much less the ambassadorship, for the sultan was away on campaign. Instead, Wyche remained in Istanbul awaiting the monarch's return until at least April 1639, and during this time the two shared both the post and the strangers' consulage.[7] Seven years later, the fruits of Charles's victory against the prerogatives of the English Levant Company were to be tested, for Crow's commission in 1646 constituted nothing less than a declaration of war against the company and its factors in the Levant.

ACTING AGAINST THE "REBELS"

Crow moved swiftly to execute his king's directives, and in the months of May and June 1646, even as Charles floundered into a religious inferno in Scotland, the English factories of Istanbul and Izmir became immersed in a self-destructive clash that hauntingly mirrored the English civil war. Correspondence about this crisis flew between ambassadors and consuls, factors and merchants, sultans and ministers.[8] Curiously, no one, whether royalist or parliamentarian, whether in England or overseas, directly implicated the king. Perhaps only royalists knew that Crow was acting as a royalist agent; perhaps everyone realized the damage that a royal intrigue with infidel Ottomans could cause both monarchy and kingdom. In any case, Crow and his henchmen took the heat. A massive cover-up shielded both the Charleses (and the monarchy itself) from the shame of conspiring with an infidel ruler and exposing Englishmen and their possessions to Islamic justice.

Crow no doubt consulted with Henry Hyde and other advisors before acting. Although Hyde's name never appears in correspondence between the ambassador and his collaborators, Crow's stratagems against his compatriots bear the stamp of the former consul's familiarity with the Levantine world.[9] Crow himself realized from earlier experiences with the English factories of Istanbul and Izmir that he could not act against first one and then the other. In this contest, he would have to strike both parties simultaneously so that neither could mount an effective counterattack. Consequently, his first move in response to Charles's directive was to dispatch to Izmir a loyal kinsman, John Hetherington (whom several dozen English merchants later described angrily as "a most lewd, debaucht, prophane, riotous fellow"),[10] together with a Greek dragoman, Lorenzo Zuma, with orders to coordinate a campaign against the English factors there with his operation against their fellow countrymen in Istanbul.

On 27 April 1646, Crow issued the first of a barrage of warrants and instructions to Hetherington and Zuma. In it, he directed his agents to proceed to the port of Izmir, where they were to seize and deliver to Istanbul "the Consul with six or eight of the chief of that Factory, and most refractorie" (they were named as John Wylde, consul, Dixwell Brent, treasurer, John Lancelot, Daniel Edwards, Samuel Barnardiston, George Hanger, James Moyer, John Bell, John Englesby, and Henry Davy) and to seal up their homes and warehouses.[11] The devices through which Hetherington and Zuma were to effect these seizures were imperial Ottoman decrees ordering either the *çavuş* (*balukbaşı*) who accompanied them to Izmir or the kadi of that town to escort them to merchants' domiciles and storerooms and help seize them and confiscate their belongings.

It is remarkable that Crow reacted so quickly to his liege's directive. It must have taken at least a month for Charles's dispatch to reach him, yet within a few days of his apprisal he had managed an audience with the grand vizier, secured an imperial firman and supporting documentation, and hatched his scheme to snatch the persons and estates of his allegedly rebellious countrymen. One can only surmise that Crow had been plotting since his receipt of Talbot's letter in late 1645 and had merely awaited the king's endorsement. Indeed, three months earlier, the ambassador, probably already intent on securing estates for the king, had convinced the Ottoman government to prevent the lading or embarkation of English ships at the ports of Istanbul and Izmir,[12] and by 26 January had himself sent out directives to this effect.[13]

Crow later constructed an elaborate defense for this dangerous blockade, which paralyzed English trade for several months. As we will see, he also helped plant in Ottoman minds the persistent and devitalizing notion that English vessels were playing a decisive role in the Venetian defense of Candia on Crete.

First, Crow insisted he had imposed the blockade in part because he feared that some English factors would secretly export their goods without paying a leviation he planned to charge upon merchants' goods.[14] Such leviations were themselves controversial. Although they had been developed as emergency impositions meant to deal with predicaments that threatened the entire English nation in the Levant, such situations were not clearly defined, and in the opinion of many factors, Crow levied them cavalierly. His excuse for imposing a leviation in 1646, for instance, concerned his treasurer, John Wolfe, who was hopelessly in debt. Crow argued that since Wolfe's creditors were powerful "Turks and Jews" who could severely damage English commerce, his indebtedness was in fact a public matter and required a general leviation. On 18 February, he ordered English factors to pay six lion dollars per cloth in order to clear a total debt of 118,109 dollars.[15] Most factors objected vehemently, maintaining that they should not be held liable for such a manifestly private lapse.[16]

Crow's justification for the embargo went beyond the matter of a leviation, however. Two years later, he maintained that it had not been his idea at all, but the Ottoman government's. The ambassador explained that the Sublime Porte had embargoed the shipping "not only of all English and other Christians, but of all Greek and Turkish vessels, their own subjects none of them being suffered to pass out of the Castles for near six months time."[17] Fearing that such vessels would help the Venetians, with whom the Ottomans were then at war, the government also sent special orders to "outports," including Izmir, to keep ships from leaving. Crow contended that the intent of his commands freezing English ships in port had simply been to protect them from Ottoman seizure.[18] In hindsight, Crow elected to ignore consultations he allegedly had with a vizier, during which he was said to have divulged that English vessels then anchored off the coast of Izmir were trafficking powder and ammunition to Venetian defenders in Candia (an allegation mimicking one that Gyles Ball had made several years earlier against the captain of the *Edward* and that these ships' captains denied just as vehemently).[19]

Ottoman rescripts issued to the kadi of Izmir establish that Crow's rumored interviews with an Ottoman pasha indeed took place. In fact, the ambassador concocted a tale that gravely compromised his compatriots in Izmir in order to persuade the grand vizier, Salih Pasha, to assist him in his embargo of English shipping. In the early months of 1646, the ambassador visited that pasha several times to discuss persistent trafficking in materiel. He suggested that members of the English factory in Izmir undertook a large share of this transport, supplying the Venetian enemy with grains, weapons, soldiers, and oarsmen. Twice he secured Ottoman rescripts forbidding the loading of English vessels at that port town.[20]

Such tactics had helped draw provincial as well as principal Ottoman officials into the feud, for English factors and ship captains had begun employing local Ottoman administrators in order to evade these directives and run Crow's blockade. A certain Captain Porter, for example, even from prison allegedly managed to empower an Armenian customs collector, Antoine, to oversee nighttime loading of his ship with prohibited cargo. The ambassador's response to this defiance had been to secure yet more condemnatory decrees from the sultan's government.[21]

Sir Sackvile Crow spun a succession of distortions, half-truths, and fabrications to mask his designs and shield his monarch. He was not content merely to bribe Ottoman officials in Istanbul; he also played upon their fears of an Anglo-Venetian alliance against the empire. The grand vizier in particular fretted that English *bertoni* (a type of wind-driven ship) piloted by "rebel" captains might aid the Venetians in their blockade of the Dardanelles and defense of Cretan strongholds. Crow convinced the chief Ottoman official to detain English bottoms in the ports of Istanbul and Izmir in order to avert such a league, fanciful though the apprehension might have been. He also heeded his monarch's counsel by further arguing before the imperial divan that antiroyalists among the Levantine merchants conspired to undermine commerce within the Ottoman Empire as part of their campaign against the king of England and monarchy in general. Crow persuaded principal Ottoman officials, including the grand vizier, to aid him against these malefactors with decrees, men, and other means.

His approach toward local officials and middlemen in Izmir was more circumspect. Crow's long experience with that little regulated port city had taught him that the consul and merchants there had cultivated and secured the trust of the local political and economic elite (the kadi and his assistants, the collectors of customs, the resident janissaries and dragomans, and the principal indigene merchants and brokers). The relationship between the English nation in Izmir and local Muslims, Jews, Armenians, and Greeks was at least as effective as was the ambassador's association with officials and notables in Istanbul. It was not enough that Crow obtain directives from the Sublime Porte; he also had to ensure that the provincial dignitaries would abide by them. Consequently, he particularly directed Lorenzo Zuma, the dragoman who acted as Hetherington's communicant with the Ottoman world, to

> (taking the Chouz [*çavuş*] along with you) ... repair to the caddie [kadi], and by the said Chouz his hand deliver such Commands to him (to bee Registred by him and after returned unto you) as accompanie these for your better aid to the effects aforesaid; and thereafter (for the Cadies greater awe, and the firmer securing him to the service and your part) you shall also in occasion shew him that Fettfaw [*fetva*] which you here with receive, declaring our absolute Interest and Authoritie by the Grand Signors grant, and so, by their Law in such cases, over all His Majestie's Subjects under our Charge, and thereon require the assistance of his powers and aid accordingly agreeable to the Imperial Commands.... [Y]ou are not to spare any reasonable Cost or Charge to make him firmly yours, and so his Naive [*naib*], or any other of Interest about him.[22]

Thus, Zuma was to employ both imperial decrees and bribes in order to secure the support and protection of the kadi and his retinue as he and Hetherington embargoed ships, sequestered goods, and imprisoned merchants. The two agents were rumored to have ensured the kadi's backing by telling him that English factors had laded the ship *William and Thomas* with wheat (which it was forbidden to export), presumably to succor the Venetians on Crete.[23]

Crow felt that even these precautions were insufficient. He suspected that people from the town's powerful Jewish and Armenian communities, or cooperative resident officials, might try to shelter English property by claiming it as their own, or they might try to expedite the withdrawal of English merchants and their estates aboard ship or into the countryside. Therefore, he enjoined Hetherington to send an "Armenian or Jew Broker about, under colour and pretence of buying or bartering, for some cloath," in order to expose the types, quantities, and values of goods stored in the merchants' homes and warehouses and, one imagines, to drag those Ottoman subjects into his scheme.[24] He also enjoined his agent to present letters from Crow and the French ambassador to Jean Dupuy, the French consul in Izmir, "praying for the Assistance of his Druggermen in your occasions; under which generals, having Order from the Consul for his Druggermen in such occasion, being a Jew, you may for money (which you are not to spare) make him yours, and work him to your ends."[25]

More than any of these Ottoman subjects, however, Crow feared the chief collector of customs (the *emin,* or customer) in Izmir, whom he called "Bogus" and whose responsibilities included the collection of duty on commodities leaving and entering the port as well as security against smuggling and other illicit ventures. This person was actually a farmer of customs rather than a direct appointee of the state, for he had purchased the position. The customer could authorize the departure of English stock despite the opposition of the kadi and other Ottoman officials, and Crow's proposal that Bogus might "at last forsake the Merchants part" suggests that he had assisted English factors in Izmir against the ambassador in the past. He urged Hetherington to visit the customer, advise him that Crow could request the grand vizier to have him taken to Istanbul, and promise him a "negotiated" gift as well as customs on all detained wares. Should all this fail to sway the customer, Hetherington was to "proceed by the Caddie, to make Arze [petition] to the Port, of his demeanure here to us."[26]

The ambassador also ventured to misguide his compatriots. He wanted not only to cloak the involvement of the king but also to lull the merchants into believing that he, Crow, was doing nothing out of the ordinary. Many ambassadors, specifically Sir Thomas Glover (served 1606–13), Sir Thomas Roe (served 1621–29), and Crow's immediate predecessor, Sir Peter Wyche (served 1627–39), had complained bitterly to the company and the king about their meager incomes and perquisites, and they had tried to exploit the prerogatives of their post to supplement their salaries. Crow was following long precedent when, in the summer of 1646, he imposed an onerous leviation upon the English communities in Istanbul and Izmir. He instructed Hetherington that when asked why he had come to Izmir, he was to "say (as true it is) that you are sent to bee a spectator, witness, and overseer, of the Druggerman and Chiouz proceeding in the Leviation … which so much concerns mee, them, and the publick interest, and that bee not bauked, or delaid, and that I might bee sure."[27] Crow knew from past cases that many merchants (particularly John Lancelot, the acting consul in John Wylde's absence, whom he sneeringly deemed "an actor") would dispute such a levy upon their goods,[28] and that Hetherington, the kadi, and other Ottoman officials could use such protests as an excuse to incarcerate them and confiscate their property.[29]

Not even Hetherington and Zuma, selected by Crow to help execute his dangerous plan, discerned the whole truth. The king's man fabricated for them a story that the Levant Company had used the occasion of the king's distress to seize 174,000 lion dollars worth of strangers' consulage (which Crow believed was rightfully his) and to sequester his lands and estates in England worth 297,000 lion dollars.[30] Although Crow knew that he could rely on these men's loyalty to their king and their ambassador, he was willing to divulge to no one Charles's personal involvement in the game.

In early May 1646, Hetherington and Zuma launched Crow's tangled design. Several of the men whom Crow most wanted neutralized—John Lancelot, Dixwell Brent, Daniell Edwards, John Pixley, Samuel Barnardiston, George Hanger, and James Moyers—were brought to the kadi's court, where they were accused of secretly lading a ship, the *William and Thomas,* with contraband grain and directing it to weigh anchor and depart, presumably to assist the Venetians on Crete. They were then secured in a room in the *balukbaşı's* home, "an offensive dark place, the doors and windowes not only shut, but nayled upon them."[31] Crow's intent surely was to make it impossible for the leaders of the factory in Izmir to communicate with their compatriots and thereby design a collective response to the ambassador's underhanded assault. The stratagem went awry, however, for the seven men appealed to their Ottoman jailor against their brutal handling, and for a present of one hundred dollars convinced him to debar the windows and allow "his Servant and twelv Soldiers that wee had from the Castle to guard them, to let in the Nation for a Dollar or two a head."[32] In this way, the merchants' leaders were able to conceive a counteroffensive before their captors could dispatch them overland to Crow's residence in Istanbul.

Impediments already were mounting in Istanbul as well. On 25 May, Crow wrote to his agents that the collector of customs in Izmir, Bogus, had somehow made his way to the capital in order to negotiate with the ambassador. The influential Ottoman collector had insisted that Crow pay customs on all English goods, in return for which he agreed to detain two English ships then riding in Izmir's harbor, to forbid their lading, and to give Hetherington *tezkeres* (receipts) for all merchandise that had been laded or was "hid and concealed from mee, in the hands, Custody, or Ware-houses of any *Jew* or others, & shall proov to be such."[33] Although Crow declared satisfaction at this outcome, he remained wary of Bogus's design.

Two days later, Crow reported that the *balukbaşı* and *çavuş* had arrived in Istanbul with the acting consul, Lancelot, and his merchants, who voiced biting protests against Hetherington and Zuma's handling of themselves and their possessions. Crow's answer was to visit the imperial divan again in order to confirm the sultan's and grand vizier's blessings, and to display the captured merchants threateningly to their compatriots in Galata (accompanied by dragoman and janissary) in order to collect leviations.

He also issued a new set of instructions to his agents. For the most part they merely reiterated earlier directives, but there were a few notable modifications. Crow suggested that the customer unlawfully had permitted nighttime loading of goods which the customer insisted belonged to "strangers" but the ambassador believed really belonged to Englishmen attempting to shield them from confiscation. Somewhat hysterically, he instructed Hetherington to remind the kadi that some merchants already had escaped on a ship captained by a Mr. Pitler, and he insisted that his agent spare no "cost whatsoever, to the Caddie or his Ministers, the Customer or his Servants, Jews, Waiters, Boatmen, or other Officers" in order to detain the Englishmen and seize their estates.[34] Finally, he reported that most English goods had been transferred into the possession of Muslim, Jewish, or Armenian merchants, and he suggested that Hetherington and Zuma might want to leave Izmir for several days, during which the rightful owners would claim their goods, only to return in order to pounce upon English possessions. At the very least, they should post their own men at night to watch the ships.

It is apparent from Crow's letters that his ambush had miscarried and his influence was swiftly eroding. Warned by the abduction of their consul and principal factors, the fractured English factory in Izmir had quietly transferred many of its goods into the possession of Ottoman traders and brokers, whom Crow could not touch. It also had begun subverting the ambassador's support among Ottoman agents in Izmir, so that many provincial officials surreptitiously frustrated even imperial decrees. Crow also had heard that ships riding in Izmir's road might abandon that harbor and anchor beyond his reach, perhaps at Aleppo's port of Alexandretta, until the risk of impoundment had ended.

Crow was so sensitive to these perils that he felt it necessary to encourage his two agents to be faithful and to remind them of the virtues of their campaign—particularly the dire circumstances confronting their king and country—and the hazards of their proceedings. Even more than merchants (who might plot but were unlikely to riot), he feared the dozens of hardened and partisan English seamen confined aboard the five vessels then at anchor in the harbor. Probably with Henry Hyde's counsel, Crow advised Hetherington and Zuma to continue pressuring the kadi and his agents to send "Arz and Maxars from time to time to the Port" and to walk the streets always with a guard of twelve janissaries.[35] How they were to pay these exorbitant expenses, however, Crow could not tell; his own purse was empty.

THE REBELS STRIKE BACK

By the beginning of June 1646, the merchant communities in Istanbul and Izmir understood that Crow was maneuvering for something beyond a leviation, but the ambassador still concealed the sweeping incarcerations and confiscations he intended. In a letter dated 8 June, he informed Hetherington and Zuma that reckless rumors were circulating through the merchant community in Istanbul, that the death of the chief customer in Istanbul, Ali Ağa, had brought Hasan Çelebi to the post, and that in view of the sudden changes and numerous alarms, Crow and his cohorts needed to act quickly.

Hetherington's response, dispatched seven days later on 15 June, explained the kadi's hesitancy to abet the seizures because a great part of the English goods were "pretended unto by Jews, Turks, Armenians, &c." It also stated that a promise of one thousand lion dollars to the kadi, five hundred to his son, and various gratuities to his servants had convinced the kadi to send his son, his *naib,* and "some 40 or 50 souldiers" to force open merchants' warehouses and board the English ship *Jonas* in order to seize unlawfully laded merchandise. The agent further reported: "Wee have imployed the most-cunningst Rogues in all the Country, to see if they can discover any other part of the Nations Estate either his or lying out, but as yet they have discovered nothing."[36]

The English agent, together with his Ottoman henchmen, launched the operation the next morning. On the evening of 16 June, Hetherington and Zuma wrote:

> this morning, the Caddies son, with his Neipe and principall Officers came ... but before wee began 'twas spoken in the Caddies own hous, & all over the Town, our design to seiz what we could finde; about 7 a clock his son came & entred the Consul hous, & opened all the Warehouses.... Before we had ended at this house, the whole Town was in an uprore, being fomented by Jews, and som of the young frie left behinde, and proclaimed in the Streets, that the Town would bee undone, the Trade lost and go to wrack, if this was suffered; so that before the Consulls door were so many of the scum of the Town, the Streets were packed thick of them. On the other side, a more unruly enemy threatned worse things, [Nicolas Terrick] the Master of the Golden Lyon [renamed the *Hopewell*] ... lands 40 men at Barnardistons house, and vowed hee would have his money or goods, or swore hee would beat down the Town.[37]

This passage exposes the ease with which the English factory in Izmir subverted Crow's design. The ambassador may have committed to his campaign many of the sultan's representatives in Izmir, but few of the town's inhabitants were servants of the state. Instead, they depended upon local, regional, and transcontinental commerce for their livelihoods. Crow's agents themselves remarked upon "the little regard these people bear to the Grand Signors commands, the Caddie, or ought els but their private ends."[38] The town's factors, brokers, baggage carriers, tavern keepers, translators, and shopkeepers could hardly concur with Crow's argument that the thriving community of English factors, who had contributed much to Izmir's development and with whom they had traded profitably for decades, would ruin commerce in that port city. Nor would English sea captains easily have permitted Ottoman soldiers to board and ransack their vessels, whatever the attitude of their ambassador. The consequences were a popular uproar and the *naib*'s temporary suspension of the operation against English traders.

The next morning, Hetherington and his Ottoman allies tried again. This time, Captain Terrick sent some "Jewes" to tell the *naib* and *çavuş* "that the Master would shoot down the Town" if they persisted.³⁹ Hetherington, seeing that his Ottoman cohorts had again fled, that all the *hamal*s (stevedores) were committed to the enemy's cause, that the townspeople were again "rowdy," and that one of the *Golden Lyon*'s boats (filled with well-armed men) was about to dock, appealed once more to the kadi. The Ottoman magistrate's response was swift. He first ordered all shops closed, then "immediatly sent for all the chief men of the Town ... and there before them all, and a great company of the Townesmen; caused the Commands to bee read, and told them how much they were bound to see the Grand Signors Commands put into execution."⁴⁰ After this forceful expression of imperial authority, the tumult subsided, and Hetherington continued his business of expropriation. His takings were rather meager; he apparently snatched approximately one hundred thousand dollars worth of English goods, which he promptly shifted to several "Turkish warehouses."⁴¹

Once he had seized the goods, however, he did not know what to do with them. The agent was compelled to relinquish some of the estate to those who had "pretended" debts out of it: to Hüseyin Ahmed Ağa, "one of the chief men in the Town," and to a Greek servant of the powerful French consul, Jean Dupuy.⁴² The remaining merchandise sat under a constant guard of twenty or thirty Ottoman soldiers. Hetherington remained anxious about the town's populace and fearful to move too far from the waterfront because of the "people of the country." He could not market the seized wares in Izmir, because prices for the lead, tin, and wire were extremely low. Removing them from the city was impossible, too. Exorbitant costs made overland transport untenable, and untrustworthy English captains closed the sea lanes to him.

Crow had no better idea how to escape the dilemma than had his agent, for the situation in Istanbul meanwhile had begun to turn against the royalists. On 18 June, two days after Hetherington had effected his action against the English nation in Izmir, the ambassador had called a court at his home in Istanbul. In attendance was the entire English factory in the capital city and many of the factory of Izmir who had been conveyed to Istanbul and, since 22 May, imprisoned in Crow's house.⁴³ Crow advised the angry gathering that the company and parliament had sequestered his estates in England. Since English factors represented the company in the Levant, he demanded from the merchants in recompense twenty-five thousand pounds sterling and thirty-five thousand lion dollars. The assembled nation retorted that no one other than the ambassador had heard of this sequestration and implored him to consider "the Estate of our principals in England, their Wives and Families, our selvs here, with many thousands that have dependance upon our wel-fares under your Honors protection."[44] Crow rashly rejoined that the merchants not only knew of the traitorous actions against him but also had been apprised that despite a pledge that the ambassadorship belonged to Crow, an ambassador-designate, Sir Peter Killigrew, had been dispatched with the king's commission to replace him.[45]

The ambassador and his countrymen had reached an impasse. Crow would not release his compatriots from confinement in his home; they would not countenance his demands for recompense. The stalemate was quickly broken, however, by four English merchants (Thomas Piggot, Morris Evans, Robert Frampton, and James Modyford—the third of whom was chaplain and the last of whom was fluent in Turkish) who had escaped from the ambassador's residence and were not present at the court on 18 June.[46] Both sides had involved rival European states in their internecine squabble. Crow had appealed to the French in his campaign; the four factors who had escaped petitioned the Dutch agent, Signor Copes, to help them against their ambassador. Through Copes's intervention and "the clamors of the Jews, and many other of the Grand Signor's subjects against this our present abuse and destruction of future trade,"[47] the English merchants obtained release from confinement after three days and attained an audience with the grand vizier. By 21 June (and at an alleged cost of 94,646 dollars),[48] the factories had escaped Crow's grasp and sent horsemen speeding toward Izmir, had intercepted much of the ambassador's correspondence with his agents there,[49] and had procured an imperial command to recover their estates. This decree, dispatched to the kadi of Izmir in late June or early July, stated that the ambassador had wrongfully secured permission to imprison his compatriots in Izmir and confiscate their goods, that he had sent a man and dragoman down to do so, and that the kadi should now prevent the seizures and secure the freedom and goods of all affected persons.[50]

The factories of Izmir and Istanbul had acted jointly to obtain this Ottoman rescript, for it was a petition from the provincial port town that had pried open the grand vizier's chambers for the Galatan nation. In the petition, the factors of Izmir protested that the English ambassador had "found a way" to secure a lawless decree and had sent a servant and translator to the town with it. These representatives had then seized and sold a portion of the English factory's property at ruinously deflated prices. Two subsequent Ottoman responses to this entreaty were even stronger than the one issued in June. They not only directed the kadi of Izmir to arrest Hetherington and Zuma, compel them to redress the damages, and dispatch them to Istanbul but also granted the English factory of Izmir absolute autonomy by preventing its ambassador from interfering with it in any way.[51]

The willingness of the Ottoman government to reverse course so casually does not bear witness to a corrupt and self-serving regime. Rather, it displays how trivial the melee within the divided English nation must have seemed to most Ottoman officials and subjects, an assessment that the virtual silence of Ottoman sources about this episode confirms. The incident also attests to the intricacy, opaqueness, and far-flung distribution of Ottoman authority in the mid-seventeenth century. Just as Hyde and Ball, in the Morea, had earlier labored to enlist both foreigners and Ottoman subjects to their factions, so now did Crow and his adversaries each draw upon the backing of their colleagues and friends, whether Ottoman or not, in their internecine conflict.

A FRACTURED NATION

In a letter to his agents in Izmir dated 1 July 1646, Crow acknowledged the calamitous outcome of his scheme, even as he asked them to rescue him. Somewhat frantically, the ambassador asserted that his "enemies" had spent thirty thousand lion dollars for a decree to release their sequestered goods and have Hetherington and Zuma seized and sent to the capital. In a biting harangue against his personal secretary, Domenico Timone, and chief dragoman, Giorgio Draperis—his two closest and most valued Ottoman subordinates—Crow also contended that

> Dominico hath been the grand Traitor to mee, and played the Devill, the Arch-devill with mee in this business, debashed, and frighted

Georgio and the rest from mee, and stoll away my Capitulations and Records, and is now Secretary to the Apprentices of Gallata; where hee and the rest keep close, and are ashamed to shew their faces; for the very boyes of the Streets hout and scorn them for their falshood.[52]

Crow's words show how truly desperate his position was, for among his confederates Domenico and especially Georgio best knew Greek, Italian, and Turkish and understood Ottoman administration. They had served as Crow's linguistic and cultural link with the Ottoman world, and without them he could not effectively intercede with the grand vizier, admiral, customs official, and other authorities.

Having been neutralized at the core of the empire, Crow veered toward its edges. In an ironic shift, in this same letter he ordered his agents to employ regional authorities in Izmir to help him in the capital. They were to try to secure a petition from the kadi to the grand vizier asking for the overturn of the new imperial command. Crow must have realized that this directive would prove unavailing; the kadi and his aides were delighted to abandon a policy that the inhabitants of Izmir so wholeheartedly opposed.

This letter not only exposes Crow's wretched situation but also intimates how much the internecine strife between the ambassador and his nation had undermined English autonomy and authority within the Ottoman Empire. An underlying principle governing English merchants overseas was that they resist interference from foreign authorities and regulate themselves. Even more essentially than representing London, consuls and ambassadors served as mediators in disputes between English factors and merchants. The first Levant Company agents had prudently drafted this privilege of extraterritoriality into their capitulations, and each treaty since the 1580s had renewed it. By 1646, however, consuls and the ambassador were fighting among themselves, and it was even unclear to whom they owed allegiance or who among them maintained the authority to act as arbitrator. It is not surprising, then, that the grand vizier, as Crow reported, suggested the dangerous notion that the English quarrel be "heard before the caddielascars [*kadiasker*s] at the Turkish Law,"[53] the very circumstance that any ambassador most needed to avoid. Crow's failure to do so closed out his career in Istanbul.

The ambassador's relationship with his merchants in Istanbul and his consuls in Izmir and Aleppo had been shaky long before this incident. Nevertheless, they had continued in uneasy allegiance until 1646. Only in that year, when the king demanded an open breech, was the English community in the Levant sucked into the battle raging at home. No event more clearly delineates the manner in which the civil war in England spilled into the Levantine world than Sir Sackvile Crow's attempt to seize the estates of his compatriots in the Ottoman Empire. His failure to do so echoed the king's failures in England, and the Levant Company's struggle to revive the English factories in Istanbul, Izmir, and even Aleppo reflected parliament's endeavors to rebuild the fractured English state.

6 / Parliament or King?

It is hard to avoid the judgment that Sir Sackvile Crow, in his blind obedience to his king, had betrayed England's primary interests in the eastern Mediterranean. Such at least was the overwhelming opinion at home. By the mid-1640s, parliamentary forces were on the ascent, and the City of London—hub of the English international commercial community—was generally antiroyalist and sympathetic toward parliament.[1] When tidings of Crow's maneuverings began reaching London in the midsummer of 1646, the company and parliament grew eager to depose the pesky meddler, whose royalism was notorious and seemingly rabid. A wrathful English Levant Company immediately sought his dismissal.

THE SEARCH FOR A SUCCESSOR

In truth, with both king and ambassador living under virtual house arrest in late 1646, there were few obstructions, either legal or practical, to removing Crow. Agreeing upon someone to take his place, however, would be more difficult. After sixty-odd years of Anglo-Ottoman relations, a certain protocol had emerged, and the Ottomans expected the English ambassador to present to their sultan letters of appointment from his king. Thus, even though many of the directors of the company were sympathetic to parliament (and some—preeminently the company's governor and leading City radical, Isaac Pennington—even served in it),[2] they had the daunting job of finding a candidate whom both Charles and the parliament would be willing to support. Indeed, the latter body might prove particularly intransigent; the directors could not be certain that parliament, insecure in its legitimacy and sensitive to global perceptions after it had rebelled against its own king and was now fumbling toward a redefinition of the monarch's constitutional jurisdiction, would accept Charles's involvement in any form. This dilemma was acute in the late summer and early autumn of 1646, for parliament was in the midst of delicate negotiations with its defeated but still obdurate king.

The company had already experienced the difficulty of appointing satisfactory candidates for lesser offices in 1644, during the first civil war, when George Ivate had resigned the important office of consul in Izmir. The directors of the company were angry that "the factory there were fallen into great extravagancies," and they were disturbed to learn on 19 September 1644 that Ivate and Crow, without consultation, had appointed John Lancelot (whose radical politics perhaps were not yet known) in Ivate's place.[3] Within a month, the directors had resolved to select their own man for the post and had established as candidates Wylde, a certain Captain Smith, Benjamin Whitcomb, John Lancelot, and George Ivate. On 19 December 1644, the company selected by a show of hands Captain Wylde, apparently a known parliamentarian, to succeed the royalist Crow's appointee.[4]

More piquantly, at a general court held on 24 October 1644, the company had decided to look for a replacement for Crow himself as ambassador.[5] Its members fully grasped the risks of their task, undertaken in the heat of civil war. Nevertheless, beginning the following week, the company's governor, Isaac Pennington, its deputy governor, William Cokayne, its treasurer, John Smith, its husband, Henry Hunt, and six other members, "all of whom are by virtue of their oaths, to be enjoined secretly, as all these now present were, in a matter of so great Concernment to the Company," began gathering every Tuesday and Thursday to search for a suitable representative and to ponder a politic means by which to discharge Sackvile Crow.[6]

These busy merchants could not have met twice weekly over the next two years. Nevertheless, the company was well prepared in the summer of 1646 when news reached them of Crow's roguery. Not only had they long deliberated upon the ambassadorship, but already by 14 May 1646 the directors had heard about and sanctioned the refusal of the English factory of Izmir to comply with Crow's demand for a leviation to finance his treasurer's debts.[7] As early as June, news had begun trickling into London about Crow's villainous activities, and in July the company began to debate intensely how to supplant him. On 25 July, the directors reviewed three candidates—Edward Barnard, the English consul of Aleppo, Robert Sainthill, the English agent at Leghorn, and Sir Thomas Bendysh, a minor aristocrat with little experience overseas, or perhaps none at all.[8]

Although the last of these nominees seemed the least qualified, records of the deliberations indicate how much Bendysh craved and lobbied for the commission (although not why he wanted it so badly). Not only did he offer to pay his own way to Istanbul and to depart immediately, but he also pledged to discontinue Crow's habit of appropriating to himself the strangers' consulage. Most temptingly for an assembly of rather antiroyalist men uncertain how to approach their captive king, Bendysh declared that he could procure letters of appointment from Charles. The company decided to gamble on this candidate, even though he earlier had openly sympathized with the monarchy (and been imprisoned for doing so). Parliament, however, proved less amenable and refused to confirm the choice.

Three weeks or so later, Sir William Killigrew, a loyal ally of Charles, presented himself to the company directors and insisted that *he* was the king's choice as ambassador to Istanbul.[9] The directors must have found Killigrew's petition embarrassing, for the House of Commons, having already rejected Bendysh, was unlikely to sanction so manifestly a king's man. Yet the company had to be careful not to anger Charles. Its three objectives were to dislodge Crow, find a suitable replacement, and avoid being crushed between the two authorities of king and parliament. So it asked for other volunteers and received self-nominations from Edward Barnard, Robert Sainthill, John Bond, Jeremiah Alexander, William Quarles, and, once again, Thomas Bendysh. By a show of hands, the directors this time nominated Edward Barnard.

This nomination failed too, mainly because Charles refused to sanction Barnard, who, he imagined, had conspired in Crow's defeat. The directors of the company believed no one could dislodge Crow without letters of credence from both king and parliament. Indeed, dispatches from Lancelot (by this time openly anti-Crow and acting as an interim English representative at the Sublime Porte) and other factors in Istanbul maintained that the Ottoman government would never recognize (and Crow could easily discredit) an ambassador without letters from the king. Yet the House of Commons, most of whose members were thoroughly fed up with their unbending monarch, persisted in its refusal to allow Charles a voice in the decision.[10] With parliament having rejected the king's choice, and the king, parliament's, the company's endeavors to appoint a new ambassador seemed frustrated and its regulation of Levantine commerce disabled.

The directors' desperate response was to initiate a frenzied campaign against Crow. Operating out of London, the company set out to warn parliament and the general public about the dire dangers to Levantine commerce that the ambassador's actions had released. On 3 September 1646, the company's directors announced the printing of the grievances of the English nation of Izmir against Crow in London's burgeoning pamphlet press. Twelve hundred copies of this damning publication were distributed.[11] On 9 September, they again presented a petition to the Houses of parliament, futilely pleading for letters from both them and the king.[12] Although parliament established a committee to discuss the question of Crow's recall (among whose members were Oliver Cromwell, other notable civil war figures, and prominent members of the company) and voted in favor of it nine days later,[13] the ruling bodies refused to approach the king, who was then wavering in anguish between the Scottish Covenant and parliament's Newcastle Propositions.

The company again petitioned parliament on 22 September, arguing that the Ottoman government could not accept the authority of the parliament and that Crow needed to be removed by Charles personally, by "whose power he had been established there."[14] It further maintained before the House of Commons that it feared Crow's continuing residence would lead to the loss of three hundred thousand pounds, ten merchant ships, three hundred pieces of ordnance, and the liberty and perhaps lives of more than six hundred Englishmen. Despite these arguments, parliament again denied the company's petition.[15] On 25 September, the Commons, after hot debate and in bitterness against the king, rejected the company's plea to involve Charles in the appointment. It did, however, "give the Company any accommodation which lay within the power of both Houses of parliament" to assist in Crow's discharge.[16]

This rejection of the king's aid distressed company officials, who on 3 November received yet another letter from John Lancelot declaring his desperate need for a mandate from the king in order to dislodge Crow.[17] The acting agent wrote again three or four weeks later, relating how he had had to expend eight thousand dollars to rescue Crow's former secretary, Signior Dominico Timone, from execution on the allegedly false pretense, devised by Crow, that he had murdered a Greek Ottoman subject.[18] The company simultaneously received an onslaught of alarming dispatches from the east that explained Crow's lock-up of English merchants, their rescue, and the impasse that had followed.

Even though the Levant Company directors were convinced that neither Crow nor the Ottoman grand vizier would accept a change of ambassador without the king's signature,[19] they concluded that something had to be done without delay and reluctantly accepted the parliament's offer to intercede. They prepared letters addressed to the sultan, the grand vizier, Signior Copes (the Dutch agent in Istanbul), and Sackvile Crow that ordered the ambassador's recall in the name of company and parliament (but not of king) and nominated a certain Francis Vernon to bear them to Istanbul and remain there as agent in John Lancelot's place.[20] Almost immediately after devising this strategy, the company's directors heard from the king that he would furnish a letter ordering the deposition of Crow, which Vernon probably carried also on his journey eastward.[21]

The company must have found Charles's willingness to abandon his ambassador surprising. In fact, there is no indication that Charles ever openly aided Crow at all. The last thing the king, already militarily and politically crushed and clinging desperately to his honor, wanted was general knowledge that the debacle in the east had been of his design. Charles was lucky that only his most loyal retainers knew of his part in that scheme. He did nothing to disabuse the company and the parliament of their faulty theory that Sir Sackvile, persona non grata in both England and the Ottoman Empire, had acted from greed alone and that he merely intended to load a ship, the *Golden Fleece*, with his seized goods and take himself, his family, his friends, and his booty to France.[22]

Having solved (or at least faced) the question of Crow's pretensions, the company turned yet again to the selection of his replacement. On 3 December, it nominated Barnard, Richard Browne, Quarles, Sainthill, Lancelot, and Bendysh and then produced a list of finalists consisting of the last three.[23] Next, the directors vainly debated the choices, after two weeks arriving only at the decision that whoever became ambassador must be "fit for the employment, not obnoxious to the Parliament, renouncing the Strangers Consulage, & giving sufficient security by members of the company to the value of 10,000 pounds."[24]

THE KING'S END GAME

There, for the directors at least, the matter rested until the new year. While they took their Christmas break, the king, idling in confinement at Newcastle, plotted one last dangerous bid to salvage his operation in the Levant. On 24 November 1646, he drafted (but probably never sent) a rather belligerent letter to sultan İbrahim.[25] In it, Charles insisted that, as the English capitulations made clear, his ambassador—Sir Sackvile Crow—enjoyed the license not only to select and discharge English consuls throughout the Ottoman Empire but also to collect consulage unmolested. Ottoman ministers, by interfering in English administration and collection, had broken this treaty. Charles accused these officials not of premeditated opposition but simply of guilelessness. Rebel merchants, he asserted, had

> by their misinformations and false suggestions so prevailed, as that they have obtained an Order or Commission from you ... not only to suspend Our Ambassador from meddling with any of our merchants' affairs ... but to appoint and authorize one John Launcellot [in Crow's place], a person unknown to Us, but by what we credibly hear of his traitorous practices and confederacies with such of the merchants of the Levant Company here, who are principal actors in, and contributors to, the present Rebellion against Us.[26]

Charles condemned Lancelot "as an imposter & traitor" and urged that he and his followers be placed in Crow's hands. He concluded that the rebels in England would "send an Ambassador to you in Our name, and with a Commission under a counterfeit Great Seal, which they have here traitorously forged." He was certain, he added, that the sultan would not countenance such actions of "a factious party of Rebels (enemies to all Monarchy)" and that continuation of these insulting actions against Crow would dissolve "the League between our Crowns."

The company knew nothing of this ominous and cunning letter, which even contained thinly veiled threats against the Ottoman state. Indeed, both parliament and company seem to have believed that the king, too, was outraged that Crow had resisted recall to England and attempted to escape to France. At exactly the time that the company was petitioning parliament and Charles was drafting his letter to İbrahim, the directors also were negotiating secretly with the king, not only for letters of dismissal but also for a letter of credence for a replacement. Perhaps to their surprise, the king had quickly agreed to supplant Crow, presumably in the hope of sharing in the determination of his successor. The truth was even more tangled. Correspondence from Sir Edward Hyde dated 14 December 1646 indicates that the king's servants continued simultaneously to help Crow ("nothing can possibly be done till we hear farther from Sr. S. Crow to whom I have sent some papers in your Name may perhaps do him good") and conspire concerning his replacement ("if Sr. S. Crow be of necessary to be recalled; Sr. W. Killigrew pretence is next, and he writes that he shall get the consent of the Company, & the parliament, and next to him you are engaged for Sr. R. Brown").[27]

Charles's plan to replace royalist with royalist faltered, however, for someone informed both proposed candidates of these schemes. On the very first day of January, Killigrew in person and Browne via a letter from Paris each informed the Levant Company that Charles had promised him the ambassadorship. Indeed, Killigrew strode imperiously into the company's court and proclaimed that

> he had long since a promise from his Majesty to succeed Sr. Sac. Crow as Ambassador at Constantinople, that Sr. Richard Browne having some pretentions that way, had endeavored with him for relinquishing his interest, But now he understood that Sr. Richard Browne intended to supplant him, encouraged thereto by some of the Company who (as he had heard) had vowed that he (Sr. William Killigrew) should not be the man; so that by this means he had exceedingly suffered in his reputation.[28]

These overtures must have terrified the directors, in part because Killigrew's and Browne's royalism rivaled Crow's own (in the previous year Charles had ordered money seized from the English nation in the Ottoman Empire forwarded not to Oxford but to Browne at Paris). Even more frightening was the possibility that both king and parliament would dispatch pretenders to the ambassadorship simultaneously, thus further confusing an already dangerous predicament.[29]

A COMPROMISE CANDIDATE

The company acted quickly to nullify Killigrew's and Browne's claims and to nominate Bendysh to replace Crow—probably because he pledged to sail immediately and as the least partisan candidate. The directors, despairing of appealing yet again to parliament, bribed "certain persons" to go up to Newcastle and extract letters from the king to Crow recalling him, to Bendysh authorizing his succession, to the sultan, to the grand vizier, and to the company.[30] At a cost of two thousand pounds, they succeeded, for they caught Charles at the perfect moment. Having ventured and failed to escape to the continent on Christmas Day, he was now under heavy guard, profoundly disheartened, and resigned to a long captivity.

On 8 January 1647, the company obtained instructions from Charles that not only discharged Crow and designated Sir Thomas Bendysh as his replacement but also conceded that "neither the Strangers Consulage, nor any undue profits whatsoever, [shall] be exacted from you, upon any pretence from Us, or precedent of former Ambassadors."[31] In Bendysh, Charles at least had a person who in the past had been supportive of the royalist cause. In return, he was prepared to forsake Crow and even to give up the control over the company incomes for which he previously had fought so hard. On 14 January, the company authorized its governor to prepare Bendysh's "Articles of Commission,"[32] and on the following day Bendysh himself came to the company's court, where he received letters from king and company and was urged to depart as soon as possible.

Sir Thomas replied that he must have a month to put his affairs in order, but that he would leave in the middle of February.[33] In letters that Charles finally wrote to İbrahim and Ahmed Pasha on 20–21 January, he maintained his tangled deceptions even as he utterly subverted Crow's position. The king specifically insisted that the sitting ambassador "return to our presence and give us satisfaction in the late differences which happened between himself and our Merchants."[34] Such language would powerfully promote Bendysh's forthcoming bid to wrest from Crow's grasp control of English commerce in the Levant.

The directors of the company now possessed official credentials from the king, but they still could not reconcile parliament to the monarch's involvement. An unsigned letter to Edward Hyde dated 18 January explained that "the King hath sent letters for revocation of Sr. Sac. Crow from Constantinople and for establishing Sr. Tho. Bendish in his place at the instance of the Turkey Company in London which is infinitely affected there with, but they are liked to be checked for sending to the King without the parliament's leave."[35] Charles may in fact have been relying upon parliamentary opposition to feign magnanimity toward the company. The directors certainly realized that parliament was likely to reject their nominee and began working immediately to assure its consent. On 27 and 28 January, they presented to the House of Commons an abundance of letters incriminating Crow, together with yet another petition to appoint Bendysh.[36] In it, the company expressed how long it had "endeavored to procure such qualification as is necessary for establishing an Ambassador at Constantinople to succeed Sr. Sac. Crow by whom they have sustained unexpressable injuries and a loss of fifty thousand pounds sterling already."[37] It further pleaded that the House grant Bendysh a commission to prevent the loss of a further three hundred thousand pounds.

The directors also decided to appoint George Vernon to rush copies of the new letters from the king to Istanbul ahead of Bendysh in order to forestall further opposition from Crow.[38] Vernon apparently spoke Ottoman Turkish, for, in a demonstration of company disquiet at the part played by dragomans in the previous year's intrigues, he was ordered to remain in the Ottoman capital to act as Bendysh's interpreter.[39]

Although parliament apparently recognized Bendysh's selection on 29 January 1647,[40] the company still could not obtain letters to ratify its choice. Nor could the ambassador-elect depart without them, because parliament now controlled not only the king (whom it had secured from the Scots in late January 1647 for four hundred thousand pounds) and the very land upon which the directors met but also the chief cities, ports, and (as it began building its navy in the late 1640s) even ships of English commerce.[41] Yet parliament still refused to supply letters ratifying a choice approved by the king, even though he was a captive, had just been deposited at Holdenby Hall in Northamptonshire, and could do little to prevent the removal of his representative. Parliament no doubt wanted to prove that it could rule without the king, and its members must have resented the company's reiterated contention that an ambassadorial selection required Charles's endorsement.

The crippling stalemate dragged on between king and parliament in the west and between royalists under Crow and parliamentarians under Lancelot in the east. Eventually, sometime in early March—almost two months after his appointment—parliament finally presented letters to Bendysh. On 18 March, he received articles from the company restating the directors' concern that the new ambassador collect the strangers' consulage for the company rather than for himself and that he seize no goods or money from Englishmen unless specifically ordered to do so by the company.[42] Bendysh boarded ship for the Levant sometime in early April, nearly a full year after the company had seriously set to work to replace Crow.

The directors of the company might have regretted their choice, and parliament its approval of it, had they known how cordial relations between the king and Bendysh remained. Even in late 1647, as Charles languished in internal exile at Carisbrooke Castle on the Isle of Wight and Bendysh settled himself in at Istanbul, at least three lengthy letters from the new ambassador reported to the king not only matters of state but also more personal concerns.[43]

7 / Pretenders to the Ambassadorship

By the autumn of 1646, Charles I's rearguard action in the Levant had thoroughly miscarried. The inability of his officials and agents either to enlist Ottoman aid against his enemies or to deliver to the king the persons and wealth of the English Levant Company factors and merchant adventurers in Istanbul, Izmir, and Aleppo constituted a serious, perhaps even fatal blow in the monarch's struggle with parliament. Just as the virtually simultaneous royalist defeat in England did not quite finish Charles, however, so did the exposure and ruin of their designs in the eastern Mediterranean not quite close the Levantine careers of Crow, Hyde, Hetherington, and their royalist companions. Although their bald lunge at their compatriots' jugulars had severed many of the political and ideological strands that had bound together the commercial and diplomatic representatives of Britain in the Levant, and although the factory in Istanbul had elected John Lancelot as the company's agent there,[1] so far as the Ottoman government was concerned (as well as the French and Venetian representatives in Istanbul), Crow remained the sole fully accredited representative of the English government. Even as an English Levant Company vessel, fittingly called the *London*, carried Sir Thomas Bendysh eastward, the disenfranchised Crow, with nowhere else to go, ensconced himself in the official residency in the Ottoman capital, together with Henry Hyde and a few other servants and advisors.

DEPARTURE FOR THE EAST

Little is known of the early life of the ambassador-designate who in the summer of 1647 voyaged toward Istanbul. Bendysh, whose family may have been involved in the fisheries off Yarmouth, was the second baronet of Steeple Bumpstead in Essex.[2] A warrant he issued against a Richard Thwaytes of St. Martin in the Fields on 30 September 1630 proves that he had served as the sheriff of Essex.[3] He also apparently began the first civil war with royalist sympathies, for he spent some time in the Tower of London for publishing a proclamation that opposed the House of Commons's plan to associate several counties.[4] Bendysh does not seem to have been a man of great wealth, for in 1643 he pleaded with Sir Thomas Barington and Sir Martin Lomby "& the rest of the Commissioners for the County of Essex" to have mercy on his meager estate of eleven hundred to fifteen hundred pounds per annum, as he languished in the Tower and his wife and children were dispersed across the country.[5] He somehow bounced back quickly, and four years later he was appointed to the prominent post of ambassador to the Sublime Porte.

The company's instructions to its ambassador-designate included a rather standard recitation of desired reforms in relations with Ottoman authorities.[6] The directors craved less lavish gifts to the sultan, grand vizier, and others, the renewal of the English capitulations, with more moderate customs charges on goods and none on monies, and better supervision over collectors of customs in Aleppo and Istanbul, who too often demanded extraordinary monies and payment in kind rather than in specie. Added to these predictable guidelines, the company demanded specific reforms in the internal workings of the English nation. For example, payment for the ambassador's and consuls' opulent entertainments were to come from leviations collected in the Levant rather than out of the company's coffer.

More irregular in these instructions were expressions of fear that the very morals of the company's factors had grown lax and hope that the new ambassador could improve them. Bendysh was to protect members of the English nation from the vices of "gaming, drinking or any other licentious course of life, whereby the Principals may receive damage, Our Nation scandal, and other young men ill example, That in such case you will inform and reclaim them."[7] He also was to reform the manner in which English trade was conducted by insisting that factors begin registering their transactions in the chancellories of Istanbul and Izmir, presumably in order to regulate the cutthroat intracommunal competition that the company believed had contributed (together with

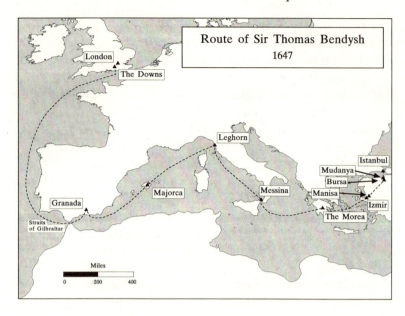

royalism) to a decay in English commerce. The factors in Istanbul were expressly to avoid entrusting cloth to Jews and others (although, curiously, those in Izmir might continue to do so). This clause presumably related not only to a long-standing English animosity against Judaism but also to the strong sense of Jews as commercial competitors that English merchants shared with their European rivals.[8] Exacerbating these tensions, perhaps, were the concurrent presences in London of a crypto-Jewish trading colony and a Puritan philo-Semitism. These were to contribute to the official readmission of Jews into England in 1657, almost four hundred years after their expulsion. For either religious or commercial reasons, then, many members of the company loathed Jews.

Finally, the instructions indicated how Bendysh was to enforce these changes, declaring that because "we have already suffered much by the refractory and dishonest carriage of some of the factors and other persons now residing within our Privileges . . . we do in special manner desire your endeavor for a speedy removal of them, by sending them home hither."[9] In short, the company granted Bendysh what four years earlier it had refused Gyles Ball—the power to seize Englishmen and deliver them to England—and suggested as targets for such actions the recalcitrant Henry Hyde and John Hetherington. In another dispatch dated 3 April, just before Bendysh's sailing, the directors advised him to reward the secretary Dominico Timone for exceptional loyalty and to send home any English divines he found still at large, particularly the minister Mr. Gotbed.[10] This curious directive may reflect the disputes over faith and doctrine that distinguished especially London in the aftermath of the first civil war and that were even then provoking ideological fissures in the parliamentary party.[11]

Armed with this sweeping commission, as well as with letters from parliament and king, and ordered "to ship out hastily,"[12] Bendysh, together with his wife, five daughters, and eldest son, embarked from the Downs aboard the *London* (captained by John Stevens), accompanied by the *Unicorne* (captained by Richard Goodlade), in April 1647.[13] Attending him was a retinue including Dr. Reyner (his personal physician), Mr. Poole (his steward), ten other attendants, and seven "potentiary" merchants.

He did not get far. In a peculiar foreshadowing of the upheavals to come, a violent storm soon greeted the two ships. As one of the accompanying factors, Robert Bargrave, recounted in his diary, "the wind grew exceedingly boistrous, making us fresh water souldiers sensible of the sudden change; so that we threw our very Galls in Neptunes face, & payd our Forfeits to the Fishes his hungry & dilligent Attendants."[14] The tempest ripped out the *London*'s mainsail, waterlogged all the vessels' provisions, and compelled the captains to retreat to the Downs for repairs. It was only after a month in port that the entourage again set sail.

This second journey, although successful, was not itself without adventure. A mere two days out, the vessels met with five Swedish men-of-war, whose commanding officer insisted that he had a commission from his queen threatening that if he "struck Flagg to any of the Parliaments Power, she would at his returne divide his body in the midst."[15] They simultaneously encountered a parliamentary man-of-war and frigate, the English naval captain of which urged the two company vessels, heavily armed to confront the myriad privateers that swarmed the Mediterranean seas, to jointly attack the Swedish fleet.

This prospect must have terrified the ambassador-designate, who, after all, had most of his family in tow. It also put him in a quandary concerning his loyalties. Should he heroically embrace the parliamentary cause and fling his vessels against the Swedish queen's squadron, or should he present his commission from Charles in an effort to escape? After a brief but ardent firefight, Bendysh chose to negotiate as the king's ambassador rather than as parliament's, thereby extricating his ships and his family from the conflict and leaving the two parliamentary vessels to fight alone (although a larger fleet soon relieved them).

This engagement was the most dramatic of several that faced the ambassador and his entourage during their journey, although his ships did on two occasions face off three French and later two "pirate" craft.[16] A month after embarking, they anchored off Gibraltar. Soon thereafter they were becalmed for ten days offshore from Granada (where the mariners watched and smelled their sheep and fowl perish and putrefy in the heat). They visited a monastery on Majorca, where the priests urged the Protestant merchant Bargrave to convert and join their isolated splendor, and sometime in June landed at Leghorn.

Considering that the English community of the Ottoman Empire desperately needed a fully credentialed ambassador in order to pry Crow from his residency, that it had taken almost a year for the company to find a replacement for Crow, and that almost three months had already passed since Bendysh's initial departure from England, it is curious that he tarried for almost a month at this Tuscan port, which English trade had only recently helped transform into a bustling commercial center.[17] The explanation seems only in part to have been that he there saw his eldest daughter married to Mr. Philip Williams, a principal merchant in the port city (much to the dismay of Bargrave, who had his own designs upon the young woman).

Additionally, the king seems to have commissioned Bendysh to recount the affairs and politics of the English community in Leghorn. Some months later, on 12 November 1647, Bendysh wrote to his liege that the English community there displayed "large expressions of duty, and affection to you[r] Majesty and so unanimously therein conjoined, as it filled me with no less admiration, than joyfulness to behold it: amongst whom none more zealous than your servant, and Agent Mr. Sainthill."[18] The king's particular concern for Sainthill, the foremost English representative in Leghorn, suggests that even after the debacle of 1646 the royal party had not abandoned its ambitions to orchestrate English commerce on the Mediterranean Sea. Bendysh seems to have been willing at least to humor Charles's plea for intelligence, and he adopted the tone of royalist agent, surveying and assessing for the king the opinions of distant compatriots about the struggles wracking England.

While in Italy, the ambassador-designate also somehow learned that Crow had obtained new letters from Charles, which Bendysh accurately deemed false, and on 26 June he wrote to the company requesting a second letter from the king condemning his rival's forgery.[19] Bendysh's supplication arrived in London in late July, and in the first days of August the directors sent the same emissary who had negotiated on behalf of the company at Newcastle to obtain such a communiqué from the king, in which he was to express his "dislike of Sr. Sac. Crow's proceedings herein, as also of the ships in the Venetian service which is likewise a great cause of avanias daily upon us in Turkey."[20] On 7 August, Charles not only delivered exactly the letter requested but also wrote to Bendysh explaining that he had done so.[21]

MEDIATING IN IZMIR

Upon departing from Leghorn, the ambassador-elect proceeded with relative haste to his post in the Ottoman Empire. After brief stops at Messina and in the Morea, his two ships anchored in the Izmir Road sometime in the middle of August 1647, where the long-besieged English factory enthusiastically welcomed him.[22] According to his letter to his king, Bendysh found the English community there profoundly demoralized and in shocking disarray. In a thinly veiled and crushing criticism of Crow, he exclaimed that "the fabric of peace, and safety to your Majesty's subjects, which was so long in building, and so well upheld by former Ambassadors was now utterly defaced, and no corner preserved either to keep your Majesty's honor or your subjects in safety."[23] He elaborated these words with a tirade against the malpractices of Ottomans in Izmir—the customs officials' abusive rates, the subject merchants' reluctance to provide the English even with bread, the frequent beatings that "Turks" administered to English merchants on the streets of Izmir—in short, the "reign of terror" under which the English community believed it languished.

These charges, of course, merely reflected the opinions of English factors in the town. As Hetherington and his English adversaries had proven the previous year, Ottoman citizens often had good reason to censure and restrain foreign inhabitants of their city. Nevertheless, however prejudiced they may have been, English convictions were persistent and shared by other outlanders. Both Venetian and French factors, for example, protested to Istanbul frequently and bitterly over alleged mistreatment by Ottoman collectors of customs, the difficulty of procuring even biscuit to supply their vessels, and sundry other offenses against their consuls, factors, and mariners.[24]

Bendysh did not set out at once for the capital city but tarried in Izmir for two or three weeks, where, just as instructed, he set about reorganizing the administration of its English factory.[25] His first action, on 16 August 1647, was to freeze all English trade by ordering ship captains to remain in port, forbidding them to load or unload commodities, and imposing a 20 percent fine upon anyone who disobeyed.[26] This action served at least three purposes. First, it forced the English community of Izmir to attend Bendysh's general courts and negotiate with him, for they were desperate for the specie and commodities which were in his ships and which he would not deliver until certain issues were resolved. Second, it temporarily stopped the threat of either Venetians or Ottomans seizing or hiring English Levant Company ships for use in their war over Crete and averted any consequent diplomatic predicament. Finally, it constituted an assertion of authority, Bendysh's notice that he could and would grasp the prerogatives of the ambassadorship.

The ploy worked. Of the perhaps thirty-five factors then residing in Izmir, an average of twenty-seven or twenty-eight attended each of the seven general courts which the new ambassador convened and over which he presided during the third and fourth weeks of August.[27] The deliberations of these assemblies concentrated first upon the ambassador still sitting in Istanbul and the calamitous internecine strife that most of the factors blamed him for instigating. For some time Crow had known that the directors had dispatched a fully accredited Bendysh to replace him, and on 25 May 1647 the entrenched ambassador had sent a letter of greeting meant to reach Bendysh during his stopover in Izmir. Crow's salutation carried veiled threats, however. Phrases such as "the worthy reports I hear of your civility, moderation, wisdom & constant good offices to all his Majesty's well wishers & loyal people" disclosed that he demanded a royalist successor. He also warned that Bendysh's fate would mirror Vernon's if he did not really have a commission from the king.[28]

Bendysh must have read and initially praised Crow's letter, for on 17 August the battle-hardened factors in Izmir unanimously exclaimed that they found naive Bendysh's sanguine appraisal that Crow, recognizing the new ambassador's letters from both king and parliament, would quietly relinquish his station. Warning him that dislodging the royalist agent would demand perspicacity as well as the guidance and funds of the English factories in Izmir and Istanbul, the factors all urged Bendysh to leave his vessels, the *London* and the *Unicorne,* in their care and proceed overland to the capital city.

Although the route across western Anatolia was slower than the sea road, the factors judged it much safer. As they no doubt explained to the new envoy, at the Dardanelles Straits, officials stopped, inspected, and imposed levies upon all vessels, whether Ottoman or foreign. The Englishmen also complained of the abuses of Ottoman bureaucrats at that place, to which many Ottoman decrees attest. As early as 1622, the Dutch, French, and Venetian envoys in Istanbul had objected to seizures and other violations at the straits; two years later the *bailo* of Venice complained that officials there collected more than their due for the Cretan honey, olive oil, beans, lemon juice, and other goods that passed through on their way to Istanbul.[29] The difficulties had not been resolved thirty years later. In September 1652, for example, an Ottoman shipmaster named Hasan objected that the commanders of the castles guarding the Dardanelles had levied more than the customary 136 *akçe*s upon his vessel. In September 1646, the French ambassador had requested that officials in these castles stop harassing Dutch ships during their passages toward the Netherlands.[30] His allies in Izmir reasoned further that once past the castles of the Dardanelles, Bendysh would lose to the Ottoman government command over his floating fortresses (and thus his most important bargaining chip) in the unavoidable conflict with Crow and his supporters.

They feared, however, that the precaution of approaching by land rather than by sea would prove insufficient, and they beseeched

> that for his better accommodation, & security his Lordship would be pleased to admit of a CapeAgee Basha [*kapıcıbaşı*] ... to accompany him, besides two druggermen to attend him ... besides a competent number of

horsemen, spahies, & Janizaries as also such number of gentlemen, and servants of his own attendance as he pleased to demand.³¹

Although Sir Thomas expressed some reluctance about dragging such an immense retinue across the rugged Anatolian plateau, he agreed, so long as no goods were removed from the vessels without his approval and they remained anchored in the Gulf of Izmir.³²

While his staff set about mobilizing the escort for its march overland, Bendysh proceeded to reorganize Izmir's English factory. He quickly detected that decreasing revenues lay at the heart of the nation's administrative difficulties, and first on 21 August and again five days later he ordered correctives in the collection of consulage. In this major reform he insisted that strangers' goods carried in English bottoms should land only at the scale of the company's treasurer (who would assess them and collect the consulage accordingly) and that nighttime transfers of goods should cease.³³

The question of consulage, especially on commodities that foreigners laded on English ships (which the company termed "strangers' consulage" to differentiate it from surcharges imposed on the goods of English merchants), had long been a sore point between the company and the king. A 1- or 2-percent surcharge was customarily imposed upon circulating English commodities in order to maintain the consul, his officers, and his administration. In 1634, Charles had authorized Crow to wrest from the directors of the company the right to collect the "foreigner consulage." More recently, growing tired of the anarchy accompanying the bitter encounter between the ambassador and the company, stranger merchants and, potentially disastrously for the company treasury, even English merchants had begun shipping their goods on Dutch or French ships, landing them at unauthorized scales or even more blatantly flouting English authorities in order to circumvent the surcharge.

Without this income, the factory had become indebted to several of its wealthier factors. Attempting to remedy this insolvency, Bendysh revised his earlier directive that the *London* and the *Unicorne* not land any money or goods and instead ordered the ship captains to dispense one thousand dollars apiece to the fourteen men who had lent the most.³⁴ At the same time, he mandated to the factory's treasurer, Dipwell Brent, the right and obligation "to make a due collection of the company's own consulage, as well as Strangers, which last having much need of, so his Majesty hath by his Royal letter to the company, acknowledged their right thereunto." Brent (and his fellow treasurer in Istanbul, Joseph Keeble) was to charge English ships one dollar per ton and interlopers "dollars 500 broke for bringing cloth, & other commodities of the growth of England."[35]

In this declaration, Bendysh not only announced to the factory at Izmir the company's total victory over Charles in the battle over consulage but also—by repudiating Charles's right to the consulage—proclaimed that he was not merely the king's man. The ambassador-designate had other motives as well. His subsequent letters to the king reveal how quickly he had realized the depth of the anger that divided the English nation in the Levant. He must have discerned with equal speed how badly he would need the advice and sympathy of these triumphant veterans of the dispute of 1646. In that struggle, the factory of Izmir had acted independently of Istanbul. It had repudiated Crow's directives, outmaneuvered his agents, and helped reverse hostile Ottoman proceedings in both Izmir and Istanbul. If Bendysh wanted to fight Crow effectively, support from these men was crucial. For this reason, he quickly bowed to the factory's desire to revise the company's attempt to reform the duties of the treasurer.

This officer was responsible for collecting and disbursing monies for the consul and the company. Although the task was vital (it called for the assessment of charges on commodities and the collection of fines for smuggling and other abuses), it also was thankless (it demanded responsibility without power and often produced rancor) and unprofitable (it was time consuming and drew the appointee away from his own business dealings). Duplicating a system that already existed in Aleppo, the directors wanted Bendysh to schedule the election of two men who had been resident in Izmir for at least two years, who would each serve for six months and would each receive a salary of two hundred dollars per annum. The factory objected to this arrangement on two grounds: first, that the salary was niggardly considering the treasurer's need to support "a bookkeeper, a Jew, a Janizary, and several Magazines, to receive Strangers Goods,"[36] and second, that the company wanted the officer changed too frequently, for commerce was growing in Izmir and the account books were complex. Consequently, Bendysh agreed that pending company approval, one resident factor should serve for an entire year with a recompense of 5 percent of the consulage. This last allowance was fundamental, for it transformed a salaried office into a virtual tax farm, and a public service into a potentially lucrative and venal enterprise.

Despite Bendysh's concessions, a candidate for treasurer was difficult to find. On 24 August, the factory first elected George Cave, who balked on the basis of ill health and an impending return to England, and then applied to Samuel Barnardiston, who consented only after a personal guarantee from Bendysh that he would indeed retain 5 percent of the consulage. At this same general court, Bendysh, having heard how steadfastly and skillfully the chief dragoman, George Honiero, had interceded with the kadi and other officials in Izmir during the previous year's crisis, agreed to raise his salary from two hundred to three hundred dollars per year. The ambassador also ratified the appointments of a certain Signor Lura and his son Oslan as dragomans, raising to three the number serving the city's English consul and nation.[37]

These reforms all assailed administrative and commercial abuses. The ambassador's mission was not only civil, however. In accordance with his instructions to safeguard the English merchants' moralities, Bendysh also probed their private worlds of faith and church attendance, in order that "the Worship of God might be duly, and carefully observed, & his name not profaned, both for the avoidance of such scandals, as by other Religions and nations, may be cast upon us, and also that God might the better prosper us."[38] Although the factory members called in their minister, Mr. Bull, to attest to their devotion to the English church, the ambassador still demanded that the entire nation regularly attend Sunday worship in both the morning and the afternoon. Failure to do so in the morning, he insisted, should return a fine of one-half dollar toward the redemption of English captives; the penalty for nonattendance in the afternoon would be one-fourth dollar. Bendysh also imposed a twenty-*akçe* (twelve-pence) fine for swearing and blasphemy.

These reforms confirm that the clash between the king's and the parliament's men in the Ottoman Empire was not only over money and power but also had a vital moral dimension. Just as the conviction that they were fighting for God helped justify the parliamentarians' cause in England, so the company and its proponents argued that Crow and his henchmen had tried to corrupt the souls of their factors in the Levant, as well as seizing their purses. The religious heterogeneity of Izmir further complicated the ethical issues. In the streets of London, it was merely exponents of various Christian heterodoxies who struggled for mastery; in Izmir's religious clutter, the dominion of Christianity itself was in doubt. In other words, the company directors dreaded not so much heresy as apostasy. Although the impetus of the godly may have originated in the exclusively Christian milieu of London, the appointment of a minister and imposition of fines for negligence and blasphemy in Izmir probably formed hedges more against Islam than against Catholicism or sectaries.

FACE TO FACE IN ISTANBUL

Having settled company affairs in Izmir and, he judged, secured the respect and support of the English factory there, Bendysh prepared to confront the more serious challenges awaiting him in the Ottoman capital. He relayed to the king worrisome reports from Istanbul. Bendysh dwelt long on the intolerable difficulties that plagued English trade in the Ottoman realm. Ultimately, however, he did not blame the Ottoman state for the disarray. He uttered not a word against individual sultans, viziers, or other state officials. In fact, Bendysh exonerated them from malfeasance, even implicitly praising the Ottoman authorities for assistance against the intransigent Sir Sackvile Crow, whom he spent several pages censuring. He blamed Crow for "Turkish" harassment of English vessels, whose cargoes were often seized, whose captains and seamen were sometimes beaten, who had to pay enormous docking fees, and whose goods were picked over and stolen in the customs shed. In short, the sitting ambassador had failed to secure his merchants' goods and persons. The situation had so deteriorated, Bendysh reported, that Ottoman officials and soldiers brazenly staved in the doors of English homes and removed their contents. For these reasons, the new appointee told his king, he had chosen to leave his "richly laden" ships in Izmir and journey overland to Istanbul.

Leaving his wife and children under the protection of the English nation of Izmir,[39] the ambassador set out on 13 or 14 September on the twelve-day trek to Istanbul.[40] According to Bargrave's diary, the party's passage took it overland, in a Kieravan [caravan] of about :100: english, together with their Servants; Our Harbingers went dayly before us to prepare all things against his Lordship came; when we had but litle to do more then to spread his Lordships tent.... On this Rhode are none but despicable Villages, nor anything of noat, but their rich immanur'd land, & their many handsom pleasant Fountaines for relief of thirsty Travellers: Only the City Bruseia [Bursa] is indeed remarkeable having formerly been an Imperiall Seate.[41]

After a brief respite in Bursa's hot-spring baths, the party continued to Montania, rowed down the Scamander River and across the Sea of Marmara, and arrived in Istanbul on 26 September 1647.

Bendysh quickly discerned that during his weeks in Izmir, Crow had been hard at work denouncing him. As Bendysh put it in his report to the king, Crow and the French ambassador had "given out that I was a traitor."[42] It seems that almost a month earlier, Sir Sackvile, assisted by the French ambassador, de la Haye (who perhaps acted at the indirect urgings of Charles I's French wife, Henrietta Maria), had attained an audience with the grand vizier and there issued a formal protest against Bendysh. He notified the Ottoman official that Sir Thomas had taken a treasonable oath against His Majesty Charles, and that although he had secured a counterfeit seal from the "rebels," he had none from the king. More curiously, Crow also asserted that Charles was even then at the head of an army, within twelve miles "of that Rebellious city of London."[43]

Crow's statement indicates either his desperation or, more plausibly, that he had been away from England too long. His was the reasoning of the late 1630s, not the late 1640s. The ambassador simply could not comprehend the fantastic changes that had taken place during the intervening decade. Of course, wild rumors, first about Charles's and then, after 1649, about his son's having mounted triumphant crusades, initially against the parliamentary rebels and later against Cromwell's regime, continued to circulate in the Levant well into the 1650s. Nevertheless, in the summer of 1647 even that royal fiasco known as the second civil war was almost a year away. One of the new ambassador's hardest and most vital chores would be to show the Ottoman administration the fallacy of his rival's contentions. By the end of September, Edward Hyde and others in the king's court already had intelligence confirming that Crow had long been at work undermining his challenger. They were convinced that Bendysh would fail to persuade the Ottomans that his credentials were authentic.[44]

Bendysh found the English factory in Istanbul in a resolute if precarious condition. John Lancelot, the agent whom the nation had appointed to lead it until a new ambassador arrived, was serving only informally because of Sackvile Crow's stubborn persistence. Although the Dutch agent Copes acknowledged and supported Lancelot, the Ottoman government did not, and both the French ambassador and the Venetian *bailo* openly snubbed him as an unlicensed rebel. Crow and his supporters, however, soon found that it was more difficult to ignore Bendysh, who not only proved to be exceedingly clever but who also carried letters from both parliament and king. In addition, Bendysh had the advantage of being an enigma. Although the *bailo,* Soranzo, had carefully followed his progress from London to Izmir and Galata, even a month after Bendysh's arrival the Venetian could ascertain neither his qualifications nor his politics.[45] Thus, rather than persist in backing Crow, Soranzo joined the French ambassador in studiously ignoring both him and the new arrival.

Despite being spurned by his peers, Bendysh astutely employed letters from the king, parliament, and company, as well as the expertise and financial resources of the community of English factors in Istanbul, to open dialogues rapidly with his compatriots and establish himself as the English ambassador. Only a day after his arrival, for example, he caused Lancelot to send a dragoman to the *bailo* in order to present a copy of his letter of credence and declare that Charles (thus did Bendysh seek to assert his authority as the *king*'s ambassador) craved cordial relations with Venice.[46] On the same day, he attempted to deliver to Crow his letter of revocation from the king. When Crow refused it, the English nation in Istanbul quickly procured six *çavuş*es from a vizier, who the next day forced it into his hand.[47]

After this incident, Sir Sackvile finally took Bendysh's letters. He did not accept their contents at face value, however. On 29 September, he acknowledged their authenticity but declared that the king, then a prisoner, must have been forced to write them, and that Bendysh thus acted as the chief of the community of rebel merchants. He further accused his challenger of the dreadful outrage of using "Turkish justice" against a fellow Englishman. At this point, Sir Thomas seems to have despaired of negotiating with Crow. As he later recounted to the king:

> when I perceived that he would not acknowledge me, but report me a deceiver, and [would assert] that the letters I brought were false, and seeing that the Merchants could not trade, nor have credit while he remained upon this place, I thought it time to require of him in your Majesty's name ... your seal, the merchants' goods, and writings, and his speedy departure from his office and place of Ambassador.[48]

The ambassador-designate resolved to mount a full-scale campaign against Crow and his pretensions.

It took Bendysh only three days after his arrival in Istanbul to determine that there could be no compromise with Crow, who almost simultaneously deduced his rival's competence and tenacity. Crow's appreciation of Bendysh's abilities is evident in a vengeful letter he penned to Charles on 30 September.[49] In it, the ambassador reiterated in a self-pitying manner the incidents of 1646–47. He bemoaned how close he had come, through presents to the *şeyhülislam*, *kapudanpaşa*, and *defterdarbaşı*, to success in carrying out the king's orders to expropriate Englishmen's estates. In fact, he had managed to seize over one million dollars from them. Then, disaster had struck: the grand vizier had been unseated, the *şeyhülislam* had passed away, and the *kapudanpaşa* had sailed away to the Venetian wars. Crow, through these misfortunes, "came to be suspended in [his] charge, only for prosecuting what was required by his Majesty."[50] He confessed that in his desperation he had used the king's seal to draft phony directives, and he recounted how, when a certain Vernon had appeared with letters from Charles to the sultan and the grand vizier and had proceeded directly "to that Arch Rebel Lancelott,"[51] Crow had persuaded the grand vizier that the dispatches were either counterfeit or surreptitiously obtained.

Crow adopted a more despairing tone in his version of developments since Bendysh's arrival. He claimed that the letter he had sent to Bendysh in Izmir had been cordial, welcoming him to the empire and requesting a copy of his commission from Charles so that he could help him settle himself. Crow contended not only that Bendysh had spurned him but also that he had heard from Paris that the ambassador-designate had secured letters only from parliament, that he had recently taken the Scottish Covenant, an oath of fealty to Presbyterianism, and that his "ungodly instructions" were to demand new capitulations under the name of king and parliament or, if these were unobtainable, to smash English trade in the Levant.

Crow ended his epistle piteously, asserting that he had been suspended from governance for sixteen months and had spent nearly fifteen thousand pounds, all in order "to defend myself and Hostages from slavery or worse, His Majesty's honor and interests from scandal against the horrid and incredible inventions and Avanious proceedings of his Rebles [sic], backed with the Common Purse of the Company and by their order prosecuted at the Turkish justice." This letter displayed the attitude of a royalist who had utterly lost perspective over events in England. Crow believed in a prerevolutionary island in which the king's authority was unquestioned and his commands unconditionally obeyed. In fact, Charles himself was no longer part of such a world. He and his counselors (Edward Hyde was receiving frequent reports on Crow's predicament) paid no heed to their servant's plea.

Neither did Thomas Bendysh. On 3 October, within a week of his arrival, he had attained an audience with the notoriously erratic sultan İbrahim, "with all the magnificence which is usually displayed on such occasions."[52] Bendysh made the most of this event, which was of enormous symbolic value in legitimizing his authority. It occurred, according to Bargrave, in a pavilion bordering the inner courtyard of Topkapı palace, to which "richly clad & bravely mounted" Bendysh "went attended by all the Merchants in gaudy Clothes & on gallant horses; & with diverse Droggomen (Interpreters) & Janizaries besides his proper Retinue, among whom were :12: gentlemen in a noble Livery." The sultan's guard admitted only ten or twelve of this company into the audience room, where

> his Lordship, being entred, was mann'd by two Turke Officers, who when his lordship bowed to the Gr^d. Signor, thrust doune his head lest he should do short Reverence. Then being sett on a Chaire opposit to the Gr^d. Signor, they interchangeably pass'd theyr complementall addresses; which done, his lordship [presented?] his letters of Credence from his Maiestie of England. These being read & conferr'd on about halfe an howers space, the Gr^d. Signor pronounc'd him Ambass^r, & presented

him a Robe of Honour.... At the Adieu, the Ambass^r was made to go backwards, till he was out of the Gr^d. Signors sight.⁵³

    Although Bargrave, loyal to his lord, did not expose the topics of the half-hour consultation, the *bailo,* Soranzo, still trying to puzzle Bendysh out, pondered the meeting. It was customary that an outgoing ambassador would accompany the ambassador-designate when he presented his letters to the sultan, and, according to the Venetian, the Ottoman ministers expressed displeasure that Crow had not done so. When they requested his attendance, however, Bendysh aggressively declared that Crow was a rebel against his king, that his credentials were forged, that many Ottoman officials, including even a Jew in the grand vizier's service, brazenly pilfered English merchandise,⁵⁴ and "that he [Bendysh] would not allow ships to come in here any more, and they would see if the old ambassador had so much power."⁵⁵ It probably was the last argument that convinced the Ottoman ministers, who cared little about England's political legitimacy but much about who controlled the powerful vessels, advanced military supplies, and rich commerce of that distant country.⁵⁶

CROW'S OBSTINACY

Although Bendysh's strong-arm tactics made a great impression upon the foreign community in Galata, they did little to discourage Crow, who continued to harass Bendysh with the accusation that he was a rebel offering fraudulent letters of credence. The very day after Bendysh's audience, his rival not only conferred with the *bailo* but also visited, unavailingly, the recently appointed grand vizier, Hezar-pare Ahmed Pasha, in order to declare the falseness of Bendysh's credentials.⁵⁷ Despite the latter's triumph in the sultan's pavilion, he felt compelled to parley with Crow, whose residency he visited on 7 October.

    The meeting accomplished little. Although Crow apparently met Bendysh at the door of his audience room and welcomed him cordially enough, the deposed ambassador straightaway retreated to his throne-like interview seat and, when presented with a letter of revocation from Charles I, "pleaded the letter either counterfeit or deceitfully obteined; & instead of submitting to it, drawes out his old Commission, & commands Sr. Thomas Bendyshe his Reverence to it."⁵⁸ Bendysh, standing before his tenacious competitor with one letter from his king ordering Crow to "return to our presence and give us satisfaction in the late differences which happened between himself and our Merchants" and a second urging Crow to comply,[59] must have felt frustrated and deeply insulted. Such at least was the case according to one witness, Bargrave, who commented that "each with theyr hatts on, they parted in Disgust and Defyance."[60]

The subsequent narrative is somewhat muddled and contradictory. Although Bendysh vehemently denied it, Crow later insisted that the new ambassador and his factory next tried to buy him out, offering him five thousand pounds to depart quietly, a proposal that he claimed to have indignantly refused.[61] Bendysh then secured a second audience with the grand vizier (on 10 October), at which it was rumored he received his vestments in return for thirty thousand reals (approximately seventy-five hundred pounds sterling) and the promise to order his well-stocked and powerful ships, still riding in the Gulf of Izmir, to proceed to Istanbul.[62] Three days later he appealed for aid from the French ambassador, who, after consulting with the Venetian *bailo*, refused.

Crow, too, was not idle. On 19 October he floated the effective rumor that a certain "Colonel Joe" had arrived with letters to Crow from the king.[63] This deception—Crow later conceded that the letters were forgeries[64]—confused the Ottoman government, upset Bendysh's maneuverings, and even gave the Venetians and French pause. The Ottoman government's confrontation with two sets of recent letters from Charles sharpened its dilemma and perhaps even forced the divan to consider closely how the civil war then raging in England might influence warfare and politics in the eastern Mediterranean. The sudden appearance of these mysterious letters certainly deceived and alarmed Bendysh, who soon thereafter penned a long letter to his king, justifying his enterprise and begging his liege's continued favor.[65] The *bailo*, in particular, feared that the English controversy—with each faction recklessly flinging currency and commitments at Ottoman officials—was fast becoming a dangerous precedent for putting embassies and foreign nations up for auction.[66]

It was Bendysh, ultimately, who took the most decisive action. On 23 November,[67] a mass of Ottoman soldiers and servants seized Sir Sackvile Crow in his garden, dragged him through the streets of Galata, displayed him before an English throng who jeered at him from the windows of

Bendysh's residence (and whom Crow mocked as "rebels" in return), and dumped him unceremoniously into a small *kayık* bound for San Stefano. From there, he was immediately transferred to an Ottoman coastal vessel and, treated very much like the bulk goods the boat customarily freighted, shipped to Izmir.[68] As Crow himself later maintained:

> in the third day of November 1647 by undue procurement of Sr. Thomas Bendysh and the factors or some of them, the Vizier sent some of the Grand Signior's officers of Justice to the said Sr. Sac., who by a Subtilty having entered his house of Residence by force of Arms apprehended his person and by like force (attended by some of the factors of the Levant Company) caused him to be embarked in an open Turkish boat for Smirna without any provision for the way, money about him, or other clothing than he was found in, no servant to attend him or suffering to send to his wife, children or family, or to take any order for their diversion, sustentation, or relief in that barbarous place.[69]

If the tense rivalry between Crow and Bendysh had dismayed the Venetian *bailo*, Soranzo, this incident must have chilled his blood. It was not so disturbing that the English factory appeared to have utterly disintegrated. Indeed, the Venetians could only have welcomed the apparent collapse of the English Levant Company, which almost seventy years earlier had exploded into the Mediterranean and set about systematically dismantling Venetian trade through a combination of innovative organization, advanced technology, and piracy.[70] It was rather the anxiety that English deeds might pull down Istanbul's entire diplomatic edifice that so troubled the *bailo* and his peers.

This fear derived from the Ottoman role in Crow's humiliating departure. Having failed to flatter, entreat, cajole, intimidate, or bribe his opponent into retirement, Bendysh had resorted to Ottoman power—surely the riskiest kind of compulsion for a diplomat, whose foremost duty was the retention of his own and his compatriots' legal and political autonomy. Even worse, the English factory did not bother to conceal the disgraceful withdrawal of the man who had led them for almost a decade. Crow's eviction was carried out in broad daylight, and English merchants guided the throng that escorted him to the sea. Indeed, it seems that by 23 November Bendysh had relinquished all control over the proceedings, for it was Ottoman officials who dragged

Crow away at the behest and according to the method of the grand vizier himself.

Even though the English Levant Company later denied wrongdoing, insisting that the transition from Crow to Bendysh was smooth, without bribery, and entirely legal,[71] Robert Bargrave, Bendysh's own subordinate, described how "the Vezir sent a Chaous [*çavuş*] ... to seaze on him, & to convey him thence: & this he did indeed in too rude & savage a manner; pulling & thrusting him till he came from his own house to the Seae side."[72] Such public impertinence against an ambassador recalls how *çavuş*es and the kadis of Patras and Izmir had fiddled with English affairs, and it set an ominous precedent for *all* ambassadors. The Venetians in particular, with their long training in eastern Mediterranean politics and trade, feared that the English fiasco might invite further Ottoman interference into the private proceedings of foreign companies and states.

OTTOMAN SCHEMES AND ENGLISH SQUABBLES

The fact is that Hezar-pare Ahmed Pasha intervened decisively in the confrontation between Crow and Bendysh, ostensibly because of a massive payoff. The Venetian *bailo* charged that the English merchants had squandered eighty thousand reals in order to get rid of Sir Sackvile, and Bargrave later confirmed that the English factory in Galata had paid the grand vizier ten thousand pounds sterling for Crow's expulsion.[73] Crow himself had dispensed over forty thousand reals, much of it borrowed from Venetian merchants, to various Ottoman officials.[74] These outlays confirmed only too convincingly the misgivings that Richard Talbot claimed to have expressed two years earlier when the king decided to seize merchant properties in the Levant rather than appeal directly to the sultan for help.[75]

Western Europeans, contending not only with religious antagonism but also with often aggressive and hostile customs collectors and other Ottoman officials, tended to deem Ottomans, all Ottomans, inescapably corrupt and venal. Accordingly, most observers imagined that the company's deep pockets had overwhelmed Crow. They were wrong. The grand vizier's resolve to support Bendysh rested only minimally upon the English factory's munificence; his principal interest was to preserve his own neck.

In the mid-seventeenth century, the position of grand vizier was notoriously tenuous and even dangerous. After the death of Murad IV in 1638, the grand vizier Kara Mustafa Pasha held the Ottoman center competently until his execution in 1644. After Kara Mustafa's demise, however, Ottoman leadership became infamously erratic and volatile. Between 1644 and 1656, eighteen men—four being executed, eleven dismissed, two resigning, and one dying of natural causes—held the grand vizierate. Indeed, Hezar-pare Ahmed Pasha's own predecessor, Kara-Musa Pasha, had held office for only five days, and Ahmed himself would last less than a year. Nor were the posts of other dignitaries any more secure. In the same period there were twelve *şeyhülislam*s, twenty-three *defterdarbaşı*s, and eighteen *kapudanpaşa*s.[76] This impermanence suggests that the grasping corruption for which Ottoman officials had become infamous derived principally from the fleetingness of their power. Furthermore, each new appointee launched massive displacements as he assigned loyal retainers to key positions in the bureaucracy.[77]

The late 1640s were among the worst of these years. Riotous crowds frequently demanded, and often got, the deposition and sometimes the execution of high officials, grand viziers, and even sultans. On 8 August 1648, protestors incited the dethronement and murder of Sultan İbrahim, whose sobriquet "the insane" was probably well deserved. Istanbul also endured frequent famine—sometimes precipitated by Venetian blockades of the Dardanelles—and bands, occasionally murderous, who ranged the city's streets. Aliens seemed particularly to fear janissary troops. Bargrave, for one, observed "the dayly hazards of being stabb'd by the drunken sottish Turkes; who supposing all to be Venetians that wore our westerne habit, (as if the world were divided between Venetians & Turkes) & they having lost in the warr perhaps some neer relations, were allways apt to mischief us."[78] The diarist's reflections suggest a profoundly disheartened, famished, and frustrated populace, impatient to strike out at "the foreigner" or any other convenient scapegoat. Before embracing his version, however, one would wish for the impressions of his "drunken sottish Turkes," which seem not to exist.

Bargrave was wrong to assume that the inhabitants of Istanbul mistook Englishmen for Venetians. The anger of the citizens of Istanbul against the Britons was not unjustified; it derived from the English role in the debilitating war over Crete. The conflict persisted for twenty-four years, from 1645 until 1669, and pitted against each other two battered and weary behemoths of the Mediterranean world. Like heavyweight fighters in the final rounds of a long bout, the Venetian and Ottoman empires alternately heaved great body blows against each other before collapsing in order to reassemble their ebbing energy. At stake, the Venetian and Ottoman governments believed, was commercial and military dominion over the eastern Mediterranean.[79]

Ironically, the future masters of commerce merely observed this contest. Renegade English vessels (often indistinguishable from company ships), haunted the harbors and recesses of the Aegean basin and acted almost as vultures in the struggle. Their captains exploited the desperation of the combatants in order to use their long experience as pirates and their strong, nimble, heavily fortified ships to supply and transport the troops of both sides. By doing so, they not only made enormous profits but also helped prolong the war and provoked ire against their compatriot merchants.

Although the Venetians could not break the Ottoman siege of their stronghold at Candia, they could use their navy to counterattack. The Venetian strategy in the 1640s and early 1650s, only sporadically effective, was to blockade the entrance to the Dardanelles in order to disrupt the Aegean network that provisioned Istanbul's several hundred thousand inhabitants. The Venetians, not wishing to provoke a disoriented giant, confronted English vessels—licensed as well as outlaw—only reluctantly. The English were therefore positioned to help decide the outcomes of these blockades.

Thus the grand vizier and his entourage confronted both domestic and foreign crises in the autumn of 1647. Hezar-pare Ahmed Pasha's tenure, and indeed his very life, depended upon the capacity of his government adequately to provision the citizens of the Ottoman capital. The route through the Dardanelles Straits to the coasts of the Aegean Sea and Egypt constituted a critical passageway for Istanbul, and English seacraft, able to break the Venetian blockade, could guarantee access to these shores. In the several audiences that Sir Thomas Bendysh secured with the grand vizier in October 1647, the ambassador not only handed him ten thousand pounds but apparently also pledged to command his heavily armed vessels, still anchored in the harbor of Izmir, to sail for Istanbul.[80] They finally anchored off the capital city on 19 December, presumably carrying Bendysh's wife and children.[81] He also may have promised to prevent English privateering captains from commissioning their ships to the Venetians,[82] a long-lived procedure which the Ottomans understandably loathed.

It was thus in the autumn of 1647 that the Ottoman government (or at least *an* Ottoman government) abandoned the royalist cause. For years, Crow had promised to regulate English shipping; for years, English ships had continued to plunder Ottoman vessels and abet the Venetian foe. The Ottomans apparently decided to see whether the untried pretender, Bendysh, who claimed to represent parliament, company, and the Levantine English nation as well as his king, could better govern his unruly countrymen. An immediate inducement to this decision may have been that as many as seventeen English ships—a potentially potent armada—were then clogging the Gulf of Izmir and awaiting Bendysh's command.[83]

The Ottoman commitment to Bendysh was absolute. Not only did the divan dispatch a band of *çavuş*es and *bostancı*s to oust and deport Crow, but it also exiled his entire retinue, including Henry Hyde, who had taken refuge in the ambassador's residence. Two days after Crow's departure, the grand vizier also pitched out Lady Crow, several months pregnant and burdened with two young children. Crow's wife, it seems, was left penniless. She appealed first to ambassador de la Haye and *bailo* Soranzo, who seem to have annoyed her by offering much less than she requested.[84] She then scraped together one thousand or so pounds from some English merchants who—perhaps sensitive to her father's powerful position in parliament[85]—secretly provided the money. Lady Crow soon joined her fellow exiles waiting on the *Margaret* in the harbor of Izmir.

AN EX-AMBASSADOR IN LONDON

Bendysh chose to deport his adversaries via Izmir in part because vessels usually embarked westward from that port city rather than from Istanbul. Moreover, it was Ottoman coastal boats rather than English seagoing ships that conveyed Crow and his family from the capital. The new ambassador, however, would never have risked giving his rival a layover in Izmir if he had not himself visited the town and felt confident in that English factory's competence and willingness to ensure Crow's repatriation. As it happened, the English nation of Izmir even weathered a decree demanding that Crow be returned to Istanbul, which de la Haye had promptly obtained from the Sublime Porte and which a *çavuş* hurried to the western-Anatolian town.[86] Perhaps the kadi and other local officials, as well as *ayan* and indigenous merchants, were themselves fed up with the ambassador's squabblings with his nation and eager to expedite his deportation.

The *Margaret* set sail from Izmir in December 1647 and, after a brief layover in Alicante (where Lady Crow, put ashore because of illness from her pregnancy, almost succeeded in having the ship seized by the Inquisition), touched port in London the following March or April. There, Crow's co-conspirator, Hyde, effectively threw himself on the mercy of the company. On 18 April 1648, William Garway and John Robinson agreed to stand a bond of four thousand pounds for him. A month later, Hyde consented to have the entire matter arbitrated by five men, two chosen by the company, two chosen by the accused, and the fifth selected by the first four. On 17 August, the company appointed Roger Vivyan and Ja. Wyche, and Hyde selected John Collyer and Oliver Clobery.[87] By 17 April 1649, Hyde had jumped his bail and fled to the continent.[88] Thus did he weather the complaints of Gyles Ball and others against him.[89] Having been arrested for his debts, paid a small bond, and spent a year or so in the City, he then followed Prince Charles into exile after the king's execution. Two years later, Hyde was to return to Istanbul, where he would again challenge Sir Thomas Bendysh's authority.[90]

Sir Sackvile Crow was less fortunate. A sergeant-at-arms had met the *Margaret* as it docked at London and conveyed him at once to the Tower of London, where he awaited indictment.[91]

Even though Bendysh was now the uncontested ambassador, the company was in no hurry to press charges against Crow. The directors met on 7 March 1648 to discuss what exactly to accuse him of, and decided simply to await expected testimony from Robert Keble, Nathaniel Barnardiston, Walter Elford, John Swift, Robert Garway, and the captains Ashley, Jordan, and Jerick.[92] A week later, their debate was over whether to take action against Crow and Hetherington at the common law for breach of covenants or to take action by petition to parliament.[93]

On 28 April, the company finally elected not to charge Crow in a court of law but to leave the accusations against him with the Committee for the Navy, a parliamentary council.[94] This decision was momentous, for it removed the case from the sphere of private law and faulted the former ambassador for crimes against the state.[95] Indeed, when Crow heard the indictment five days later, he was outraged, presumably because it constituted an onslaught upon his monarch's authority. In his lengthy written response to the company's charges, he insisted that he had been the king's ambassador, not parliament's (he was right that parliament was not authorized to appoint envoys), and he asserted that the company's complaints against him were of no concern to the state but belonged within the realm of private law. Crow was bitterly aware that the civil war had violently cleaved established bonds between king and state, and that the victors even then were demanding that the captive Charles accept a much diminished position in government. Crow's point-by-point refutation of the company's charges against him reads almost as an afterthought to this paramount concern.

Crow's attempt to associate public law with the king—and simultaneously to dissociate his litigation from the state—drove the company into the dangerous and uncertain terrain of state legitimacy. The simplest response of the company directors would have been to insist that the king no longer had the right to appoint ambassadors and that Crow consequently had managed Levantine trade illegally. But the second civil war was still months away, parliament had not yet been purged, and it had not yet so sweepingly repudiated its sovereign. The directors did not want to budge from the careful perch between king and parliament that had led to Bendysh's appointment. So they chose a different tack. Although the body of their reply to Crow was a detailed and carefully documented rebuttal of each of his justifications, it began with the markedly modern declaration that

> commerce and trade with foreign Nations ... is the life of every Commonweal; and the destruction of such trade ... tends to the dishonor and impoverishing thereof, is of public damage & concernment: So are the Parliament the patriots, and conservers of the Liberties & properties of England, the proper Judges of the breaches thereof, and of those injuries done by the said Sr. Sac. to this Nation, Company, and their factors and estates there residing.[96]

In these lines, the company directors not only intimately linked state and commerce but also, in order to refute Crow's contentions concerning common law, proclaimed parliament to be the protector of that trade and therefore the proper judge over it. Most arrestingly, the company resorted to modern concepts concerning the English "nation" and "patriot" in order to skirt issues of authority and parliamentary versus monarchical jurisdiction.[97]

Even after this seemingly decisive skirmish, however, the company did not vigorously prosecute its claim. The case had not been resolved even by 1658, and almost yearly after his arrest Crow requested the company or the government or both to support his release from the Tower of London so that "he might be enabled to solicit his occasions and a subsistence for himself & family."[98] Finally, he vigorously seized the initiative in his battle against the company. On 25 August 1654, he emerged from the Tower to argue in the presence of the protector, Oliver Cromwell, that revenue from the strangers' consulage belonged to the state rather than to the company, as did the prerogative to appoint ambassadors to the Sublime Porte.[99] Two years later, in November 1656, he orchestrated from the Tower the arrest of Zachary Browne, the master of the *Margaret,* which had carried him home from Izmir almost a decade earlier, and several members of the company on charges of indebtedness.[100] These entreaties and assaults availed him not at all. The former ambassador spent virtually the entire interregnum imprisoned in the Tower. Nor did he ever recover either his authority or his resources. Indeed, Crow's deportation from the Ottoman Empire in 1647 marked the end of his public life, and several plaintive and cloying missives to Charles II and various ministers during the 1670s and well into the 1680s exhibit that not even the restoration could revive his career.[101]

THE CIVIL WARS IN THE OTTOMAN WORLD

During the 1640s, English proceedings in the Levantine world reflected the civil wars that at the same time consumed society at home. The most striking feature of the English presence in the Ottoman Empire during those years was that community's intensifying disarray and the consequent tension between it and the Ottoman state and society. At first, the strains exhibited themselves principally along the imperial frontiers, far from Ottoman centers of economic and political power. Henry Hyde's clash with Gyles Ball in the Morea during the early 1640s pitted against each other two pretenders to a relatively insignificant consulship. Although their conflict engaged diverse local foreigners, Ottoman subjects, and officials, the dispute involved the English ambassador only marginally and the Sublime Porte hardly at all.

Such was not the case a few years later. Sir Sackvile Crow's assault upon the English nation in the Levant during the mid-1640s struck closer to the heart of the English presence in the empire. Crow, Hyde, and their cohorts drew important Ottoman subjects and officials—indeed, the inhabitants of an entire Ottoman city—into their intrigue. They also thoroughly engrossed the directors of the English Levant Company in London and forced that organization to take harsh measures against its principal appointee in the eastern Mediterranean. Despite the sense of crisis that gripped English Levantine commerce in its aftermath, however, the main dramas of this contretemps took place in the outlying city of Izmir; it failed fully to engage the sultan's administration in Istanbul.

With Sir Thomas Bendysh's appearance in the capital city in late 1647, the English civil war finally burst into the Ottoman world at the highest possible level. Two ambassadors, each claiming to represent the government of England—whatever that may have been in the late 1640s—squared off in the presence of sometimes partisan high Ottoman officials. Through their desperate actions, they not only made themselves dramatically visible in the Ottoman capital but also forced England's political crisis upon the consciousness of the Ottoman state and commercial society. With Crow's expulsion, Bendysh, left at the head of a shattered nation of merchants, had gained the attention of notable portions of the Ottoman trading community as well as the imperial council itself. With these eyes upon him, he also gained an opportunity to reconstruct and perhaps even revise the English presence in the Ottoman world.

8 / Adapting to the Ottoman Commercial World

Sir Thomas Bendysh endeavored to consolidate his position during his first years as ambassador. He attempted to unite three divided, deeply suspicious, and incessantly litigious assemblies of English merchants in Istanbul, Izmir, and Aleppo. Before Crow's expulsion, a common enemy had united them, but with that ambassador's defeat, a multitude of ideological, personal, and commercial tensions manifested themselves. One result was increased strain between the English and other groups residing in the Ottoman Empire. A second consequence was a succession of intense quarrels among the three English factories. Yet a third was the formation of disputatious factions within each community. The new ambassador expended much time and effort trying to close these fissures and build a consensus among his Levantine factories.

ENGLISH AND OTTOMAN MERCHANTS

In the last of his three extant letters to Charles I, Sir Thomas complained bitterly that the written records of the day-to-day management of the English factory in Istanbul had vanished together with his predecessor, Sir Sackvile Crow. He noted the difficulty of administering that factory without access to the precedents established by previous ambassadors and the histories of current cases.[1] Despite this and other obstacles, he immediately had to begin adjudicating the sundry quotidian problems confronting the community as well as contend with the many complaints and disagreements that had piled up during Crow's last months in office.

One of the ambassador's foremost duties was to protect the rights and privileges of the English community against incursions from outside.

Since divisions within Ottoman society tended to be communally based rather than class based, such protection often meant coping both with Ottoman subject merchants as members of millets and with foreign competitors as members of factories. Squabbles among the English, Dutch, French, and Venetian nations were endemic, and Bendysh took great pains to maintain English precedence and foil the ambitions of England's rivals, particularly the French, in Levantine trade.

Yet the greater menace to English commerce rested with Ottoman communities, especially the Armenian, Greek, and Jewish ones. As integral components of Ottoman society, these millets were involved in Ottoman administration as well as in trade. They had developed indigenous commercial networks that were intricate and almost impenetrable and with which foreign communities had to associate. They also controlled the position of dragoman, the translators through whom foreigners and Ottomans customarily conversed.[2] In short, Ottoman subject groups effectively dominated both internal trade and communications between foreign traders and the Ottoman bureaucracy. The ambassador had no alternative but to accommodate (and occasionally confront) the power of these communities, a power that permeated the Ottoman economy and administration.

Bendysh also had to grapple with the partialities of the English Levant Company's directors, many of whom exhibited the deep-seated religious prejudices of English society and thus opposed fraternization with Muslims and Jews and even with members of rival Christian denominations. Particularly widespread among the English (and other western Europeans) was a belief that Jews wielded immense power in the Ottoman bureaucracy. The English probably inherited this conviction from the Venetians and other Mediterranean trading partners to the Ottomans, whose rivalries with Sephardic Jews for control of eastern Mediterranean commerce coincided with the sixteenth-century Ottoman settlement of Spanish Jews, who soon gained leverage particularly as collectors of customs in Ottoman port cities.[3] In 1532, for example, the disheartened Venetian consul in Alexandria, Nadalin Contarini, wrote: "This scoundrel, the Jewish customs-farmer Abraham Castro, is the source of all our troubles. . . . All the consuls have complained about him to the Sublime Porte, but to no avail. . . . The Pasha does nothing without his advice."[4] English attitudes soon reflected Venetian ones. As early as 12 March 1631, Ambassador Sir Peter Wyche professed to his friend

Lord Dorchester that "as all these Ministers are bought and soulde, wee speede the worse, the Jewes beinge our adversaries, doe make it a generall business amonge them, and have extraordinarie favour within the Seraglio."⁵

Such antipathy toward the Ottoman Jewish community persisted. Recorded in the English Levant Company's instructions to its new ambassador in 1647 was the proscription against all English factors in the Ottoman Empire trusting "out cloth to Jews,"⁶ largely because the directors feared their influence at the Sublime Porte. Observing how interwoven into the Ottoman economy its Jewish community was, and considering that virtually every English, French, Dutch, and Venetian factor employed Jewish (not to mention Armenian, Greek Orthodox, and Muslim) translators, brokers, and middlemen and dealt symbiotically with Jewish distributors, Bendysh quickly realized the futility of this directive.

The new ambassador never tried to implement the company's edict against Jewish merchants. Nevertheless, the habitual nature of commercial relations between Englishmen and Jews inevitably led to occasional conflict. Just such a clash climaxed on 11 October 1652, when the ambassador received a petition from three English merchants, Roger How, Nathaniel Man, and John Hurt, protesting the intentions of a compatriot, William Pearle, to resort to an Ottoman court of law in order to achieve redress against a Jewish firm owned by a certain Benjamin Perists.⁷ Pearle, it appears, believed that his friends among Ottoman officialdom would ensure the success of his suit. The three petitioners feared that the case would only expose the disarray within the English factory in the city. They suspected Pearle would be out of his depth before "Turkish justice" because the Jews' experience and influence in that arena were far greater than his, and they worried that the Ottoman magistrate's acceptance of verbal testimony would further advantage the Englishman's adversaries (the Jews presumably could rely upon their coreligionists, who enjoyed the powerful advantage of knowing the Ottoman language and being a part of that culture, to support them). How, Man, and Hurt insisted that "whereas Mr. Pearle's chiefest hopes are to prevail by making friends, it may justly be feared that the Jews will be too hard for him therein, having already gained the Vizier's [ear], & his Jew being also most likely to favor those of his own tribe."⁸ Finally, they deemed it likely that both sides would resort to bribery, and they judged the Jews' pockets far deeper than Pearle's.[9]

The Englishmen's fears were not unfounded. In fact, one of the first incidents with which Bendysh had to contend concerned Jewish influence among the Ottoman elite. Several years earlier, in February 1646, the English factors John Rydley and William Osborne had closed a deal with the Jewish partnership of Saguen and Sermony.[10] The Englishmen, acting on behalf of the merchant Frances Reade, who had left Izmir for Leghorn after winning his dispute with Richard Lawrence in 1639, as well as for themselves, agreed to sell the Jews 1,860 pikes of flowered satin, in partial compensation for which they were to receive 918 *okka*s of grogram yarn. This agreement seems at first to have proceeded satisfactorily, and Osborne then negotiated independently to sell several bales of paper to another Jewish partnership comprising "Yachiel the Cape," Isaak Yemamo, Braani Coen, Isaak Coen, and "Tarakee."[11]

Both arrangements, however, soon turned sour. On 13 September 1648, Osborne petitioned the ambassador against the Coens' firm, complaining that it had reneged on an agreement to buy ten bales of paper at forty-five dollars each. The Englishman demanded that Bendysh order a battulation against them (that is, a boycott against all English commerce with them) and that the ambassador's Jewish dragoman, Jantoph, direct two other of the Coens—David and Moseh—to attend Bendysh's court to explain their comportment. About a year later, on 19 November 1649, Rydley complained to Bendysh that Osborne had cut him out of the previously negotiated deal for grogram yarn by renegotiating with Saguen and Sermony.

Osborne, not surprisingly, objected to Rydley's complaint, insisting four days later that he had merely confirmed the old agreement with Saguen and Sermony upon the death of Isaac Sermony.[12] The factor explained that he had fretted about having only Jews (who, he asserted, were notoriously unwilling to testify against each other) to witness the previous agreement and had several times asked Rydley to accompany him, unavailingly. Rydley's name was not mentioned in the new agreement simply because none of the goods were his.

In the Ottoman Empire, ethnoreligious communities and foreigners routinely sought to construct common fronts against trading rivals. One of the English nation's most frequent maneuvers was the battulation, or factorywide boycott, intended to punish individuals, partners, or entire communities for attacks upon English commerce. Bendysh resorted to this exigency often: on 30 November 1649, for example, he ordered a battulation against the Jew Isaac Soreson and his son David for not paying William Gibbs for some cloths, and on 8 January 1650, he ordered one against the Jew Joseph Aluffe and Company.[13] In response to Osborne and Rydley's complaint against the Coens, Bendysh decreed that any Englishman who associated with that partnership would face a fine.

Battulations, however, often were ineffectual, as the ambassador learned in late 1648. On 25 October, Bendysh ordered a battulation against the Jews Jacob and Samaria Jannie because James Modyford claimed four thousand dollars against them, only to have Modyford reappear with the complaint that the two had simply employed the Rabbi Abram Yami to transact their business with the English factory.[14] Bendysh, perhaps in some frustration, reiterated the battulation, included Yami in it, and ordered the English nation to enforce it more diligently. This action, too, was probably inadequate; even blanket battulations against entire millets often proved useless in a world where merchants could compete only by crossing such communal lines. Despite mutual contempts that were doctrinal and deep-seated, Ottoman diversity demanded frequent alliances between Jew and Briton, Armenian and Venetian, or Greek Orthodox and Frenchman.

In the case of the Coen family, Bendysh felt obliged not only to blacklist the Jewish partnership but also to summon the Jews to the judicial court that he maintained over his factory, presumably to be examined and chastised and perhaps to be judged by the overlord of the English nation in the Ottoman Empire. Osborne, meanwhile, continued contracting with various Jewish partnerships and even conspired with them against his compatriots. In 1649, when Rydley accused Osborne of defrauding him and his master, Osborne defended himself by claiming to have been compelled to forge a commercial agreement with Saguen and Sermony because the witnesses to their first agreement had been "only Jews, and such as by the experience I had found, would not give in testimony against their own nation."[15] Osborne unquestionably believed, if not entirely accurately, that millets were impermeable and that just as he petitioned his ambassador for assistance against rivals, so would another people throw its support unquestioningly behind a compeer.

This Englishman seems not to have learned much from his encounters with Jewish commercial establishments. Two years later, in 1651, he protested the stratagems of the Jewish partnership of Isaak Cargashan, Abraham Hekem, and Isaak Useph.[16] When that company became insolvent, Osborne maintained, Useph had had him dragged before the kadi of Istanbul, where the merchant unjustly demanded from him 3,587 lion dollars as payment for 644 buffalo hides. When Osborne balked, Useph procured from the kadi an order to seal the Englishman's house with all his goods inside. Osborne countered on the next Saturday by going to the public divan. There, Useph again outmaneuvered him "with a bribe of $300.00." Osborne next was dragged to the *kadiasker*'s house, clapped in irons for five days, and forced to acknowledge that he had received from Useph the 644 buffalo hides and still owed four and one-half dollars for each. Osborne finally escaped his predicament after a payment of twelve hundred lion dollars, a disbursement that he termed an *avania* and requested the English Levant Company to repay.

On the one hand, the company was sympathetic to such appeals against a hated "tribe." On 6 February 1651, for example, it ordered its ambassador to "procure justice" against Jews who owed money to members of the English factory and who hid behind the "lies" of their compatriot brokers, "who refuse to testify the truth of bargains."[17] On the other hand, it is doubtful that the tightwad company was so supportive as to dole out money. The directors invariably recoiled from paying such bills, which were incurred often and which it termed "private" *avania*s. Ambassador Bendysh likely responded in the only way he could, by imposing yet another battulation against Useph and his collaborators.[18]

This series of incidents reflects the almost unfathomable commercial organization in the Ottoman capital, which involved all communities, both subject and foreign. Throughout his tenure, Bendysh kept up a running battle with his French rival, and he often had to act against non-Jewish Ottoman servants and associates as well. On 6 October 1649, for example, he battulated a certain Hatchooke, an Armenian servant to the factor William Pearle, for slandering and abusing some of the ambassador's own servants,[19] and on 14 March 1650 he battulated the dragoman Giorgio Draperis (who had abandoned Sir Sackvile Crow three years earlier) from all "discourse or communications" with the English factory, under penalty of five hundred dollars.[20] Despite such quarrels with Ottoman employees, Englishmen and other foreigners, at a disadvantage in the Ottoman legal morass, had little choice but to hire natives, whether as dragomans, brokers, or in some other capacity, to represent them. Sometimes the foreigners were very much reliant on such employees. Despite Bendysh's animosity toward Draperis, by 1658 the translator was again serving as his dragoman, both conversing with the Ottomans on his behalf and betraying him to the Venetians and others.[21]

INTRAFACTORY DISPUTES

It was not solely in regard to rival commercial communities, however, that Bendysh resorted to the battulation. He also employed it against hostile fellow countrymen. The Istanbul factor Marmaduke Pickett was such a fomenter against his authority. In late 1649, the ambassador ordered Edward Maplesden, the commander of the *Laurell,* to carry Pickett to England because of "misdemeanors" against the ambassador. When the commander refused, Bendysh disciplined Maplesden by ordering that no one should lade any ship he mastered, under a penalty of five hundred dollars.[22] In addition, the ambassador ordered his consuls and vice-consuls to imprison Maplesden unless he paid one thousand dollars to the Levant Company. This incident suggests the ambassador's need for constant diligence not only against competing communities but also against his own compatriots.

Indeed, Osborne's quarrel had been as much with his English colleague Rydley as with rival Jewish merchants, and Bendysh's most consuming task probably was policing his own factory and mediating domestic feuds. Crow had been within his theoretical rights when he imprisoned compatriots in 1646, and Bendysh's commission made explicit his authority to confine English factors. Nor did he balk at claiming this right, as the following incident illustrates.

On 22 August 1648, John Rydley burst into the ambassador's public court together with several other English merchants to denounce a certain Maurice Evans. Evans, it seems, had broken into James Wyche's warehouse in Pera and sold several barrels of his red and white lead. They also insisted that some time earlier Rydley and Evans, along with Thomas Birkley, had accepted a consignment of twenty-five cloths and thirty-five bales of paper from Frances Reade at Leghorn.[23] When

Birkley suddenly died, the two merchants had given Bendysh a bond for four thousand dollars and rented an empty magazine in Galata from a Frenchman until a contract for the merchandise could be drawn up with the Jew Abraham Wachill. Reade meanwhile asked that his goods be transferred to the care of Alexander Myers. Although Rydley attempted to comply immediately with Reade's request, Evans, the group contended, first procrastinated and then broke into the warehouse and stole the cloth, thereby purloining the four thousand dollars' worth of goods that Frances Reade had dispatched earlier. Evans later returned to the warehouse and removed the thirty-five bales of paper as well.[24] According to Bendysh's information, the burglar also owed Michael Francis and several other creditors seventeen thousand dollars.[25] Notably, although the case engaged both Frenchmen and Ottoman Jews, each of the charges came from and was leveled against Englishmen.

On 12 September 1648, Bendysh detained Maurice Evans in the ambassador's residence. The English Levant Company's intent in granting its ambassador such a right of constraint was not to install a tyrannical regime over its factories (the purpose to which Sir Sackvile Crow had turned it) but to establish the predominance of English law within the Levantine nation in order to shield it from other, perhaps more capricious, self-serving, or unfathomable legal regulations. To this end, two days after Evans's confinement Bendysh granted the factor an occasion to justify his deeds. Evans appeared in a panic and some bewilderment. Not entirely realizing the seriousness of the charges against him, he pleaded that both he and his principals would lose a great deal were he not released, because he needed to recover loans to Jews and other people in Istanbul totaling one hundred fifty thousand dollars. He assigned great urgency to this appeal by claiming that the plague then raging in the capital city might carry off some of his debtors, or they might take the opportunity of his imprisonment to escape the city.

Bendysh had his clerk register these arguments, but he also invited other English merchants to testify against Evans. On 20 October, John Rydley and Alexander Myers did so, adding to previous complaints the allegation that Evans had whisked away two cases of gold satins consigned to Thomas Birkley and promised to John Pixley, a factor in Izmir.[26] Three days later the ambassador again summoned Evans, who then had been in detention for nearly one and one-half months, to answer these various accusations. When the factor finally appeared on 23 October, he vainly declared that Birkley, not he, had been Reade's factor and that Birkley's death merely provided Evans's rivals an opportunity to make a scapegoat of him.[27]

Only a month later did Evans finally find a creditable rebuttal to his accusers. In a petition presented on 21 November, he denounced a houseboy, Thomas Simonds, who had worked for Birkley.[28] Evans claimed that the previous year Simonds had purloined silver and gold from his chambers, that he had stolen a picture from a certain Lazaro Thorntone, and that he had cheated an apothecary named Andrea of money which the English factory had given for the burial of William Greere. It seemed likely, Evans concluded, that it had been Simonds, who inexplicably now had money for "cards, dice, and gaming," rather than he who had absconded with the stock from Birkley's warehouse. We do not know whether Bendysh accepted Evans's accusations or whether Simonds ever admitted the crimes, but it is likely that the houseboy's apparent malfeasances afforded the ambassador a convenient resolution to the dispute between Rydley and Evans.

Evans's subsequent actions support this conjecture, for he soon began making commercial claims himself. The factor had been one of Ambassador Crow's chief opponents, and on 25 January he asserted that during the uproar marking Crow's last months, the grand vizier, Ahmed, had sent his "Jew," Aaron Amon, to seize goods valued at twenty-one thousand dollars from Evans's warehouse in Galata.[29] These wares belonged to two principals, Frances Reade of Leghorn and Edward Beale of Messina, and Bendysh decreed proportional compensation to each.

Rydley had not yet finished with petitions to the ambassador. After routing Evans and securing his confinement, on 28 October he initiated yet another complaint. This time, despite the recent strife between the two men, Osborne stood with him against Frances Reade.[30] They explained that during the last months of Sackvile Crow's administration, this prominent merchant of Leghorn had shipped to Istanbul several cases of silk in the *Lewis*.[31] He then had consigned that freight to his two factors, Rydley and Osborne, whom he charged sixty-six hundred dollars at the Istanbul dock. The factors later insisted that they had not had such funds and that they had been unable to procure the money because Crow's malfeasances had so eroded trust in the nation. This predicament forced them to borrow from a Jewish moneylender and use the silk itself as security. A year or so later, the cases of fabric still languished in a Jewish-owned warehouse.

Compatriots often clashed in ways that entangled members of Ottoman millets, even if inadvertently, and obliged the ambassador to reach decisions that were bound to anger someone. At times, the boundaries between English and Ottoman culture became blurred even in a single identity. On 27 August 1649, for example, Arthur Bedford and John South denounced each other.[32] Bedford insisted not only that South had threatened to go to the "Turks" to ensure that Bedford export nothing from the empire, but also, more ominously, that South had accused him of being a fugitive (renegade?) from Christendom. Bedford demanded that the ambassador protect him from his harasser.

Three days later, South countered that Bedford was a charlatan who had arrived in Istanbul only recently and had unlawfully claimed the privileges of membership in the Levant Company.[33] South's principal grievance, however, was that his rival had demanded funds from the estate of the deceased Birkley and thereby endangered South's own rights to the assets. As for South's accusations concerning Bedford's apostasy, the latter declared only that he had fled England after the king had routed the parliamentarian forces. He would not deny that he was an antiroyalist but insisted that he was no heretic.

In one sense, the lawsuits that erupted after Birkley's death show a deep relief that Crow's despotic obstructionism had ended. These and other factors expected the new administration to settle the factory's many discords, some of which had festered for years. The Britons of Istanbul had borne the brunt of Crow's aggression and had almost singlehandedly defeated his designs. They did not hesitate to demand swift verdicts and compensation. It was Birkley's death, however, that precipitated these many grievances. Like greedy relatives, Rydley, Osborne, and Evans hovered around the deceased factor's estate. Bendysh's responsibility was to protect it, ascertain its true heirs, and ensure an equitable division of the spoils.

That Birkley had died intestate in the Ottoman realm further complicated things. Bendysh knew that Ottoman law denied rights of inheritance to the heirs of persons who died intestate and made "any goods in the house of the debtor liable to the creditor."[34] Despite capitulations that granted Englishmen exemption from this statute, Birkley's contracts with both Ottomans and Englishmen made the situation potentially awkward and even risky. When he heard that Birkley had died, the ambassador did not immediately sequester his merchandise but first distributed many of the deceased man's wares among the warehouses of other factors (while demanding bond from them) in order to protect them from "Turkish justice," that is, to keep them out of the hands of Ottoman subjects with claims against Birkley.

Such Ottoman claims *were* made against Birkley. Curiously, these claims came not through the Ottoman courts but via Bendysh himself. On 26 March 1649, for example, the *baltacı* (halberdier) Mehmed Ağa sent his proxy to Bendysh in order to explain that Dixwell Brent, a factor in Izmir, the previous year had requested that Birkley pay the *baltacı* two bills of exchange, the first for 3,149 dollars and the second for 2,000 dollars.[35] The Ottoman agent proclaimed that only part of the second bill had been honored. Bendysh, aware of the importance of satisfying high Ottoman officials, acted quickly. He immediately contacted Birkley's Jewish broker, Jacob Aben Shushin, who not only repaid the debt but also gave Mehmed Ağa's servants an additional ten dollars.

From the ambassador's perspective, such actions were at least prudent and probably imperative. Nevertheless, Bendysh's prolonged and deliberate ordering of Birkley's affairs generated an alarming bottleneck in English trade. Many English and other merchants had dealt with the factor, and some, in correspondence with directors of the English Levant Company, tried to hold the ambassador responsible for damages resulting from the impoundment of his estate. In an angry retort, Bendysh insisted that his sealing up of Birkley's warehouses accorded with English capitulations, that it was necessary in order to thwart seizures by "Turks, Jews, or other Grand Signior's subjects," and that given the affair's complexities, he had followed the only course possible.

AN EROSION OF AMBASSADORIAL AUTHORITY

The ambassador also reopened old disputes, which entangled him in even more complex webs. One of the most explosive of these had been the feud between Frances Reade and Richard Lawrence that had consumed so much of Ambassador Crow's and the factory of Izmir's energy in the late 1630s and early 1640s.[36] Bendysh's long investigations into Reade's many commercial alliances with English factors in Istanbul, launched by Birkley's death, seem to have aroused his curiosity about Reade's past activities. On 9 June 1649, he wrote to John Wylde, consul at Izmir, informing him that Lawrence still owed Reade twelve thousand dollars and ordering that the consul "secure all the goods & estate of the said Richard Laurence" until he should either pay or provide a sufficient reason not to do so.[37] He also wrote to Reade in Leghorn requesting a clarification and addition to previous statements.

Lawrence, unsurprisingly, proved reluctant to reopen the ancient conflict. Rather than traveling to Istanbul as Bendysh desired, he simply wrote a terse justification, which the ambassador read together with Reade's petition, Crow's previous judgment, and the attestations of twelve merchants from Izmir. The ambassador's decision was to acquit Reade of all past charges and declare Lawrence guilty and "unfit to have any vote or suffrage in the Courts of the Nation."[38] Bendysh next composed a warrant for Wylde to sequester Lawrence's goods to the value of twelve thousand dollars. Should the factor not have such funds, Wylde was to imprison him.[39] This harsh judgment against Lawrence, who had ensconced himself among Izmir's English elite, shocked many factors in Izmir and created for Bendysh an embittered, experienced, and determined adversary. Lawrence was the first of several English factors whom Bendysh estranged and who quietly began working through both foreign and Ottoman allies to undermine his authority.

The tales of Birkley's death, Rydley's feuds with Osborne, Evans, Reade, and other compatriots, and Bendysh's treatment of Lawrence represent many other such accounts threaded through Bendysh's five-hundred-odd-page book recording communal petitions and ambassadorial decisions for the years between 1648 and 1652. The parade of squabbles that the book chronicles not only must have consumed much of his time and energy but also reflects a gradual communal disintegration. It is apparent, furthermore, that as Bendysh's term lengthened, resentment against him swelled.

In his record book, the ambassador openly expressed exasperation with several of his associates. On 14 September 1649, he specifically named Richard Pickett, John Abney, Robert Frampton, Gyles Davis, John South, Jonathan Davies, and Richard Charleton, all comrades in the factory at Galata, as his chief tormentors.[40] He denounced them for sending scandalous letters to the Levant Company in order to cause a breach between the directors and their ambassador and for refusing to heed him except when his directives conformed precisely to the company's instructions. This scheme, Bendysh avowed, exposed him to the derision of Ottoman ministers and subjects, and these English miscreants constituted "the true incendiaries and only causes" of his afflictions.

FACTORY VERSUS FACTORY

Lawrence's wrathful letters to consul Wylde suggest that Bendysh had begun to alienate other English factories as well as Galata's. Indeed, several incidents confirm that the English nation of Izmir had begun to withdraw the loyalty that the ambassador earlier had so carefully cultivated. The loss of a common opponent with Crow's expulsion to England was only one of several reasons for this unraveling of consensus. More systemic was that the requirements and aspirations of the three factories of Istanbul, Izmir, and Aleppo simply rarely coincided. After 1648–49, the aspirations and objectives of factors in these cities began quickly to diverge.

Bendysh's image of his position in regard to the provinces reflected the Ottoman government's, which envisioned an empire in which Istanbul served as both political and economic hub. The capital was to issue orders and the provinces were to comply. Provincial powers had always resisted this paradigm, which never had been fully implemented.[41] Realities in the mid-seventeenth century were singularly removed from the ideal. The central authority seemed distant and weak, and provincial notables in Izmir and Aleppo routinely contested (or at least ignored) Istanbul's centrist vision. In the middle decades of the seventeenth century, for example, the Sublime Porte futilely sought to control Izmir's rapid economic growth, to which both Ottoman subjects and foreigners contributed. Just as Bendysh's attempts to dominate the English factory of Izmir reflected Istanbul's attitude toward that city, so did the English consul and nation's defiance of their ambassador emulate the attitudes of their provincial hosts toward their central government.

The very structure of English Levantine trade and Bendysh's peculiar place in it further confused matters. The Levant Company itself was ill defined. Whereas it had been born as an independent chartered company under Queen Elizabeth I, the wealth of Levantine trade and the influence of the Ottoman Empire in European politics brought the English monarch more and more to interfere in its affairs. This intrusion had come to a head in the mid-1640s, when Ambassador Crow polarized the English nation in the empire by affiliating himself with the monarch and dissociating himself from the parliament, the company, and its representatives in the Levant.

Bendysh's appointment, together with the conclusion of the first English civil war, only briefly resolved the issue of state interference in Levantine trade. Many English merchants in Izmir, more than their compatriots in Istanbul, presumed that in 1646 (and especially after January 1649) they had routed not only Crow but also the idea of a centralized administration in the Levant. Many anticipated that the political consensus that would emerge in postmonarchical England would embrace a decentralized design for Levantine trade and thus grant relative autonomy to their factory.

The consul of Izmir and his factors thus received a rude shock when the new ambassador began intruding on their decisions and ventures. Some of these encroachments occurred in areas that unquestionably were within the ambassador's jurisdiction. Just as a Muslim, Jewish, Armenian, or Greek lawbreaker might flee Istanbul for a provincial town, so might an English malcontent take refuge in the factories of Aleppo or Izmir; and just as the Ottoman central government might order provincial authorities to apprehend a fugitive Ottoman subject, so might the English Levant Company or the ambassador direct his consuls to apprehend an English runaway. Thus, the company ordered the English consul of Izmir to imprison Richard Charleton, who had fled from Istanbul with the help of "certain ill-disposed persons of this Factory," should he reach that city.[42] The consul and factory of Izmir could scarcely question the rights of the company and the ambassador over such an outlaw.

The appropriateness of ambassadorial meddling could be much less clear, however, and the ambiguities of English lines of authority are displayed in clashes between Bendysh and the consul in Izmir, John Wylde. In late 1648, it seems, Samuel Barnardiston, the reluctant treasurer for the factory at Izmir, had requested that Bendysh secure personal license from the grand vizier and other chief Ottoman officials to purchase, load on vessels, and ship various fruits and cuit (a wine product) in Izmir.⁴³ The ambassador, perhaps eager to prove his worth to the factory that had so helped his assumption of power, complied with Barnardiston's request. He must have been amazed when Wylde then opposed his treasurer's scheme, which the consul believed would allow the treasurer to monopolize commerce in those comestibles.

The consul and his factory ignored a whole flurry of directives on the matter that Bendysh issued in late 1648 and early 1649, and the ambassador grew increasingly irritated, particularly about the implied defiance. In emulation of the Sublime Porte's convention of sending *çavuş*es across the empire carrying decrees and invested with special authority, he dispatched his servant, Paul Haggatt, to ensure that the English factory of Izmir understood and heeded his order. Bendysh had not reckoned with that port city's accustomed freedoms and his compatriots' temperaments, however. Not only did some English factors there spread "malicious reports" against Haggatt, but they also attacked him verbally and even physically.⁴⁴

Bendysh had begun to taste the frustrations of supervising his fractious countrymen (similar provocations had helped thwart Crow). Contempt for authority distinguished and indeed constituted the chief strength of the community of English merchants in Ottoman domains, and particularly those in Izmir. Unlike his predecessor, however, Bendysh did not endeavor to bully the factory of Izmir into submission. Trying no doubt to build on initial good faith and shared interests, on 13 March he instead protested to the consul, ordering Wylde to protect Haggatt and render justice against his oppressors.

On the same day, Bendysh denounced a particular factor, George Hangar, whom he charged with breeding disturbances and subverting ambassadorial authority through hostility toward Haggatt.⁴⁵ He further claimed that Hangar had complained to some Ottoman ministers about English abuses of the strangers' consulage. This last charge was serious, for the ambassador was accusing the factor not only of rupturing the judicial walls that shielded the English nation from Ottoman intrusion but also of jeopardizing the financial heart of local company management. The abuses Bendysh referred to must have been smuggling, and such trafficking, as the Ottomans easily surmised, decreased the empire's as well as English revenue.

Bendysh directed his consul to discipline Hangar. He was to fine him one thousand dollars—to be doubled if unpaid within a week. Should

Hangar fail to pay the fine at all, Wylde was to sequester the factor's estates and deport him to England. The ambassador judged that such violations endangered all Britons and England's commerce, and in his retribution Sir Thomas proved a stern but perhaps fair master. Although Wylde and his factory probably resented Istanbul's interference, it was certainly not arbitrary or inequitable.

The ambassador, however, also badgered the factory of Izmir in less impartial ways. One of the outcomes of the stoppage of trade during Crow's last months in Istanbul and the continuing Veneto-Ottoman war had been that goods piled up (and in some cases rotted away) in that city's warehouses. The English factory there pressured Bendysh to find ships to transport this idle stock. In late 1647, he had ordered to Istanbul vessels tarrying in the Gulf of Izmir. The problem of insufficient shipping resurfaced in early 1649, and he scoured the eastern Mediterranean for available English bottoms.

In May or June 1649, Bendysh heard that the *Elizabeth,* bound for Izmir, was scheduled next to go directly to Mawola (Marvola) in order to load the goods of Jews and other foreigners. He regarded the appearance of this ship as a chance to ease Istanbul's bottleneck and immediately wrote to Wylde, directing it diverted to the capital, with the excuse that the need for transport was great and that English officials should "promote the trade of the English before all foreigners."[46]

From Bendysh's vantage point, these arguments seemed sound. From the perspective of Izmir, they appeared despotic and destructive. That the *Elizabeth* would leave town loaded with foreign rather than English goods suggests that a lack of business plagued the English factory there (perhaps a caravan had failed to arrive from the east). If so, then Izmir's factors were unlikely to sympathize with compatriots in a mart overflowing with goods. Nor did the factory wish to lose either the consulage or the goodwill that would attend the vessel's lading of strangers' goods. The factors of Izmir must have interpreted Bendysh's order as favoritism or even spite, and thoroughly resented it.

The question of leviations further eroded bonds between the ambassador and the provincial English factories of Izmir and Aleppo. Several regular incomes, including customs revenue (particularly from strangers) and fines, covered most company expenses. Nevertheless, extraordinary outlays, perhaps deriving from an imperial accession, the need for an imperial decree, or an extraordinary demand for monies (*avanias*), sometimes created budgetary crises. In order to overcome such shortages, the ambassador could impose upon his factories special tariffs, the despised leviations. His habit was to announce such a shortfall and direct each factory to render a certain percentage of it. The method of collection customarily was left to the consuls and their nations.

Of course, no one liked this procedure. Not only did it mean dipping into one's own pockets, but each factory also invariably believed that it surrendered the lion's share of the donation. Furthermore, in the late 1640s factors were especially sensitive to the leviation as a method for collecting money, for this very device had justified Sackvile Crow's plunder of the estates of English factors in 1646.

Deep suspicion and resentment thus greeted Bendysh when he announced a leviation in late 1649. Rumors swirled in all the factories that it was unnecessary and inequitably distributed. Some openly denounced it. Bendysh learned that a factor in Galata had even cried out to a compatriot that the leviation was a "sham," and news of this opinion quickly spread. The ambassador worked hard to stanch the dangerous gossip. He first called a general court in Istanbul, where the Galata factors utterly denied such talk, and then turned again to his consul in Izmir. On 19 February 1650, he issued a warrant against the factor of Izmir, Thomas Newsam, who had spoken against the ambassador in open court and, insisting that such talk was "likely to breed a very great disturbance (both in the collection of the Leviation, and in the affections of several of both Factories [Istanbul and Izmir])," ordered Wylde to call a court and publicly expel Newsam "as a fomenter & raiser of faction & division."[47] An open expression of disaffection over an onerous surcharge hardly deserved a humiliating and career-threatening public expulsion from the factory, and whether or not the consul complied, the harsh directive must have troubled English traders in Izmir.

The following months brought heightening tensions between Bendysh and the factory. In order to deal with his mounting expenses, which derived largely from several showdowns with the grand vizier and other Ottoman officials,[48] the ambassador both borrowed from his more prosperous English associates in Galata and pushed harder and harder for financial assistance from the allegedly affluent factory at Izmir. Jonathan Dawes, the treasurer in Istanbul, a loyal supporter of Bendysh, and a wealthy factor, spearheaded this venture.

In early 1651 the treasurer charged the factory of Izmir fifteen hundred dollars for expenses that had accompanied the appointment of the new grand vizier, Melek Ahmed Pasha, in August 1650.[49] The bills, however, came back "protested and unpaid," leaving Istanbul's factory "destitute." Bendysh then asked Dawes to advance money from his private estate for the management of the nation, but the treasurer was understandably reluctant to do so without guarantees. The circumstances were particularly desperate because the grand vizierate seemed about to change yet again, which would induce even more disbursements from the English treasury. Bendysh ordered Spencer Bretton, the new consul in Izmir, to accept two bills of fifteen hundred and two thousand dollars, or else the ambassador would "use the help of Turkish Justice for obtained thereof."[50]

By not only insisting on money from Izmir but also threatening those who defied him with "Turkish justice," Bendysh seemed to be emulating his notorious predecessor. In an almost comic unintentional mimicry, Bendysh continued down this road. On 11 September 1651, the ambassador wrote to Bretton concerning Dawes's continuing inability to come up with sufficient monies to cover even basic expenses.[51] He declared that he feared an insurrection among his factors at Istanbul, who refused further payments into the general funds without parallel deposits from Izmir. He also confessed his factory's deep suspicions against Izmir's English factors, to whom, Bendysh suggested, the entire trade of the Levant came, leaving their compatriots in Istanbul unemployed and almost destitute. Finally, the ambassador enjoined Bretton to assemble his nation and arrange either a loan or a leviation for Istanbul. Failure to comply would mean confinement until Bendysh could hear the grounds for their resistance.

When the factory in Izmir disregarded these commands, the ambassador turned to the Ottomans in order to force compliance. He arranged for an Ottoman messenger to travel to the port city carrying a letter dated 11 February 1652 that ordered Bretton to call together all persons who refused to pay their leviations and send those who still resisted to Istanbul under the care of the *çavuş*. Once again, the frustrations of governing a community in which authority was uncertain and mutable and which flourished through initiative and independence had brought an ambassadorial plea for relief to the Sublime Porte.

THE DIURNAL CHORES OF AN AMBASSADOR

On 20 April 1649, Bendysh issued a right of passage into "Christendom" to Isiodoro, a Christian of the Latin church on the island of Sio who had served the nation "faithfully and well" for some twenty years.[52] A year later he wrote a letter of transit on behalf of Seydee Mohi Yedee, an Ottoman ambassador to the "Indies," directing all English captains, masters, commanders, and other officials met en route to render the Muslim every possible assistance.[53] These two actions remind us that Bendysh was not only an agent of the English Levant Company. He also was responsible for representing, protecting, and extending the power and authority of the English state in the Ottoman Empire, a duty that must have consumed a good part of each day.

Even though the composition of the English government was uncertain during the early years of his service as ambassador, Bendysh accepted the idea that he was the embodiment of his state. He also imagined himself to be the protector of English society and took seriously his role (granted in his commission from the Levant Company) as bearer and defender of English culture.[54] He labored hard to safeguard his compatriots' moral character, which meant diligence especially in matters of religion. On 2 May 1651, for example, the ambassador ordered a certain Fethergall, master of the English merchant vessel the *Thomas*, not to let his ship's officers and seamen visit any Ottoman taverns or board Ottoman ships because "diverse Renegadoes do resort aboard your ship, and entice your Mariners to turn from their religion."[55] Bendysh, it seems, had heard that several English sailors went ashore regularly and kept "company with such apostates in taverns & other scandalous houses."

Such "renegades"—converts to and from Christianity and Islam—helped define the maritime community of the Mediterranean world throughout the late sixteenth and the seventeenth centuries. They consorted particularly with the corsairs of the Barbary Coast—whose predecessors had helped organize the Ottoman navy—and Malta, and they achieved notoriety as pirates and fame as transmitters of technical information to and from the Christian and Ottoman worlds.[56]

Bendysh's warning to Fethergall, in addition, illustrates a less celebrated but perhaps more menacing consequence of such apostasies. In all but religion, the renegades remained English (or Venetian, or Arab) and fraternized with English mariners along the wharves and in the taverns and brothels of Ottoman port towns. In these settings, they served as persuasive emissaries for Ottoman culture as well as for Islam itself.

The ambassador zealously sought to protect his countrymen against the entreaties of such persons, who sometimes even served aboard English vessels. Nicholas Terricks, the commander of the *Hopewell*, complained on 11 March 1650 that William Trednocks, whom seven months earlier he had redeemed from captivity at Tunis, met with an English renegade in Istanbul and promptly "turned Turk."[57] Terricks was angry that Trednocks had repudiated his deliverance; Bendysh's principal worry was that the renegade had spent seven months in close contact with the *Hopewell*'s other sailors, perhaps even whittling away at their faith.

The threat of his charges "turning Turk" (that is, converting to Islam) was one challenge facing Bendysh as he worked to preserve his community's cultural autonomy. A second and probably more insidious one was the risk that his young, lonely, and ingenuous factors might marry Ottoman subjects. His concern was not so much that they would marry Muslim or Jewish women but that Armenian and Greek Christians, with whom many more regularly fraternized, might captivate them. There was no legal obstacle to such a marriage in the Ottoman Empire (as there certainly was to union with Muslim women), and the ambassador's fear was that a young and impressionable Englishman might embrace his betrothed's religion, and thus her culture, as a communal prerequisite to marriage. Such unions occurred more and more frequently in Ottoman port cities and were perhaps the main catalyst in the creation of the "Levantine" culture that so marked the eighteenth- and nineteenth-century eastern Mediterranean world. The ambassador dealt with one such situation in early 1650, when John Plummer, "late of the factory of Galata," married an Ottoman subject, renounced his affiliations, menaced the English factory, and allegedly behaved scandalously against the English religion and nation.[58] Bendysh ordered his immediate and absolute battulation.

This last incident suggests how easily "deviant" Englishmen could become a threat to their compatriots in this complex foreign environment.

In Istanbul itself, it was particularly easy to stray into behavior that Bendysh and his circle considered a danger to the English nation and consequently degenerate. As the nucleus of the eastern Mediterranean commercial world, the city was thick with eating houses, taverns, and brothels offering a celebrated assortment of enticements. The most infamous and stimulating of these were nestled in the murky and tantalizing back streets of Galata, and frustratingly obscure allusions to English rendezvous in these iniquitous haunts riddle Bendysh's record books. Although we possess few specifics, it was under such conditions that English and Ottoman cultures most commonly met, clashed, and sometimes converged.

AN ENVOY AND HIS NATION

The challenges that beset his first years as ambassador show that Sir Thomas Bendysh's troubles did not end with his rout of Sir Sackvile Crow. Before his rival's fall, Bendysh had relied upon the solidarity that widespread antagonism had generated. From its beginnings, however, the English community of the Levant had flourished on competition, and harmony could not long survive Crow's political demise. After the autumn of 1647 the English unity of purpose simply disintegrated. Bendysh struggled, apparently futilely, to hold together a cantankerous nation that seemed determined to crush not only its Ottoman and foreign rivals but also each other, and especially its ambassador.

The rivalries that were natural to the cutthroat world of Levantine commerce were only one aspect of the disarray with which Bendysh had to contend. His most troublesome hindrances were those very authorities from whom he had obtained his post. The ambassador could rely upon neither the English nor the Ottoman state for a consistent direction or even for coherence in sovereignty. In England, Charles I's execution closely followed the second civil war and led first to rule by a purged parliament and then to the Cromwellian protectorate. In the aftermath of İbrahim's execution, meanwhile, the Ottoman imperial household fashioned and refashioned a succession of administrations. These uncertainties kept Bendysh (and many others) anxious and bewildered.

9 / The Sublime Porte, the Ambassador, and the Provinces

Even as he vainly toiled to organize and supervise his factors in Istanbul, Izmir, and Aleppo, Bendysh also confronted an Ottoman host government that was chronically unstable, that had witnessed a certain vengefulness in his compatriots, and to which he had made perhaps undeliverable promises concerning his authority and his own government's ability to manage the English merchant marine and navy. As he worked his way through Istanbul's labyrinthine politics seeking to reestablish English standards of conduct and construct a consistent English policy through which to influence his hosts, Ottoman governmental fragility forced the ambassador over and over to refashion and revise political alliances.

He also struggled to deal with a home government that underwent a dramatic metamorphosis almost immediately after his selection as ambassador. Although the English Levant Company had appointed Bendysh as a compromise candidate in an extraordinarily volatile time for English politics, during his early tenure the situation in England quickly stabilized. The armies of the parliament—the authority that had hesitated the most over his appointment—emerged victorious over royalist forces. Indeed, a rump of that body, albeit the army's agent, soon arranged the execution of the king, for whom Bendysh felt much sympathy. After his monarch's death, however, the ambassador did not set out to demonstrate his fidelity to the young Charles Stuart. Nor did he at once display that he would competently and loyally serve the fledgling commonwealth. These were only some of the responsibilities to be faced and decisions to be made as Bendysh administered his new office in the Ottoman capital.

The Sublime Porte, the Ambassador, and the Provinces 147

CHALLENGING THE SUBLIME PORTE

In December 1647, Sir Thomas Bendysh ordered to Istanbul the English vessels that the summer before had carried him to Izmir, even though neither he nor the merchants of the English factory of Istanbul were certain that the Sublime Porte, still battling the Venetians on Crete and in the Aegean, would honor its promise to keep its hands off the ships. Despite these worries, the ships anchored in the "river," as the English referred to the Golden Horn, because the factors of Galata were determined to have the valuable craft and Bendysh, during his negotiations over the expulsion of Sackvile Crow, had promised the grand vizier to free them from idle anchorage in Izmir's gulf.

The ambassador soon regretted his decision. In the late winter of 1647–48—the time of year when feeding Istanbul's population was most difficult—a Venetian squadron of eight ships resumed its blockade of the Dardanelles and cut off delivery of grains and dried fruits to Istanbul from Egypt and the Aegean. The population of the city grew restive and the Ottoman government more desperate. According to the Venetian *bailo,* in early March Ammar-zade Mehmed Pasha, the *kapudanpaşa,* called the Dutch, English, and French dragomans into his presence and demanded that each state provide ten ships to assist the Ottoman navy in breaking the Venetian blockade.[1]

The envoys all refused this demand. Bendysh, however, was particularly incensed over it. Not only had he three months earlier extracted a promise from the grand vizier, Hezar-pare Ahmed Pasha, that the Ottoman government would not interrupt the free passage of English vessels, but he also had contended with incessant complaints from his nation against the extortions of Ottoman customs officials. In response to this new demand, he first protested to the grand vizier and then, dissatisfied with that minister's response, hurried the entire English factory aboard the eight English ships riding in Istanbul's port, ordered the vessels primed for battle, and had them piloted to a menacing location just beneath Seraglio Point. There, "all of them fell fairly downe, before the Seraglio walls; setting on fire Potts of Pitch at theyr maineyard Armes: which Token qualified with the white Flaggs, and closs Ports, signified that they sought redress of some great Injuries."[2]

Bendysh's undertaking—an affront (and possibly even a direct threat) to the ruler of perhaps the most powerful empire in the world—was brazen. It also seems to have been effective, for both English and Venetian sources report that a multitude swarmed along the European and Asian banks of the Bosphorus's mouth to see the magnificent display of eight fully panoplied English war vessels. The grand vizier, in a frenzy that Sultan İbrahim (himself soon to suffer a violent death) not detect the same sight, rushed out to the ships and immediately agreed to order the head customs collector of Istanbul to repay the money he had wrung from English merchants. On top of that, he promised to free all English slaves in the city (one of the vexing contradictions for English factors was that enslaved compatriots inhabited the same Ottoman cities in which they freely and gainfully lived and traded).

The larger challenge of whether or not—and how—to charter English ships to the Ottoman and Venetian navies was not so easily resolved. Nor was it clear how English commerce could thrive in a region afflicted with chronic naval warfare. Although in July 1648 Bendysh finally obtained permission from both the grand vizier and the Venetian *bailo* for his eight ships to depart the city, he was unable to obtain more sweeping privileges from either.[3] Thus he had to request from the *bailo* a special passport enabling the ships anchored in Izmir to sail up the Dardanelles.[4]

He also had to contend with a stream of pesky complaints such as the *bailo*'s insistence in October 1648 that the English ship *Buonaventura* had illegally transported a *çavuş* to Izmir in order to hire English ships for the Cretan war. A month later, Captain William Ashley declared that he could not fulfill his current commission because of the Venetian blockade and his fear that the Ottoman navy might seize his ship, the *Sampson*. And there was Frances Reade's protest that Bendysh had debarred Captain John Mervin's ship, the *John*, from entering the Dardanelles, at a loss of twenty-four thousand dollars and four months' time, even though Reade had commissioned him to do so and had spent three thousand dollars securing authorization from the Ottoman government.[5]

The adventures of the *Laurell*, though, epitomized the frustrations of the English carrying trade in these years. The vessel's captain, Edward Maplesden, languishing in Izmir for most of 1648 as a result of the Veneto-Ottoman war and Bendysh's actions against him, had finally appealed for relief to John Wylde, the English consul of Izmir, on 30 November of that year. He complained that despite Bendysh's assurances that English ships would be allowed entry through the Dardanelles, he twice had sailed for Istanbul, as commissioned, only to be turned back by the Venetian fleet. Recently he had received a letter from a factor in Istanbul, Bermet Mayne, asking that he yet again proceed to that city. Maplesden did not want to go, maintaining that the Ottomans might conclude that, given his frequent visitations to the Venetian fleet, the *Laurell* "went up only to victual and furnish their enemies with provisions (which they do already mutter and begin to report) so by that means may not only bring an Avania upon himself and ship, but also upon the whole nation."[6] The captain requested permission to disregard Mayne's order and license to lade in Izmir, since he could not do so in Istanbul.

Maplesden's request, once it reached Bendysh, left the English ambassador with a dilemma. He could not disprove the captain's statement, which sworn statements from Witt. Hodges and Robert Salmon confirmed.[7] Nor could he deny that the presence of English ships among the Venetian navy—for whatever reason—enraged the Ottoman *kapudanpaşa,* Mehmed Pasha, or that the *Laurell*'s idleness damaged her captain's reputation and threatened to reduce severely the earnings of those who had commissioned her. Nevertheless, Istanbul remained the capital of the empire; it was imperative for political as well as commercial reasons that the English maintain a presence there. Furthermore, one of Bendysh's principal obligations was to that city's factory, and to assent to Maplesden's entreaty meant to confess the futility of commercial undertakings in Galata. Although the ambassador did periodically browbeat Ottoman authorities with the threat of abandoning Istanbul, neither he nor his factory or company could afford actually to desert the city (nor did they want to do so). So he denied the captain's request to circumvent the Ottoman capital.

Instead, Bendysh redoubled his efforts to liberate the city's seaborne commerce. In December 1648, he pried out of the grand vizier (now Sofu-Mehmed Pasha) a signed pledge to permit free trade that "quietly permitted all our ships (formerly restrained by him) to pass freely out of this port."[8] With this document in hand, the ambassador could direct to Istanbul the *Laurell,* the *Sampson,* and other English vessels anchored in Izmir and other outlying ports, and the factory in Galata could hold ship captains responsible for all losses because of further delay. Several English factors indeed protested against William Ashley of the *Sampson*, insisting that he had refused to deliver goods from merchants of the Levant Company to their factors in Istanbul by the fraudulent reasoning that the port was "unfree."[9]

This quarrel between the factors of Istanbul and English sea captains exemplified a fierce tussle for limited cargo space during the Cretan war. The dispute had little to do with ideological divisions. James Modyford, for example, one of the factors who condemned Captain Ashley, became closely associated with parliament, whereas another, John South, was ardently to defend the exiled Charles Stuart. The denunciation of Ashley reflected, rather, the dashed expectations of a factory that under Sir Sackvile Crow had suffered through an internecine conflict and now was helplessly watching the fortunes of its compatriot rivals in Izmir rise seemingly unchecked because Venetian ships and Ottoman policies blocked the approach to Istanbul.

Not that the English factory alone faced such obstacles. In late June 1649, the ambassador of France, de la Haye, secured an imperial order that the *naib* and *voyvoda* of Gallipoli, the kadis and commanders of the fortresses defending the Dardanelles, and the captains of Ottoman and Barbary vessels not disrupt French shipping.[10] Despite such decrees, the situation at the Dardanelles seemed to worsen as Istanbul's population grew more desperate. Five years later, the French ambassador denounced kadis, commanders, and customs collectors there for routinely detaining French ships and shredding their cargoes of leather and wool in a vain search for grains and other provisions, even though they had already secured passes from the chief customs collector in Istanbul.[11]

The English factory, however, was concerned with its own predicament; it wanted only to move its goods. The Englishmen lashed out at the captains and the ambassador, from whom they desperately needed assistance.

BETWEEN WARRING PRINCIPALITIES

Bendysh was caught between the warring states. The Venetian Senate feared that the "free trade" which the English ambassador so craved from Venice's foe would produce a dangerous Anglo-Ottoman alliance.

The Sublime Porte, meanwhile, suspected that the fully laden English vessels leaving Ottoman domains carried men and provisions for the beleaguered Venetian garrisons on Crete. Demands increased and suspicions deepened as the stalemate between Venice and the Ottoman Empire persisted. In late 1648, the Ottoman government demanded that Bendysh provide English ships for its navy. When he refused even to discuss the possibility, the grand vizier, Mehmed Pasha, and the *kapudanpaşa*, Voynuk-Ahmed Pasha, detained the vessels in port and threatened to force them into service.[12] The Venetian Senate, meanwhile, which had initially agreed to allow ships to pass through the Dardanelles to Istanbul so long as an equal number passed out again, continued to harass English vessels such as the *Laurell*, the *Sampson*, and the *Thomas and William*. These ships now almost routinely landed their letters, men, and goods at Izmir and dispatched what they could overland.

The *bailo* understood that Bendysh was under great pressure from his factory and his company to deliver Istanbul's commerce. The English ambassador many times had visited the Venetian representative, Soranzo, who sat out much of the Veneto-Ottoman war in a Black Sea prison, with requests for passports granting English vessels freedom to navigate the Dardanelles.[13] Indeed, in March 1649 the *bailo* warned the Venetian Senate against the assemblage of English ships at Izmir and the threat that Bendysh, following his successful display of seapower before the sultan's palace, might use them as leverage against the Venetians or even to settle his difficulties with the Ottomans.[14] On 25 April, he reported that Bendysh had mysteriously obtained the release of his ships and exemption from all payments of customs at Istanbul and Izmir, and he warned that the English ambassador had promised to charter to the Ottomans twenty-five English ships for three thousand to five thousand reals per ship.[15] Soranzo further recounted that a French "renegade" named Bairan had departed for Izmir in order to close the bargain.

Soranzo's information, although a bit garbled, was not entirely wrong. The grand vizier (who now was Kara Murad Pasha) and Bendysh had for some time been negotiating the hiring out of thirteen English ships to ferry "provisions and passengers" from Izmir to Candia on Crete.[16] This Anglo-Ottoman pact was not arranged without English resistance, however. Some, indeed, judged it satanic. John South was one Galatan factor who opposed it; he later even advised the *bailo*'s secretary that English ships had sailed to support the Ottoman fleet off Candia.[17] Several members of the English factory in Izmir also resisted it.

In order to supervise the operation and browbeat the rebellious among the English nation of Izmir, their ambassador had dispatched not a French renegade, as Soranzo reported, but the English merchant Roger Fowke, together with an Ottoman *çavuş*. Bendysh, through his agent, insisted that without this venture English trade in the Levant would collapse. He later declared disingenuously to his factory that the Venetians should not have protested the action because the ships merely conveyed people and goods from one Ottoman port to another.[18] He also proclaimed to Soranzo himself (after having helped secure the Venetian's release from Ottoman imprisonment) that he had surrendered the vessels because the Ottomans would not otherwise allow them to "revictual," and their mariners had been starving.[19]

The simultaneous fitting out in the Golden Horn of a vast Ottoman armada, which took to sea at the end of April 1649,[20] lent considerable urgency to Soranzo's dispatch concerning an Anglo-Ottoman rapprochement. The launching of the mighty fleet was

> one of the most glorious sights the City yeelds: It consisted then of about :60: Gallies, & Gally-grosses, & :30: Shipps, all which were richly guilded, painted, & furbish'd, new out of theyr Arsenall, full laden with Men, Gunns & Provisions, & clad from Stemm to Sterne with most glorious Bandiers: (theyr Gunns all thundred together, wth such an Eccho as the World has scarse the Like: theyr numerous trumpetts, Drumms, & other warrlike Instruments made a rattling Chorus, & above all Many thousands of Men, in a generall Shout, made a dreadfull noise: so that All together they fill'd the Aire with Clouds, & with Thunder; as if Mars & Bellona were celebrating a triumph with theyr Sonns of Thunder.[21]

This fleet's first business was to break the Venetian blockade of the Dardanelles, which it succeeded in doing.[22] It then proceeded to Crete, where, according to the *bailo*'s intelligence, thirteen English ships from Izmir, together with three French and four Flemish vessels that the Ottomans also had pressed into service, were to join it.[23]

Meanwhile, in Izmir, negotiations between Fowke, the Ottoman *çavuş*, and the English ship captains were in trouble, for the Ottoman representative considered immoderate the captains' demands for two thousand reals in advance and the conveyance of only one hundred fifty Ottoman soldiers per vessel.[24] They also insisted upon written orders from Bendysh (which they eventually did receive) and a guarantee that they would not be asked to sail beneath any castles, for fear of being blasted from the ramparts. These demands apparently were finally met, for the English ships did set sail for Crete. Indeed, rumors soon began swirling about the prominent role they played in subsequent Ottoman actions, including the perhaps fraudulent report that in a naval action off Zia, the *kapudanpaşa* had spearheaded his attack with Barbary and English ships and then fled.[25]

THE SCHEME MISCARRIES

Difficulties, however, were besetting Bendysh's intrigue in other arenas. On 20 May, the Venetian Senate ordered its representative in London, Salvetti, to denounce the Englishman's "un-Christian" proceedings to the English Levant Company and to pressure its directors to order its ships not to serve the Ottomans.[26] The company agreed to direct its representative to comply and, amid the alarming distractions of regicide and an increasingly autocratic rump parliament, began the process of censuring its principal agent in the east.

Even more calamitous for the ambassador's scheme had been the dismissal of the grand vizier and his replacement by Kara Murad, the *ağa* of the janissaries.[27] This event had occurred in mid-May, and within two weeks Bendysh was in audience with the new Ottoman head minister trying to explain away the ineffectiveness of English ships, demanding confirmation of his agreement with Murad's predecessor, and requesting Ottoman gratitude for his contribution of English ships and an additional reduction in tariffs.[28]

Bendysh's posturing belied the fact that his countrymen had done little to help the Ottoman cause. The thirteen English ships had indeed sailed from Izmir with Ottoman men and supplies and had landed them on Crete near Candia. With this action, however, Fowke (who remained with the fleet) and the English sea captains considered their obligations fulfilled. Rather than combining with the Ottoman fleet in subsequent actions, the vessels had shied off and returned to Izmir, leaving Voynuk-Ahmed Pasha, the *kapudanpaşa,* alone not only to confront (and suffer a humiliating defeat at the hands of) the Venetians off the coast of Foça but also to fail in his plan to conquer the city of Candia—and to die of a gunshot wound at the castle of Suda.[29]

This debacle infuriated the grand vizier, and the perceived English role in it seriously undermined Bendysh's relations with the Ottoman government. Most damaging of all, according at least to the English witness Bargrave, the streets of Istanbul echoed with mutterings that the English captains had treacherously informed the Venetians of their withdrawal, so that the Venetian captain general at sea had known exactly when the Ottoman fleet was weakest. Bargrave and other members of the English community, fearing association with and even blame for the Ottoman disaster and anxious about the shadowy, teeming lanes of Galata, scurried fearfully from shelter to shelter and grew increasingly embittered against their conniving ambassador.[30]

Englishmen more justifiably feared reprisals from official Istanbul, and the grand vizier, Murad Pasha, acted against their factory in early August. He imposed a heavy *avania* upon and threatened further proceedings against Roger Fowke, whose response was to flee for Christendom and to whom the ambassador provided helpful letters excusing him from both blame and debts.[31] The Ottoman official also reportedly demanded the return of the sixty thousand or so reals disbursed in payment for the English ships, and when Bendysh secured an audience with him on 18 August 1649, he harangued the ambassador savagely. He allegedly denounced the English nation for betrayal, blamed it for the defeat and burning of the Ottoman fleet, and threatened to throw Bendysh into a dungeon should he not immediately recompense the Ottoman government for its entire loss of some one hundred vessels. Finally, Murad Pasha dispatched to Izmir a *çavuş* with orders to seize the captains and sequester the goods of the thirteen culpable English ships.[32] The young and impressionable English factor Bargrave, alluding to the Ottoman government's assault upon Englishmen in these months, wrote that "the Ball of Opression roll'd till it became intolerable great."[33] The canny *bailo,* Soranzo, reported that the English factory intended to resist Ottoman demands, even if to do so meant abandoning the city of Istanbul.[34]

Bendysh, utilizing his painstakingly maintained network of Ottoman friends (including the *şeyhülislam,* Haci Abdurrahim Efendi, and others in the imperial divan who intervened on his behalf), was able to weather this crisis. Indeed, by late October he had succeeded not only in avoiding paying compensation to the Ottomans for their lost vessels but also in securing his ships at Izmir, where there were reportedly fifteen lading "in the normal way."[35] Nevertheless, the ambassador could not lay the business to rest. He still had to contend with the lingering presence of English merchant vessels and privateers (often one and the same) in the Aegean combat zone, where their escapades yielded persistent discord with both the Venetians and the Ottomans. Bendysh scrambled to maintain English commerce despite the war. On 23 October, the Venetian Senate agreed to allow up to (but not more than) three English ships to pass through the Dardanelles. A few days later, English and Flemish vessels serving in the Venetian fleet (and there were many) refused to assist in blockading the Dardanelles. The following month Bendysh again felt obliged to turn several English ships away from Istanbul for fear that the Ottoman government would seize them, and in March 1650 the *bailo* angrily reported to his doge that an Ottoman embassy to Barbary would embark on an English ship at Izmir rather than at Istanbul from fear of the Venetian fleet (the Venetian's informant was the captain of an English ship, the *Thomas and William*).[36]

The ambassador's willingness to convey an Ottoman emissary to Algiers had originated in an appeal from an English ship captain. Bendysh's most perplexing quandary continued to be the Venetian and Ottoman habit of pressing into service all available vessels. The root of the crisis of 1649 had been Bendysh's acquiescence in the Sublime Porte's attempt to normalize the long-held Mediterranean practice of hiring ships, men, and materiel as required. Nor was the habit of seizing the vessels of "neutrals" broken when this venture collapsed. In fact, the very next spring Bendysh received a complaint from William White, captain of the *George,* that off the coast of Modona he had encountered a combined Algerian, Tunisian, and Tripolitan fleet of twenty-nine sails on its way to join the Ottoman fleet at Crete. The Barbary admirals had demanded that the *George* join them and serve against the Venetians.[37] White claimed to have at first resisted this proposal, but finally he signed a standard contract concerning prepayment, monthly recompense, and the freedom of ship and mariners.

According to White's appeal to Bendysh, however, this agreement soon was broken. While anchored off the port of Rhodes, the admiral of Algiers had seized the captain and confiscated his ship and sailors. When the other English ship captains in Ottoman service had protested to the *kapudanpaşa* Haydar-Ağa-zade Mehmed Pasha, he had promised, but never undertook, to restore the men and the ship, which was fired and lost in service at an estimated cost of fifty thousand dollars. White supposedly had spent the next six months in Istanbul vainly awaiting recompense before finally soliciting Bendysh for assistance.

It was partially in order to act upon this appeal that in late March 1650 the ambassador agreed to appropriate an English ship to convey an Ottoman envoy to Barbary, in return for which the Ottoman government offered White compensation for the loss of his ship. A second motivation was pressure from the directors of the English Levant Company to expedite the redemption of English slaves held by the Algerians and Tunisians. In the previous year, it had taken a show of force for Bendysh to wrest from the Sublime Porte a decree (probably never implemented) freeing English slaves in Istanbul. Emancipation for those held by the Barbaries, whom the Ottomans governed only nominally, was even more problematic. Nevertheless, in late 1649 the ambassador indignantly denied company accusations that he was doing too little and beseeched "your Honours to Esteeme of me, as of one so much a Christian, as not to give cause of any complaint of this nature so justly odious to God, and all good men."[38] He also remarked that it was naive to expect the grand vizier, who depended so much upon the corsairs for his war against Venice, to act against them, and he confessed that in any case dissension within the English factory in Istanbul had crippled his authority.

Indeed, the imbroglio of 1649 had determined several of Bendysh's compatriots to resist his management of their factory. Some had earlier felt uneasy when the ambassador had insisted upon punishing the religiously heterodox in both Izmir and Istanbul.[39] In 1649, perhaps stunned by the king's execution, Sir Thomas also had begun cracking down on the pervasive partisanship that the English civil wars had engendered. In late April, after several merchants had initiated proceedings against a factor of Galata named Jeffrey Keeble for expressing quarrelsome opinions about the conflict, Bendysh ordered "him to be committed to prison, and there abide, until such time as his Lordship could take convenient course to send him into England: as resolving not to suffer such a contentious & disquiet member in this Factory."[40]

Keeble, it seems, had remarked at a dinner party in Pera that he concurred with the alleged opinion of a certain Lord Downes that if Charles II did not submit to parliament, the Duke of York should be crowned in his stead. Bendysh wanted to punish Keeble not so much for the opinion itself as for the possibly slanderous and certainly damaging implication that it had been expressed by Lord Downes. Nevertheless, to some merchants the ambassador's response, bundling Keeble off to a volatile England where he might be hanged for treason, seemed imperious and tyrannical. Although the panicked factor averted this fate by beseeching both Downes and Bendysh to accept his apologies, the ambassador's ruthless reaction warned the entire factory not to meddle in disputes concerning king, parliament, or the English army.[41]

An earlier incident may have provoked the ambassador's harsh penalties for such idle talk. The Venetians, it seems, had caught wind of his intention to provide the Ottomans with ships not only from their *bailo*'s reports but also from an Englishman named Morgan Read, who was forced to take refuge with the French ambassador in Istanbul when his letters about the collusion were printed and widely distributed in Venice.[42] This publication, which advised the general public of the English ambassador's "un-Christian" comportment, thoroughly embarrassed Bendysh. Indeed, his "devilish fraternization" so angered some of the English factory that by October they were menacing him with the same treatment that two years earlier had sent Sir Sackvile Crow to the Tower.

10 / An Ambassador Besieged

Events outside their control soon granted the English factory in Istanbul an opportunity to act against its ambassador. Even after the execution of his monarch and patron on 30 January 1649, Bendysh had refused to declare for either parliament or king, an irresolution that simply was no longer viable after the regicide. Charles I's death deepened and multiplied the political rifts that divided England, and both monarchy and parliament now demanded unconditional fealty from state servants. Indeed, on 12 March the Council of State issued an order to the English Levant Company requiring it "not to send abroad public Officers without the approbation of that Councell under their seal."[1] As a petition prepared for the council several months later verified, the state now obliged the company to obtain confirmation even for appointments to the relatively humble consulships of Aleppo and Izmir.[2] Thus, when the English ambassador—whose selection two years earlier had occurred under profoundly different circumstances—gave no clear signal concerning his attitude toward the new government in England, both sides began scrutinizing his procedures and considering whether and how to replace him.

HYDE AT THE KING'S COURT

The new king, Charles II, already overseas at The Hague when he learned of his father's execution on 4 February, was in a desperate plight, perhaps in shock, and certainly distressed at ascending to a stateless throne. His inaction reflected his almost hopeless predicament; initially, he did nothing but dispatch envoys—to little advantage—to solicit aid from all the major (and several minor) states of Christian Europe.[3] What has not been fully appreciated is that even as he agonized over whether to allow a Christian compromise with the Scots over the Covenant,[4] he also sent an emissary to that most un-Christian of potentates, the Ottoman sultan. Soon after moving to France in June, the king met with and ordered to Istanbul that same Henry Hyde whom Thomas Bendysh had vanquished and dismissed two years earlier.

Hyde, having escaped punishment for his role in the ambassadorial struggles of 1647, had remained in England after his eviction from Ottoman domains.[5] He probably had assisted the royalists in the last months of the civil war and perhaps had even witnessed the parliamentarians' irrevocable triumph over his monarch in early 1649. After Charles's execution, Hyde escaped the realm and joined the throng of exiled royalists gathering in Paris awaiting Charles II's arrival.

Just what Hyde told his new liege about Ottoman affairs, or whether or not he even spoke directly with him, rather than acting through an intermediary (Charles II, after all, was not yet twenty in the early months of his reign, and still under the sway of his father's advisors) is murky. The factor Robert Bargrave, perhaps not wishing to think ill of the king and certainly poorly informed, later recorded in his diary that "through his frends assistance & his own well fram'd pretenses, [Hyde] procur'd a Letter from his Matie: Charles the Second to my Lord Ambass^r Sr. Thomas Bendyshe, obligingly desiring Sr. Thomas to restore Sr. He: Hide to his former Possessions in the Morea, & to make him once more Consul for our Nation there."[6] Hyde's "frend" at court may have been his illustrious uncle, Edward Hyde, whom he had known since boyhood, who had been a member of Charles I's inner circle during the intrigues of 1646–47, and who was now in Madrid on a similar errand, pleading with the Spaniards for financial and military assistance against the parliamentarian usurpers.[7] It is certain, at least, that tidings already were trickling in from across Europe of the futility of the royalists' requests for help (only the czar of Russia and a Danish envoy offered anything of substance, and the latter gesture was considered a diplomatic error and quickly withdrawn). The royalist camp already was in despair and eager to grasp even the remote possibility of Ottoman patronage. Furthermore, neither Charles nor his counselors—far from the commercial networks of the City of London—could reliably substantiate or contradict Henry Hyde's claims that Bendysh's standing with the English nation in the Levant, as well as with the Ottoman government, was shaky.

Hyde's arguments must have been persuasive, for Charles heeded them and on 19 September 1649 sent the former consul detailed instructions on how to proceed in the Levant.[8] The exiled monarch's foremost concern seems to have been that his new appointee not anger actual or potential European allies, and he ordered Hyde particularly to treat the Venetian *bailo* and other emissaries politely. He also moved to rebuild the bridges with the English nation in the eastern Mediterranean that his father had so recklessly ripped down, explicitly exempting from leviations and other taxes all sympathetic English merchants residing in Ottoman port cities. In Hyde's instructions, Charles further pronounced that all directives issued by the English Levant Company since the previous January should be considered invalid, and he implied that through his envoy he intended to appropriate the company's prerogatives. In return for his labors Hyde would receive not the ambassadorship but the lucrative consulship of Izmir. As the beset monarch explained:

> we have granted the consulship of Smyrna onto you, as a reward for your service in carrying Our letters to the Grand Signor at your own charge, we hereby declare that Our intention is to allow you all that public salary & allowance which the Turkey Company do allow to the Consul there for the time being and now do by these presents authorize you to determine the same in your hands out of the Consulage which we have authorized you to receive as well from Our own subjects or Strangers trading under Our banners and likewise to defray all public charges in that place of Smyrna.[9]

Hyde probably had requested this posting specifically, for after his ordeals as Sackvile Crow's strategist he must have fully grasped the power of the consulship of Izmir. That Charles was willing to bestow upon Hyde not only the commission but also the consulage of this rich port, over which his father's agent, Crow, had so bitterly fought, was a bonus.

The monarch demanded considerable service in return for this plum posting. His envoy was to proceed to Istanbul, the site of his humiliating rout some two years earlier, and solicit aid from his principal nemesis,

Sir Thomas Bendysh, by presenting imperial letters to the Ottoman sultan and grand vizier. Charles's wish was for a fat loan from the sultan in order to finance his impending assault upon England. Should Bendysh prove reluctant to assist, the monarch's letter granted Hyde authority to "use such other means as you shall think fit & necessary for our service."[10]

Sir Henry (for Charles also conferred knighthood upon him as part of the bargain) thus journeyed eastward, empowered to investigate English affairs in the Ottoman capital and perhaps also to act in the monarch's name. The English court in exile exerted pressure upon the French and Venetian governments to support its envoy. Paris seems to have done so unhesitatingly and even to have ordered its representative in Venice to urge that republic's Senate to follow suit. By 23 October 1649, evincing eagerness to "keep warm the friendly disposition of his majesty" the king of England, Venice, too, had ordered its *bailo* to cooperate with the royal initiative.[11]

Charles departed for Jersey almost immediately after dispatching Hyde and soon became mired in Irish and especially Scottish intrigues. Royalist interest in Hyde's venture nevertheless seems to have persisted. On 23 November, the Venetian ambassador in Paris, Morosini, informed Henriette Maria, the young king's mother, that the Venetian Senate had sanctioned Hyde's mission.[12] Nor was Edward Hyde the only royalist urging Charles's court to work the eastern Mediterranean sphere of English affairs. John Berkeley, who had been a principal candidate for the ambassadorship in 1646, in early 1650 informed Hyde of his wish to replace Bendysh. Whereas it is likely that a rage for revenge had inspired Henry Hyde's actions, Berkeley seems simply to have wished to vanish into the remote East. As he confessed to Hyde: "If I could get that retreat I should envy no man and I hope be envied by no man."[13] In fact, it appears that knowledge about and interest in Hyde's scheme spread rapidly, for by 9 November the English Levant Company directors were already drafting fresh instructions to Wylde and Bendysh for coping with the new pretender.[14]

RETURNING TO THE SITE OF THE CRIME

Even though Henry Hyde did not reach Istanbul until May 1650, by December of the previous year Bendysh had learned about his mission and received instructions for dealing with his obstinate opponent, the news of whose imminent arrival must have been most unwelcome. It is true that Bendysh, having personally intervened on behalf of the Venetian *bailo,* Soranzo, in the divan and secured his release from prison, was now on "perfect terms" with this clever diplomat.[15] Nevertheless, we have seen not only how Charles I's execution had jarred the foundations of English commerce in the Levant but also how Bendysh's actions over the previous two years had angered many of his compatriot factors. The nation he governed had shattered into myriad factions, some of which, Bendysh must have realized, would zealously promote an emissary from Charles II.

As if it were not enough that he faced such challenges from the community of English factors in the Levant, personal distress also beset him. The death of his monarch, to whom he often had declared devotion, was only the first of several blows. Sometime in the summer of 1649, the ambassador's eldest son, together with his personal physician, Dr. Reyner, boarded the ship *Talent* to begin a pilgrimage to Jerusalem. They did not get far, for during an engagement with a French ship they were drowned.[16] Soon thereafter, Bendysh's wife also died, leaving him with two daughters and two younger sons.[17]

Furthermore, on the very eve of Hyde's arrival, a serious rupture occurred between the English factories of Istanbul and Aleppo. Some years before, the Aleppine factors, contesting the supposed abuses of a domineering Armenian collector of customs and his Jewish successors,[18] had appealed to Ambassador Crow and several factors of Galata to help secure a *hatt-i şerif* as the best insurance against further tyrannies.[19] The grand vizier, Mustafa Pasha, had provided this document only at considerable expense to a number of factors of Galata, whom the Aleppine factory had promised to repay through a self-imposed leviation. According to a petition submitted to Bendysh by William Chappell, Roger Fowke, William Pearle, and Robert Frampton, the English factory of Aleppo, perhaps frustrated that the imperial decree proved unavailing, had stopped payments on the debt. On 8 May 1650, the ambassador tried to order the factory there to raise one-third of its duties on behalf of these creditors (within months, the company had disallowed this leviation). Some time later, he lashed out at this factory, declaring that he should be very sorry to find, that your Scale should make advantage of any such order [from the imperial divan], so badly to requite your friends of Galata, who have so well deserved at your hands; both by their procuring at your instance & entreaty the Hattsheriffe, & by staying so long without their monies, to the very great prejudice of some of them, and manifest injury to them all.[20]

No one relishes such censure, and Bendysh's rhetoric fueled the fires of resentment and helped turn the English factory of Aleppo against him.

Hyde, arriving in Istanbul on 9 May, refused Bendysh's invitation to his home, paid a courtesy call instead on the ambassador of France, and lodged with his old confederate the dragoman Giorgio Draperis, who must have resented terribly Bendysh's recent battulation against him.[21] Only on 10 May did Hyde finally dine with the ambassador of England, and he openly faulted his host for allowing the singing of psalms in his chapel and for not praying for the king (with the designation "Charles II"). On 12 May, he again dined with Bendysh and admitted that he was in Istanbul merely as an observer and would report to Charles his assessment of the ambassador's performance. That same evening, however, Hyde announced that he intended to play a more active role by demanding that no Jew serve as dragoman to the English, that the Levant Company repay him the twelve thousand dollars ostensibly owed him since his tenure as consul of the Morea, and that the king be given control over consulage and authorized to appoint all English consuls in the Ottoman Empire.

These sundry demands and observations combined personal and royal objectives. The dogged determination that an old debt be repaid fell into the former category, and the resurrected insistence that the king receive consulage monies, into the latter. It is unlikely, however, that in the chaotic circumstances of 1649 and 1650 Charles's council concerned itself with Jewish translators in the distant Levant. In urging the exclusion of Jews from English service, it is possible that Hyde acted on behalf of his Greek friend and host, Draperis.

After this dinner, the conflict between Bendysh and Hyde sharpened. On 13 May, Bendysh held a court of the entire factory, over which—or so Hyde's servant Coleman (who had been with him since his consulship in the Morea) bruited about the factory—he no longer had authority to preside. On that same day Hyde told the ambassador that he carried a letter from Charles II appointing him consul over Greece and the islands (but made no mention of his appointment at Izmir), and on the following day he proclaimed himself extraordinary ambassador and demanded an audience with the grand vizier.[22] Bendysh then challenged Hyde's credentials, called another court at which he requested a solemn oath of support from the factors of Galata (which all but eight men provided),[23] battulated his rival, and prepared a petition to prevent him from appearing before the grand vizier.

These actions stirred up the already profoundly divided English factory, which Hyde concurrently had been inciting against the ambassador's dwindling party. Robert Bargrave, acting as secretary to the most powerful English factor in the city, James Modyford, found himself dramatically dragged into the ensuing tumult. He had accompanied Bendysh to Istanbul in 1647 and considered the ambassador an adept and honorable official, a man "whom we all knew to have Commission from the King deceas'd, to have been a Prisoner in the Tower in testimony of his Loyaltie, to be a person of much Honour, true Worth, & spottless Reputation."[24] Nevertheless, he, no less than most, had been dismayed and confused at the news of Charles I's execution and instinctively was drawn to a man who had recently met with and now claimed to carry letters from the king's successor. In order to probe the authenticity of Henry Hyde's credentials, Bargrave invited to dinner Dr. James Hyde, Hyde's brother, with whom he had had a slight acquaintance at Oxford. Even though Dr. Hyde refused the invitation (from fear of being poisoned, Bargrave suspected), Bargrave did call on him and promised that both he and Modyford would support his brother if he indeed had letters of appointment as extraordinary ambassador from the king. Dr. Hyde admitted that such letters did not exist, at which Bargrave became thoroughly disillusioned and undertook a vigorous campaign—which he began by securing Modyford's backing—against Hyde and his faction. The episode not only confirms Hyde's cunning improvisations but also suggests that in the aftermath of the regicide, royalist sympathy had swept through the Levantine factories. Charles II had made a decisive error by not granting his agent plenipotentiary powers.[25]

AN ENGLISH RABBLE BRAVES THE DIVAN

Although Hyde had lost any chance to gain Modyford's support, he remained an able and veteran adversary who soon gathered around him a circle of talented English factors, among whom Richard Pickett, Robert Frampton, Gyles Davis, and John South already had challenged Bendysh's authority. Even more alarming was Hyde's proven ability to penetrate and thrive in the world of Ottoman politics and administration. As Bargrave later recalled,

> we had certein Information even from those great Rebells who then undertook the greatest Villainies, & were to Performe this Exploit: that he had made a Contract with them; on theyr parts, to install him Ambass^r, & to give into his power the merch^{ts}, persons & Estates, & on his p[romise], to give them there out the Summe of $70,000 . . . for theyr so doing.[26]

The "rebels" to whom Bargrave referred were not English but Ottoman. Just as the English sought political stability after Charles's execution—and fleetingly found it in Oliver Cromwell—so did the Ottomans lurch through the early 1650s before uncovering their own political strongman in Köprülü Mehmed Pasha. As Bargrave's passage implies, in the years following Sultan İbrahim's murder it was not the palace alone that determined who held power at the Ottoman core. The tendrils of principal factions reached far beyond the palace and city walls. Military leaders, the citizenry of Istanbul, or some combination of the two could exert great pressure upon, unseat, or murder a grand vizier, a *valide sultan* (the sultan's mother), or even a sultan and his retinue. If Bargrave is right, Henry Hyde tried to capitalize on these fissures in Ottoman rule in order to overturn the English order in the Levant. The diarist here accuses Hyde of negotiating with "rebels," who might even have been important Ottoman officials currently in disfavor—such as Melek Ahmed Pasha, who was to attain the grand vizierate three months later. Bendysh felt compelled to outbid his rival for the backing of such Ottoman "rebels."

Meanwhile, Hyde did not give up on the sitting grand vizier, Kara Murad Pasha, on 18 May attending him in public divan, where, with some help from the French ambassador (under orders from Paris to assist him), he had secured an audience. His stratagem foundered. Although

Hyde had arrived before the gates of Topkapı Palace at eight o'clock in the morning, Bendysh and a mass of his partisans were there ahead of him. They convinced the grand vizier to allow them to accompany Hyde to the private audience, to be held that afternoon at one o'clock.

Hyde seems to have realized that Bendysh had again outmaneuvered him and did not even bother to appear before the divan, sending instead his brother and Paul Haggatt—the same man who had previously defied the English factory of Izmir on Bendysh's behalf.[27] Haggatt's subsequent double-dealing, and the prominent part he was to play in Hyde's undertaking, illustrates the misgivings and disorientation that the events of 1649 had visited upon many Englishmen. Dr. Hyde and Haggatt explained to the grand vizier that Henry Hyde brought greetings from the new king of England, wanted to renew England's capitulations, and was empowered to investigate Bendysh's handling of English affairs. Bendysh's delegation rebuked these contentions, reminding the grand vizier of Hyde's villainies in the Morea and as Ambassador Crow's colleague. It protested that Hyde had brought no credentials from England, and in any case, the king of England had been dead for over a year.

No doubt annoyed at the quarrelsome foreigners, Kara Murad summoned Hyde, who appeared with a retinue of Frenchmen, a Mr. Bosteale, and a Mr. Plummer ("who a little before had renounced his King & Country & declared himself a subject of the Grand Signior").[28] At this point, Bendysh, James Modyford, and a throng of English merchants dashed into the divan, and Modyford at once began to vilify Hyde "openly to the Vezir in the Turkish Language."[29] Crushingly, he observed that Charles II himself was not in England but in exile with neither ships nor money, and that Hyde's entourage, suspiciously, consisted almost exclusively of Frenchmen. Upon hearing these words, the grand vizier, evincing little concern for the niceties of English legitimacy, replied, "I must have shipps & merchants" and threw Hyde out.

This public display of intracommunal turmoil sharpened English factionalism, and the conflict grew "strangely high; insomuch to wherever our parties were, they were even at Daggers drawing."[30] John Abney, the treasurer to the Levant Company in Istanbul and sympathetic to the monarchy if not to Hyde, refused to disburse money to Bendysh and his supporters, at which the ambassador wrote to Samuel Barnardiston in Izmir not to accept any draughts or bills of exchange from Abney unless expressly directed to do so by Bendysh, James Modyford, Jonathan Dawes, or John Erisey.[31] Hyde himself compounded his mistakes by combing the city of Istanbul for patrons and trying to buy off whomever he met, even pledging to supportive Ottoman officers twice the money they currently received from Bendysh. The feud possibly led even to murder, for on 21 May Hyde's long-time attendant Coleman was found dead in Giorgio Draperis's home. The former dragoman vainly tried to involve Bendysh in this nasty affair by complaining to the city's *voyvoda* that Coleman had been poisoned in the ambassador's residence and then dumped in his dwelling.

THE COUNTERATTACK

Bendysh, of course, had not been idle during these intricate intrigues. His men shadowed Hyde everywhere, and he seemed able to best his opponent's every ploy among the English factors, in the divan, on the streets of Pera, and with the so-called Ottoman rebels. The ambassador even projected his attack beyond the capital city by sending a letter to the consul of Izmir ordering the factory there to secure from the kadi a petition (*arz*) censuring Hyde. He perhaps was overoptimistic to expect support from these discontented factors, who resented the heavy-handed and centrist methods they judged him to favor. Nevertheless, the immediate dispatch of this appeal attests that Bendysh discerned the leverage this provincial factory was able to employ and that he did not underrate his rival's considerable talents.

Indeed, the greatest regional threat to Bendysh's tenure came not from the English nation in Izmir but from the kadi and the ingenious French consul there, Jean Dupuy. On 26 May, a mere eighteen days after Hyde's arrival, news reached Istanbul that the kadi of Izmir, helped to his decision with a one-hundred-fifty-dollar gift from Dupuy, had refused to petition the Sublime Porte against Hyde. These tidings must have alarmed Bendysh, particularly because Hyde's faction had somehow obtained this same intelligence and hurried an agent, Paul Haggatt, to Izmir to urge the English factory there to adopt Hyde's agenda.[32]

The ambassador's standing in the provinces became even more tenuous two weeks later, when Thomas Newsam arrived from Izmir, ostensibly with the signatures of twenty-five partisans of Hyde, whose party in Galata also had swelled. When Hyde again solicited the Ottoman divan on 11 June, seventeen adherents attended him. These men declared to the grand vizier that although it was true that Charles I had been executed, England nevertheless still had a monarch—Charles's son—who had assembled a mass of troops in Scotland and was on the point of reconquering his homeland. Kara Murad seems to have grown weary of Hyde's continual badgering, however, for after conferring with an advisor named Mustafa Çavuş, who had been to England as an emissary and who considered the faction's assertions absurd, he told Hyde "that when his master recovers the kingdom [then he] will acknowledge him for king" and had the whole contingent thrown out.[33]

Had the grand vizier known of concurrent events in Scotland, he might not have been so hasty, for Hyde's intelligence, if incautious and somewhat premature, was surprisingly precise. Charles was, after all, king of the Scots (as well as of the Irish) and on 11 June was actually in Breda hammering out a compromise (treacherous and humiliating though it may have been) over religious doctrine with representatives of Scotland's parliament in preparation for his Scottish coronation and an attack upon England.[34] It is unclear whether Charles, Edward Hyde, or some other royal advisor had divulged these arrangements to Henry Hyde; perhaps his assertion was simply sensible foresight (from where else could Charles have mounted an invasion?). It really made no difference, for the parliamentarians, too, had grasped the monarch's strategy, marked his landing in Scotland on 21 June, aggressively ordered an army under Oliver Cromwell to hunt him down, and, with his defeat at Worcester, driven him out of Great Britain and into ignoble, wandering, penurious exile.

Consequently, Kara Murad had made the politically expedient choice, if only through chance, in dismissing the king's man. His action did not daunt the uncommonly bullheaded Hyde, who the very next morning was again wandering the streets of Istanbul seeking assistance from "people of quality." He even convinced one of his supporters, Roger Howe, to pass himself off as the captain of the ship *Northumberland*, then in port. Howe asserted to any Ottoman official who would listen that he and his entire crew supported the royalist pretender, although a Jewish broker soon recognized him as a factor of Galata. When the real captain, Trenchfield, appeared, this feeble stratagem was exposed. Its aim probably had been to convince the grand vizier that even though the English factors of Galata were divided between king and parliament, the English mariners who controlled the vessels that could smash the Venetian blockade of the Dardanelles and serve in the conquest of Candia were all loyal to Charles II.

With his second ejection from the divan, events had begun to turn against Hyde. On 13 June, letters arrived from Izmir pledging to Bendysh the support of that port's consul and twenty-six of forty or so factors. They also reported that upon arrival there, Paul Haggatt had proclaimed that Bendysh had poisoned Coleman and that Hyde was now ambassador in his place. Consul Wylde's daring response had been to lock Haggatt up, which produced yet another uproar, with the French consul and a group of Hyde's partisans marching to the kadi in protest.[35] Two days later, back in Istanbul, the French ambassador himself approached the grand vizier on behalf of Hyde, at which Kara Murad bluntly rebuked him for interfering in English affairs and ordered Hyde expelled. On the next day (16 June), Mustafa Çavuş forcibly ushered him onto a ship bound for Izmir.[36]

Soon Bendysh began tracking down Hyde's adherents, who had scattered. Although Wylde and the factory of Izmir already knew about Hyde's rebellion, Edward Barnard, the consul of Aleppo, apparently did not. On 10 July, the ambassador advised him to apprehend and ship to England any of the fugitives Roger Howe, John South, Richard Pickett, Marmaduke Pickett, Richard Charleton, Thomas Newsham, Robert Frampton, Gyles Davis, and James Hyde, should they seek sanctuary in Aleppo.[37]

Although detached from the heart of Ottoman power, Hyde still did not yield. Instead, he tried to exploit the semi-independent power structure in the provinces. Upon his arrival in Izmir, the French consul rescued him and deposited him aboard a vessel riding in the harbor. From this refuge, on 5 July, Hyde wrote a note ordering John Wylde and his entire factory to render him obedience as the appointed consul over "Smirna & Natolia, Scio and Mittiline."[38] He also proclaimed Bendysh a traitor "for his delaying and denying obedience to his Majesties demands Exhibited unto him under his Royall Signature ... and all other theire Adherents and abetters in the Combination, Mutiny, Rebellion & Insurrection perpetuated in Constantinople and this province against his Majesties Royal dignity and Authority."[39] Hyde, however, had misrepresented the truth too many times to convince anyone that the younger Charles had appointed him consul of Izmir (even though it was the simple truth), much less of Anatolia and the Aegean, or that he had authority to pursue his charges of sedition (which was even more doubtful). The consul and most of his factory believed instead that Sir Henry had given himself this fictitious title in a desperate final bid to elevate his influence and authority over them.

Despite such deep distrust, Hyde's ploy did produce some commotion among English factors in Izmir. It took almost a month for the consul to pen a letter of repudiation, in which he cuttingly addressed Hyde's bid to "seduce" the factory "to that wicked and groundlesse rebellion" against the ambassador. Wylde angrily charged that the pretender had made "the port of Smirna [Izmir] the stage to vent more of your Mountebanke delusions, further to deceive the Nation, to summon us to your obedience, and to belch out your lyes & Rabshakeh [ramshackle?] language against our Ambassador."[40]

The consul was not content with mere words, however. He simultaneously had Richard Charleton, Paul Haggatt, and others of Hyde's key supporters in Izmir arrested, and he arranged for the *Lewis* to carry them away to England.[41] He also managed to mount a raid against the French, snatch Henry Hyde from them, and whisk him onto the *London Dragon* and off to London.

The *London Dragon,* with Sir Henry Hyde aboard, anchored at the port of London in early January 1651. The directors of the English Levant Company had spent the previous weeks preparing a case against their troublesome agent and were ready for his arrival. Already in December they had condemned Hyde in a letter to the Committee for the Admiralty,[42] and in a detailed statement forwarded to the Council of State in the second week of January they described and denounced as treasonous his unflagging support for Charles II.[43] The company convinced commonwealth officials of Hyde's sedition. In February he was tried for treason before the judges of the Admiralty and condemned, and on 4 March 1651 he was executed in the City of London.[44]

Hyde's final utterances on the scaffold in Cornhill displayed his convictions about his king, his religion, and his deeds in the Levant. He upbraided the England that had condemned him, declaring that "to learn a New-Religion, and New-Ways (that I must say Master Sheriff to you, and all others that hear me) I cannot dispence with my Conscience." He also censured the man and the organization who had defeated him with the comment that

> if I thought it were satisfaction to Sir Thomas Bendish, and all the Company, or any who think they have offended me, I am come Master Sheriff to pay that Obedience willingly; that Debt I owe to Nature, to pay it upon the score of a Subject; because Conscience within me, tells me not, that for the intentions of serving my Prince, that I could deserve such a Death, though Ten thousand times more other ways.[45]

Henry Hyde died on 4 March 1651, convinced to the end that his cause had been honorable and his actions proper. Just as his tenacity in life had mirrored Charles I's, so did his noble death duplicate his monarch's.

Having secured its bloody revenge, the company quickly composed itself. In response to a petition submitted by one of Hyde's adherents on 19 March 1651, the directors benevolently replied two days later that "the Levant Company hath nothing further against Richard Charleton, or any persons now in prison about the design of Hen. Hyde, than what was formerly mentioned in the charge delivered in by them to this honorable Councell against the said Hen. Hyde."[46] At the same time, the company agreed to release from all charges Hyde's brother, Dr. James Hyde, and his two servants, and even to consider disbursing two hundred fifty sequins for funeral expenses.

THE AFTERMATH

Wylde had forced Hyde, the mastermind of all the agitation, to board the *London Dragon,* which embarked for London in mid-August 1650. His departure did not at once end the intrigues but rather had quite the opposite effect. The French ambassador, de la Haye, in particular was incensed that Hyde had been spirited away from Istanbul, perhaps out of concern that he had so thoroughly bungled his directive from Paris to protect the pretender. In any case, he went to great expense and trouble to secure from Melek Ahmed Pasha, who had just succeeded Kara Murad, a decree, hurried by a *çavuş* to Izmir, that Hyde be restored. Nor could the French consul, Dupuy, and several English merchants in Izmir believe that Hyde was truly departed; they insisted that the English simply had hidden him. Securing the support of the kadi and other Ottoman officials, the members of the French factory in Izmir proceeded to tear the town apart, futilely searching for the phantom schemer.

At the heart of this seesaw contest between supporters of Bendysh and Hyde was Ottoman irresolution, as yet another grand vizierial crisis came to a head. On 5 August, while Hyde languished aboard a French ship in the Gulf of Izmir, the sultan dismissed Kara Murad Pasha, who twice had heard the English pretender's petition and who had engineered his expulsion from Istanbul. Both the French ambassador and Hyde's English supporters in Istanbul moved swiftly to persuade his replacement, Melek Ahmed Pasha, to reverse his predecessor's rulings.[47] Thus, Bendysh perhaps wrote too hastily on 6 August when he informed the directors of the English Levant Company that he had frustrated the designs of the "disorderly" people who had agitated against him.[48]

Indeed, Hyde's party initially enjoyed remarkable success. It was rumored that the French ambassador, out for revenge (and possibly having promised the grand vizier aid against the Venetians),[49] had even secured an Ottoman decree ordering James Modyford's execution. Bendysh himself later reported to the directors of the Levant Company that the new Ottoman government had threatened him with chains, death, "and whatsoever else might terrifie me."[50] On 20 August, before news of Hyde's sailing for London could have reached Istanbul, four *çavuş*es and two janissaries did arrive at Modyford's door, which Roger Midleton, seeing them approaching, quickly slammed shut even as Robert Bargrave demanded from the Ottomans an edict that would legalize their entry. Şaban, the chief *çavuş*, at once produced such a document.

This assertive response by Modyford's servants was meant as a delaying tactic, and it allowed their master a daring escape through a back window and over some houses to the safety of a French friend's home. His attendants, however, were not so lucky. Jonathan Dawes had elected this moment to make a house call and was at once seized and dragged through Galata, across the Golden Horn, and into Melek Ahmed Pasha's villa. That evening, Bargrave was seized as well, grilled by the grand vizier's lieutenant, and dumped into a pitlike room—the bedroom of Melek Ahmed Pasha's tailor—with Dawes, who was "fast in the Stocks, under the Tailors bed, where he could not so much as sitt upright, but lay on his back, upon broken bricks & Stones, woried by a myriad of Fleaes."⁵¹

Thus did Bargrave and Dawes start an adventure (at the behest, it should be recalled, of their own compatriots) that might have verified all the horrific accounts of Ottoman bestiality had their chief antagonists not been English and French. Even as Modyford disguised himself in woman's garb and slunk away to Bendysh's house, where he hid for several weeks before emerging unharmed, his two friends spent the night in a fetid little room. Although their stocks were removed, fleas and other vermin continued to torment them, and Bargrave, who styled himself a young dandy, fended off "proffers of kindness" from the tailor that were "unfit to Discourse, & horrid to remember." After this miserable night, janissaries conveyed them to the palace of Bektaş Ağa, one of the grand vizier's confederates. The next day, 22 August, the two factors began a coerced trek overland to Izmir.

Hyde's faction had hatched the scheme for this kidnapping. It had hoped to exchange Bendysh's chief lieutenant, Modyford, for Hyde, but was willing to make do with Bargrave and Dawes. The French ambassador sent an Englishman (Taylor Stevens), a Frenchman, and a janissary to the pier in Istanbul to give orders to the *çavuş*es assigned to accompany the two men to Izmir. The French and English representatives directed the Ottoman messengers to chain their captives to the bottom of the boat while crossing the Sea of Marmara, to make them sleep enchained, and to chain their legs together under the bellies of their horses as they rode. The *çavuş*es were to deliver them to Dupuy, the French consul in Izmir, who was to hold them in chains until Hyde was restored. Should the rumors that the English had already dispatched Hyde to England prove true, Dupuy was to send Bargrave and Dawes to France, where their punishment would mirror the English parliament's treatment of Hyde.

At first, the *çavuş*es seemed willing to comply, even crying out when the hostages refused to finance their own captivity: "Doggs, you shall runn on foot & we will beat you before us."⁵² They soon checked their tempers, however. Despite Stevens's presence on the journey to Izmir, the Ottoman agents did not bind Bargrave and Dawes as their English and French tormentors had urged. Indeed, they treated their prisoners rather courteously. As Bargrave later observed sardonically: "This [cruel handling] these french Xtians [Christians] were so Turkish to propund, but the Turks so Xtian, not to execute."⁵³

Furthermore, upon arriving in Izmir, the *çavuş*es did not at once deliver their charges to the French consul. Instead, one of them confined Bargrave and Dawes in pleasant surroundings at his own residence. Then the *çavuş*es rowed out to one of the English ships anchored in the harbor, where Spencer Bretton, who had recently replaced Wylde as consul, had sought refuge from vengeful Ottoman and French officials. From aboard ship he defied them, asserting that although they were "priveledg'd on Shoare," they enjoyed no jurisdiction over the ships.⁵⁴

This impertinent pronouncement confirms that Izmir was popular with foreign merchants in part because of the ease with which they could retreat to heavily armed vessels—which they perceived as projections of their homelands—anchored in the harbor. The assertion was impolitic, however, considering that hostages had been taken, and it put Bargrave and Dawes at considerable risk. The offended *çavuş*es, who, as representatives of the Sublime Porte, held considerable authority, at once moved to mobilize the city against the English. They dragged Bargrave to the customs house on the wharf and ordered Izmir's kadi, assistant kadi (*naib*), captain of janissaries (*serdar*), commander of the castle (*hisar ağası*), and various other community elders to attend. There they apparently directed the Englishman to pen a note to the obdurate consul "that he must not delude himselfe, but give back Sr. Hen: Hide, who was not yet departed: which if he did not, our Ambass. would be imprisoned at Constᵖˡᵉ: the merchants all be hang'd, & theyr Estates confiscat."⁵⁵ They allegedly also threatened to hang Bargrave at once should he not comply, which the factor claims to have refused to do even then. Although he was not consequently executed, he and Dawes were delivered to the French consul, where they were held in chains.

During the next three days, the English and French nations of Izmir erupted in open conflict. First, several Englishmen seized Hyde's adherent Taylor Stevens as, accompanied by some Frenchmen, he strolled the city's streets. After an exchange of small-shot with the French (one pellet from which injured an English mariner), they hustled Stevens aboard an English ship. Then, these same Frenchmen rushed to Bargrave and Dawes, imprisoned at the French consul's house, "& running furiously at us with theyr Rapiours, stopp'd them at our breasts; crying =Par Dieu, vous meritez la mort=."⁵⁶ The French next handed Bargrave and Dawes back to the *çavuş*es, who pledged that they would suffer for the afflictions they and their English colleagues had visited upon the French and the Ottomans. The agents dragged Bargrave and Dawes up the hill to Kadifekale, the castle that loomed above Izmir, and "threw [them] into a dismall, darke, & noisome Dungeon: & lay'd [them] in the Stocks" amid rats, stench, human bones, and filth.[57]

It is difficult to discern what the French and Ottoman deputies were thinking as they tossed the two hostages back and forth between them. Dupuy probably feared that the imbroglio would ruin French trade in Izmir, a trade which the English factory had already eclipsed and threatened to engulf. The *çavuş*es and their associates had orders to comply with French wishes. Nevertheless, they had just beheld a throng of foreigners brawling in the streets of their city, must have realized that the dispute had little to do with the Ottoman state, and merely wished it quickly and quietly resolved.

It was the Ottomans who, as Bargrave was fond of saying, did the "Christian" thing. After leaving him and Dawes a mere ten hours in the dungeon, the *hisar ağası* settled them in more comfortable quarters and soon befriended his two charges. During the next month or so, Bargrave and Dawes remained safe and comfortable in the castle, while in the town below the French and English, who by now must have known that Hyde was en route to England, battled over them. The *hisar ağası* reported to his new comrades various French plots to seize them yet again, including one foiled attempt to rush them off to France aboard a French ship lurking behind Giocomo Point, just outside Izmir's harbor. The Ottoman commander also described the kidnapping of Monsieur Manzarat, one of the chief French factors in Izmir, in exchange for whom the English consul demanded Bargrave and Dawes's release.

This ruckus finally was settled when the English and French parties gathered at Izmir's customs house for an exchange of prisoners. Bargrave later recounted this episode:

> At the Day appointed for us to be exchanged, the Grandees, & a great part of the City repair'd to the Custome=house, whither we were sent for; & from over the Railes where we stood, we had the glad greetings of our frends, all arm'd in theyr Boats beneath us: & now counting each tedious moment till we were free; the Surly Chaouses demand as well Stevens to be surrendred, as the French Prisoners; swearing that unless they had

> him with them, to carie back to the French Ambass^r they would not yet give us up: & streight crying to our Keepers=Away with us again!=But I resolv'd rather to leap into the Seae then returne to the Castle; & to this end, I agreed with Mr. Dawes, & call'd to some of my frends in English to save me: but as I was mounting over, Mr. Dawes doubted he might faile in the attempt, & caught hold of me to stay me. Our frends mean while threatned that if they baffled any longer, they would fire among them: but Mazarat p[er]ceiving theyr resolutions, interpos'd, by taking on himselfe to answer for Stevens; & salv'd up all: when being one by one exchanged, & we amongst our frends; our Flaggs of Defyance were soon turn'd into Ensignes of Joy; & our Gunns that were charg'd in Enmitie, we let fly in Triumph: speaking our wellcome to our frends, & theyr [and] our Gladness for our Liberty.[58]

In these spirited lines, Bargrave displayed the elation of someone delivered from perdition. His description, however, also conjures up the rather comic vision of picaresque English and French adversaries swaggering onto center stage as Izmir's citizens, no doubt astonished and bemused, assembled to watch. One cannot help wondering at the impressions such a display must have imprinted upon the minds of the observing "grandees" (the kadi and his assistants, the captain of the janissaries, the customs collectors, the *çavuş*es, and the chief Muslim merchants of the town), as well as "a great part of the City" (perhaps several hundred Muslim, Greek Orthodox, Armenian, and Jewish merchants, brokers, shopkeepers, artisans, vendors, and mariners).

Thus did Bargrave, Dawes, Stevens, Manzarat, and probably several others win their freedom. The first two of these captives did not remain long in Izmir but soon returned to Istanbul, where their ambassador had not only checked the grand vizier's resolve to send him to Charles II for trial but had even persuaded him to rescind his decrees handing Bargrave and Dawes over to the French and ordering Modyford's execution.[59] According to de la Haye, Bendysh had gained the latter reversal by promising to write to England urging the withdrawal of English ships from the Venetian fleet, as well as securing vessels for the Ottoman navy.[60]

11 / The Commonwealth and the Levant

Both the Venetian bailo *and the French ambassador were now convinced* that the English ambassador was a committed parliamentarian, an opinion which his every action seemed to confirm. He regularly corresponded with London, and never with the exiled Charles Stuart. He had labored energetically to deport Hyde—a royal emissary, however shady he may have been—to a hostile and bitter England. And he recently had received letters from the directors of the English Levant Company condemning South, Howe, and several other well-known royalists for their roles in the recent debacle. These epistles empowered Bendysh to force his adversaries to pay all expenses brought on by the struggle, fine those who had sought foreign protection, and send home the most troublesome of them.[1]

The ambassador acted at once on these orders, busying himself tracking down supporters of Hyde. On 27 October 1650, he dispatched to Spencer Bretton, the new consul in Izmir, a warrant against John South (who, it seems, had recently fled to that port town) for laboring on behalf of Hyde, causing great outlays of money, putting himself under the protection of the French, and helping French ambassador de la Haye in his endeavors to overturn England's capitulations.[2] He also tried to locate Robert Frampton and Gyles Davis, who "most maliciously & wickedly have been from time to time the chief instruments, contrivers, & fomenters of these late unhappy factions & divisions."[3] Unable to find them, the ambassador declared sequestered and confiscated the money owed them by the Levant Company. Bendysh also worked to compensate those loyal to him, granting to Jonathan Dawes, for example, a sequestration for nine thousand dollars in compensation for some goods that Hasan Ağa, the chief collector of customs at Istanbul, had allegedly seized from the absent merchant's warehouse while he was locked away in the citadel in Izmir.[4]

PARLIAMENTARY POLICY IN THE LEVANT

Throughout this period, Bendysh insisted to his directors that the Veneto-Ottoman war lay at the root of English woes in the Levant. Indeed, he reported on 14 January 1651 that the continuing presence of English ships in the Venetian fleet had so angered the grand vizier that the Ottoman government might cut off English trade entirely.[5] The ambassador's persistence in his campaign to steady English policy in the eastern Mediterranean seems finally to have made an impression, for on 3 December 1650, the company sent a delegation to the Committee for the Admiralty to request a new commission for Bendysh. This document was not only to confirm him as ambassador, state that his actions against Hyde had been proper, grant him the power to send home troublemakers, and enjoin English ministers and factors to take the Oath of Engagement of 1649 but also to forbid all English ships from serving against the Ottomans in the Venetian fleet.[6] Six days later, a follow-up petition to the Committee for the Admiralty requested that Henry Hyde, expected to arrive in London at any moment, be put on trial, that Bendysh receive a new commission, that the ambassador renew the Anglo-Ottoman capitulations, that the government compose letters of protest against Ottoman actions contrary to the capitulations, and, most dramatically, that the naval fleet, scheduled to escort company vessels into the Mediterranean, sail up to "the Castles of Constantinople" as a show of force.[7]

The company's request for a display of parliamentarian naval power was a spectacular divergence from its past caution in negotiations with the Ottomans. The policy change may have derived in part from the often decisive role English war vessels played in Veneto-Ottoman engagements. Bendysh's earlier effective use of English merchant vessels off Seraglio Point may also have helped convince the directors that gunboat diplomacy could be persuasive. The Committee for the Admiralty's acquiescence in this tactic in late 1650, however, had little to do with such considerations. Its justifications were more global.

Parliament's troops had just humiliated a Scottish army and sent Charles I's son scurrying into exile. Its navy was expanding rapidly and was even then hunting down the remnants of the royalist fleet under Prince Rupert. The fledgling commonwealth was busy formulating a global policy that would lead to direct conflict with Spanish, Dutch, and other European navies.[8] The new government's determination to challenge Ottoman mastery of the eastern Mediterranean was principally a manifestation of this expansionist poise and fervor.

Rumors concerning Dutch incursions into the Levant, as well as the retooling of the Ottoman fleet, lent urgency to the English government's decision. Bendysh himself reported the appointment of a new Dutch consul and the presence in Izmir of a Dutch vessel packed with goods. He also observed that the Ottomans recently had built fifteen or twenty great ships, "in the Dutch fashion," each of which carried twenty-five, forty, or fifty brass guns.[9] Robert Bargrave elaborated that it was a Flemish renegade who had supervised the construction of thirty such ships in Istanbul's imperial shipyards, adding, however, that the new fleet's flagship had recently been launched and immediately foundered, and that none was yet seaworthy.[10]

Considering these developments, the directors of the English Levant Company probably foresaw that the Committee for the Admiralty would order the Mediterranean fleet to promote and protect English commerce vigorously. Indeed, the committee acceded to all their requests, except for the renewal of Bendysh's commission. The stated reason for this one denial was that some members of the company had "expressed their desires that some other person might be sent to succeed in that employment."[11] This logic formed a useful excuse. In actuality, the government's reluctance to grant the commission was, as much as its willingness to risk Ottoman rage through the arming and dispatching of a fleet, a reflection of its newfound confidence. Whereas in 1647 the company had appointed Bendysh as a compromise between the parliamentarians and a still viable king, four years later parliament could impose upon the company someone of proven loyalty.

Although the company was dismayed that the committee refused its ambassador a new commission, and it chastised the government for listening to particular persons rather than "the public weal of the Company,"[12] the politics of the current ambassador simply seemed too equivocal to many members of parliament under post–civil war circumstances. Not only had Bendysh earlier sympathized with Charles I, but he also had never openly proclaimed for parliament. Furthermore, hints began trickling in that many factors in both Istanbul and Izmir now openly opposed Bendysh's governance, which they increasingly perceived as despotic and oppressive. Several letters describing the recent disturbances substantiated these allegations of treasonous tyranny. One such epistle from Izmir, which perhaps arrived in London on 26 March 1651, contended that in the aftermath of the Hyde affair, one of Hyde's abettors had been stabbed to death by a servant and another had been wounded. The anonymous letter also noted that Bendysh had contracted new capitulations in the name of the renegade monarch Charles II and complained against the ambassador that "the *Turkish Authority* he hath at his beck; & threatens to fetch up to *Constantinople* all that disobey his commands . . . whilst he . . . speakes & acts altogether contrary to the present powers in *England*."[13] Meanwhile, John Pixley, who had been the first man for Hyde in Izmir, tried to hang himself.

Two undated memos seconded these allegations. A short note from a Mr. Dodington claimed that two men, Mr. Isaackson and Mr. Hamilton, had recently carried a private note from Bendysh to Charles II.[14] A second, more extensive memorandum contained articles of treason against the ambassador, including the charges that he had permitted his chaplain to pray that "the King of the Scots" would be restored to his English throne, that he had wickedly delivered his merchants and estates to the "Turks and Jews," that he habitually accepted bribes, that he exercised an arbitrary government in Istanbul, that he had delivered several Englishmen into Ottoman slavery, that he had promised the Ottomans a fleet to employ against the Venetians, that he endeavored to serve as Charles II's ambassador and corresponded with the exiled king and other enemies of the commonwealth, that he had promised ships and ship carpenters to the Ottomans, that he had imprisoned several factors and demanded that they accept him as Charles's ambassador, and that he had procured new capitulations in the name of Charles II.[15]

Although unable to judge the accuracy of such denunciations, which Bendysh vehemently denied, neither the company nor the government could afford to ignore them. Indeed, the company's directors hastily withdrew their unconditional endorsement of Bendysh's proceedings. On 6 March 1651, they insisted that English factors be allowed to speak freely in their courts and assemblies, even if their remarks proved prejudicial to the ambassador or the company, and that any "exorbitancy" proclaimed or enacted should be dealt with in England rather than in Bendysh's court.[16] They also stripped the ambassador of another effective instrument of management and potential oppression: factors no longer had to go through his court in order to recover debts and call debtors to justice. The company directors instead authorized English merchants operating in the Ottoman Empire to hire their own intermediaries—janissaries and dragomans—at company expense to do so.

This sudden policy shift disoriented relations between factors and their ambassador and made untenable Bendysh's harsh penalties against those he deemed responsible for the recent ambassadorial crisis. Although he judged John South, who had fled to Izmir, to have been one of Henry Hyde's principal partisans, in late July 1651 Bendysh nevertheless felt compelled to release South's sequestered estate, following the company's orders that he no longer molest or hinder factors who had put themselves under the protection of the French ambassador and other foreigners because of Hyde or for other reasons.[17]

AN EROSION IN AUTHORITY

Bendysh must have resented terribly the directive to suspend his prosecution of the despised South and his other rivals. He had little choice but to do so, however, for he found himself perilously close to the complete alienation that had brought down his predecessor, Sir Sackvile Crow. Even as he faced rampant disaffection among his factors and diminishing support from his home government, his links with the Ottoman court also deteriorated. On 10 June 1651, the ambassador related to the directors of the Levant Company that his "old enemy the Muftee [*şeyhülislam*]" had recently loosed a tangled design against him.[18]

The kadi who had contended with the turmoil that the Hyde-Bendysh clash had unleashed upon Izmir was a certain Hashimizade, rumored to be the nephew of this *şeyhülislam*, Bahai Mehmed Efendi.[19] Soon after Bargrave and Dawes were rescued from French and Ottoman captivity, it seems, this kadi had reopened an old lawsuit between an Armenian and an English merchant, ruled against the Englishman, seized Consul Bretton, and had several English merchants hurled bodily down a staircase. He also charged the consul with insulting the sultan and threatening the town of Izmir, demanded two hundred thousand *akçes* from him in recompense, and related these allegations to his uncle, Bahai Mehmed Efendi.[20]

News of these events and accusations reached the grand mufti in the early summer of 1651. He at once called the English ambassador into audience and demanded the immediate removal of Bretton, something to which Bendysh, being not only the chief defender but also a friend and comrade of the consul's, refused to accede. Indeed, given the restrictions that London had lately imposed upon him, it is doubtful that the ambassador possessed the authority to dismiss Bretton even had he wished to do so. The instant consequence of his defiance was a sensational clash with the *şeyhülislam,* which Mustafa Naima, a contemporary Ottoman memorialist, recounted with relish. He reported that Bahai Mehmed had lashed out at Bendysh verbally, proclaiming: "You are an irreligious cursed one. What kind of ally are you, who never ceases from perfidy against religion and the state? How many galleons and how much help have you given to the Venetian infidels? Do you suppose that I do not know of your intrigues?" The Ottoman official physically abused him by shackling and punching him. For the ambassador, the interview ended with an unpleasant three-hour imprisonment in Bahai Mehmed Efendi's summer house and the expectation of being cast into the dungeon in the notorious Black Sea castle where the Ottomans had occasionally confined Venetian *bailo*s during Veneto-Ottoman wars.[21]

Bendysh's long experience in Istanbul, however, and in the deep-rooted factionalism of Ottoman politics combined to rescue him. The *şeyhülislam*'s threats against him proved to be a political blunder, for, as Naima laconically if inaccurately observed, "the King of England is one of the great lords of Europe. He is the possessor of much property, soldiers, ships, and weapons of war." Bahai Mehmed's many enemies—principal among whom were the grand vizier, the janissary *ağa,* and the *kaymakam*[22]—used this public blunder as an excuse to depose and replace him—if only briefly—with his rival, Abdülaziz Efendi (whom Bendysh, with inadvertent irony, proclaimed a Christian "for this Justice done on a Christians complaint").[23]

Upon his release, Bendysh moved quickly to comply with company directives, displaying both restraint and shrewdness as he acted to remove the many resentments against him. On 29 July 1651, he released

John South's sequestered estate. More drastically, he ordered Jonathan Dawes, one of the players in the recent conflict with Henry Hyde and now acting treasurer, to provide South with bills charged upon the English nation of Izmir.[24]

The ambassador also was unexpectedly lenient with John Abney, who had been the English Levant Company's treasurer in Istanbul during the recent uproar. From Bendysh's perspective, Abney's actions over the previous few months must have seemed treacherous, if not treasonous. Not only had the treasurer refused to disburse monies to him during the crisis months of late 1650, but he also had fled Istanbul for Belgrade, "taking his pleasure, and following his sports whilst his fellow factors were here striving to defend their lives & their principal's estates."[25] Even more damningly, Bendysh accused Abney of subscribing company funds to Hyde even as he withheld resources from the duly appointed ambassador. And all this during a time when, Bendysh insisted, he was desperate for supplementary funds because of the abrupt and costly change of the grand vizier and other chief Ottoman officers, the arrival of Hyde, and the lock-up of the English consul and factors in Izmir. Despite these many misdeeds, on 12 September 1651, Bendysh sullenly authorized the restoration to Abney of his entire estate.

This uncharacteristic benevolence derived both from the company's injunction that Bendysh show forbearance toward his enemies and from his recognition of a need to broaden his base wherever possible because of the continuing tenuousness of his position vis-à-vis both the Ottoman Empire and England. For example, even after Bendysh's face-off with the *şeyhülislam,* the sultan's government continued to pressure the ambassador to provide warships against the Venetians. In late summer 1651, the Ottoman navy compelled Samuel Chamlet's vessel, the *John Bonaventure,* to carry Ottoman troops to Candia.[26]

Soon thereafter, the grand vizier, Gürcü Mehmed Pasha, just appointed and to be deposed within a matter of months, summoned into his presence the French, English, and Dutch envoys because of the continuing presence within the Venetian fleet of ships flying their flags. This audience led, perhaps inevitably, to a crisis of protocol. Both the English and French ambassadors, eager to establish preeminence with each new grand vizier, ventured to sit on that minister's right side. Bendysh arrived first and claimed the prestigious spot. While he was "respectfully" standing and chatting, however, the French ambassador approached and, as the mocking Bargrave later recounted, "the small Great man silently slipt behind my Lord Bendysh into his chair; my L^d not Perceiving it, as he retir'd backwards, sitt on the Fr. Ambassadors Lap, but finding his Cusheon thus chang'd clapt his hand on the Fr. Amb^{rs} neck & threw him out of his Seat."[27] This disgraceful episode only confirmed the new Ottoman minister's views of western European boorishness and ineptitude. It further soured relations between the representatives of the two European powers and may have given the Ottoman government some leverage to use against them.

In any case, the old rumor had resurfaced in London that the Sublime Porte was negotiating with Bendysh for warships. Amerigo Salvetti, the agent for the Grand Duke of Tuscany, related to the allegedly astonished directors of the Levant Company that he had heard from the Venetian ambassador at Paris, Michele Morosini, that Bendysh had offered the grand vizier thirty vessels for operations against the Venetians. The Ottoman official supposedly had countered with a proposal for English exemption from all duties in the Ottoman Empire in return for sixty ships.[28] Salvetti also learned, to his satisfaction, that the company had already decided to have Bendysh recalled.

THE BID TO RECALL THE ENVOY

By late 1651, Bendysh's influence in London had dissipated. As Cromwell and his New Model Army expanded their authority in 1650 and 1651, and as tensions between the English and the Dutch escalated, the company's ability to manage its own affairs weakened and its finances suffered. One result of the shifts in domestic politics was a company proposal in October 1651 to replace Bendysh with an agent of unquestionable loyalty who, it was hoped, would be less extravagant than the sitting ambassador.[29]

Within days, an initiative from Cromwell's Council of State also called for Bendysh's dismissal. Paulucci, the Venetian secretary in England, concluded optimistically that the English government was rebutting the ambassador's insistence that company vessels serve the Ottomans in the Cretan war. He even wrote to Sagredo, the Venetian ambassador in Paris, that parliament intended to send an ambassador extraordinary to Istanbul to investigate the allegations and "would take the earliest opportunity of punishing such an offence as it deserved."[30]

The Council of State, however, was urging Bendysh's recall not because of the company's indigence at home or the ambassador's collusion abroad but because "of a disaffection alleged to be in the present Ambassador towards this Government & State."[31] Indeed, several months later Sir Oliver Fleming, the chief councillor of state, told Paulucci that "during the civil wars the Commonwealth was by no means satisfied with the actions of the English ambassador at the Porte."[32] Commonwealth authorities had long suspected their evasive and enigmatic envoy, and Cromwell himself, having served on a committee to consider the recall of Sackvile Crow in 1646,[33] knew Bendysh personally and was cognizant of his uncertain politics. Yet it was anxiety about the Dutch that finally decided the rulers to act. The Council of State particularly feared a Dutch design to dispatch to the Levant an ambassador together with thirty-five ships "with intent (if possible) to supplant this Nation of so considerable a trade."[34] Should England choose to act against this peril, it would hardly do to have a suspect ambassador conducting its policy in the eastern Mediterranean.

The selection of a replacement was not easy. On the one hand, the company wanted only to save some money and end the destructive squabbling within and among the factories of Istanbul, Izmir, and Aleppo. On the other, the government demanded the appointment of a proven parliamentarian with the leverage and capital to help realize the overseas policies of the commonwealth, particularly in regard to the Dutch. Consequently, when on 20 January 1652 the company selected one of its members, a certain Mr. Mithwold, as agent to succeed Bendysh, parliament not only rejected his appointment but also (and for the continued autonomy of the English Levant Company, menacingly) designated its Committee of Foreign Affairs to review the company's letters patent and capitulations.[35]

Bendysh soon was informed of these proceedings and in February 1652 took the drastic step of drawing fourteen hundred lion dollars from the treasury in Izmir to finance the dispatch to England of two servants—one of whom probably was his son, John—to plead for a renewal of his commission.[36] Rather than the ambassador's deputation, however, disputes within parliament and between that institution and the company saved him, at least for the moment. It was not until September that the company found another candidate—the civil war veteran Major Richard Salway—who was acceptable to both parties, and it was not until February 1653 that anyone at all arrived in Istanbul to replace Bendysh. Salway himself caused the delay. He had been out of the country when selected on 1 September 1652.[37] On 12 October, when he finally appeared before a general court of the company, he thanked the assembly for the nomination and then postponed his departure indefinitely because of uncertainties caused by the Anglo-Dutch war.[38]

The major's worries were not unfounded, for the Dutch were active in the Mediterranean and, despite parliament's systematic use of convoys, were disrupting English commerce and inconveniencing English factors throughout the basin. On 24 December, the company received information about one of several Dutch strikes against English shipping.[39] Eight months previously, on 10 April, the company vessels *Sampson, Levant Merchant,* and *Mary* had departed in a convoy from Izmir. Although they anchored safely at Leghorn on 20 June, a week later four Dutch men-of-war approached and threatened to attack the English ships even as they crowded under the protection of the castle's guns. The Duke of Tuscany ordered his galleys to protect the English vessels, whose captains then proceeded to empty their holds of their cargoes of silks, grosgrain yarns and cloth, mohairs, wormseed, cottons, gallnuts (used in leather tanning), and other goods, some of which were perishable, and store them in Leghorn's lazaretto, which they had rented for this purpose. The company's principal predicament, it seems, was that the three English merchant vessels were at once converted into men-of-war in order to confront the Dutch, which left their rich freight moldering in a lepers house at great loss to the company, its merchants, and its factors.

The company's response to this crisis, on 7 January 1653, was to petition the Council of State to send a powerful convoy through the Straits of Gibraltar, hastily approve Major Salway as ambassador-designate, and appoint an agent to represent him until the seas of the Mediterranean world were again cleared and secure.[40] Although the council quickly agreed to these recommendations, it was unwilling to pay for the convoy, insisting instead that the company, as the most interested party, underwrite its hefty expenses.

The directors balked at this demand, in part, no doubt, because of impoverishment, but also because the government's directive uncomfortably reminded them of Charles I's mangled efforts to tax company revenue and supervise its procedures.[41] They cautiously discussed various justifications for refusing to finance the convoy, including prevailing taxes, costly current obligations, recent outlays because of Sackvile Crow and Henry Hyde, and the company's lack of liquid wealth on account of merchandise that lay idled by the war in the warehouses of Aleppo, Istanbul, Izmir, Leghorn, and other places.[42] They also offered to the state the six or seven ships then bound for the straits (after they had unloaded their goods), while asserting that the Dutch, by adequately protecting their own commercial vessels, were consuming Levantine trade. They finally claimed, disingenuously, that since the war was "national," and since the company's stock belonged to "clothiers, lenders, widows, & orphans of the whole Nation," it was the state's duty to defend company interests as national interests. Such arguments were dangerous, for they could easily be used to overturn the company's monopoly on Levantine commerce: if the company truly represented the nation, it could be claimed, then surely all English citizens should have access to Mediterranean sea lanes and port facilities.

YET ANOTHER PRETENDER IN ISTANBUL

Most of these arguments and interests were long-term, however. The company and state's immediate purpose was to replace Bendysh quickly and quietly. On 21 January 1653, the company proposed that Richard Lawrence be commissioned as agent by parliament and company to carry letters of revocation to Bendysh and to represent the English nation in Istanbul until Salway could come. Parliament promptly agreed.[43]

This selection was not very shrewd. The English government had decided to pry Bendysh from his post in the unprecedented and thus dangerous manner of appointing in his place an agent rather than an ambassador. It was injudicious to further offend the old battle-hardened hand by designating a successor who not only had experienced a long and litigious Levantine career but also had previously clashed with Bendysh. Four years earlier, the ambassador had found Lawrence guilty of serious transgressions, pronounced him unfit to vote in the court of the English factory in Izmir, sequestered twelve thousand lion dollars from him, and even threatened him with imprisonment.[44] The company and the English government chose to ignore this contentious history, and on 2 February 1653 appointed Lawrence to go to Istanbul with letters and instructions to remain as agent. Six days later, the company ordered him to depart with all expedition.[45]

The zealous envoy did so, arriving in Istanbul within a month, armed with a packet of letters to Bendysh, the Ottoman sultan, Mehmed IV, and his grand vizier, who at that time was Derviş Mehmed Pasha. The dispatch from the company to Bendysh recalled him to England and appointed Richard Lawrence to remain in Istanbul as "agent," a reorganization that the company directors justified with reference to the dreadful state of English commerce.[46] Letters from parliament to the sultan and grand vizier reiterated Bendysh's recall, asking them to "dismiss the said Sr. Thomas Bendish that he may return hither to give an account of his negotiation."[47]

Bendysh, of course, did not want to return to England, where he feared exchanging the great power and authority he enjoyed in Istanbul for impoverishment, imprisonment, or even death. The threat from Lawrence, however, differed from and was more awkward than those he had faced from Henry Hyde or Sir Sackvile Crow. During the crises of 1651 and, especially, 1647, Bendysh had been able to pose as the fully credentialed moderate alternative to virulently partisan pretenders to the ambassadorship during times of exceptional political uncertainty. By 1653, the royalists had been decisively crushed both in England and on the high seas, Charles II was a penniless fugitive, the Cromwellian commonwealth was in the final phase of its consolidation, and the new administration had dispatched its own commissioned and accredited delegate to replace him. It was no longer feasible to be nonpartisan.

Bendysh realized how much the political climate had changed. In a letter penned to Cromwell's secretary, John Thurloe, on 4 March 1653, he not only posed as the wise old master mentoring the neophyte rulers of England in their relations with the Islamic giant to the east but also brandished a new and marked spirit of sympathy with the commonwealth.[48] The ambassador politely warned Cromwell that the cloying tone of parliamentary dispatches to the Ottoman rulers would harm the commonwealth and its representatives in the Levant. These letters, the envoy declared, "being full of thanks, and acknowledgments for courtesies, and respects done (which they [the Ottomans] were never guilty of to any) and desires of continuance of the same (which I fear they will easily grant) for upon the reading of the letters, they will not only use us as they have done, but (if possible) worse."[49] These lines reveal that Bendysh somehow sensed that although Oliver Cromwell might have been able to conduct and win a war against the Dutch, his grasp of international diplomacy remained shaky. The soon-to-be protector, understanding the tenuousness of his government's position overseas, labored to sound regal in his correspondence with other heads of state. His representative in Istanbul advised Cromwell that he had failed in this undertaking and carefully intimated that only the sitting ambassador could protect him from further faux pas.

Bendysh adroitly eased from this topic into a discussion of Richard Lawrence, whom he claimed to have welcomed with "due honor," offering to arrange an audience for him with the grand vizier. Then, in the same letter, he quickly changed tack. The lame duck ambassador rebuked the company's determination to downgrade its envoy from "ambassador" to "agent" (which he insisted was contrary to the capitulations and would greatly damage English influence at the Sublime Porte), and he launched a detailed appraisal of the position of Richard Lawrence, who, he argued, was caught between the desire for a prompt imperial audience and a desperate lack of funds. Bendysh contended that an ambassador-designate must raise at least eight or ten thousand lion dollars for such an occasion and that unless several well-stocked English merchant vessels were unexpectedly to anchor off the ports of Istanbul and Izmir, the English factories in those cities could not possibly supply such a sum. The ambassador shrewdly explained that he had reluctantly advised Lawrence to delay his audience, and he declared, "I assure your Honors although I may not be so happy as to ease this charge longer entrusted with me, yet it would grieve my heart in my absence to hear of the death and pain in [preserving] and bringing up" the English presence in Ottoman lands.[50]

Brilliantly, Bendysh thus was able to freeze the ambitions of his challenger without destroying his own position in Istanbul. Although Cromwell began referring to Bendysh as "our late Ambassador," the Ottoman government never acknowledged Lawrence's commission and continued to negotiate with his predecessor.[51] Despite this failure, Lawrence refused to return to England, even though the company, tiring of the double charge of supporting both him and Bendysh, finally requested on 19 February 1655 that Cromwell reconsider Bendysh's removal. His Highness's response nine days later was to recommend the recall of both men, whereupon (in a striking display of disorder and division) the company on 8 March selected, six days later withdrew, and on 19 March again nominated William Garway as their replacement.[52] Finally, on 3 June 1656, over one year after these events, it sent letters of revocation to Lawrence, including an agreement to allow four thousand dollars per annum for his residence in Istanbul.[53]

In a curious echo of Crow's devotion to Charles I, Lawrence insisted that a directive recalling him to England could come only from the potentate himself—in this case, Oliver Cromwell.[54] Indeed, he remained in Istanbul for several years and wrote his own intelligence dispatches to the protector. On 7 November 1654, for example, he related that the Dutch agent had died and that Bendysh was trying to force the Dutch to ship under English protection. On 26 November 1654, he recounted Bendysh's failure in his bid to gain control of Dutch commerce.[55] It was Lawrence's wife, Joanna, longing to end her husband's ludicrous pretense and no doubt homesick for England, who finally pleaded with Bendysh to petition that Cromwell write a letter of recall.[56] In early April 1656, Bendysh complied.

THE PROTECTOR JOINS THE FRAY

Meanwhile, a letter that Cromwell wrote to Sultan Mehmed IV on 25 March 1654 displayed how quickly the protector had adjusted to and learned his part as chief of state.[57] The epistle not only insisted on free trade for English ships but also vehemently condemned Ottoman treatment of Cromwell's subjects. It named the case of Commander William White and his ship the *George,* which the Barbary fleet had forced into service and abandoned under the castle of Rhodes, where it was seized and later destroyed. Cromwell forcefully condemned Ottoman inaction in this case and seconded Bendysh's demand that Commander White be fully compensated for the loss of his vessel.

The protector's endorsement of Bendysh's appeal on behalf of White did not denote any amendment to his judgment of the ambassador's inconstancy. Despite reports that Bendysh finally had abandoned his pragmatic neutrality and declared himself ambassador in the protector's name, "and hath baffled Lawrence as coming in the name of parliament,"[58] Cromwell desultorily continued pushing for his removal. Indeed, consideration of Bendysh's station served to reopen the old debate between monarch (that is, protector) and the English Levant

Company over rights of appointment and collection of duties. On 7 July 1654, a large contingent from the company hastily decided to attend upon Cromwell to defend the company's prerogatives in selecting ambassadors.[59] Several weeks later, the protector informed the company that, following the precedent by which the last parliament had recalled Bendysh and appointed Lawrence in his place, he now intended to elect and appoint Richard Salway as ambassador-designate.[60] Cromwell directed the company to draft letters of credence on Salway's behalf to the sultan and grand vizier.

By securing consent from both Cromwell and the company to withdraw from the ambassadorial appointment because of the death of a friend, Major Salway himself resolved the immediate crisis concerning the rights over his appointment.[61] Nevertheless, the general issue remained, and on 25 August the governor of the company reported that he had attended the Council of State to defend the company's privilege not only to appoint ambassadors but also to collect the strangers' consulage. Incredibly, among those who joined the attorney general in arguing the protector's license in these cases were two battered royalists—Sackvile Crow (who, it seems, had been released from prison for the occasion) and Paul Haggatt.[62]

Crow's sudden support of the man held most culpable in the regicide of his beloved Charles I was not so exceptional. By 1654, many royalists, resigned to the demise of their monarchy, bereft of patronage, and eager for a strong centralized authority, were drifting into promotion of Cromwell's increasingly authoritarian vision of the English state. Bendysh, himself an old royalist, was also doing so. Crow had the additional motives of a deep and enduring hatred for the English Levant Company and the possibility of fulfilling his dream of securing the ambassadorship and consulage for his sovereign, even if he be a pseudo-king such as Oliver Cromwell.

Such support for the protector (or resignation that he had to be dealt with) extended across the seas, too. Even before the first Anglo-Dutch war ended, in April 1654, Venice had begun scheming to drag England into its conflict with the Ottoman state. The Catholic republic's representative in London, Paulucci, quaintly urged a Protestant crusade against the "Turk," pondering as early as July 1653 how easy it would be "for England to pass into the Mediterranean with 40 or 50 men of war. These, with others easily procurable from the Dutch, might rid the Levant of the barbarians and carry the fear of the Christian arms to Constantinople itself."[63] Early in the following year, he argued that Cromwell "had long considered the most serene republic the strong bulwark against the most potent enemy of the Christian faith."[64]

This stratagem may suggest a Venetian ignorance of English culture, but it was not entirely quixotic. The English naval presence in the Mediterranean had grown dramatically during the recent war (although the Dutch had prevailed in that arena), and Cromwell was considering more carnage almost before the ink had dried on his treaty with the Netherlands. Of course, the prey was to be Catholic and not Muslim, and the target was to be the West Indies and not the eastern Mediterranean. Nevertheless, the ideological rationale for the campaign was resistance against any "universal monarchy," which might have been Islamic or even Protestant (in the case of Sweden) as easily as Catholic.[65] Indeed, the Islamic menace was more ancient, more firmly rooted, and (after 1648 at least) probably greater than was the Catholic one, and Venice, still laboring to secure an English fleet, longed to persuade Cromwell that to confront Islam was more noble an enterprise. In short, the Venetian Senate believed that the Western Design, which was launched in December 1654, might just as credibly and far more laudably have been an Eastern Design.

The Venetians persisted in their counsel even after the English assault against the Spanish West Indies. In late 1655 the Senate drafted an appeal to Cromwell, blatantly couched in the language of holy war, for assistance in the republic's lengthy conflict with the Ottoman Empire over the island of Crete.[66] In it, the Venetians wrote of "these most barbarous Infidells, whoe have noe other end but the oppression of Christendome." The Ottomans, they explained, "doe multiplie their forces utterly to subiugate the Kingdome of Candie, beinge the bullwarke of Italy, and an entrance, wherby the most insidious nation of the Turks may thrust themselves forwards to the oppression of the better part of Europe."

According to the Venetians, the moment was right to launch a counterassault against the mighty Muslim foe: "Never will there be seene a more propitious conjuncture to suppresse the Ottoman Empire, being nowe tired under the burthen of eleven yeares warre, directed by the counsell of women, exhausted of souldiers and money and can hardly resist the comonwealth alone." The sickly empire may have been on the verge of a dramatic recovery (its last siege of Vienna was still almost thirty years away), but at the time, the Senate's assessment of Ottoman impotence seemed accurate. Not only were the futilities of the Veneto-Ottoman war manifest in Istanbul, but in 1655 the empire was also suffering a particularly paralyzing atrophy at its political and administrative core. Between May of that year and October of the following, no fewer than seven grand viziers (one of whom served a mere four hours), six *şeyhülislam*s, and five *kapudanpaşa*s whirled into and out of office.

The Venetians suggested that Oliver Cromwell seize this opportunity to strike. As a great Christian ruler, he could be the noble champion of a crusade against the corrupt, bankrupt, and devitalized Ottoman polity:

> You cannot make your name more immortall, nor crowne the last actions of your life with greater glory, than to send a fleete of this state, which united to the fleet of our commonwealth comes to be a buckler to the Christian faith, violently assaulted by the power of the Turke.... [I]t wilbe an action soe Illustrious, and soe heroique to show yourselfe the only defender of the ghospell, and the oppougner of infidelitie, that it will exalt your Highnesse's name to the supremest degree of glory and applause and crowne your sword with immortall lawrell.[67]

In effect, the disheartened rulers of the Venetian state were inviting Cromwell, so recently a pariah to Christian Europe, to lead a latter-day crusade against their Muslim foe.

It was a barren plea. The English ruler found himself in the midst of a war against Spain even as he settled into a more conventional dominion. Moreover, Bendysh at Istanbul, Charles Longland at Leghorn, and other career diplomats had helped convince him of the commercial risks of overt hostility against the Ottomans. In any case, even had Cromwell and the English risen to the glorifying Venetian rhetoric, the English might not have been able to deliver salvation. Although the Venetian navy had so far won most of its engagements against the Ottomans and the following year would enjoy a spectacular victory at the Dardanelles, the Islamic empire even then was beginning to regroup and soon was on the offensive again in both the eastern Mediterranean and southeastern Europe.

12 / Uniformity Restored

Whereas before 1653 the ambassador's chief correspondent in England had been the English Levant Company and its directors, after its failure to recall him Bendysh seems to have reduced his communications with that body considerably. Thereafter, he engaged instead in an extensive and prolonged correspondence with Cromwell and his secretary, John Thurloe. Ironically, this shift established just the assertion of state control over Levantine diplomacy and commerce that Charles I had so desired, worked so hard to realize, and failed to attain. Much to Cromwell's and Bendysh's credit, the transfer worked. During the final seven years of commonwealth control, the ambassador became the linchpin in an unforeseeably stable and productive association between Cromwellian England and the Ottoman Empire under Köprülü Mehmed Pasha (who assumed the helm in 1656), an association that thoroughly circumvented the English Levant Company.

THE CHAMELEON CHANGES HIS SHADE

During these years, Bendysh's correspondence with Thurloe was voluminous.[1] It also was occasionally amiable, as when the ambassador declared in 1655 that "some passages have here fallen out which I shall only impart to you being unwilling so soon to trouble his Highness [Cromwell] with more letters."[2] Considering Bendysh's royalist and thus suspect upbringing, his long absence from a revolutionized England, his indirect and often hearsay knowledge of happenings there, and his lack of intimate acquaintance with either Cromwell or Thurloe, his masterful grasp and even manipulation of their personalities was striking. By the time Cromwell had consolidated his power, Bendysh's political acumen was sharp. Indeed, the ambassador's correspondence with the rulers of commonwealth England suggests that despite their initial plan to remove him from his ambassadorship, he handled them almost effortlessly.

His ability to do so probably derived as much from his multifarious encounters in the Ottoman capital as from his own innate caginess. In Istanbul, Bendysh faced a ragtag assembly of English defenders of a bewildering variety of beliefs and ambitions—including oddballs such as Sackvile Crow and Henry Hyde. He also was forced almost daily to test his political savvy against clever and determined Dutch, French, and Venetian political and commercial rivals.

Even more challenging for someone from uniform England was the profoundly unpredictable Ottoman backdrop against which Bendysh and his peers operated. During his early tenure, which coincided with the apogee of the condescendingly and misleadingly labeled "sultanate of the women," the sultan İbrahim was deposed and murdered, only to be succeeded by a timid youngster. The consequent vacuum at the political center did not much threaten the Ottoman state. Indeed, the imperial family and its retainers continued to govern, sometimes quite competently, by way of factions that extruded from the palace. A mature and merit-based Ottoman bureaucracy kept the administration running even through the frequent political upheavals of that time.[3] Nevertheless, it took enormous cultural discernment for the outsider, especially someone who did not even know the Ottoman language, to identify which faction was failing and which was in the ascendant, particularly since the summits of these political blocs lay in the inaccessible and shadowy imperial harem. Such circumstances had forced Bendysh to stretch and refine his diplomatic and political craft enormously.

It was not only Bendysh's craft that sustained his position, however. Domestic problems and wars with Spain also distracted the protector's government. Indeed, the tendency of the ambassador's letters to engulf the recipient in obscure and rambling details suggests that he feared becoming marginalized or even ignored. It is difficult to imagine that Thurloe was particularly concerned with local Aleppine politics. Nevertheless, in November 1655 Bendysh devoted a lengthy epistle to an encounter between the notoriously brutal Side Ahmed Pasha and the notables of that city.[4] Three months later, he reported on the Ottoman mobilization of an army four hundred thousand strong, for some still-veiled purpose.⁵

The English rulers certainly had not solicited such tidbits of information. In fact, Bendysh himself acknowledged the futility of such reports:

> I have now wrote your Honor rather to show that I am awake (as a public Minister, being, as is well fancied, the eye to his Majesty should always be) than that I have made any considerable discoveries, or observations, which indeed without information whither, on instructions how his Highness' interest were intermixed with that of any Prince, whose Agents, or allies, are resident and conversing here) how can I better do. Uncommissioned I am no more than spectator.⁶

Even though Bendysh had foiled Lawrence's bid to unseat him, he never did receive a new commission, for which he blamed his routed rival. As late as December 1657, the ambassador groused in a letter to Cromwell that Lawrence had "written so many groundless and apparent untruths against me, as I believe he was unwilling to see me, nor can he speak a good word of me without taxing his own reputation, yet I never gave him the least occasion."⁷ Without specific instructions from his government, he had little to do. Subsequent dispatches, such as his plea in April 1657 of "a readiness to obey, whenever his Highness shall think fit to command," or his grumble that he desired only intercession against the continuing Venetian pestering of English vessels at the entrance to the Dardanelles, reveal a dynamic and pragmatic personality forced by the silence and disinterest of his new sovereign into a plaintive prose (eerily reminiscent of Crow's) and detested inactivity.⁸

PLUNDERERS AND PROSCRIPTIONS

An alarming resurgence of corsair ventures in the summer of 1657 obliged the protector finally to take notice of the eastern Mediterranean. On the Muslim side, seven Tripolitan vessels under the direct command of the *kapudanpaşa* apparently waylaid the *Resolution* near Candia (the ship was bound for Aleppo's port, Alexandretta) and spirited her off to Cyprus, together with her crew and a rich cargo of cloth, tin, lead, and money.⁹ On the Christian side, Charles Longland, the state's agent at Leghorn, warned Thurloe on 27 July that Spanish men-of-war were prowling the seas around Alexandretta, Cyprus, and Alexandria, and two weeks later advised him that four Majorcan warships had attacked the English merchant vessels *An Persy* and *Eastland-merchant*, torched the former, and pursued the latter to Egypt, where they captured her.[10] Longland, Bendysh, and the company itself all reiterated their old plea that a strong naval squadron be dispatched to the Mediterranean, and on 11 August 1657, Cromwell (upon obtaining the company's agreement to procure several of his cherished Arabian horses for him) demanded from Sultan Mehmed restitution for the *Resolution* and the suppression of such plundering operations.[11]

The Britons ranged this moral high ground only briefly, however, for in the autumn of 1657 William Ell, the master of the *Little Lewis*, absconded with goods belonging to the sultan valued at seventy-five thousand lion dollars. His audacious deed severely damaged the reputation of England in the Ottoman Empire. According to Bendysh's report to Cromwell in October, the pasha of Cairo had commissioned Ell to carry the commodities to Istanbul; instead, he took them to Leghorn, where he secured a forged license to market them.[12]

Ell had long experience in the Mediterranean Sea, having sailed Levantine waters since before 1651. A ruinous Ottoman embargo against his vessel during the summer of 1656 may have provoked him to retaliate against the sultan. On 12 July of that year, Jonathan Dawes declared in Bendysh's court that Robert Manley, a merchant of London, had commissioned Ell's ship to transport woolens to Istanbul. As a result of the embargo, the *Little Lewis* was unable to deliver its cargo, and Dawes now claimed damages against Ell and the vessel's owners.[13] Some three weeks later, Dawes, again representing Manley, claimed that on 5 August 1656, just as the *Little Lewis* was about to set sail for Leghorn, fully laden, the sultan's government again had detained the ship. Bendysh's treasurer insisted that Manley should not pay his tariff for the ship during the embargoed period.[14] Finally, on 9 August Bendysh made Ell pay security for eight barrels of damaged tin he had brought from Leghorn.[15]

It probably was the interminable Veneto-Ottoman war that induced the Ottomans to embargo the *Little Lewis*. It also is possible that the Sublime Porte was responding to the running of fugitive slaves. At the very same time that Dawes was representing Manley, he also was acting on behalf of another London merchant, Francis Clarke, against Samuel Warren, master of the ship *Hopefull Imployment*.¹⁶ This vessel was under commission to Clarke, and sometime after 14 June Bendysh had secured its release from the Ottoman embargo. A routine inspection at the castles of the Dardanelles, however, uncovered "fugitive slaves in her, whom the said master had privily received into his said ship, & bestowed closely under his lading in the hold."¹⁷ The Ottoman commander imprisoned the entire crew.

English factors had long shared Ottoman cities with English slaves. To recover such persons legally was honorable, but to steal their freedom could be catastrophic for the English nation, and Warren's endeavor left Bendysh in a predicament. Ell himself had been known to redeem English slaves from the Ottomans. On 26 August 1656, Bendysh certified that the master had paid $315 for Thomas May, $155 for Thomas Corte, $225 for Joh: Mills, and $255 for Hen: Barnes, and he communicated with the directors of the company that when Ell landed in England he should be reimbursed out of monies collected for just this purpose.¹⁸ Yet the daily sight of compatriot slaves in the streets of Istanbul may have been too much for him, and it is possible that he had joined Samuel Warren in resorting to less legal means to rescue them.

In 1657, when he absconded with the sultan's goods, William Ell may have had a grudge against the sultan or may have been running English slaves. Or he may simply have been a loose cannon. One of the greatest threats to the English presence in the Ottoman Empire had always been the ventures of independent men, and Ell had a reputation for bullheaded detachment. During the first Anglo-Dutch war, for example, he had spurned the plodding naval convoys and braved the Dutch- and French-infested Mediterranean alone.¹⁹ His flight in 1657 was a direct affront against Ottoman majesty, however, and both the ambassador and the English Levant Company feared reprisals against English commerce.²⁰

The English government seems to have understood this danger, for Cromwell at once dispatched letters both to Longland requesting the Duke of Tuscany to seize Ell and his vessel and to the sultan and grand vizier apologizing for the affront.²¹ The duke unhesitatingly agreed, sequestering the *Little Lewis* and its commander in November.²² By the end of the year, an English ship was awaiting only fair weather (and news that the seas had been swept clear of pirates) before embarking with the sultan's provisions for Izmir.²³ The vessel, carrying goods that by now were rotten, finally arrived in Istanbul in March 1658.²⁴

QUIET TIMES IN ISTANBUL

Though he may have been reduced to pleading for convoys—usually futilely—and dealing in horseflesh to feed Oliver Cromwell's obsession, Bendysh's faculties certainly did not falter in these years. In one of a series of perceptive letters to Thurloe, this one dated 8 May 1656, he reported on the changes then sweeping Ottoman politics. Partly in response to the dreadful impact of the interminable Venetian blockade of the Dardanelles upon the inhabitants of Istanbul, the young Sultan Mehmed had just had the chief customs collector, Hasan Ağa, and seven of his cohorts executed,

> and finding his people noway disturbed thereat, takes heart, and every day goes disguised about the city with only one servant appearing with him, and where he sees any injustice done, or any violation made of his orders in selling, buying, or exchanging money, he immediately chops off their heads having his Executioner to that purpose not far off.²⁵

Bendysh rightly perceived the sultan's sudden aggressiveness as indicative of a spectacular change in Ottoman political and military fortune.

He further observed how directly this political shift had touched his compatriots. For several years, foreign (particularly Christian) communities had dreaded demonstrations and more threatening displays of displeasure by the sometimes starving citizens and underemployed soldiers who endured in the Ottoman capital (and other early modern European cities). In May 1656, the ambassador deduced an end to this "tyranny of the masses," remarking that

> less than a week past no Christian could well pass in the streets without some danger of being wounded or affronted by impudent soldiers, and renegades, now no such persons are to be seen, but are caught up, beaten, and put into the Gallies.... [A]ny man may safely, and securely now pass through the city without any affront or molestation at all.

The sultan, the correspondent concluded, "is now absolute, and what word he speaks is now a law, whereas the other day no one valued him otherwise than a child."[26]

Bendysh's observation was prophetic, for a new steadiness gripped the Ottoman helm, not so much under the young sultan as under the soon-to-be-appointed octogenarian grand vizier, Köprülü Mehmed Pasha. This efficient and ruthless administrator and his heirs would reassert central authority, rebuild the Ottoman military, conquer Candia, definitively break the intermittent Venetian blockade of Istanbul, and even launch an attack against Vienna. Indeed, the company later (and self-deludingly) would recall the twenty-year administration of this man and his son as a golden age for English trade in the Levantine world.[27]

It was a quiet and privileged time for the English ambassador. As both the Ottoman world under Mehmed Pasha and the English one under Cromwell recovered from civil turmoil and settled into conservative and restrained continuity, past transgressions were forgotten. On 15 June 1658, for example, the general court of the company calmly accepted a petition that two nephews of Sackvile Crow's notorious dragoman, Giorgio Draperis, serve as translators for Bendysh.[28] Three months later, the company passively reappointed its controversial ambassador to a third five-year term.[29] Bendysh took advantage of this tranquil moment to ship his two daughters, who had spent the previous decade with him in Istanbul, back to England.[30]

By 1660, Bendysh had spent over twelve years in the Ottoman capital and had become the senior foreign statesman there. As the Venetian secretary, Ballarino, reported on 6 March 1660: "The high spirit of this gentleman had certainly won him a great place among them here, and even in the past his name has stood high, but he was not previously favoured or protected in any unusual way."[31] Three months later, the same correspondent wrote: "One thing is certain that the English ambassador thirsts for an absolute dominion over the marts of the Levant to the exclusion of France because this would mean the greatness of his house and fortune."[32] This observation—that Bendysh's aspirations on behalf of his offspring only increased in the final years of his posting—was not so far-fetched. Not only did the diplomat still have at least two unwed daughters, but he also had two sons who were just launching their careers as factors in the Levant.

Bendysh may have been happy, but his work must have seemed tedious. For one thing, conservative regimes in the Ottoman Empire and England had much reduced opportunities for Bendysh and other ambitious Englishmen who had inhabited the turbulent commercial frontier between the Ottoman and British Empires. Even before the restoration of Charles II to the throne of England in 1660, it became harder to find fortune and power on the marches between these two no longer crisis-ridden states. Furthermore, disturbing rumors from Bendysh's homeland began drifting eastward. On 4 July 1659, the Venetian resident in England advised his government that the English seemed about to recall all envoys currently accredited to foreign princes because they were judged to be "the creatures of the Secretary Turloe [*sic*]."[33] The English coronation of Charles in May of the following year crystallized these rumors of a Stuart restoration.

KING OVER COMPANY

Charles II carried painful memories with him when he triumphantly claimed the English throne in 1660. Among these, recollections of the Levantine world and the Englishmen who inhabited it must have loomed large. One of his father's last strategies had involved the seizure of goods in the Ottoman Empire; the English ambassador at Istanbul, Sir Sackvile Crow, was to have been his agent. One of his own first endeavors after his father's execution had involved the attempted seizure of these same estates, for which he had appointed a royalist pretender to the ambassadorship, Henry Hyde, as his agent. Each scheme had failed because of the proceedings of the English Levant Company and the actions of its ambassador, Sir Thomas Bendysh.

In 1660 and 1661, Charles II sought to discipline the company for its offenses by recalling its envoy and divesting it of much autonomy. The restoration of the monarch's sovereignty had happened quickly. On 14 April 1660, Charles promised amnesty to all Englishmen who had opposed him. On 8 May a "Convention Parliament" proclaimed him king, and on 29 May he returned to London. Within a month, on 27 June, the new king had dispatched Heneage Finch, the Earl of Winchelsea and a close advisor, to a general court of the English Levant Company with a letter revoking Bendysh's commission and recommending that the carrier of the letter be appointed in his place.[34]

The company, knowing that the appointment of a steadfast and noble supporter of the king would cost much more than Bendysh and would furnish the monarch even more control over its agent in Istanbul than Oliver Cromwell had secured, tried to block Winchelsea. The directors informed him that they would call a special court to discuss the matter, which they did on 19 July. The result was a petition declaring the company's wretched condition because of its losses, advising that Winchelsea was too noble a gentleman for such a posting as Istanbul, pleading for a continuance of Bendysh as ambassador, and requesting Charles's confirmation of the company's charter and privileges.[35]

The king's prompt and determined reply displayed his intent to bring the company to heel and exposed his particular dislike of Bendysh. On 26 July, a general court heard that

> his Majesty had been pleased to promise a ratification of the Company's privileges, with addition of what else should be reasonably proposed, yet he adhered to his purpose of sending the Earle of Winchelsea, Ambassador to Constantinople, unless the Company had any just exception to him . . . and would nevertheless recall Sr. Thomas Bendyshe.[36]

The company leaped at this chance to retain its charter, and with it, its monopoly, and at once voted to jettison Bendysh and approve Charles's recommendation of Winchelsea as ambassador. One consequence of this action was finally to give the state absolute control over this influential posting, a full eighty years after Elizabeth I had consented to company supervision in the person of England's first agent in Istanbul, William Harborne.[37]

Once the decision was made, the directors treated Winchelsea well. On 5 September, the governor presented him with a warrant for three hundred pounds sterling and promised him seven hundred more. The company also pledged to give his wife two hundred pounds, and wined and dined him at Drapers Hall.[38] Winchelsea at once began preparations for his journey: on 27 August 1660 and again the following month he requested that the secretary of state, Edward Nicholas, assist and support in every way Sir Edward Dering, whom he had named trustee to manage his estates during his absence.[39] To Dering, Winchelsea assigned the task of decommissioning and disarming his companies of foot soldiers and cavalry, still enrolled from his years as leader of the royalist underground in Kent, counseling him to "be very secret in it, & quick, that none may have time, or notice to embezzle their arms."[40]

Winchelsea received his instructions from the king in September. They left administration of commerce to the company, the principal themes of the ambassador's commission being religion, loyalty to the monarchy, and the normalization of monarchical relations with the Ottoman government. Charles emphasized not only that all English factors must embrace "the true Protestant Religion established in the Church of England" but also that none of "our Subjects under your charge . . . shall by word or deed express any disaffection to Our person or government."[41]

In order to undo the damage to monarchical legitimacy of a twelve-year hiatus, Winchelsea in his first audience with the Ottoman sovereign was to "let the Grand Signor understand how wonderfully it hath pleased God to restor Us to Our throne" and to emphasize the "affections of Our people to that temper and obedience that We may reasonably believe Ourself as happy therein as any of Our Royal Predecessors."[42] He was to stress and help project English sea power while assiduously guarding against the shameful employment of English vessels by the "Turk" against Christians. The new ambassador also carried Bendysh's letters of revocation, which emphatically ordered him to help settle his replacement in Istanbul and then return immediately to the king's presence. Charles II addressed similar letters to the sultan and the grand vizier.[43]

The company's new charter, issued on 2 April 1661, relied principally upon the Letters Patent granted by James I.[44] Most of the few modifications actually gave the company additional authority or security. For example, trying no doubt to elude recurrence of the crises of the civil war years, the government ordered the company to keep eight thousand pounds always in the treasury for "Debts, Arrearages, and Charges due and owing, or otherwise formerly growing upon the said Trade for the charge of the Ambassador and consuls." It also granted English consuls the right to "chastize, and correct by imprisonment, or otherwise by fine, Amerciament, or other reasonable punishment," to enter houses, ships, warehouses, and cellars in order to seize goods in lieu of fines, and to expel to England all but the ambassador (who could himself take such action) and other persons appointed especially by the king. This last rider probably was inserted to deter another violent deportation like Sackvile Crow's or Henry Hyde's.

The company directors must have realized a great sense of satisfaction from another clause confirming their monopoly over the entire Mediterranean trade other than the coasts of Spain, France, and Tuscany. Curiously, the reason given for this mandate was cultural rather than economic. The government apparently accepted the company's argument that interlopers, in their ignorance of Ottoman customs, had damaged Levantine trade in the past and might irreparably harm it in the future. More surprisingly, Charles granted to the company, after a brief tussle,[45] all rights over consulage, even that of strangers, either because he did not want to resurrect his father's misery over this surcharge, because the royal treasury no longer needed it, or because it was now considered too negligible a revenue to be worth a fight.

Both the state and the company had learned a great deal from the tumultuous experiences of the 1640s and 1650s about administering and protecting a far-flung and monopolistic commercial network. The charter several times expressed this comprehension, as it did in its denunciation of the progenies of the English civil war in the Levant, those

> divers persons Our Subjects of refractory and perverse minds, seeking as much as in them lyeth to disturb the said Trade by wilfull refusall to accompt with their principalls, and to pay the Companies Duties, and otherwise by Attempting and practicing to violate, break or make voyd the priviledges of the said Company, or any of them; And being of scandalous Life, do appeal oftentimes from the Justice of the English Ambassadour, or Consuls, and vice Consuls, to Turkish Judicature and Justice, to the great prejudice of the said Company and Trade, and Dishonour of the English Nation and Scandall to their Religion.[46]

Paradoxically, these remarks describe and condemn the very persons who, through their daring, ingenuity, and willingness to fraternize with Ottoman subjects and rulers, had sustained and even invigorated English commerce in the Mediterranean world. Such loose cannons, of course, had no place in the stable, sober, and weary atmosphere of restoration England or its imperial projections.

Bendysh followed these developments as best he could from his distant vantage point. By 10 August 1660, he knew of Charles's return to London,[47] and soon thereafter must have learned of Charles's resolve to recall him. He must also have heard about such disquieting episodes as the meeting between the Venetian Giavarina and Secretary of State Nicholas, during which the influential royal counselor, ostensibly scandalized at being told that Bendysh had tried, on his own authority, to negotiate an Anglo-Ottoman treaty, blurted out that the king "had not and never would give such orders and if the minister there has made such proposals of his own caprice he may pay for it with his head."[48] In response to such disturbing statements, Bendysh transformed himself into a gracious and magnanimous diplomat, which the Venetians ascribed to "his wish to leave as few enemies here as possible, since he has to leave for London and he is very uneasy about the favour of his king whom he disobeyed openly when the affair of Henry Ider [Hyde] was dealt with twelve years ago."[49] The ambassador must surely have dreaded his impending return home.

Nevertheless, he could not delay forever. The *Plymouth* anchored at Izmir with Winchelsea aboard in early January 1661, soon sailed for Istanbul, and on 17 March returned westward, now carrying Bendysh.[50] After a brief stop at Zante, the vessel continued to Leghorn, from which the former ambassador made an excursion to Florence. From there, he journeyed on to England, arriving in London in late July or early August.

CONSOLIDATING AMBASSADORIAL CONTROL

In Istanbul, one of Winchelsea's first achievements was to contain and regulate the infamously independent and reckless factory of Izmir. On 29 January 1661, Richard Baker, the consul there, called a court in reaction to the new ambassador's demand (as requested by the directors of the English Levant Company) that his factors swear to pay their consulage and other duties in full. There certainly was no consensus in the responses of these frontiersmen. Eleven factors eagerly agreed to the directive, claiming that they currently paid more than their share because of the frauds of others. Seven suggested a 50 percent reduction in consulage on personal goods in return for such an oath; six would swear only in return for a 10 percent reduction in all consulage; and nine would swear only if every other member of the factory did likewise.

Ten indignantly refused to swear at all, proclaiming the demand an insult and insisting that they always had and would continue to turn in a true entry of their commodities in any case. Three would swear only that their entries were true within 8 percent of their value. Four exclaimed that they currently paid three times the consulage in order to avoid suspicion of fraud and would gladly pay fully in future. Three equivocated, and one simply stated that there was no need for him to swear, for he was leaving the place anyway.[51] Altogether, fifty-four men found nine distinct ways in which to respond to Winchelsea's simple request.

This fractured answer reflected not only defiance of the company's call for an oath but also an estrangement of the factors from their consul. Indeed, Winchelsea first sent his personal secretary, Anthony Isaacson, to investigate, and then, on 13 April 1661, received a petition from the factory at Izmir denouncing Baker's inexperience, his defamations of character, and his slanderous letters to Istanbul and England.[52] No fewer than thirty-one of the fifty-four or so factors then resident in Izmir (including three members of the powerful Barnardiston family) had signed this complaint.

Obviously, the battle for hierarchical uniformity would be a hard one, particularly with prosperous, self-governing, and fractious factories like Izmir's to manage. In any case, Winchelsea soon tired of Baker's ostensible distortions, excuses, and incompetence. On 11 June, he issued a warrant to discharge the consul, arguing that

> by his Ma:ties comission, & Instructions, wee are impowred to discharge all such of any office, or employment, & to punish all person of what qualitie, or condition soever, that are subiects to his Ma:tie within the Turkish dominions, whom wee find to bee obstructours of the comon peace, & trade, or to embarke them for England.[53]

Such a directive must have dismayed the factory in Izmir, however much it might have loathed its consul, for these words represented considerable growth in ambassadorial authority at the factory's expense. Some two months later, there followed a warrant to ship Baker to England to answer charges before "the Councell table."[54]

On 20 August 1661, Winchelsea wrote directly to Charles's secretary of state, Edward Nicholas, that he was incensed against Richard Baker the Consul of Smyrna, for his ill carriage in his trust, as being a fomentour of factions, & a bad manager of the Companies interest besides those scandalls & aspersions with which hee hath traduced mee, & dishonoured his Ma:^ties power in mee; I have ... removed him from office, and shipped him for England.[55]

By 10 September, the company had learned of this undertaking and heard the explanation that Winchelsea had discharged the consul on account of "the interest and advantage of the company, and for his venting of seditious words reflecting on his Majesty and the Lord Ambassador."[56] Although the directors rejected this logic, the operation was a fait accompli, and they set about looking for a suitable replacement for Baker.

It is noteworthy that Winchelsea not only could act so swiftly and decisively against a consul but also could replace him (as suggested in the new charter) with his own man, in this case his personal secretary, Isaacson.[57] Baker, his factory, and even the directors of the company perhaps had imagined that they were still in the chaotic and opportunistic world of the 1640s and 1650s, when their quarrel with the ambassador might easily have spawned a protracted, knock-down struggle involving myriad English and Ottoman local and state authorities. Conditions were quite different in the 1660s, when the ambassador could count on support from both Ottoman and company officials or simply circumvent them and appeal directly to the king. Indeed, had he landed at London, poor Richard Baker would have found himself face to face with Charles's council itself. Instead, he mysteriously vanished.[58]

On the matter of the oath to pay the consulage, however, the company and the ambassador were in perfect agreement. The directors learned in the summer of 1663 (over two years after Winchelsea had first demanded it) that twenty-eight factors of Izmir (including Bendysh's son Andrew) had recently declined to take the vow.[59] In retribution, on 19 June the company ordered that none of its members deal with those men, under penalty of a "consulage extraordinary." This order constituted a virtual battulation against them.

In general, the company's ability to answer the ambassador's actions and charges was severely limited because Winchelsea's correspondence, following Bendysh's precedent with Cromwell and Thurloe, was almost exclusively with the English court.[60] Furthermore, notices about vagabond factors, rebellious consuls, and other internal difficulties in his reports were few. In their place were pronouncements upon the Ottoman government, its wars, and the personalities of its principal officials. This ambassador was very much the king's man rather than a representative of the company, and his papers reflect the affairs of state rather than of commerce.

Of course, the company did continue to correspond with the king's ambassador. The tone of its letters, however, became supplicating, and their contents overwhelmingly concerned with "frugality" and the limits of company responsibility. In 1663, for instance, the directors several times wrote to Winchelsea to reject liability for "personal" *avania*s, arguing that most of them derived from the "jollity & recreation of the factors."[61] They also pleaded with him to intervene with the factory at Aleppo, which the company believed to have expended "vast sums in feasting and extravagant entertainments, in Avanias upon particular men, whereas we are not concerned, and in such a variety of innovations and unusual charges."[62]

The most awkward correspondence involved the expenditures of Winchelsea himself. Even though the new ambassador was clearly an appointee of the king, he maintained the fiction that he represented the company as well and continued to draw upon its treasury for his expenses. When, in late 1663, he claimed monies for a visit to the sultan's court in Edirne and for a journey his secretary, Paul Rycaut, had made to the king's court in London,[63] the directors refused to cover them, explaining that surely "it doth not stand with the pleasure of his Majesty & Councell, that the company should furnish monies toward the affairs of State" and humbly suggesting that Winchelsea draw such expenses from the Lord High Treasurer.[64] Although the royalist representative promised to be more frugal, the dispute dragged on at least into late 1664.[65] Ironically, this penny-wise reluctance to pay the ambassador's and his secretary's expenses probably accelerated the company's forfeiture of control to the state, which picked up the purse and with it absolute authority over its ambassador.

FADING INTO RESTORATION ENGLAND

And what of Winchelsea's two predecessors, Sackvile Crow and Thomas Bendysh? Although Crow finally gained his freedom shortly before the restoration, he still could not find the political promised land. The obdurate royalist certainly intended to rebuild his shattered career. Indeed, in May 1660, even before the king had reentered London, he solicited Edward Hyde's assistance in doing so.[66] But perhaps his years in prison had finally defeated him, for his prose had become unpleasantly sycophantic, and his ambitions, quixotic.

In his letter to Hyde (which accompanied a long and now seemingly lost recitation of his misfortunes), Crow lamented that "I am looked upon by the world as a most remarkable sufferer ... and ... if his Majesty knew the particulars of my sufferings, as well before my going into Turkey and since, that it is not doubted ... but his Majesty will have a compassion for me." Crow's aim, which must have echoed the aspirations of many other devoted servants, was a position in the king's household. Or, as he put it to Sir Edward, he would appreciate "any reasonable place that first presents itself, either as a Carver, Cupbearer, server, or Pensioner, or other which may give you but the name of a domestic servant, title for a gentleman."

Crow secured nothing. Edward Hyde, now the Earl of Clarendon, himself was ignobly ousted from the royal court in 1667,[67] and the king's other advisers must have dreaded (or simply filed away unread) the ex-ambassador's letters written over the next decades. Although he lived at least into the 1680s, Crow never did receive his coveted position in the king's household (or, apparently, any other appointment), even though as late as 9 June 1686 he was still entreating an unnamed patron for favors on behalf of friends.[68]

Bendysh's fortunes in tranquil England, while perhaps less pitiable, were not much better. He arrived in London shortly before 14 August 1661, on which date the governor of the company paid him a courtesy call and offered to accompany him to an audience with the king.[69] Nevertheless, gratitude for his services quickly evaporated into a cloud of suspicions that company resources had been misspent during his long administration. By May 1662, a court of assistants had ordered auditors to scrutinize Bendysh's accounts and those of his treasurer, Jonathan Dawes.[70] On 2 October, a general court concluded, perhaps with justification, that Dawes was sheltering himself "under the authority & orders of the Ambassador Sr. Tho. Bendysh," and on 12 December 1662 Bendysh found himself at the company's court, trying to explain away various expenses.[71]

The directors' sudden notice of Bendysh's accounts probably originated in their simultaneous conflict with his successor. Just as the company was to claim that Winchelsea's journey to Edirne in 1663 was on the king's business and should be financed by the king's treasury, so it argued that a journey Bendysh had taken to Edirne in 1657 had been on Cromwell's account.[72] Bendysh challenged this contention (along with the charge that he had routinely overpaid his dragoman), insisting that the occasion for his visit to the Ottoman court had nothing to do with high diplomacy but had been to denounce the seizing of a company ship, the *Resolution,* by Barbary corsairs.

We do not know whether or how this quarrel was settled. It is likely that the company (in typical committee fashion) simply shifted its focus to the more urgent hemorrhage of Winchelsea's mounting expenditures. Nor do we know much more about Bendysh's other projects, although one might assume that in a general way he joined Crow (and so many other interregnum politicians and administrators, both royalist and parliamentarian) in internal exile, barred from service to king or state.

When Bendysh returned to England, his son Andrew apparently remained in Izmir as a factor, and the father worked vigorously to further his progeny's career. For example, he probably helped convince Winchelsea to reestablish an English factory at Cairo and to nominate Andrew as its consul.[73] The new settlement was short-lived, however, for the company first revoked the young Bendysh's appointment and then disallowed the very founding of such a factory because of memories of past English failures there and concerns about the infamous Egyptian *avania*s and other nuisances.[74]

Andrew had other problems, too. Even the former ambassador realized that his son was indolent and perhaps also a bit of a profligate. On 10 April 1662, the elder Bendysh penned a letter to George Oxinden (then probably in Izmir), somewhat cryptically but suggestively thanking him for rescuing Andrew from "his assaulters and getting him on shipboard." Displaying the abiding faith of a father, Bendysh added that "your favour may ... make him more industrious and less supine in his future undertakings."[75] Almost a year later, Bendysh showed the constancy that had helped make him an adept diplomat when he again thanked Oxinden and wished him success in his new posting in the Indian port town of Surat.[76]

Andrew apparently followed his benefactor to India, where Oxinden's support continued, a patronage the father greatly appreciated even as he found the need for it dispiriting. On 8 March 1666, Bendysh, still in London, wrote a bittersweet thanks to Oxinden, confessing that whereas in earlier years, as ambassador, he had "done very good services for unworthy & ungrateful persons. . . . what now grieves me most is, that I am in no capacity to serve you to whom I am so extremely obliged for your Countenance, & great favour to my son."[77] Bendysh's letters express despondence, disillusionment, and bitterness, the emotions of a dynamic, creative, and effective professional put out to pasture. A career diplomat who had held, protected, and even energized a vital post through a dozen turbulent years surely might have expected some regard and leverage. In restoration England, Bendysh seems to have enjoyed neither.

13 / Domestic Politics and Worlds Overseas

> Had I, born in Japan, no choice but to sing Japanese songs? Was there a Japanese song that expressed my present sentiment—a traveler who had immersed himself in love and the arts in France but was now going back to the extreme end of the Orient where only death would follow monotonous life? . . . I felt totally forsaken.
> — Nagai Kafu, "Twilight in the Mediterranean"

The early-twentieth-century Japanese intellectual Nagai Kafu captures in this epigraph the intense emotions experienced by the traveler who becomes marginalized in his own country by long sojourns in foreign lands. He wrote "Twilight in the Mediterranean" in 1908 while steaming across the Mediterranean Sea en route to Japan after five years of travel and study in the United States and France.[1] Kafu, seeking to express his heartache, turned to the artistic genius of the West. He thought of the opening aria of the Italian opera *Cavalleria Rusticana* as a fitting vehicle for his passion. Unfortunately, he was unable to recall the song's words. Nor was the tune that the sailor sings on the mast at the beginning of *Tristan und Isolde* helpful, because he could recall only the libretto. Kafu experienced great anguish, but it was not something lacking in Japanese culture that kindled his feeling. It was, rather, his encounter with the limitations of his own civilization and his recognition that his cultural innocence had forever been lost.

THE TRANSCULTURAL INDIVIDUAL

It was the West that transformed Kafu. When most of us imagine cross-cultural relationships, we envision the influences of the West—that is, Europe and its cultural offshoots—upon the rest of the world. English historians of the British empires, for example, tend to focus their attention on how the English "engendered" those they encountered, overpowered, and exploited.² Such transfigured persons also dominate many novels dealing with the former British Empire (indeed, the "postcolonialists" who write them are the archetypal products of the encounter between the European and the "other"). In such novels, conflict, for both European and non-European central characters, often involves clashes between indigenous and imperial modes of thought and behavior.³

Nevertheless, the enterprise of a journey from the "darkness" of the East into the "blinding light" of European civilization—to use the imagery of another Japanese writer, Shusako Endo⁴—can and often has been reversed. George Orwell, for example, famously recorded how his sojourn in Burma jolted his convictions and dragged him out of the darkness of his cultural bigotries.⁵ Before and since Orwell's writings, a whole genre of travel literature that investigates the knowledge gained through adventures in other cultures has emerged. This literature often is sensitive and revelatory, although such travel sometimes simply magnifies prejudice, as it occasionally seems to do for Paul Theroux and certainly does in the case of V. S. Naipaul's popular investigation into the world of Islam.⁶

Historical scholarship has accomplished much less than literature in piercing cultural divides. It is true that Donald Lach and others have thoroughly explored how the non-European world stimulated and altered the *mentalité* of early modern Europe.⁷ Yet the thought processes of the European overseas—particularly the Englishman overseas—have been little examined, perhaps because he was so dominating and seemed so much more to fashion than to be fashioned by the colonial setting. Even the best historical studies of individual Englishmen in eastern Mediterranean settings pay little heed to the influences of Ottoman society upon their subjects.⁸ One wonders how the long sojourns of Henry Hyde, Sackvile Crow, and Thomas Bendysh in the Ottoman world could have failed to affect them. Indeed, it seems likely that the Ottoman experience unsettled minds and produced a disquietude about England that paralleled Kafu's and Endo's expressed apprehensions about monotonous Japan. Such Englishmen certainly did not dominate their surroundings, and one intent of this book has been to argue that dense and opaque environments overseas not only profoundly influenced individual Britons but also were endlessly diverse and thus recast each personality uniquely.

ENGLISH INFLUENCES OVERSEAS

The two most prominent overseas companies in early modern England were those that monopolized the Levant and the East Indies.[9] They also were the greatest of rivals, although by the eighteenth century the latter had outdistanced its competitor. The economic (and certainly most important) cause for the success of the English East India Company was its capture of some of the principal sources of silk and spices; however, domestic, and particularly royal, politics also played its part. Charles I clashed with the Levant Company over consulage and later plotted to seize the property and persons of company factors. The royalist navy forced the steady attention of the parliamentarians upon the Mediterranean Sea, and both Charleses focused their gazes greedily upon Ottoman military power and fiscal resources.

English diplomatic and political concerns began seeping into the Mediterranean basin in the 1630s, 1640s, and 1650s, even as tempests of radical politics and ideology battered the British Isles. The vortex of the storm may have been London, but most historians now concur that its origins can be found in, and its repercussions touched, both Scotland and Ireland. Although there is less agreement concerning its impact upon Europe, many scholars acknowledge that civil war innovations in politics and warfare induced responses that altered the political and societal structures of other western European states. The revolutionary nature of parliamentary rule also drew hard glances from the governments and peoples of states bordering the Atlantic and the Mediterranean.

How far did the gale actually drive? Had the turbulence occurred a few decades earlier, one probably could state categorically that it would hardly have been felt beyond continental Europe. By the 1640s, however, the English presence touched the Americas in the form of colonies and possessions, and Asia in the shape of commercial networks. The consequences of English turmoil in North America are manifest, for England's colonists, many of whom sailed in those decades (Cromwell himself maintained personal links with some of them and even contemplated joining them), carried the conflict in their historical imaginations and invented societies and states partially in its image.

The civil war's influences in Asia are less obvious. Not only was the English presence in the east limited and untested, but Englishmen also encountered hegemonic and almost impenetrable empires in much of the old world.[10] Nevertheless, survivors of the rule of Charles I and the British civil wars, many of them outcasts, did embark for southeast Asia, India, and the Middle East and carried with them memories of those volatile decades ruthlessly etched into their senses. The English clerics, factors, and diplomats who set out during this period—often to escape the very turmoil that had molded them—helped construct the imperial model that would so influence relations between Europe (particularly Britain) and the rest of the world in later centuries.

A WANDERING BRITON

The Britons who lived and worked in the Ottoman Empire were not mere forerunners of nineteenth-century imperialists, however, as the career of Isaac Bagire convincingly illustrates. This intensely royalist Anglican cleric arrived in the Levant in 1646, just after the climax of the first civil war and in the heat of the Puritan bid to cleanse English religion of its Laudian elements and create a new national church.[11] He spent the next fourteen years in exile, mostly in the Ottoman realm.[12] In Bagire's seemingly aimless wanderings, which left him divided from his wife and five children for the entire period, he carried with him a strong sense of his spiritual and political purpose in the world and also spied for the royalist camp. Over the years, Bagire wrote several long reports to that same Richard Browne who in 1647 had stood for the ambassadorship against Bendysh.

He described, from the comfort of an Aleppine factory, his sojourn and proselytizing in Zante, where he had produced "a vulgar Greek translation of our church's catechism."[13] This enterprise had led to his forcible removal to the Ottoman Morea, where, undeterred, he preached and presented to the Greek Orthodox Metropolitan of Achaia a Greek-language copy of the Anglican catechism. After a brief return to Italy and travels through Sicily, Bagire found his way to Aleppo, where he chatted with the patriarch of Antioch and left him an Arabic version of the catechism, and to Jerusalem, where he had long discussions with both Orthodox and Latin clerics and gained entrance into the Church of the Holy Sepulchre (for control over which those two Christian creeds frequently quarreled). He also passed into the Mesopotamian valley, where he discussed religion with Armenian bishops and arranged (through Ambassador Sir Thomas Bendysh) for the preparation of a Turkish translation of the catechism.

After wintering in Aleppo in 1652–53, Bagire finally set out for Istanbul by land, traveling "without either servant, or Christian, or any man with me that could so much as speak the Frank language; yet, by the help of some Arabic I had picked up at Aleppo; I did perform this journey in the company of 20 Turks, who used me courteously, the rather, because I was their physician, and of their friends."[14] Bagire claims to have mastered doctoring while visiting Padua, persuaded to do so by the dominance of Jews in this profession. Most arresting in his account, however, is the image of a steadfast English divine pushing across Syria and Anatolia in the company of twenty Muslim Turks. Traveling with this infidel throng, to whom, alone of all those encountered, he dared not preach, seems to have troubled him not at all.

In Istanbul also, where Bendysh served as his host, Bagire found a flock to whom to preach—an assembly of exiled French Protestants. Despite their devotion to the Genevan creed, these people were willing to pay him "a competent stipend," and he officiated for them according to the Anglican catechism, which he promptly had translated into French. Not that the restless preacher was now content to settle down. He ended his letter to Browne with the proposal of communion between the English and Greek churches and the announcement that he was preparing to depart for Egypt to "take a survey of the churches of the Coptics."[15]

This divine was a doughty and determined drifter. Just as remarkable as the man, however, was the realm in which he wandered. Unlike the Venetians, who banished Bagire from the island of Zante, the Islamic Ottomans placed few constraints upon this committed Anglican missionary. Nor was the government's sanctioning of Bagire's ventures so unusual. Indeed, Ottoman sources describe a domain that must have seemed almost crowded with Christian proselytizers. For example, Istanbul diligently defended from Greek and Serbian Orthodox slander and from abuse by local Ottoman officials the Dubrovnikan and Venetian priests who ranged across the Ottoman Balkans, as well as the many Catholic monasteries situated there.[16] The Sublime Porte also protected Capuchin priests who wandered across the empire, ostensibly tending to French factories in Egypt, Jerusalem, Aleppo, Damascus, and elsewhere.[17] The image that springs from such sources is one of

Protestant divines such as Bagire invading Ottoman lands to do battle with Catholic and Greek Orthodox priests for the souls not of Muslims or Jews but of Ottoman Christians. The only part that the Ottoman authorities assigned themselves in this combat was to provide ground rules and act as referees.

Bagire finally returned to England with the restoration of 1660. In the meantime, he continued to serve as an informant for the exiled Charles II, as he confessed in a letter penned in Transylvania in August 1659: "Being still, in my Heart, firmly tied unto your Royal Cause, and Person, by the sacred Bond of Religious Allegiance, I have thought it my duty, (as formerly I have done, more than once,) to acquaint your Royal Highness with the present state of these parts."[18] Undoubtedly he also continued to hurl himself into the Ottoman world with eagerness and curiosity.

Bagire probably visited Aleppo en route to Jerusalem. Indeed, the city's proximity to this hallowed place further complicated—even as it enriched—the lives of English merchants there, for it meant that the religious, both accomplished and neophyte—and almost always zealous—regularly passed through the city. These devout folk complained bitterly against Greek Orthodox control over the Church of the Holy Sepulchre in Jerusalem and the Church of the Virgin Mary in Bethlehem, decrying their decayed state.[19] They also enthusiastically "raised a great sound" during worship in the factories of Aleppo and thereby, to the dismay of the resident English consul and factors, stirred up Muslim dwellers against the foreign infidels and their proselytizing.[20]

The worldly merchants who objected to their compatriots' pious zeal were not utterly profane, however. Indeed, some were exiles of conscience from war-torn England. Furthermore, Richard Frampton, chaplain to the English nation of Aleppo in the 1660s, reported in two letters to Ambassador Winchelsea (who himself planned such a journey) that almost every resident English factor undertook at least one pilgrimage to the holy sites.[21] These tours typically occurred in the spring. The pilgrims would have preferred to travel by ship from Alexandretta to Acre and thence by caravan to Jerusalem. Since the Alexandretta-Acre route was little sailed, however, most trekked overland. This expensive excursion (five hundred lion dollars at least) necessitated the hiring of an Ottoman official (*kapıcı*) and the wearing of the "Turkish habit" as protection against exorbitant charges and bedouin attacks. Eagerness to visit the holy sites thus drew virtually every English merchant in Aleppo out of his secluded *khan* and into an extended and intimate association with Ottoman garb, victuals, shelter, and dispositions.

BRITONS IN A KALEIDOSCOPIC LAND

Of course, the Ottoman world was neither monolithic nor unchanging (no civilization can ever be either) but disparate and contradictory. Englishmen in Izmir or Istanbul, for example, did not routinely outfit themselves and others for the pilgrimage (although the overland journey between the two cities was perhaps not so different an experience). They had to learn the peculiarities of whichever Ottoman city they found themselves in, and when they traveled between Ottoman towns they had to be able to adapt quickly and competently to a new environment.

Considering the rigid homogeneity of English society, such flexibility must normally have been exceedingly rare. The 1640s and 1650s, however, were not normal times for Britons, and the British civil wars and interregnum could train the wanderer well indeed. England (and the rest of Britain) was fumbling toward new definitions of leadership, struggling to design new constitutional frameworks, founding new military institutions, proposing, disputing, and publishing the wildest of political and religious visions (after the collapse of the Puritan effort to impose uniformity in 1646), quarreling over the relative merits of Presbyterianism and sectarianism, and exploring how it might better (or more aggressively) relate to the rest of the world, even as it executed its king. The remote Ottoman realm must have seemed almost a relief to the adventurer fashioned in such a caldron!

Henry Hyde, in his appointments as both consul and *voyvoda* near the Islamic-Christian frontier, certainly stepped easily into this alien world. He even seemed able to manipulate Ottoman society in his talent for crossing the ethnoreligious barriers that helped define it. Indeed, the English Levant Company's attempt to dislodge him with the appointment of Gyles Ball initiated a brawl that swept into the Ottoman world, ultimately involving Frenchmen, Venetians, Jews, Greeks, Turks, and a plethora of Ottoman officials.

As consul of the Morea, however, Hyde acted on the political and geographic fringes of the Ottoman Empire. Sackvile Crow moved

Ottoman involvement to center stage when he sought to expropriate the goods and seize the persons of "rebel" English factors. In this dubious and self-destructive act, the ambassador broke through at least two hallowed barriers. For one, Charles I's connivance signified a spilling over into the Levant of the first English civil war. For another, Crow's request for assistance from high Ottoman officials bespoke a reversal of Hyde's manipulations; Crow, whose principal goal as ambassador should have been the preservation and advancement of English commerce in the Levant, had elected to solicit the aid of an implacable doctrinal foe in order to ravage the English Levant Company in the name of political ideology.

One problem with Crow's plot was that he did not comprehend the complexities of Ottoman administration, particularly in the provinces. In Izmir, for example, the consul and merchants had close relations with the regional political and economic elites. Consequently, the English factory there managed to solicit Ottoman aid to subvert Crow's design. The main point is that few of that town's inhabitants served the Ottoman state directly, so they could defy its commands with some impunity. The results of Crow's offensive in the English world were manifold. In the Ottoman world, it precipitated a popular uproar—the gathering of a seditious "crowd"—and produced the startling image of an Ottoman magistrate, steeped in the principles of Islam, confronting and seeking to calm his townsmen on behalf of a Christian king.

The struggle between Crow and Bendysh, initiated in London and played out in the cultural borderlands the following year, wholly enmeshed company, parliament, king, and a host of Ottoman statesmen and officials. Only by gathering the full force of the English factories in both Istanbul and Izmir, and by seeking help from numerous Ottoman officials and subjects, did Bendysh manage to defeat his royalist rival. With this engagement, the English nation of the Levant and many of its associates became utterly absorbed in the battle raging at home. Just as Crow's collapse echoed the king's breakdown, so the resultant disorders reflected the simultaneous disintegration—particularly marked in the years immediately proceeding Charles I's execution—of tradition and legality in Britain.

Ironically, Englishmen in the Levant used the catastrophe at home to hone their understanding of the Ottoman world. Indeed, Bendysh's career in the late 1640s and 1650s indicates not only that by mid-century the Briton had learned well how to cope with the Ottoman quagmire but also that the most astute expatriates had learned how deliberately to disguise their politics and beliefs. An anonymous hagiography of Charles II, published in celebration of his enthronement in 1660, displays that even a decade after the events of 1647–50, Bendysh's motives remained enigmatic. The writer describes how

> about this time Sir *Henry Hide* being sent over to *England* from *Constantinople* (whither he had been sent as Ambassador from his Majesty to the *Grand Seignior*) by Sir *Thomas Bendysh* his means, who was then Ambassador for the Republick in *England* (but yet deem'd a person of more loyalty to his Prince, then to have sent his Ambassador to be murder'd, if he could have avoided it) after somewhat a formall tryall, he suffered death on a Scaffold, before the Royal Exchange in *London,* for having taken Commissions from his Soveraign.[22]

The apologetic tone of this passage no doubt derived in part from a pervasive ache to restore a shattered realm. Nevertheless, the remoteness of the Ottoman Empire, the strangeness of that territory, and the intentional ambiguity of Bendysh's motives and actions made it much easier to absolve the just-recalled ambassador of being an accessory to premeditated murder. Bendysh adapted himself as situations changed in London, Istanbul, and Izmir—in fact, throughout the English and eastern Mediterranean worlds. His chameleonic abilities, so typical of English state servants during the British civil wars and interregnum, are evidenced in his overlapping correspondences with the exiled Charles Stuart in France, the directors of the "Turky Company" in the City of London, and Oliver Cromwell.

Neither company nor commonwealth could dislodge Bendysh, although both wanted to, largely because of his ability to gain the patronage of important Ottoman officials and convince the company—and even Richard Lawrence, who was sent to replace him—that only he, Bendysh, could provide the company, the commonwealth, and the protectorate with the authority and guidance that would present the facade of legality the illegitimate regimes so desperately craved. The ambassador apparently was right. By the end of Oliver Cromwell's life, Bendysh, by all accounts, had become the most influential foreigner in Istanbul and had helped reestablish English commerce and re-create English diplomacy in the Ottoman Empire.

TRAVERSING FRONTIERS

The ragtag assortment of Englishmen who ventured into the Ottoman Empire during the mid-seventeenth century excelled at accommodating themselves to a profoundly foreign society. The experiences they had gained in a homeland racked with civil war and extremist fervor were decisive in enabling them to realize their objectives. These experiences helped Britons construct a commercial and institutional network that their successors would forge into a great empire in Asia. It is important to understand, however, that such heirs, with their acute fantasies of first economic and then racial preeminence, could never have punctured the Ottoman world of the 1640s and 1650s. There, English exploits depended upon cross-cultural and even multicultural discourse and accommodation as much as upon organization and commercial acumen. These Englishmen were but feeble and barely countenanced outlanders and could hardly have aroused, much less co-opted, the massive and refined Ottoman state and its people or economy. The English diplomats, merchants, and even clerics who ventured eastward had little choice but to fuse themselves into that great diversity which was the Ottoman realm.

Notes

1 / THE PROTO-IMPERIALIST

1. The classic study is that of Alfred Wood, *A History of the English Levant Company* (Oxford: Oxford University Press, 1935), but see also Sonia Anderson, *An English Consul in Turkey: Paul Rycaut at Smyrna, 1667–1678* (Oxford: Clarendon Press, 1989).

2. Bharati Mukherjee, *The Holder of the World* (New York: Ballantine, 1993), p. 181. Critics such as Neel Chowdhury ("Indian Camp," *Far Eastern Economic Review*, 26 May 1994, p. 47) who attack this intelligent work for its "inauthentic" depiction of India confuse the author's ancestry with her personal, transcultural upbringing. Mukherjee and other "postcolonial" novelists need to be judged for what they write about, which usually is intersections between and the disenfranchised within civilizations, rather than for what Indian, English, or other nationalists deem acceptable. I believe, though, that the author fails to distinguish between the seventeenth-century English imperialist and his more infamous nineteenth-century heir.

3. Bernard Bailyn and Philip D. Morgan, eds., *Strangers within the Realm: Cultural Margins of the First British Empire* (Chapel Hill: University of North Carolina Press, 1991), p. 18. The authors borrowed this terminology from J. G. A. Pocock (whom they later cite), "British History: A Plea for a New Subject," *Journal of Modern History* 47 (1975): 627, where he writes of the English as "an expanding and imperial people, who exist in the relations between themselves and other peoples, whom they encounter and whom (particularly in the case of 'British history') they also engender."

4. Derek Hirst, "The English Republic and the Meaning of Britain," *Journal of Modern History* 66 (1994): 470 and 484.

5. Robert Ashton, *Counter-Revolution: The Second Civil War and Its Origins, 1646–1648* (New Haven, Connecticut: Yale University Press, 1994).

6. Steve Pincus, "England and the World in the 1650s," in *Revolution and Restoration: England in the 1650s,* ed. John Morrill (London: Collins and Brown, 1992), pp. 129–47.

7. Pocock, "British History," p. 610.

8. Pocock, "British History," pp. 605–6.

9. A related conviction forms the essence of Cemal Kafadar's writings on the frontier between Byzantium and the first (that is, pre-Timurid) Ottoman Empire. See his *Between Two Worlds: The Construction of the Ottoman State* (Berkeley: University of California Press, 1995), especially pp. 19–28.

10. Bailyn and Morgan, *Strangers within the Realm.*

11. See particularly Karen Ordahl Kupperman's various writings, such as *Settling with the Indians: The Meeting of English and Indian Cultures in America, 1580–1640* (Totowa, New Jersey: Rowman and Littlefield, 1980), *Roanoke: The Abandoned Colony* (Savage, Maryland: Rowman and Littlefield, 1984), and *Providence Island, 1630–1641: The Other Puritan Colony* (Cambridge: Cambridge University Press, 1993).

12. On which see Kenneth R. Andrews, *Trade, Plunder and Settlement: Maritime Enterprise and the Genesis of the British Empire, 1480–1630* (Cambridge: Cambridge University Press, 1984).

13. British historians and other authors have commemorated the heirs of such dissimulators, who disguised themselves and penetrated deep into enemy territory in Central Asia and elsewhere during the "Great Game" of the late nineteenth and early twentieth centuries.

14. See, for example, Richard White, *The Middle Ground: Indians, Empires, and Republics in the Great Lakes Region, 1650–1815* (Cambridge: Cambridge University Press, 1991), whose notable contribution is not the concept that frontiers (a term that still works in other historiographies) can be "middle grounds" but an elegant exploration of the Indian-European borderlands and the recognition that a period of balance was formed, lingered, and—tragically for Native Americans—perished there. For a contrary stance, see James H. Merrell, *The Indians' New World: Catawbas and Their Neighbors from European Contact through the Era of Removal* (Chapel Hill: University of North Carolina Press, 1989). It is interesting that despite the sophistication of these works, neither author seems to probe much beyond his own subdiscipline by way of the extensive and sophisticated literature on frontiers, marchlands, and borderlands outside North America.

15. S. C. Chew, *The Crescent and the Rose: Islam and England during the Renaissance* (Oxford: Oxford University Press, 1937); and Wood, *History of the Levant Company.*

16. Wood, *History of the Levant Company,* p. 53.

17. Dorothy M. Vaughan, *Europe and the Turk: A Pattern of Alliances, 1350–1700* (Liverpool: University Press, 1954), p. 241.

18. Andrews, *Trade, Plunder, and Settlement,* p. 100. Even more indicative of the narrowness of Andrews's vision than his contention that Englishmen pretty much ignored their Ottoman hosts during that period is his use of terms—"Turks" and "Turkey"—that did not even exist in the early modern Ottoman mind.

19. On whom see also Colin Heywood's ground-breaking "Sir Paul Rycaut, a Seventeenth-Century Observer of the Ottoman State: Notes for a Study," in *English and Continental Views of the Ottoman Empire, 1500–1800,* by E. Kural Shaw and C. J. Heywood, pp. 31–59 (Los Angeles: William Andrews Clark Memorial Library, 1972); and Linda Darling's theoretically notable "Ottoman Politics through British Eyes: Paul Rycaut's *The Present State of the Ottoman Empire,*" *Journal of World History* 5 (1994): 71–97.

20. Anderson, *An English Consul in Turkey,* pp. 248–87.

21. Robert Brenner, *Merchants and Revolution: Commercial Change, Political Conflict, and London's Overseas Traders, 1550–1653* (Princeton, New Jersey: Princeton University Press, 1993). Although the City of London certainly was central to the development of international commerce in Britain, we need to broaden our base and examine more thoroughly than does Brenner both the nexus between company merchants and their agents overseas and the nexus between these expatriates themselves. Brenner bases his case principally upon statistical research, asserting, for example, that the English Levant Company was conservative and royalist simply because the majority of those English Levant Company merchants *whose politics we know* seemed sympathetic to royalist rather than parliamentarian positions (pp. 374–79). It is hard to see, though, how either the many antiroyalist actions of company officials and agents during the civil war years or the Charleses' various bunglings in the eastern Mediterranean are merely "exceptions to the generalization that the Levant–East India Company merchants held antiparliamentary, anti-Puritan positions" (pp. 378–79).

22. This is a sort of arrogance that an influential strand of Turkish historiography reflects in its recent efforts to appropriate and ahistorically equate Ottoman and Turkish history. The flip side of the contemporary Turkish

position dominates the historiographies of virtually every other Ottoman successor state (and formerly characterized also the Turkish one) in their sterile (and sometimes dangerous) insistence that the centuries of Ottoman control over their regions constituted nothing but a black hole in their national histories. Writings in both the Arab and Balkan worlds repeatedly represent this period as a "Turkish yoke" that choked off the spirit and creativity of their peoples. Because of the war of Yugoslavian succession and other recent conflagrations in the Balkans, the issue of the Ottoman legacy has received much attention. See, for example, L. Carl Brown (ed.), *Imperial Legacy: The Ottoman Imprint on the Balkans and the Middle East* (New York: Columbia University Press, 1996), particularly Maria Todorova's "The Ottoman Legacy in the Balkans," pp. 45–77.

23. Benjamin Arbel, *Trading Nations: Jews and Venetians in the Early Modern Eastern Mediterranean* (Leiden: Brill, 1995), pp. 95–168.

24. These mentions are in Başbakanlık Osmanlı Arşivi (Ottoman National Archives, hereafter BOA), Ecnebi Defterleri (Registers of Foreign Matters, hereafter ED) 26/1, p. 50, no. 1 (*İngiliz elçisi namında olan Bendiş*); and Mustafa Naima, *Tarih-i Naima,* 6 vols. (Istanbul: n.p., 1864–66), vol. 5, pp. 64–67. Indeed, this incident is repeated by others, and it became a chestnut of Ottoman chroniclers. Joseph von Hammer-Purgstall (*Geschichte des Osmanischen Reiches,* vol. 5, [Pest: C. A. Hartleben's Verlage, 1829], p. 512) cites Naima as the source for his only references to Bendysh. Other mentions of these persons in Ottoman documents are indirect and usually general. For example, we possess copies of Ottoman decrees, discussed in chapter 5, responding to Ambassador Crow's request in 1646 that English goods in Izmir be sequestered and English factors seized (preserved in BOA, Mühimme Defterleri [Registers of Important Matters, hereafter MD] 90, pp. 43, no. 139; 44, no. 140; 82, no. 260; and 90, no. 285). These rescripts are extremely vague and conventional, however, and only a reconstruction of the story through British sources communicates their meaning.

25. On the intriguing and difficult "new historicism," developed more by literary critics than by historians, see H. Aram Veeser (ed.), *The New Historicism* (London: Routledge, 1989). Two adaptations of its methods to historical writings, the first more successful than the second, are Jonathan Spence's *The Death of Woman Wang* (New York: Viking Press, 1978) and Simon Schama's *Dead Certainties (Unwarranted Speculations)* (New York: Vintage Books, 1991). Edhem Eldem has employed some of these techniques in his "Istanbul: From Imperial to Peripheral Capital," in Eldem, Daniel

Goffman, and Bruce Masters, *Three Ottoman Cities: Aleppo, Izmir, and Istanbul* (forthcoming). Gender is a particularly enticing arena in which to raise such imagined narratives, for our sources tell us virtually nothing of the lives of women who inhabited the early modern Anglo-Ottoman frontier. Although we know, for example, that in the 1650s Ambassador Bendysh's wife and five daughters lived with him in Istanbul (and his wife died there), we know nothing more. For a later period, Billie Melman, in her *Women's Orients: English Women and the Middle East, 1718–1918 (Sexuality, Religion and Work)*, 2d ed. (Ann Arbor: University of Michigan Press, 1995), has utilized the writings of English women to discuss how a marginalized gender in a dominant society envisioned and interacted with a dominated culture in an imperial setting.

26. Some extremely imaginative and productive uses of Ottoman sources have recently been made. They give us at least traces of Ottoman personalities. See, for example, Leslie P. Peirce's sketches of the royal household (*The Imperial Harem: Women and Sovereignty in the Ottoman Empire* [New York: Oxford University Press, 1993]); Robert Dankoff's translated fragments from Evliya Çelebi (*The Intimate Life of an Ottoman Statesman: Melek Ahmed Pasha [1588–1662] as Portrayed in Evliya Çelebi's Book of Travels,* [Albany: State University of New York Press, 1991]); Cemal Kafadar's manipulations of Ottoman autobiography and dream literature ("Self and Others: The Diary of a Dervish in Seventeenth Century Istanbul and First-Person Narratives in Ottoman Literature," *Studia Islamica* 69 [1989]: 121–50, and "Mütereddit bir Mutasavif Üsküplü Asiye Hatunun Rüya Defterleri, 1641–43," *Topkapı Sarayı Yıllığı* 5 [1991]: 168–222); and Cornell Fleischer's multifaceted biography of Mustafa Ali (*Bureaucrat and Intellectual in the Ottoman Empire: The Historian Mustafa Âli [1541–1600]* [Princeton, New Jersey: Princeton University Press, 1986]).

2 / THE ENGLISHMAN AND THE OTTOMAN OTHER

1. This topic has drawn wide interest. See as examples Fernand Braudel, *The Mediterranean and the Mediterranean World in the Age of Philip II*, trans. Siân Reynolds, vol. 1 (New York: Harper and Row, 1972), pp. 543–642; Jonathan Israel, *Dutch Supremacy in World Trade, 1585–1740* (Oxford: Clarendon Press, 1989); and Niels Steensgaard, *The Asian Trade Revolution of the Seventeenth Century* (Chicago: University of Chicago Press, 1974).

2. See Frederick C. Lane, *Venice: A Maritime Republic* (Baltimore: Johns Hopkins University Press, 1973), pp. 377–89 and 407–21.

3. Neils Steensgaard, "Consuls and Nations in the Levant from 1570 to 1650," *Scandinavian Economic History Review* 15 (1967): 13–55.

4. Arthur Leon Horniker, "Anglo-French Rivalry in the Levant from 1583 to 1612," *Journal of Modern History* 14 (1946): 289–305.

5. See Wood, *History of the Levant Company*, pp. 89–92; and Mark Charles Fissel, "Law and Authority in the Collection of the Strangers' Consulage, 1621–1647," in *Law and Authority in Tudor and Stuart England*, eds. Buchanan Sharp and Mark Charles Fissel (forthcoming).

6. Just as the term "factory" had a precise and distinctive meaning in its seventeenth-century context, so did the term "nation." As used in seventeenth-century correspondence between the English Levant Company and its agents, the phrase "English nation" referred not to the citizenry of England but either to the community of Britons living in the Ottoman Empire or to those dwelling in a single city within that empire. A precise and sophisticated discussion of the etymology of this term is in Liah Greenfeld, *Nationalism: Five Roads to Modernity* (Cambridge, Massachusetts: Harvard University Press, 1992), pp. 4–9.

7. Lane, *Venice*, passim.

8. Eldem illustrates this attribute keenly in his "Istanbul," where he reconstructs a day in the life of a dragoman to the French ambassador.

9. On millets, see Michael Ursinus, "Millet," *The New Encyclopaedia of Islam*, new ed. (Leiden: E. J. Brill, 1960); Daniel Goffman, "Ottoman *Millet*s in the Early Seventeenth Century," *New Perspectives on Turkey* 11:2 (1994): 135–58; and Aron Rodrigue, "Difference and Tolerance in the Ottoman Empire," interview by Nancy Reynolds, *Stanford Humanities Review* 5 (1995): 80–90.

10. This tendency dominates both Ottoman and rabbinic scholarship. It may derive in part from the nationalist's temptation to reorder and reinterpret in order to legitimize his or her own nation-state. On this phenomenon historically, see especially Benedict Anderson, *Imagined Communities: Reflections on the Origin and Spread of Nationalism* (London: Verso, 1983); E. J. Hobsbawm, *Nations and Nationalism since 1780: Programmes, Myth, Reality* (Cambridge: Cambridge University Press, 1990); and, for the Ottoman instance, Selim Deringil, "Legitimacy Structures in the Ottoman State: The Reign of Abdülhamid II (1876–1909)," *International Journal of Middle East Studies* 23 (1991): 345–59.

11. Cemal Kafadar takes issue with other "natural aspects" of Ottoman society in his "On the Purity and Corruption of the Janissaries," *Turkish Studies Association Bulletin* 15 (1991): 273–80, and elsewhere in his work.

He describes a related phenomenon as the "'lid model' whereby at least some empires (the oriental ones?) are conceived as lids closing upon a set of ingredients (peoples) that are kept under but intact until the lid is toppled and those peoples, unchanged (unspoilt, as nationalists would like to see it), simply reenter the grand flow of history as what they once were" (*Between Two Worlds*, p. 21).

12. See BOA, ED 13/1, p. 115, no. 2; BOA, ED 14/1, p. 62, no. 62 (5–13 April 1630); BOA, ED 14/1, pp. 114–15 (7–16 October 1640); and BOA, ED 14/1, p. 146, no. 1 (1–10 February 1642).

13. Nevertheless, the Ottomans apparently preferred the term *taife* for any distinct congregation of people. See Goffman, "Ottoman *Millet*s," pp. 139–41; and Halil İnalcık, "The Ottoman State: Economy and Society, 1300–1600," in *An Economic and Social History of the Ottoman Empire, 1300–1914*, eds. Halil İnalcık with Donald Quataert (Cambridge: Cambridge University Press, 1994), pp. 190–92.

14. On these terms, see particularly Halil İnalcık, "Imtiyazat," *Encyclopedia of Islam*.

15. BOA, ED 13/1, pp. 29, no. 4; 28, no. 6; and 35, no. 5.

16. BOA, ED 26, pp. 144, no. 3; and 54, no. 3.

17. See particularly Ali İhsan Bağış, *Osmanlı Ticaretinde Gayri Müslimler, Kapitülasyonlar-Beratlı Tüccarlar, Avrupa ve Hayriye Tüccarları (1750–1839)* (Ankara: Turhan Kitabı, 1983); and, for the Syrian context, Bruce Masters, "The Sultan's Entrepreneurs: The *Avrupa Tüccarı*s and the *Hayriye Tüccarı*s in Syria," *International Journal of Middle East Studies* 24 (1992): 579–97.

18. On the resulting religious ferment, at least domestically, see particularly Christopher Hill, *The World Turned Upside Down: Radical Ideas during the English Revolution* (London: Penguin Books, 1974), especially 87–106. John Morrill and others have presented persuasive counterarguments, particularly for the provinces. See his article in Morrill (ed.), *Reactions to the English Civil War, 1642–1649* (New York: St. Martin's Press, 1982).

19. See Daniel Goffman, *Izmir and the Levantine World, 1550–1650* (Seattle: University of Washington Press, 1990), pp. 93–118.

20. Robert Bargrave, *A Relation of Sundry Voyages & Journeys made by mee*, fo. 11^r. I am preparing a critical edition of this diary, which is preserved in the Bodleian Library as Rawlinson MS C.799.

21. Bargrave, *Relation*, fos. 30^v–31^r.

22. Bargrave, *Relation*, fo. 31^r.

23. Generally, however, Bargrave's diary seems quite matter-of-fact, concurs with other sources, and probably was not intended for publication (this section of it never has been).

24. On which, for the imperial household at least, see Peirce, *The Imperial Harem*.

25. The Public Record Office (hereafter PRO), State Papers (hereafter SP) 110/111, passim.

26. It is inventoried in PRO, SP 105/175, fos. 27^v–32^r (22 May 1657).

27. PRO, SP 105/175, fos. 27^v–32^r. The spellings of names in this and other documents are retained.

28. Arvieux, *Mémoires du Chevalier d', Envoyé Extraordinaire du Roy, etc.*, ed. J. B. Labat (Paris, 1735), vol. 1, p. 101, as quoted in W. H. Lewis, *Levantine Adventurer: The Travels and Missions of the Chevalier d'Arvieux, 1653–1697* (New York: Harcourt, Brace and World, 1962), p. 35.

3 / THREE ENGLISH SETTLEMENTS

1. See Wood, *History of the Levant Company*, pp. 1–18; and Susan A. Skilliter, *William Harborne and the Trade with Turkey, 1578–1582: A Documentary Study of the First Anglo-Ottoman Relations* (London: Oxford University Press, 1977). Skilliter summarizes some of the major points in this book in "William Harborne, The First English Ambassador, 1583–1588," in *Four Centuries of Turco-British Relations: Studies in Diplomatic, Economic and Cultural Affairs*, eds. William Hale and Ali İhsan Bağış (Beverly, North Humberside: Eothen Press, 1984), pp. 10–25.

2. On Aleppo, see the various works by Bruce Masters, especially his *The Origins of Western Economic Dominance in the Middle East: Mercantilism and the Islamic Economy of Aleppo, 1600–1750* (New York: New York University Press, 1988); and, for the slightly later period, Abraham Marcus, *The Middle East on the Eve of Modernity: Aleppo in the Eighteenth Century* (New York: Columbia University Press, 1989). Also see Ralph Davis, *Aleppo and Devonshire Square: English Traders in the Levant in the Eighteenth Century* (London: Macmillan, 1967). All three of the cities discussed in this chapter receive more thorough treatment in Eldem, Goffman, and Masters, *Three Ottoman Cities*, and although my arguments may at times be at variance with theirs, I am greatly indebted to Bruce Masters and Edhem Eldem for their enthusiasm and for the ideas set forth in what follows.

3. Halil İnalcık, "Ottoman Methods of Conquest," *Studia Islamica* 2 (1954): 112–22.

4. Bruce Masters persuasively argues that Aleppo and its surroundings, unlike the rest of the Arab world, achieved an unusual balance between Ottoman and Arab cultures. Following White's conceptualization in his *Middle Ground,* Masters also refers to this situation as a "middle ground" (see his essay "Aleppo" in *Three Ottoman Cities*).

5. Abdul Karim Rafeq, "Changes in the Relationship between the Ottoman Central Administration and the Syrian Provinces from the Sixteenth to the Eighteenth Centuries," in *Studies in Eighteenth Century Islamic History*, eds. Thomas Naff and Roger Owen (Carbondale: Southern Illinois University Press, 1977), pp. 53–73.

6. The literature on Istanbul is immense, but curiously fragmented. Indeed, no reliable general study exists. For the present, see particularly Besim Darkot et al., "İstanbul," *İslam Ansiklopedisi* (Istanbul: Milli Eğitim Basımevi, 1967); Halil İnalcık, "Istanbul," *Encyclopedia of Islam;* İnalcık, "The Policy of Mehmed II toward the Greek Population of Istanbul and the Byzantine Buildings of the City," *Dumbarton Oaks Papers* 23–24 (1969–70): 231–49; Robert Mantran, *Istanbul dans la seconde moitié du XVIIe siècle* (Paris: Librairie d'Amerique et d'Orient Adrien Maisonneuve, 1962); and Eldem, "Istanbul."

7. Kafadar, *Between Two Worlds*, p. 17.

8. The most thorough, if somewhat biased, study of the conquest remains that of Steven Runciman, *The Fall of Constantinople* (Cambridge: Cambridge University Press, 1965).

9. Philip D. Curtin, in *Cross-Cultural Trade in World History* (Cambridge: Cambridge University Press, 1984), discusses these and other "trading diasporas," including the Armenian, Chinese, and Portuguese examples.

10. See İnalcık, "Policy of Mehmed II."

11. On these resettlements, see İnalcık, "Istanbul"; and Joseph Hacker, "The Impact of the 'Sürgün'-System on Jewish Society in the Ottoman Empire in the Fifteenth through the Seventeenth Centuries," paper presented at the Fourth International Congress for the Economic and Social History of Turkey (1071–1922) (Munich, 4–8 August 1986).

12. Istanbul's consuming and seductive nature is illustrated in its persistent trade imbalance—many more imports than exports (Mantran, *Istanbul dans la seconde moitié*)–and in the writings of such of its denizens as Mustafa Ali, Evliya Çelebi, and Robert Bargrave.

13. On these boats, their owners, and the elaborate system of their operation, see Cengiz Orhonlu, "İstanbul'da kayıkçılık ve kayık işletmeciliği," *Tarih Dergisi* 21 (1966): 109–34.

14. Venetian bailo in *Calendar of State Papers and Manuscripts Relating to English Affairs Existing in the Archives and Collections of Venice, and in Other Libraries of Northern Italy* (hereafter *CSP, Venice*) (London: Longman, 1864–1947), vols. 24–27, passim.

15. BOA, MD 90, p. 152, no. 479.

16. On seventeenth-century Izmir and its hinterland, see also Suraiya Faroqhi, *Towns and Townsmen of Ottoman Anatolia: Trade, Crafts, and Food Production in an Urban Setting, 1520–1650* (Cambridge: Cambridge University Press, 1984); Goffman, *Izmir and the Levantine World;* and Necmi Ülker, "The Rise of Izmir, 1688–1740" (Ph.D. diss., University of Michigan, 1974).

17. There is a large literature on the Aydınoğlus. In this context, the most valuable work is that of Halil İnalcık, "The Rise of the Turcoman Maritime Principalities in Anatolia, Byzantium, and the Crusades," *Byzantinische Forschungen, Internationale Zeitschrift für Byzantinistik* 9 (1985): 179–217, reprinted in İnalcık, *The Middle East and the Balkans under the Ottoman Empire: Essays on Economy and Society* (Bloomington: Indiana University Turkish Studies, 1993), pp. 309–41.

18. On these transformations, see in particular Steensgaard, *The Asian Trade Revolution.*

19. Goffman, *Izmir and the Levantine World,* pp. 68–75.

20. On the relationship between commerce and power, see Frederic C. Lane, "Economic Consequences of Organized Violence," *Journal of Economic History* 18 (1958): 401–17. On piracy in the Mediterranean, see Maurice Aymard, "XVI. yüzyılın sonunda Akdeniz'de korsanlık ve Venedik," *İstanbul Üniversitesi İktisat Fakültesi Mecmuası* 23 (1962–63): 219–38; and Alberto Tenenti, *Piracy and the Decline of Venice, 1580–1615,* trans. Janet and Brian Pullan (Berkeley: University of California Press, 1967).

21. On the silk trade, see Fahri Dalsar, *Türk sanayi ve ticaret tarihinde Bursa'da ipekçilik* (Istanbul: Sermet Matbaası, 1960); Murat Çizakça, "Price History and the Bursa Silk Industry: A Study in Ottoman Industrial Decline, 1550–1650," *Journal of Economic History* 40 (1980): 533–50; and İnalcık, "The Ottoman State," pp. 218–55. On communal trading networks, see Curtin, *Cross-Cultural Trade.* On Armenians specifically, see R. W. Ferrier, "The Armenians and the East India Company in Persia in the Seventeenth and Early Eighteenth Centuries," *Economic History Review,* 2d ser., 26 (1973): 38–62.

22. On this change, see Goffman, *Izmir and the Levantine World*, pp. 59–64; and Goffman, "Demise of a Trading Center: Chios after the Ottoman Conquest," *Mediterranean History Review* (forthcoming).

23. See Goffman, *Izmir and the Levantine World*, pp. 87–90.

24. BOA, ED 26/1, p. 17, no. 1.

25. BOA, ED 26/1, p. 22, no. 2.

26. On such notables, see Özer Ergenç, "Osmanlı klâsik dönemindeki 'Eşraf ve Â'yan' üzerine bazı bilgiler," *Journal of Ottoman Studies* 3 (1982): 105–13; Gilles Veinstein, "'Ayan' de la région d'Izmir et commerce du Levant (deuxième moitié du XVIIIe siècle)," *Etudes Balkaniques* 12 (1976): 71–83; Suraiya Faroqhi, "Crisis and Change, 1590–1699," in İnalcık with Quataert, *Economic and Social History*, pp. 565–68; and Bruce McGowan, "The Age of the *Ayans*, 1699–1812," in İnalcık with Quataert, *Economic and Social History*, especially pp. 658–72.

27. An entire series in the Ottoman archives—the *Ecnebi Defterleri* (Registers of Foreign Matters)—is devoted to such complaints. On this source, see Goffman, *Izmir and the Levantine World*, appendix 1.

28. In 1618, for example, the Venetian nation in Izmir received permission to rebuild a church that had been vacant since before the Ottoman conquest. See BOA, ED 13/1, p. 186, no. 2.

29. This situation changed only in the late 1650s, when the Ottomans finally constructed a fortress at Izmir's gulf to help regulate shipping. See Goffman, "Izmir: From Village to Colonial Port City," in *Three Ottoman Cities*.

30. See Halil İnalcık, "Military and Fiscal Transformation in the Ottoman Empire, 1600–1700," *Archivum Ottomanicum* 6 (1980): 283–337.

31. On which see Fissel, "Law and Authority."

32. PRO, SP 97/16, fo. 88^r.

33. Curtin, *Cross-Cultural Trade*, pp. 1–14 and 179–206.

34. Curtin, *Cross-Cultural Trade*, p. 11.

4 / ENGLISH TRADERS ON THE OTTOMAN FRONTIER

1. This dispute is reconstructed from PRO, SP 97/16, fos. 242^r (Frances Reade to Sackvile Crow), 242^v (Crow to Edward Stringer), 243^{r-v} (English merchants of Izmir to Crow), 244^{r-v} (Crow to Stringer), 245^r (merchants of Izmir to Crow), 245^v (Stringer to Crow), and 246^r–247^v (Crow to Stringer). We know that the religious "millets" were in no sense politically or economically

independent before the nineteenth century (see Benjamin Braude, "Foundation Myths of the *Millet* System," in *Christians and Jews in the Ottoman Empire: The Functioning of a Plural Society*, vol. 1: *The Central Lands*, eds. Benjamin Braude and Bernard Lewis [New York: Holmes and Meier, 1982], pp. 74–83). As much as various authorities—whether rabbinic or Ottoman—might have striven to secure communal autonomy, the walls they built were extremely porous (see Jacob R. Hacker, "Jewish Autonomy in the Ottoman Empire: Its Scope and Limits. Jewish Courts from the Sixteenth to the Eighteenth Centuries," in *The Jews of the Ottoman Empire*, ed. and intro. Avigdor Levy [Princeton, N.J.: Darwin Press, 1994], pp. 153–202). It might even be argued that some of Ottoman Jewry's success derived from its ability to maneuver outside the Jewish world and that, paradoxically, the leadership's growing ability to seal the breaches into that world contributed to the community's loss of vigor and decline in the eighteenth and nineteenth centuries.

2. On the association between London merchants and Aleppine factors, see Davis, *Aleppo and Devonshire Square*.

3. PRO, SP 110/111, fos. 22^v–23^v.

4. PRO, SP 110/111, passim.

5. "Hoggia" is an anglicized form of *hoca*, an honorific for the head of a household, an elder, or a teacher.

6. PRO, SP 97/16, fo. 243^r.

7. PRO, SP 97/16, fo. 246^v.

8. PRO, SP 97/16, fo. 247^v.

9. İnalcık, "Imtiyazat."

10. British Library (hereafter BL), Egerton MS 2541, fos. 300–2 and 316.

11. *CSP, Venice*, vol. 28, no. 360 (Bembo to Doge and Senate: 17 November 1649).

12. *CSP, Venice*, vol. 27, nos. 1, 22, 25, and 90. Hyde probably was instrumental in securing this boycott, an effort that was self-serving because during it, all company currants came from territory under his jurisdiction.

13. The pertinent documents refer to Hyde's position as "basdarlik." My thanks to Christoph Neumann for suggesting that this was the anglicized *bacdarlık*. The granting of positions such as the *bacdarlık* to foreigners was not unprecedented and may have been quite usual. See Halil İnalcık, "Tax Collection, Embezzlement and Bribery in Ottoman Finances," *Turkish Studies Association Bulletin* 15(2) (1991): 333 for the case of an Italian-named individual, Luvizo, who received "a public office in the city of Tripoli with a daily salary of fifteen *akçe*s." Luvizo, however, may have been an Ottoman subject, a

type later known as a "levantine"; Hyde certainly was not. In any case, the securing of a high administrative post such as that of *voyvodalık* probably was less ordinary.

14. A later consul, William Foulke, hosted Robert Bargrave at this mansion during Bargrave's travels in 1652. See his *Relation,* fo. 164^v.

15. Another anglicization, this time of *sipahi,* referring to an Ottoman cavalryman. Bodleian Library, Clarendon MS 45, fo. 73^r (Joseph Kent to Killigrew [?]: 31 January 1653). During the first Anglo-Dutch war a decade later, the Dutch captured this ship while it was lading currants at Zante, and took it to Leghorn.

16. PRO, SP 105/150, fo. 5^v.

17. PRO, SP 105/150, fo. 13^v. This remark is the earliest indication of a decade-long association between Crow and Hyde, on which see chapters 5–8.

18. PRO, SP 105/150, fo. 36^r.

19. PRO, SP 105/143, fo. 95.

20. PRO, SP 105/150, fo. 42.

21. PRO, SP 105/150, fo. 48^v (General Court: 17 November 1643).

22. PRO, SP 105/150, fos. 47^v (5 October 1643), 57^r (7 March 1644), and 60^v (15 April 1644).

23. PRO, SP 105/143, fos. 101^v–102^r.

24. See, for instance, PRO, SP 97/17, fos. 5^r and 6^r. He repeated the call even on the scaffold itself, moments before his execution. See Mark Charles Fissel and Daniel Goffman, "Viewing the Scaffold From Istanbul: The Bendysh-Hyde Affair, 1647–51," *Albion* 23(3) (1990): 443.

25. BL, Egerton MS 2541, fo. 312.

26. PRO, SP 105/143, fo. 111^r.

27. BL, Egerton MS 2541, fo. 315 (Thomas Prichett, Hen. Campion, Bray Chowne, Tho Colman, John Younger, John Wyld, Tho. Gundrey, and Wm. Wombwell to Crow: 2 October 1644).

28. For the second petition, see BL, Egerton MS 2541, fo. 314 (John Bromhatt, William Tredway, James Childe, Lambert Pitches, Henry Campion, Theophilus May, Will Wombwells, Thomas Prichett, Bray Chowne, Thomas Harman, Thomas Gundry, John Wilde, and John Younger to Company Directors: 25 November 1644).

29. BL, Egerton MS 2541, fo. 313^r.

30. BL, Egerton MS 2541, fo. 313^v.

31. BL, Egerton MS 2541, fo. 315.

32. BL, Egerton MS 2541, fo. 314^v (John Bromhatt, William Tredway, James Childe, Lambert Pitches, Henry Campion, Theophilus May, Will Wombwells, Thomas Prichett, Bray Chowne, Thomas Harman, Thomas Gundry, John Wilde, and John Younger to Company Directors).

33. PRO, SP 105/150, fo. 71.

34. PRO, SP 105/150, fo. 73^v.

35. BL, Egerton MS 2541, fo. 318^r (Ball to Crow: 22 December 1644).

36. BL, Egerton MS 2541, fo. 318^r.

37. This is presumably an anglicized spelling of Holumiç (Greek: Chlomoutsi), an Ottoman town and region along the island's western coast. See Donald Edgar Pitcher, *An Historical Geography of the Ottoman Empire from Earliest Times to the End of the Sixteenth Century* (Leiden: E. J. Brill, 1972), maps 14 and 26.

38. BL, Egerton MS 2541, fos. 318^v–319^r.

39. Italian translations of the Ottoman originals, which I have been unable to locate, are in BL, Egerton MS 2541, fos. 324^r, and 324^{r-v}.

40. Italian translations of the Ottoman originals are in BL, Egerton MS 2541, fos. 324^v–325^r and 325^v.

41. BL, Egerton MS 2541, fo. 320^v. To be "siggiled" (*sicil*) was to be recorded in the kadi's register.

42. BL, Egerton MS 2541, fo. 320^v.

43. BL, Egerton MS 2541, fos. 321–323.

44. BL, Egerton MS 2541, fo. 311 (Henry Hunt to Hyde: 28 March 1645).

45. BL, Egerton MS 2541, fos. 298–99.

46. BL, Egerton MS 2541, fo. 299^v.

47. BL, Egerton MS 2541, fo. 299^v.

48. BL, Egerton MS 2541, fo. 299^v.

49. BL, Egerton MS 2541, fo. 306^{r-v}.

50. BL, Egerton MS 2541, fo. 306^v.

51. See BL, Egerton MS 2541, fos. 300–2.

52. See BL, Egerton MS 2541, fos. 326 and 327 (Thomas Day, Robert Corbin, and Jeremy Fisher's testimony given to John Lancelot, consul of Izmir: 12 July 1645).

53. BL, Egerton MS 2541, fo. 307^r (Crow on Ball's complaint: 19 July 1645).

54. BL, Egerton MS 2541, fos. 307^v–308^r.

55. BL, Egerton MS 2541, fo. 308^r.

56. BL, Egerton MS 2541, fo. 309^r.

57. BL, Egerton MS 2541, fos. 303–5.
58. BL, Egerton MS 2541, fos. 304–5.
59. PRO, SP 105/150, fo. 83^v–84^r.
60. PRO, SP 105/150, fo. 87^r and 89^v.
61. BL, Egerton MS 2541, fo. 310.
62. PRO, SP 97/17, fo. 5^r.
63. PRO, SP 97/17, fo. 6^r.
64. Bargrave, *Relation*, fos. 32^v–33^r.
65. *A Brief of the State of the Case of Walter Elfords Complaint against Sr. Sackvile Crow, which is to be reported to the Parliament* (Broadsheet, December 1649 [?]).
66. PRO, SP 105/150, fo. 61^v (Meeting of the General Council: 30 April 1644).
67. Fissel and Goffman, "Viewing the Scaffold," pp. 428–30.

5 / THE AMBASSADOR'S GAMBIT

1. Much has been written on the king's situation at Oxford. A concise and clear account is in Charles Carlton, *Charles I: The Personal Monarch*, 2d ed. (London: Routledge, 1995), pp. 294–300.
2. Even recently, historians of the English civil war and biographers of Charles I have not imagined that he would have negotiated with the Ottomans. Carlton, for example, in his thorough and convincing biography, remarks that Charles's "efforts to obtain help from Ireland, Scotland, Wales, France, Portugal, Denmark and Spain, from Catholic and covenanter, from Arminians and Independents, show how he made desperate, and frequently disparate, efforts to win men and money wherever conceivable" (*Charles I*, p. 245)—wherever conceivable, that is, other than in an Islamic state.
3. This manuscript, carrying the title "A Narrative of the Venetians tender of assistance to K. Cha. 1st in his Civil Wars. And the Disappointment of it. As likewise of the design of confiscating the English Merchants Effects in Turkey to his Majty's use," is in the Bodleian Library (MS.Eng.hist.C.312, fos. 1–6). The Venetian agent against whom Talbot complains is Gerolamo Agostini. His correspondence is in *CSP, Venice,* vols. 26 and 27, passim.
4. BL, Egerton MS 2533, fos. 438 and 439.
5. Wood, *History of the Levant Company*, pp. 89–92; and Fissel, "Law and Authority."
6. PRO, SP 105/109, fos. 178–79.

7. PRO, SP 105/109, fo. 177 (Charles I to Peter Wyche and Sackvile Crow: 20 April 1639).

8. Two important pamphlets dealing with these events exist. The company's offering is *Subtilty and Cruelty: or a true relation of Sr Sackvile Crow, His Designe of seizing and possessing himselfe of all the Estate of the English in Turky. With the Progresse he made, and the Meanes he used in the execution thereof.* A first edition was published in London in 1647. Several copies of it are in the British Library. A second edition "with such other papers as are since discovered related thereto" appeared ten years later (see PRO, SP 105/151, fo. 155^r [23 April 1657]). The British Library possesses only one copy of this more exhaustive version. This pamphlet seems to be an accurate compilation of Crow's correspondence with his henchmen. Since they were captured papers later published by his enemies, however, censorship or forgery or both cannot be entirely ruled out. G. F. Abbott cited what may be an earlier version of this same pamphlet in his *Turkey, Greece and the Great Powers: A Study in Friendship and Hate* (New York: Robert M. McBride and Company, 1917), p. 94n1. Crow's defense (in which he never questioned the earlier pamphlet's authenticity), was presented in *Sr. Sackvile Crow's Case as it now stands with his request to the Parliament 1 July 1652* (London, 1652). Petitions concerning the controversy from both the company and Crow are in PRO, SP 105/143, fos. 143–58. The narrative that follows depends principally upon these sources.

9. Hyde's enemies certainly believed his role prominent. The factors general in Istanbul wrote to the company directors on 28 June 1646 that "his Lordships chief Counsellor, in these his undue proceedings, is Mr Henry Hyde, of whose good service in your former occasions at the Morea, wee need not to give testimony; but can assure your Worships, that since his coming hither, hee hath occasioned great disturbance amongst the nation; and how at last, (had the design before mentioned taken effect) might have raised his decayed fortunes, by the ruine of yours and our Estates; but thanks bee to God, the Counsel of Achitophel is turned into foly" (*Subtilty and Cruelty*, p. 84).

10. *Subtilty and Cruelty*, p. 78 (Factors General to Levant Company: 28 June 1646).

11. *Subtilty and Cruelty*, p. 3 (Crow's warrant to Hetherington and Zuma: 27 April 1646). See also PRO, SP 105/143, fo. 143^{r-v}, where it is stated that the first seven merchants were dispatched to Istanbul on 30 April.

12. These ships were the *Rainbow, William and Thomas, Tryangle, Jonas,* and *Hopewell* at Izmir, and the *Sampson, Smirna Merchant, Lewis,* and *Phinix* at Istanbul. See PRO, SP 105/143, fo. 144^r.

13. PRO, SP 105/150, fo. 112^v.
14. PRO, SP 105/143, fo. 152^v. He ordered this leviation on 18 February.
15. PRO, SP 105/150, fo. 112^v.
16. PRO, SP 105/143, fos. 155^v–156^r, and elsewhere.
17. PRO, SP 105/143, fo. 153^r.
18. PRO, SP 105/143, fo. 153^r.
19. PRO, SP 105/143, fo. 149^r.
20. BOA, MD 90, p. 43, no. 130 (Sublime Porte to kadi of Izmir: 17 April–17 May 1646).
21. BOA, MD 90, p. 44, no. 139 (Sublime Porte to kadi of Izmir: 7–17 May 1646).
22. *Subtilty and Cruelty*, p. 19 (Crow's instructions to Zuma: 30 April 1646). A *fetva* was a canonical decision issued by the principal Ottoman religious authority (the *şeyhülislam*); a *naib* was an assistant to the kadi.
23. PRO, SP 105/143, fo. 143^r. Gyles Ball had tried this same ploy in the Morea (see chapter 4).
24. *Subtilty and Cruelty*, p. 16 (Crow's instructions to Zuma: 10 April 1646).
25. *Subtilty and Cruelty*, p. 19 (Crow's instructions to Zuma: 30 April 1646). The attitude toward Jews displayed in this passage was typical, on which see chapter 2 and, more generally, Jacob Katz, *Exclusiveness and Toleration: Jewish-Gentile Relations in Medieval and Modern Times* (Oxford: Oxford University Press, 1961).
26. *Subtilty and Cruelty*, p. 20.
27. *Subtilty and Cruelty*, p. 20 (Crow's instructions to Hetherington: 30 April 1646).
28. *Subtilty and Cruelty*, p. 24 (Crow's instructions to Hetherington: 30 April 1646).
29. Crow suspected specific merchants. Of the sixty-five persons then residing in Izmir, he named twenty-six: John Langham (alderman), Richard Chambers, Farnam Beamonte, William Davis, Joseph and Robert Keble, Humphrey Brown, Cordewell Farrington, Richard Milward, John Smith, Robert Davis, William Ashwell (alderman), John Langly, William Limbrey, William Edwards, Thomas Dorkely, Humphrey Bowater, Sir Thomas Soames, William Harlowe, John Rowles, Richard Cranely, Sam. Moyer, Bennet Mayne, Hugh Norris, Tho. Barnardiston, and Thomas Hodges (see *Subtilty and Cruelty*, p. 25 [appendage to Crow's instructions to Hetherington: 30 April 1646]). He then added to this list, surprisingly, three women: Edwine Browne, Alice Gibman, and Elizabeth Harvy.

30. Together worth approximately 130,000 pounds sterling!

31. *Subtilty and Cruelty*, p. 79 (Factors General to Levant Company: 28 June 1646).

32. *Subtilty and Cruelty*, p. 34 (Hetherington to Crow: 13 May 1646).

33. *Subtilty and Cruelty*, pp. 35–36 (Crow to Hetherington and Zuma: 25 May 1646).

34. *Subtilty and Cruelty*, p. 41 (Crow to Hetherington and Zuma: 25 May 1646).

35. *Subtilty and Cruelty*, p. 50 (Crow to Hetherington: 28 May 1646).

36. *Subtilty and Cruelty*, pp. 57–58 (Hetherington and Zuma to Crow: 15 June 1646).

37. *Subtilty and Cruelty*, pp. 60–61 (Hetherington and Zuma to Crow: 16 June 1646).

38. *Subtilty and Cruelty*, p. 61 (Hetherington and Zuma to Crow: 16 June 1646).

39. *Subtilty and Cruelty*, p. 62 (Hetherington and Zuma to Crow: 19 June 1646).

40. *Subtilty and Cruelty*, p. 63 (Hetherington and Zuma to Crow: 19 June 1646).

41. PRO, SP 105/143, fo. 144^r.

42. On Dupuy, see Goffman, *Izmir and the Levantine World*, pp. 120–32.

43. Those from the factory in Istanbul were Thomas Barkely, William Chappell, Roger Fowke, John Tye, William Pearle, William Gough, John Swift, John Abney, Francis Ashwell, Giles Davies, James Davison, William Osborne, Richard Stroade, Nathaniel Brandwood, Jonathan Dawes, and Robert Pickett; those from Izmir were John Lancelot, Dixwell Brent, John Pixley, Daniel Edwards, Samuel Barnardiston, George Langer, James Moyer, John Ball, Henry Davey, Phillip Farwell, Nathaniel Barnardiston, and John Ingoldsby. See PRO, SP 105/143, fo. 143^v.

44. *Subtilty and Cruelty*, p. 74 (petition of English nation in Istanbul to Crow: 20 June 1646).

45. The king was indeed to propose Peter Killigrew as ambassador-designate, although parliament and company never ratified the nomination. Thus, the rumor that he was on his way was false. Ironically, Killigrew was in any case just as thoroughly a king's man as was Crow. See chapter 6.

46. PRO, SP 105/143, fo. 143^v. Robert Frampton's seemingly antiroyalist interests in this and other such incidents is one indication of the ideological and personal muddle that characterized the British world in those years. This

strong-willed individual in 1672 was to preach two highly critical sermons before Charles II, despite which the king granted him the Bishopric of Gloucester. See Simpson Evans (ed.), *Life of Robert Frampton, Bishop of Gloucester* (1876), as cited in Richard Ollard, *The Image of the King: Charles I and Charles II* (London: Hodder and Stoughton, 1979), p. 111.

47. *Subtilty and Cruelty*, p. 82 (Factors General to the Levant Company: 28 June 1646). See also PRO, SP 105/143, fo. 144^r.

48. PRO, SP 105/143, fo. 144^r.

49. The company collected and published these intercepted letters in *Subtilty and Cruelty*. See chapter 6.

50. A copy of this decree is preserved in BOA, MD 91, p. 79 (25 June–4 July 1646).

51. BOA, MD 90, p. 82, no. 260; and 90, no. 285 (Sublime Porte to kadi of Izmir: 2–12 August 1646).

52. *Subtilty and Cruelty*, p. 71 (Crow to Hetherington and Zuma: 1 July 1646).

53. *Subtilty and Cruelty*, p. 71 (Crow to Hetherington and Zuma: 1 July 1646).

6 / PARLIAMENT OR KING?

1. But see Robert Brenner, "The Civil War Politics of London's Merchant Community," *Past and Present* 58 (1973): 53–107. The author elaborates the arguments of this article in *Merchants and Revolution*.

2. On Pennington's politics, see Brenner, *Merchants and Revolution*, especially pp. 323–24.

3. PRO, SP 105/150, fo. 69^v.

4. PRO, SP 105/150, fos. 73^r–75^r. His letter of appointment is in PRO, SP 105/143, fos. 105^v–108^r. The sympathies of the company are strongly suggested by its loan of eight thousand pounds to parliament in 1644 and probably again in the following year. See PRO, SP 105/150, fo. 94^v; and Wood, *History of the Levant Company*, p. 52, where doubt is expressed that the loan was ever made. Brenner has some trouble explaining away such loans, which baldly contradict his thesis of royalist Levant and East India companies. Without clear supporting evidence, he proposes that they "can be understood only in terms of the company merchants' anxiety to be sure that their charters would be renewed" (see Brenner, *Merchants and Revolution*, p. 376).

5. PRO, SP 105/150, fo. 71.
6. PRO, SP 105/150, fo. 71.
7. PRO, SP 105/150, fo. 112^v.
8. PRO, SP 105/150, fo. 118^{r-v}.
9. PRO, SP 105/150, fo. 119^{r-v}.
10. See PRO, SP 105/150, fos. 126^v–127^r.
11. PRO, SP 105/150, fo. 121^v. This pamphlet consisted of the incriminating correspondence between Crow and Hetherington, which hostile English merchants had seized in transit between Istanbul and Izmir. It was printed under the title *Subtilty and Cruelty*. A second and more extensive edition was issued a decade later. See note 8, chapter 5.
12. PRO, SP 105/150, fo. 122^r.
13. This committee met on 17 September and, according to PRO, SP 105/109, fo. 188, consisted of Mr. Dennis Bond, Mr. Holles, Mr. Ralle, Mr. Harvey, Sr. Arthur Hisilrig, Mr. Martin, Mr. Ald. Penington, Mr. Swinson, Mr. Edward Ash., Mr. Salway, Sr. Gilbert Girrard, Mr. Ashhurst, Mr. Wm. Allenson, Mr. Nath. Fynes, Mr. Robinson, Mr. Ellis, Mr. Oliver Cromwell, Sr. Wm. Lewes, Mr. Boone, Mr. Alex. Bince, Sr. Sam Rolle, Sr. Wm. Armin, Mr. Sildin, Mr. Vassill, Sr. John Northcott, Mr. Wilson, Sr. Sim Dineds [?], Sr. Phil. Stapltone, and Sr. Tho. Soame.
14. PRO, SP 105/150, fo. 123^r.
15. PRO, SP 105/143, fo. 116^r; and SP 105/150, fos. 124^v–125^r.
16. PRO, SP 105/150, fos. 124^v–125^r.
17. PRO, SP 105/150, fos. 126^v–127^r.
18. PRO, SP 105/150, fo. 137^v.
19. PRO, SP 105/143, fos. 114^v–115^r.
20. PRO, SP 105/150, fos. 124^v–125^r.
21. PRO, SP 105/150, fo. 128^r.
22. *Subtilty and Cruelty*, p. 85 (Factors General to Levant Company: 28 June 1646).
23. PRO, SP 105/150, fo. 130.
24. PRO, SP 105/150, fo. 131^v.
25. BL, Additional MS 15,856, fos. 17–18. This copy is a draft. We cannot be certain, though, that it was never sent. Crow's subsequent actions against Bendysh (see chapter 7) declare that he at least knew of it. The two monarchs, Charles I and İbrahim, were to share the fate of violent death some three years later.
26. BL, Additional MS 15,856, fo. 17^{r-v}.

27. Bodleian Library, Clarendon MS 97 (catalogued in Clarendon MS 29), no. 2373, fo. 59.

28. PRO, SP 105/150, fo. 132^r.

29. Variations on exactly this occurrence plagued English representation in Istanbul during the early 1650s. See chapter 11.

30. One of these negotiators was a Mr. Lowe, on whom see chapter 7.

31. PRO, SP 105/143, fo. 117^r.

32. PRO, SP 105/150, fo. 134^{r-v}.

33. PRO, SP 105/150, fo. 135^r.

34. PRO, SP 105/143, fos. 120^{r-v} and 121^r.

35. Bodleian Library, Clarendon MS 29, fo. 72^r.

36. PRO, SP 105/150, fo. 137^v.

37. PRO, SP 105/143, fo. 118^{r-v}.

38. PRO, SP 105/150, fos. 138^{r-v} and 141^r. The directors had already sent George Vernon's relative (brother?), Francis Vernon, to Istanbul to act as agent in Lancelot's place.

39. This decision, perhaps never enacted, is an early indication of English frustrations at having to communicate through middlemen. A century later, the problem led to an emphasis on language training and helped promote British philology. See Allan Cunningham, "Dragomania: The Dragomans of the British Embassy in Turkey," *St. Antony's Papers* 11 (1961): 81–100.

40. PRO, SP 105/143, fo. 116^v.

41. Bernard Capp, *Cromwell's Navy: The Fleet and the English Revolution, 1648–1660* (Oxford: Clarendon Press, 1989), pp. 15–41.

42. PRO, SP 105/143, fo. 124^r.

43. These are BL, Additional MS 15,750, fos. 29^{r-v}, 31^r, and 32^{r-v}. They are discussed more fully in chapter 7.

7 / PRETENDERS TO THE AMBASSADORSHIP

1. According to the account Crow later presented to the Council of the Admiralty (PRO, SP 105/143, fo. 152^r), those who voted to appoint Lancelot were the factors John Wyld, John Lancelot, Thomas Barkeley, Dixwell Brent, John Moyer, Nicholas Barnardiston, James Mudford, Dan. Edwards, William Chassell, Roger Fowke, Giles Ball, John Tyghe, John Ball, William Pearle, John Pixley, Samuel Barnardiston, John Swift, William Gough, Thomas Piggot, John Awbury, Francis Ashwell, Robert Frampton, Giles Davies, John Plomer, James Davison, William Osborne, Henry Davye, Richard Stroade, Phillip Farewell,

John Erisby, Jonathan Dawes, Ralph Gosnoll, Robert Keble, Thomas Lancelot, John Wyld Junr., Laurance Chamber, William Oxwick, Arnold White, Daniell Bassano, William Whitlock, Robert Dawes, and Samuel Bruning, as well as the ship masters Nicholas Read (*Smirna Merchant*) and William Ashley (*Sampson*) and the dragoman Dominico Timone.

2. Wood, *History of the Levant Company*, p. 91n3.
3. PRO, SP 46/78, fo. 166.
4. Wood, *History of the Levant Company*, p. 91n3.
5. BL, Egerton MS 2647, fos. 18–19 (Sir Thomas Bendysh to Sir Thomas Barington: 5 July 1643).
6. PRO, SP 105/143, fos. 126–31.
7. PRO, SP 105/143, fos. 128^v–129^r.
8. On Veneto-Jewish rivalries in the eastern Mediterranean, see Arbel, *Trading Nations,* passim.
9. PRO, SP 105/143, fos. 129^v–130^r.
10. PRO, SP 105/143, fo. 131^r.
11. On Religious Independency in particular, see Brenner, *Merchants and Revolution*, pp. 412–27.
12. PRO, SP 105/143, fo. 126^v.
13. Unless otherwise cited, the information on Bendysh's passage to Istanbul is gleaned from Robert Bargrave's *Relation*. This young merchant, adventurer, writer, and composer of hymns and sonnets accompanied the ambassador-designate to Istanbul and remained there in his service for several years. In 1660, he set out again to serve Ambassador Winchelsea but died en route at Izmir (see Anderson, *An English Consul In Turkey*, pp. 25–26). On the two captains, see also PRO, SP 105/109, fo. 192. Bendysh's two younger sons joined him later (see chapter 11).
14. Bargrave, *Relation*, fo. 2^r.
15. Bargrave, *Relation*, fo. 3^r.
16. On piracy in the Mediterranean Sea in early modern times, see Tenenti, *Piracy and the Decline of Venice*.
17. Fernand Braudel and Ruggiero Romano, *Navires et marchandises à l'entrée du port de Livourne, 1547–1611* (Paris: A. Conlin, 1951).
18. BL, Additional MS 15,759, fo. 29^r.
19. PRO, SP 105/150, fo. 163^r.
20. PRO, SP 105/143, fo. 139^r. This service cost one hundred fifty pounds, and the emissary, Mr. Lowe, claimed another one hundred pounds for his trouble. See PRO, SP 105/150, fo. 164. The meeting with Charles probably

took place at Caversham. One cannot be certain, though, for Charles was being dragged around the English countryside during the months of June through August 1647.

21. PRO, SP 105/143, fos. 139^v, 140^r, 140^v, and 141^r.
22. Bargrave, *Relation,* fo. 10^v.
23. BL, Additional MS 15,750, fo. 29^r.
24. The Ottoman archives provide many examples. See, for instance, BOA, ED 13/1, pp. 30, 1605–6, in which the Venetian *bailo* complained that collectors demanded more than 5 percent on cotton gathered in Izmir's hinterland; Maliyeden Müdevver Defterleri (hereafter MM) 6004, p. 25, no. 1, 1621–22, in which the Venetian ambassador complained that janissaries in Izmir had punished Venetians for the crimes of others; ED 26/1, p. 50, no. 2, 1650, in which the French ambassador accused an Ottoman subject of murdering a French resident of Izmir; and ED 26/1, p. 100, no. 1, 1664–65, in which the French ambassador complained that the collector had held merchandise in the customs shed and made French ships lose favorable winds. Even though these examples are from the Ottoman archives, they tell us, unfortunately, little about Ottoman perceptions of these incidents; in each case it was an ambassador rather than an Ottoman subject who initiated the proceedings. Abstracts of these and many other, similar examples are in Daniel Goffman, "Izmir as a Commercial Center: The Impact of Western Trade on an Ottoman Port, 1570–1650" (Ph.D. diss., University of Chicago, 1985), appendix 3.
25. His reforms are recorded in PRO, SP 105/109, fos. 191–97.
26. PRO, SP 105/109, fos. 192^r and 192^v.
27. Those who attended at least one session were Sam. Barnardiston, Sam. Barton, Dipwell Brent (treasurer, Izmir), Sam. Brosoinge, John Bull, George Cave, Henry Davey, Robert Dowre, Joseph Edwards, Phillippe Farwell, Roger Forobe, Arthur Garway, William Gibbs, Wm Gough (treasurer, Istanbul), George Hanger, Francis Hill, Lewis Hodges, Tho. Lancelott, George Lawe, James Moyre, Tho. Newsam, Antho. Nicholetts, Thomas Pentloe, John Pixlie, John Robinson, J^o. South, Richard Wattson, Captain John Wyle (consul), John Wyle Junior, and Martin Wynille.
28. BL, Egerton MS 2533, fo. 433. We do not know what happened to Vernon. One can infer, however, that Crow somehow blocked his attempts at audiences with the grand vizier and other Ottoman officials.
29. BOA, MM 6004, pp. 26, no. 1; and 103, no. 1. The latter decree relates that the commanders of the castles customarily received payments of 200 *akçe*s

per ship, the kadis 100, the *voyvoda* of Gallipoli 180, the cannoneers 100, and the custodians and other servants 110. The aggregate assessment was meant to be no more than 1,090 *akçe*s.

30. See BOA, Şikayet Defterleri 2, p. 10, no. 38; and MD 90, p. 110, no. 345.

31. PRO, SP 105/109, fo. 192^v.

32. There also were many expenses and hazards on the overland route. The handlers of Ambassador Lord Trumbull, preparing to embark in 1680, first protested to the king that it was safe to sail an English warship into the harbor at Istanbul, then remarked that disembarkation at Izmir cost much time and money, and finally argued that "for an Embassador to go from Smirna to Const.ple by land, is vastly chargeable, & very dangerous; those parts of Asia being much infested with thieves; & that way, he must goe 100 Miles by Sea, in small Boates, wch is altogether impracticable. To goe by Sea from Smirna on Turkish vessels, there are none that have any convenience for a person of farr lesse quality then an Embassador, besides the danger of Corsairs. To meet with Christian vessels proper for that occasion is next to an impossibility; all ships, generally, goeing there, being obliged by Chart & party for their voyages, wch they cannot alter, nor dispose of themselves. And should there be any other ships then English, it would bee very indecent, & a matter of much talke, for an Embassador to embark on them, when he had a man of Warre with him" (Bodleian Library, Rawlinson MS A.189, fo. 306^{r-v}). This passage not only suggests an awareness of the ignominious events of the 1640s but also exhibits a particular sensitivity to English and ambassadorial honor.

33. PRO, SP 105/109, fo. 196^r.

34. PRO, SP 105/109, fo. 193^r. These factors were Mr. Jn^a. Ball, Sam. Barnardiston, Henry Davey, Joseph Edwards, Arthur Garway, George Hanger, Francis Hill, Lewis Hodges, Dipwell Kent, James Moyre, John Pixlie, Jn^a. Robinson, Tho. Sampson, and George Sane.

35. PRO, SP 105/109, fo. 193^v.

36. PRO, SP 105/109, fos. 193^v–194^r.

37. PRO, SP 105/109, fo. 194^v.

38. PRO, SP 105/109, fo. 195^r.

39. *CSP, Venice,* vol. 28, pp. 20–22, no. 43 (Giovanni Soranzo to Doge and Senate: 19 October 1647).

40. BL, Additional MS 15,750, fo. 29^r (Bendysh to Charles I: 12 November 1647).

41. Bargrave, *Relation*, f. 12^r.

42. *CSP, Venice*, vol. 28, pp. 20–22, no. 43. See also PRO, SP 105/143, fo. 154^r, where Crow expresses anger that Bendysh never sent him a copy of his letter from the king.

43. BL, Egerton MS 2533, fo. 436.

44. Bodleian Library, Clarendon MS 30, fo. 77, scrawled in the margin of which is: "Sackville Crowe will not present the new ambassador and has so made his way with the G. S. [sultan], that he will not accept of him."

45. *CSP, Venice*, vol. 28, pp. 16, no. 25; 16, no. 30; and 20–22, no. 43.

46. BL, Additional MS 15,750, fo. 29^r.

47. BL, Additional MS 15,750, fo. 29^r.

48. BL, Additional MS 15,750, fo. 29^v.

49. BL, Egerton MS 2533, fo. 431^v. Thus the king, renowned for his misuse of loyal subjects, was receiving information simultaneously from both Bendysh and Crow.

50. This rather oblique reference seems to have been the closest the ambassador ever came to confessing Charles's involvement.

51. On the company's decision to dispatch Vernon with these letters, see chapter 6.

52. *CSP, Venice*, vol. 28, p. 21, no. 43 (Soranzo to Doge and Senate: 19 October 1647). There is some confusion concerning Bendysh's audiences. The *bailo* reports that he met with the grand vizier at this time and that it was only on 18 October that he obtained an audience with the sultan "at a lodge on the sea shore" and "kissed the king's hand." Bargrave, who accompanied Bendysh, insists on the earlier date.

53. Bargrave, *Relation*, fo. 13^r.

54. One of these merchants was Maurice Evans, on whom see chapter 8.

55. *CSP, Venice*, vol. 28, p. 21, no. 43.

56. On which see chapter 10; and Fissel and Goffman, "Viewing the Scaffold."

57. *CSP, Venice*, vol. 28, pp. 21–22, no. 43. This grand vizier, a native of Istanbul, became notorious for becoming the sultan's son-in-law by marriage to his two-year-old daughter.

58. Bargrave, *Relation*, fo. 13^v.

59. Copies of these letters are in PRO, SP 105/143, fos. 120 (21 January 1647) and 141^r (7 August 1647).

60. Bargrave, *Relation*, fo. 13^v.

61. On Crowe's charge, see PRO, SP 105/143, fo. 154 (Crow's answer to the company's complaints: 1648). Bargrave, who was a dependent of Bendysh's, confirms it in his *Relation,* fo. 13ᵛ.

62. *CSP, Venice,* vol. 28, p. 22, no. 43.

63. See *CSP, Venice,* vol. 28, p. 20, no. 43 (Soranzo to Doge and Senate: 19 October 1647).

64. Crow probably learned this trick from Henry Hyde, who had forged the king's seal some years earlier during his consulship in the Morea. See Fissel and Goffman, "Viewing the Scaffold," p. 426n15.

65. BL, Additional MS 15,750, fo. 32ʳ⁻ᵛ.

66. *CSP, Venice,* vol. 28, p. 222, no. 43.

67. Crow later recorded that this event took place on 3 November. All other witnesses, however, mark that it was the twenty-third.

68. There are several descriptions of this incident. See particularly Bodleian Library, Clarendon MS 30, fo. 170. See also *CSP, Venice,* vol. 28, pp. 27–29, no. 56 (Soranzo to Doge and Senate: 28 November 1647); PRO, SP 105/143, fos. 154ᵛ–155ʳ and 158ʳ; and Bargrave, *Relation,* fo. 14ʳ. Abbott briefly described it in his *Turkey, Greece and the Great Powers,* p. 94. This episode was also dealt with in Fissel and Goffman, "Viewing the Scaffold," pp. 429–30. Abbott covered several other episodes involving English diplomats in the Ottoman Empire during the civil wars and restoration, including Hyde's attempt to wrest the ambassadorship from Bendysh in 1650 (pp. 95–96) and Bendysh's quarrel with the *şeyhülislam* in 1651 (pp. 100–2). In these short narratives, though, the active agents invariably were Englishmen, and Ottoman officials were caricatured as greedy buffoons.

69. PRO, SP 105/143, fos. 154ᵛ–155ʳ.

70. See chapter 2; Steensgaard, "Consuls and Nations"; and especially Andrews, *Trade, Plunder, and Settlement,* pp. 356–64.

71. PRO, SP 105/143, fo. 158ʳ. In the company's words: "The Grand Signior ... directed to the Capigi Bassa, & Saban Chious ... to take him the said Sr. Sac. Crow out of his house and to carry him to Smirna to be put aboard an English ship ... but not in any violent manner as is by him pretended." In a cloying letter that Bendysh penned on 26 November and that repeated much of his clash with Crow, Bendysh himself apologized to the king for involving the Ottomans, something which Charles, it seems, had explicitly ordered him not to do. See BL, Additional MS 15,750, fo. 31ʳ.

72. Bargrave, *Relation,* fo. 14ʳ. There are other descriptions of this deed. The most accessible is that of Alfred Wood, *History of the Levant Company,*

p. 92. Probably the most colorful is an anonymous account preserved in the Bodleian Library, Clarendon MS 30, fo. 170, no. 2643, where it is described how "the Chaouses immediately tooke hold on [Crow], telling him that he was the man they came for.... Sir Sackville thus frighted out of his deceived hopes, called to have his Gates shutt, but all the Turckes drawing their Daggers danted the Porter from the performance of his Office and without any further delay forced him out with his beloved Companion Mr. Hide" (cited in Fissel and Goffman, "Viewing the Scaffold," p. 430).

73. See *CSP, Venice*, vol. 28, p. 29, no. 56; and Bargrave, *Relation*, fo. 14^r.

74. *CSP, Venice*, vol. 28, p. 29, no. 56.

75. See chapter 5.

76. See Robert Mantran, "L'état ottoman au XVIIe siècle: stabilisation ou déclin?" in *Histoire de l'empire ottoman*, ed. Robert Mantran (Paris: Librarie Artheme Fayard, 1989), p. 237.

77. Evliya Çelebi's description of Melek Pasha's career exposes a striking example of this system of patronage. Relevant passages from it are skillfully gleaned and translated in Dankoff, *Intimate Life of an Ottoman Statesman*, passim. Bendysh was fully informed about Ottoman disarray. As he wrote to his king in late December 1647 or early January 1648, "a Prince indisposed and unfit for managing of public affairs, referring all things to the Administration of such his officers, as purchasing th[ ] Rates their several Commands, take to themselves an intolerable latitude in execution of them" (BL, Additional MS 15,750, fo. 32^r). For a penetrating analysis of this period that looks beyond personality and corruption at the fundamentals of a transforming Ottoman political world, see Peirce, *Imperial Harem*.

78. Bargrave, *Relation*, fo. 22^v.

79. See Richard T. Rapp, "The Unmaking of the Mediterranean Trade Hegemony," *Journal of Economic History* 35 (1975): 499–525; and Rhoads Murphey, "The Ottoman Resurgence in the Seventeenth-Century Mediterranean: The Gamble and Its Results," *Mediterranean Historical Review* 8 (1993): 186–200.

80. His ships, the *London* and the *Unicorne*, were accompanied by a third. See *CSP, Venice*, vol. 28, p. 33, no. 65 (Soranzo to Doge and Senate: 19 December 1647).

81. *CSP, Venice*, vol. 28, p. 33, no. 65.

82. Such at least was Crow's contention. See PRO 105/143, fo. 158^r.

83. *CSP, Venice*, vol. 28, p. 11, no. 20 (Contarini at Rome to Doge and Senate: 24 August 1647). This source speaks of thirty English and Dutch ships

at Aleppo, Izmir, and Istanbul available for the Ottomans to expropriate. Not that the Ottomans could control these ships' ingress or egress. The government did not construct Sancak Kalesi, the castle at a narrow point of the bay, until the later 1650s. See BOA, Bab-i Asafi Dosyaları (Dossiers from the Bab-i Asafi) A.DVN 30, doc. 76 (22 April 1659); and Goffman, "Izmir," in *Three Ottoman Cities*.

84. *CSP, Venice*, vol. 28, p. 28, no. 56 (Soranzo to Doge and Senate: 28 November 1647).

85. *CSP, Venice*, vol. 28, p. 28, no. 56.

86. See Fissel and Goffman, "Viewing the Scaffold," p. 430.

87. PRO, SP 105/150, fos. 176^v–177^r, 187^v, and 193^{r-v}.

88. PRO, SP 105/151, fo. 16^r.

89. PRO, SP 105/150, fos. 175^v, and 176^v–177^r (11 April 1648).

90. PRO, SP 105/112, fos. 39–40; and PRO, SP 105/150, fo. 173^v. See also Fissel and Goffman, "Viewing the Scaffold," pp. 431–32; and chapter 10.

91. PRO, SP 105/143, fo. 142^r.

92. PRO, SP 105/150, fo. 171^{r-v}.

93. PRO, SP 105/150, fo. 172.

94. On which see D. E. Kennedy, "The Establishment and Settlement of Parliament's Admiralty, 1642–1648" *Mariner's Mirror* 48 (1962): 276–91.

95. PRO, SP 105/143, fo. 145^r.

96. PRO, SP 105/143, fo. 155^v.

97. This appraisal coincides with Greenfeld's in *Nationalism*, pp. 71–78.

98. PRO, SP 105/151, fo. 55^v (petition to the company: 11 February 1651); SP 105/151, fo. 72^{r-v} (petition to the company: 20 January 1652); SP 105/151, fo. 105^r (petition to the lord protector, forwarded to the company: 9 March 1654).

99. PRO, SP 105/151, fos. 109^v–110^r (25 August 1654). The company appointed a committee to defend itself; it still was busy doing so in 1658 (see PRO, SP 105/151, fo. 164^v).

100. PRO, SP 105/151, fo. 150^v (19 November 1656). It was probably in response to this attack that the company expanded and reissued its pamphlet of documents relating to Crow's attempts to seize the goods and persons of company factors in the summer of 1646 (see chapter 4).

101. Wood, citing John Burke, *A Genealogical and Heraldic History of the Extinct and Dormant Baronetcies of England* (London: 1844), p. 143, states in his *History of the Levant Company*, p. 92n1, that Crow died in 1683. As late as 9 June 1686, however, Crow still was writing in his tiresome prose

to an unnamed lord. See Bodleian Library, Tanner MS 41, fo. 23; and chapter 12.

8 / ADAPTING TO THE OTTOMAN COMMERCIAL WORLD

1. BL, Additional MS 15,750, fo. 32^{r-v}.
2. On the millet system and dragomans, see chapter 2.
3. For a provocative argument on the centrality of commercial matters in early-sixteenth-century Venetian and especially Ottoman state policy, see Palmira Brummett, *Ottoman Seapower and Levantine Diplomacy in the Age of Discovery* (Albany: State University of New York Press, 1994).
4. Marino Sanuto, *I Diarii*, vol. 56 (Venice, 1879–1903), col. 85; as quoted in Arbel, *Trading Nations*, p. 37. Arbel's book is replete with such examples of the Veneto-Jewish competition.
5. PRO, SP 97/15, fo. 80^v.
6. PRO, SP 105/143, fo. 127^r. See also chapter 7.
7. PRO, SP 105/174, pp. 521–23.
8. PRO, SP 105/174, p. 522.
9. It is difficult to ascertain whether this perception of great wealth constituted a stereotypical assumption, in the tradition of Shylock, or was grounded in historical truth. We do know that during this period several Jewish concerns—including the one of Cargashan, Hekem, and Useph to be mentioned shortly—confronted bankruptcy and ultimately extinction.
10. PRO, SP 105/174, p. 346 (19 November 1649).
11. PRO, SP 105/174, pp. 48–49.
12. PRO, SP 105/174, pp. 347–48 (23 November 1649).
13. PRO, SP 105/174, pp. 353 and 365.
14. PRO, SP 105/174, p. 116, doc. 1; and p. 160.
15. PRO, SP 105/174, p. 347. This communal loyalty manifests a self-defense mechanism that is exhaustively documented among Jewish communities in Christian Europe (see, for instance, Jacob Katz, *Tradition and Crisis: Jewish Society at the End of the Middle Ages* [New York: Schocken Books, 1971], pp. 18–28 and 35–42) as well as in the Ottoman Empire (see, for instance, Aryeh Shmuelevitz, *The Jews of the Ottoman Empire in the Late Fifteenth and Sixteenth Centuries: Administrative, Economic, Legal and Social Relations as Reflected in the Responsa* [Leiden: E. J. Brill, 1984], pp. 68–73).
16. PRO, SP 105/174, pp. 495–96.
17. PRO, SP 105/151, fo. 54^v.

18. See, for instance, PRO, SP 105/174, pp. 353–54, where Bendysh battulated Isaac Soreson and his son David for not paying to William Gibbs 776 lion dollars in recompense for some cloths; and p. 365, where he battulated "Joseph Aluffe Jew and Company." As we saw when Ambassador Crow announced a leviation to settle an *avania* against his treasurer (chapter 5), most factors also objected when "private" *avania*s were made "public."

19. On the rivalry between the French and the English in this period, see Wood, *History of the Levant Company*, pp. 55–56; and Paul Masson, *Histoire du commerce français dans le Levant au XVIIe* (Paris: Hachette, 1911), pp. 118–35. On Hatchooke, see PRO, SP 105/174, p. 308.

20. PRO, SP 105/174, p. 382, doc. 1 (14 March 1650).

21. See *CSP, Venice*, vol. 31, pp. 166–67 (Ballarino, Venetian secretary at the Porte, to Doge and Senate: 17 February 1658); and p. 187, no. 159 (Ballarino to Doge and Senate: 19 April 1658).

22. PRO, SP 105/174, pp. 357–58 (8 December 1649).

23. This same Reade had resided in Izmir a decade earlier and had clashed with Richard Lawrence. See chapter 4.

24. PRO, SP 105/174, pp. 109–11.

25. PRO, SP 105/174, pp. 58–60 (16 September 1648).

26. PRO, SP 105/174, pp. 109–11.

27. PRO, SP 105/174, p. 112. The clerk penned "Michael Frauncis" rather than "Frances Reade." The context, however, indicates a scribal error.

28. PRO, SP 105/174, pp. 155–56 (21 November 1648).

29. PRO, SP 105/174, p. 179 (25 January 1649).

30. PRO, SP 105/174, p. 113 (28 October 1648).

31. On which, see chapter 12.

32. PRO, SP 105/174, p. 275 (27 August 1649).

33. PRO, SP 105/174, pp. 278–79 (30 August 1649). On English interlopers into company monopolies, see Wood, *History of the Levant Company*, pp. 51–52.

34. PRO, SP 105/174, pp. 130–31.

35. PRO, SP 105/174, p. 197 (26 March 1649).

36. See chapter 4.

37. PRO, SP 105/174, pp. 229–30 (9 June 1649).

38. PRO, SP 105/174, pp. 261–63 (14 August 1649).

39. PRO, SP 105/174, p. 263 (15 August 1649).

40. PRO, SP 105/174, p. 286 (14 September 1649).

41. Most contemporaneous European commentators never understood (or chose not to understand) such provincial authority but preferred to display the

Ottoman state as paradigmatically despotic. See, for example, Paul Rycaut's *Present State of the Ottoman Empire* (London: John Starkey and Henry Brome, 1668, reprint, Westmead, England: Gregg International Publishers, 1972); and Linda Darling's discussion in "Ottoman Politics through British Eyes," pp. 71–97.

42. PRO, SP 105/174, p. 385 (25 March 1650).
43. PRO, SP 105/174, pp. 200–1 (7 February 1649).
44. PRO, SP 105/174, p. 210 (13 March 1649).
45. PRO, SP 105/174, pp. 210–11 (13 March 1649).
46. PRO, SP 105/174, pp. 228–29 (May–June 1649).
47. PRO, SP 105/174, pp. 375–76 (19 February 1650).
48. See chapter 9.
49. PRO, SP 105/174, pp. 454–55 (25 October [?] 1651).
50. PRO, SP 105/174, p. 455.
51. PRO, SP 105/174, pp. 493–94 (11 September 1651).
52. PRO, SP 105/174, p. 220 (20 April 1649).
53. PRO, SP 105/174, p. 404 (23 June 1650).
54. See chapter 7.
55. PRO, SP 150/174, p. 455 (2 May 1651).
56. See particularly Tenenti, *Piracy and the Decline of Venice*, pp. 16–31; and Braudel, *The Mediterranean*, especially vol. 2, pp. 886–91.
57. PRO, SP 105/174, p. 381 (11 March 1650).
58. PRO, SP 105/174, p. 396 (25 April 1650).

9 / THE SUBLIME PORTE, THE AMBASSADOR, AND THE PROVINCES

1. *CSP, Venice*, vol. 28, p. 49, no. 107 (Soranzo to Doge and Senate: 20 March 1648).
2. Bargrave, *Relation*, fo. 19ʳ. The Venetian *bailo* recounts that all of the English ships moved to the middle of the channel, "all their guns drawn in, the ports closed and a white flag at half mast" (*CSP, Venice*, vol. 28, p. 49, no. 107).
3. *CSP, Venice*, vol. 28, p. 67, no. 159 (Soranzo to Doge and Senate: 21 July 1648).
4. *CSP, Venice*, vol. 28, p. 67, no. 159.
5. *CSP, Venice*, vol. 28, p. 77, no. 194 (Soranzo to Doge and Senate: 13 October 1648); and PRO, SP 105/174, p. 145, doc. 2; and pp. 269–70.
6. PRO, SP 105/174, pp. 149–50.

Notes to pages 149–153

7. PRO, SP 105/174, pp. 150–51.
8. PRO, SP 105/174, pp. 161–62.
9. PRO, SP 105/174, p. 167. The factors were William Gough, James Modyford, William Pearle, John Abney, Samuel Pentlow, John South, John Erisey, and Jonathan Dawes.
10. BOA, ED 26, p. 44, no. 1.
11. BOA, ED 26, p. 79, no. 1.
12. PRO, SP 105/174, pp. 177–78 (24 January 1649).
13. See for example *CSP, Venice*, vol. 28, p. 67, no. 159; and vol. 28, p. 92, no. 249 (Soranzo to Doge and Senate: 22 March 1649).
14. *CSP, Venice*, vol. 28, p. 92, no. 249.
15. *CSP, Venice*, vol. 28, p. 96, no. 261 (Soranzo to Doge and Senate: 25 April 1649).
16. PRO, SP 105/174, pp. 266–67 (17 August 1649).
17. *CSP, Venice*, vol. 28, p. 98, no. 268 (Alberti, Venetian secretary at Istanbul, to Doge and Senate: 5 May 1649).
18. *CSP, Venice*, vol. 28, p. 98, no. 268.
19. *CSP, Venice*, vol. 28, pp. 112–13, no. 317 (Soranzo to Doge and Senate: 20 August 1649).
20. Bendysh (PRO, SP 105/174, pp. 220–22) reported that the Ottoman fleet left port on 21 April 1649; Soranzo (*CSP, Venice*, vol. 28, p. 98, no. 268) recorded that it did not depart until nine days later.
21. Bargrave, *Relation*, fo. 20^v. On the Ottoman naval yard (*tersane*) in Istanbul during the seventeenth century, see İdris Bostan, *Osmanlı bahriye teşkilâtı: XVII. yüzyılda tersâne-i âmire* (Ankara: Türk Tarih Kurumu Basımevi, 1992), especially pp. 7–13.
22. *CSP, Venice*, vol. 28, p. 100, no. 275 (Alberti and Vianuol, Venetian secretaries at Istanbul, to Doge and Senate: 19 May 1649).
23. *CSP, Venice*, vol. 28, p. 98, no. 268.
24. *CSP, Venice*, vol. 28, p. 99, no. 272 (Alberti and Vianuol to Doge and Senate: 15 May 1649).
25. *CSP, Venice*, vol. 28, p. 111, no. 312 (Soranzo to Doge and Senate: 31 July 1649).
26. *CSP, Venice*, vol. 28, p. 101, no. 278 (Venetian Senate to ambassador at Munster: 20 May 1649).
27. On which see İsmail Hakkı Uzunçarşılçı, *Osmanlı Tarihi*, vol. 3, pt. 1 (Ankara: Türk Tarih Kurumu Basımevi, 1951), pp. 247–49; and *CSP, Venice*, vol. 28, p. 100, no. 275 (Alberti and Vianuol to Doge and Senate: 19 May 1649).

28. *CSP, Venice,* vol. 28, p. 102, no. 282 (Alberti and Vianuol to Doge and Senate: 1 June 1649).

29. *CSP, Venice,* vol. 28, no. 325.

30. Bargrave, *Relation,* fo. 22ᵛ.

31. PRO, SP 105/174, pp. 266–67 (17 August 1649).

32. *CSP, Venice,* vol. 28, pp. 112–13, no. 317 (Soranzo to Doge and Senate: 20 August 1649).

33. Bargrave, *Relation,* fo. 18ᵛ.

34. *CSP, Venice,* vol. 28, pp. 112–13, no. 317.

35. *CSP, Venice,* vol. 28, p. 122, no. 343 (Soranzo to Doge and Senate: 17 October 1649).

36. *CSP, Venice,* vol. 28, p. 123, no. 347 (Contarini to Salvetti: 23 October 1649); p. 124, no. 350 (Mocenigo, Venetian general-at-sea, to Doge and Senate: 27 October 1649); p. 125, no. 355 (Salvetti to Contarini: 22 November 1649); and p. 142, no. 395 (Soranzo to Doge and Senate: 27 March 1650).

37. PRO, SP 105/174, pp. 380–81 (11 March 1650).

38. PRO, SP 97/17, fo. 23 (13 December 1649).

39. See chapter 7.

40. PRO, SP 105/174, pp. 220–22 (27 April 1649). Those who lodged the complaint were John Dodington, William Peters, William Aylosse, Samuel Rogers, Thomas Campion, John Tye, Anthony Isaakson (who, a decade later, was to become Ambassador Winchelsea's personal secretary and serve briefly as consul in Izmir), Thomas Mabbs, Thomas Bunten, and Nicholas Hobart.

41. PRO, SP 105/174, pp. 222–23 (29 and 30 April 1649).

42. *CSP, Venice,* vol. 28, p. 122, no. 343 (Soranzo to Doge and Senate: 17 October 1649).

10 / AN AMBASSADOR BESIEGED

1. PRO, SP 105/150, fo. 16ʳ.

2. PRO, SP 105/150, fo. 27ᵛ.

3. These included the Netherlands, Spain, France, Portugal, the Vatican, Russia, Sweden, Denmark, various Italian and German states, and even the Duchy of Courland. See Ronald Hutton, *Charles the Second, King of England, Scotland, and Ireland* (Oxford: Clarendon Press, 1989), p. 35. Hutton lists the names of most of these emissaries on p. 470n3.

4. Hutton, *Charles the Second,* pp. 53–60.

5. See Fissel and Goffman, "Viewing the Scaffold," p. 431.

6. Bargrave, *Relation*, fo. 31^v.

7. Perhaps, however, the fact that Edward was not on the spot supported Hyde's case, for he knew his nephew well. He later wrote to Charles II's adviser Edward Nicholas: "I hearde of the misfortune of poore Harry Hyde before your letter, and did not much wonder at it, for I thought from the beginninge it would fall out no otherwise, and did dissuade him from undertakinge so much, which I saw him inclined to, rather I thinke out of his owne vanity, then the persuasions of others, but he had so stronge a prejudice to Common lawyers, that he trusted me with little of his designes." See Clarendon MS 41, fo. 177^v (9 February 1651). My thanks to Mark Charles Fissel for this citation. Charles II may have ordered Edward Hyde to Spain more to remove himself from the domination of his father's most trusted advisor than in any real hope of aid from the Spaniards (see Ollard, *Image of the King*, p. 72).

8. BL, Egerton MS 2542, fo. 9.

9. BL, Egerton MS 2542, fo. 9.

10. BL, Egerton MS 2542, fo. 9.

11. *CSP, Venice*, vol. 28, p. 123, no. 345 (Venetian Senate to ambassador in France: 23 October 1649). Venice was careful not to offend the powers in England. On the same day it ordered this cooperation, it also granted the English Levant Company's request that three company ships be allowed to slip through the Venetian blockade of the Dardanelles. See chapter 9.

12. *CSP, Venice*, vol. 28, p. 126, no. 358 (Morosini, ambassador in France, to Doge and Senate: 23 November 1649).

13. Bodleian Library, Clarendon MS 39, fo. 122^{r-v}.

14. PRO, SP 105/151, fo. 26^v.

15. *CSP, Venice*, vol. 28, no. 317; and p. 126, no. 356 (Soranzo to Doge and Senate: 22 November 1649).

16. Bargrave, *Relation*, fos. 14–16. On the occasion of the drowning of Bendysh's son, Bargrave, who seems to have fancied himself a renaissance man in the tradition of George Sandys (see Jonathan Haynes, *The Humanist as Traveler: George Sandys's 'Relation of a Journey begun An: Dom: 1610'* [Rutherford: Farleigh Dickinson University Press, 1986]), composed a poem from which come the following couplets:

> To His Lordship Sr. Tho: Bendyshe Ambassador, &c, & to his virtuous Lady:
>
> Art, Witt, & Nature, fallen at Strife, / which had most interess in the life / of your priz'd Sonn; at last agree / their Debts were payd with Usury: / confessing what they barely lent / Hee had enriched with

Ornament / Now let them change their Theme, & All / strive for Interess in his Fall! / The Wreath of Beyes (above her head) / ready to crown Art's, withered / Desert Witt is faine to rome, / banish'd now its dearest home: / and Nature (now to seek for One) / has lost, in him, her Paragon: [15^r] / Virtue is in Summe despoil'd / of hers, in this your oldest Child. / Is there a Hart, or be there Eyes / can see this & not sympathize? / Can Such news arrive the Ears / of any, & produce no tears? / Lives there a man so void of Sence, / on whom this has not Influence? / to heare this direfull dolefull Sound / (and be himself) Squire bendyshe drownd?

17. He had left England with five daughters. One was married in Italy in 1647; I do not know what became of the other two.

18. On this dispute, see Daniel Goffman, "The Ottoman Role in Patterns of Commerce in Aleppo, Chios, Dubrovnik, and Istanbul, 1620–1650," in *Decision Making and Change in the Ottoman Empire,* ed. Caesar E. Farah (Kirksville, Missouri: Thomas Jefferson University Press, 1993), pp. 139–48.

19. PRO, SP 105/174, pp. 397–99.

20. PRO, SP 110/55, p. 5 (Bendysh to nation of Aleppo: 20 November 1650).

21. PRO, SP 97/17, fos. 38–42. This is the principal source for the following account of Bendysh's encounter with Hyde, a more exhaustive discussion of which is in Fissel and Goffman, "Viewing the Scaffold," pp. 435–40. On Giorgio Draperis's role in the events of 1646, see chapter 6. On Bendysh's battulation against him, see chapter 8.

22. Bargrave, *Relation,* fo. 32^v; and PRO, SP 97/17, fo. 38. Hyde claimed also to possess a letter from Charles appointing him consul in Izmir.

23. Apparently, only Perkett Senior, South, Howe, Davies, Frampton, Haggett, Molteah, and Perkett Junior refused (see PRO, SP 97/17, fo. 39). Among these, Frampton and Haggett had three years earlier supported Bendysh against Crow.

24. Bargrave, *Relation,* fo. 32^v.

25. How incongruous it would have seemed had the exiled king, destitute and soon to be bouncing from German state to German state like the proverbial wandering Jew, found refuge with the terrible Turk!

26. Bargrave, *Relation,* fo. 32^v.

27. See chapter 8.

28. PRO, SP 97/17, fo. 40.

29. Bargrave, *Relation,* fo. 33^r.

30. Bargrave, *Relation,* fo. 32^v.

31. PRO, SP 105/174, p. 418 (25 May 1650). These three men, it seems clear, were the ambassador's most loyal supporters.

32. PRO, SP 97/17, fo. 41. This must be the same Paul Haggatt whom, in the previous year, Bendysh had trusted enough to send to Izmir on a similar mission (see chapter 8). Haggatt's dramatic switch of alliance indicates the shock of the regicide upon these Englishmen, or perhaps merely their fickleness or rapaciousness.

33. As reported by Sagredo from Germany. See *CSP, Venice,* vol. 28, p. 154, no. 422 (Sagredo, Venetian ambassador in Germany, to Doge and Senate: 3 September 1650).

34. Charles II was as notoriously cynical about his religion as Charles I had been ardent. See Ollard, *Image of the King,* pp. 103–14.

35. Those English factors of Izmir who supported Hyde were said to have been Pixley, Lancelot, Alway, Meyer, Newsam, Newsom, Hawthorne, Gainsford, Wyual, Vesey, Bayly, Davis, Man, and Jolly (See PRO, SP 97/17, fo. 41).

36. Hyde's sensational expulsions from Istanbul and Izmir, and his trial and execution in London, receive more thorough attention in Fissel and Goffman, "Viewing the Scaffold."

37. PRO, SP 105/174, p. 408.

38. PRO, SP 97/17, fo. 31.

39. PRO, SP 97/17, fo. 31.

40. PRO, SP 97/17, fo. 33 (3 August 1650).

41. The others were John Pixley, Samuel Davis, John Vizey, Walter Newsam, Marmaduke Wival, James Moyer, William Muey, Nicholas Gainsford, Samuell Joyly, Adrian Death, William Bayley, Thomas Hathorne, and Hemend News. See PRO, SP 97/17, fo. 37 (7 August 1650).

42. PRO, SP 97/17, fo. 44.

43. PRO, SP 97/17, fo. 55.

44. *Calendar of State Papers, Commonwealth,* 1651, vol. 3, p. 14. A more detailed account of this incident, with further citations, is in Fissel and Goffman, "Viewing the Scaffold," pp. 440–47.

45. John Hinde, *A True Copy of Sir Henry Hide's Speech on the Scaffold Immediately before his Execution before the Exchange, on the 4th of March, 1650. Taken in Short-hand from his mouth* (London: Peter Cole, 1651), p. 10. The frontispiece of this pamphlet is reproduced in Goffman, *Izmir and the Levantine World.*

46. PRO, SP 105/151, fos. 61^v–62^r.

47. On these grand viziers, see İsmail Hami Danişmend, *İzahlı Osmanlı Tarihi Kronolojisi,* 2d ed., vol. 5 (Istanbul: Türkiye Yayınevi, 1971), p. 38; and Uzunçarşılı, *Osmanlı Tarihi,* pp. 245–52. On Melek Ahmed Pasha's life and personality, see Dankoff's translation into English of pertinent passages from Evliya Çelebi's *Seyahatname* in *Intimate Life of an Ottoman Statesman.*

48. PRO, SP 97/17, fo. 35.
49. Bargrave, *Relation,* fo. 32^v.
50. PRO, SP 97/17, fos. 57–58 (14 January 1651).
51. Bargrave, *Relation,* fo. 34^v; and PRO, SP 97/17, fos. 57–58.
52. Bargrave, *Relation,* fo. 35^v.
53. Bargrave, *Relation,* fo. 35^{r-v}.
54. Bargrave, *Relation,* fo. 35^v.
55. Bargrave, *Relation,* fo. 36^r.
56. Bargrave, *Relation,* fo. 37^r.
57. Bargrave, *Relation,* fo. 37^r. See also PRO, SP 97/17, fos. 57–58.
58. Bargrave, *Relation,* fo. 38^{r-v}. The diarist also composed a song to commemorate the English triumph:

Upon Mr. Dawes his & my Release from our Imprisonment
in Smirna Castle Anno: 1650

Fortunes wheele is runn about, / & has kindly turn'd us out, to / scourge the Renegado Rout: / Sr. Janifed (1) & Mendax (2) know / We for the witless Envy vow, / to bang yee to repentance now: / That you both may see, we now are free, / in fright of the Ballukgi=bassi (3)

(1) Janifed, one Hoow a licencious Papist & (2) Mendax, one South, a notorious lier who both were the chief Procurers of our Sufferings, & (3) Ballukgi=Bassi, Cape of the Ballukgi's, a term of disgrace by wch frenchmen are call'd

Verse: 2^d

Recall those wrongs that we endur'd / when with Theeves & Rogues secur'd / in the Stocks, by you procur'd! / And look yee when our angry feet / with either of your britches meet, / that theyr revenge be full & Sweet. / And then yee shall see, that we are free &c.^{a}

Ve:3^d.

Fr: Amb:

Those Impes your Ape=fac'd master sent / to see us tortur'd as we went / declare Good S^{rs}, your kind Intent: / But Officious [Stevens] doubting of his Pay / for his good service on the way / has made it sure unto a day (in the pomp Chaines) / And you all shall see, that we &c.^{a}

The Double Fetters that we wore / and all those Iniuries we bore / from your Smirna Pescadore [French Consul], / Your empty purse & adle Braines / may soon repent, when heavier Chaines / more iustly may reward your Paines. / And then yee shall see &c.ᵃ

The Rope wherein they bound & drew / us rudely through the publique vieu / like arrant Rogues, or elce like you; / take heed yet ner' be led therein / by Derick, to bewaile your Sinn / upon / his fatall Triple Gin! [Tiburne] / And there to see &c.ᵃ

But above all the dismall Cave / where we were layd, black as the Grave / or Hell, some due Revenge must have: / Which having fool'd your selves away, / tis like that Yee in Kind will pay, / & both (All) succeed us where we lay: / when the world shall see, what [pi?]tards yee be / to trust to your Ballukgibassi.

59. *CSP, Venice*, vol. 28, p. 159, no. 433 (Sieur de la Haye to Doge and Senate: November 1650); and Bargrave, *Relation*, fo. 40^r.

60. *CSP, Venice*, vol. 28, p. 159, no. 433.

11 / THE COMMONWEALTH AND THE LEVANT

1. PRO, SP 105/151, fo. 39^v (21 August 1650); and fos. 41^v–42^r (4 October 1650).
2. PRO, SP 105/174, p. 425.
3. PRO, SP 105/174, pp. 445–46 (24 January 1651).
4. PRO, SP 105/174, pp. 437–38.
5. PRO, SP 97/17, fos. 57–58.
6. PRO, SP 105/151, fos. 47^v–48^r. There were two "engagements" made during the 1640s. One was the agreement between Charles I and the Scots in late 1647 for a Scottish army in return for suppression of the many anti-Presbyterian sects then emerging in England. Here the reference is to another "engagement," the Oath of Engagement of 1649, which stated: "I do declare and promise that I will be true and faithful to the Commonwealth of England as the same is now established, without a King or House of Lords" (see Antonia Fraser, *Cromwell: The Lord Protector* [New York: Donald I. Fine, 1973], p. 297).
7. PRO, SP 105/151, fo. 49^{r-v}.
8. See Capp, *Cromwell's Navy*, pp. 73–114.
9. PRO, SP 97/17, fo. 64 (1 March 1651).
10. Bargrave, *Relation*, fo. 20^v.
11. PRO, SP 105/150, fo. 51^r.

12. PRO, SP 105/151, fo. 51ʳ.
13. PRO, SP 97/17, fo. 65.
14. PRO, SP 97/17, fo. 74.
15. PRO, SP 97/17, fo. 76.
16. PRO, SP 105/151, fos. 58ᵛ–59ʳ.
17. PRO, SP 105/174, pp. 481–82 (29 July 1651).
18. PRO, SP 97/17, fo. 66.

19. On whom, see Naima, *Tarih-i Naima,* vol. 5, pp. 64–68; and Uzunçarşılı, *Osmanlı Tarihi,* pp. 468–69. Fissel and I have written on this incident from a slightly different angle in "Viewing the Scaffold," pp. 445–46. There is also a brief biography of Bahai Mehmed in İsmail Hami Danişmend, *Osmanlı Devlet Erkani* (Istanbul: n.p., 1971), p. 532. On this incident, see also Madeline C. Zilfi, *The Politics of Piety: The Ottoman Ulema in the Postclassical Age (1600–1800)* (Minneapolis: Bibliotheca Islamica, 1988), pp. 150–51, and 178n87.

20. PRO, SP 97/17, fo. 66.

21. Naima, *Tarih-i Naima,* vol. 5, pp. 64–68. For Bendysh's report on the episode, see PRO, SP 97/17, fo. 66. This is perhaps the only incident involving Bendysh upon which Ottoman chroniclers report.

22. A lieutenant governor. The document reads "keyaubey."

23. PRO, SP 97/17, fo. 66.

24. PRO, SP 105/174, pp. 481–82.

25. PRO, SP 105/174, pp. 490–92 (12 September 1651). For Abney's rambling defense, see PRO, SP 105/174, pp. 487–89 (5 September 1651).

26. PRO, SP 105/174, p. 501 (11 November 1651).

27. Bargrave, *Relation,* fos. 19ᵛ–20ʳ. See also PRO, SP 97/17, fo. 70 (22 December 1651).

28. *CSP, Venice,* vol. 28, pp. 211–12, no. 554 (Salvetti to Morosini: 12 January 1652). See also PRO, SP 105/150, fo. 53ʳ⁻ᵛ.

29. PRO, SP 105/151, fos. 68ʳ (17 October 1651) and 69ʳ (30 October 1651).

30. *CSP, Venice,* vol. 29, p. 10, no. 12 (Paulucci to Sagredo in France: 17 January 1653).

31. PRO, SP 105/151, fo. 69ᵛ (10 November 1651).

32. *CSP, Venice,* vol. 29, p. 55, no. 77 (Paulucci to Sagredo: 12 April 1653).

33. See chapter 6.

34. PRO, SP 105/151, fo. 69ᵛ.

35. PRO, SP 105/151, fo. 72ʳ⁻ᵛ and 78–79ʳ.

36. PRO, SP 105/174, p. 513. Bendysh had two sons—John and Andrew—who remained in the Levant after his recall. It is sometimes difficult to

ascertain which one was doing what, for they both seem to have been referred to as "Bendysh the younger."

37. PRO, SP 105/150, fos. 83^v–84^r. The other nominees were Spencer Bretton, Henry Elsing, and a Mr. Harington.
38. PRO, SP 105/151, fos. 85^v–86^r.
39. This incident is described in PRO, SP 105/151, fos. 90^r–91^r.
40. PRO, SP 105/151, fo. 91^v.
41. On which see Fissel, "Law and Authority."
42. PRO, SP 105/151, fo. 93^{r-v} (21 January 1653).
43. PRO, SP 105/151, fo. 93^{r-v}.
44. See chapter 8.
45. PRO, SP 105/151, fos. 100^r and 100^v. The second document states that the company ordered Lawrence's departure on 8 September; his arrival in March, however, proves that statement to be an error.
46. Bodleian Library, Tanner MS 52, fo. 35 (16 August 1653). See also Wood, *History of the Levant Company*, pp. 93–94.
47. Bodleian Library, Tanner MS 52, fos. 37^{r-v} (to the grand vizier) and 39^{r-v} (to the sultan).
48. Bodleian Library, Rawlinson MS A.12, pp. 105–6.
49. Bodleian Library, Rawlinson MS A.12, pp. 105–6.
50. Bodleian Library, Rawlinson MS A.12, pp. 105–6.
51. See, as examples, Bodleian Library, Rawlinson MS A.261, fos. 38^{r-v} (25 March 1654) and 16^{r-v} (14 August 1654); and John Thurloe, *A Collection of the State Papers of John Thurloe* (hereafter *Thurloe State Papers*) (London: n.p., 1742), vol. 2, p. 716 (7 November 1654) and p. 742 (26 November 1654).
52. PRO, SP 105/151, fos. 122^r, 123^r, 124^r, and 124^v.
53. PRO, SP 105/151, fo. 145^{r-v}.
54. Bodleian Library, Rawlinson MS A.30, p. 379.
55. *Thurloe State Papers*, vol. 2, pp. 716 and 742.
56. Bodleian Library, Rawlinson MS A.37, p. 238.
57. Bodleian Library, Rawlinson MS A.261, fos. 38^r–39^r.
58. Bodleian Library, Tanner MS 285, fo. 145 (Herbert Ashley of Leghorn to John Hobart: 20 June 1654).
59. PRO, SP 105/151, fo. 109^v.
60. Bodleian Library, Rawlinson MS A.261, fo. 14^{r-v} (14 August 1654).
61. PRO, SP 105/151, fo. 120^{r-v}.
62. PRO, SP 105/151, fos. 109^v–110^r.
63. *CSP, Venice*, vol. 29, p. 92, no. 124 (Paulucci to Sagredo: 4 July 1653).

64. *CSP, Venice*, vol. 29, p. 177, no. 214 (Paulucci to Sagredo: 31 January 1654).

65. For a brief discussion of the Western Design, and particularly of Sweden (but not the Ottoman Empire) as an alternative to it, see Pincus, "England and the World," pp. 139–46. See also Karen Ordahl Kupperman, "Errand to the Indies: Puritan Colonization of Providence Island through the Western Design," *William and Mary Quarterly* 45 (1988): 88–99.

66. Bodleian Library, Rawlinson MS A.31, pp. 13–15. See also *CSP, Venice*, vol. 30, pp. 159–60 (Sagredo, Venetian ambassador in England, to Doge and Senate: 31 December 1655).

67. Bodleian Library, Rawlinson MS A.31, pp. 13–15.

12 / UNIFORMITY RESTORED

1. These correspondences are in the Rawlinson Collection of the Bodleian Library. They were collected and published with many other letters in *Thurloe State Papers*.
2. Bodleian Library, Rawlinson MS A.32, p. 33.
3. Peirce, *The Imperial Harem*.
4. Bodleian Library, Rawlinson MS A.32, p. 33.
5. Bodleian Library, Rawlinson MS A.47, fo. 213^r.
6. Bodleian Library, Rawlinson MS A.47, fo. 213^r.
7. *Thurloe State Papers*, vol. 6, pp. 699–702.
8. Bodleian Library, Rawlinson MS A.37, p. 391.
9. PRO, SP 105/109, fo. 203 (Cromwell to Sultan: 11 August 1657).
10. *Thurloe State Papers*, vol. 6, pp. 406–7 and 429.
11. PRO, SP 105/109, fo. 203; and PRO, SP 105/151, fo. 158^{r-v}.
12. Bodleian Library, Rawlinson MS A.43, pp. 233–34.
13. PRO, SP 105/175, fo. 4.
14. PRO, SP 105/175, fos. 4^v–5^r.
15. PRO, SP 105/175, fo. 5.
16. PRO, SP 105/175, fo. 7.
17. PRO, SP 105/175, fo. 7 (25 August 1656).
18. PRO, SP 105/175, fo. 8^r.
19. R. C. Anderson, "The First Dutch War in the Mediterranean," *Mariner's Mirror* 49 (1963): 249n1.
20. Bodleian Library, Rawlinson MS A.43, pp. 233–34; and PRO, SP 105/151, fo. 158^{r-v}.

21. PRO, SP 105/151, fo. 159^v.
22. *Thurloe State Papers*, vol. 6, p. 584 (Longland to Thurloe: 9 November 1657).
23. *Thurloe State Papers*, vol. 6, pp. 612–13 (Longland to Thurloe: 23 November 1657).
24. *CSP, Venice*, vol. 31, p. 190, no. 165 (Monsieur de Meaulx to Ballerino: 11 April 1658).
25. Bodleian Library, Rawlinson MS A.38, p. 179.
26. Bodleian Library, Rawlinson MS A.38, pp. 179–80.
27. Bodleian Library, Rawlinson MS A.256, fos. 557–58.
28. PRO, SP 105/151, fo. 168^r.
29. PRO, SP 105/151, fo. 172^r.
30. *CSP, Venice*, vol. 31, p. 190, no. 165 (Monsieur de Meaulx to Ballerino: 11 April 1658). What must it have been like for two English girls to grow up in Istanbul during that time!
31. *CSP, Venice*, vol. 32, pp. 123–24, no. 123 (Ballarino, secretary at the Porte, to Doge and Senate).
32. *CSP, Venice*, vol. 32, p. 154, no. 154 (Ballarino to Doge and Senate: 10 June 1660).
33. *CSP, Venice*, vol. 32, p. 38, no. 37 (Giavarina to Doge and Senate).
34. PRO, SP 105/151, fo. 193^r.
35. PRO, SP 105/151, fos. 193^v–194^r.
36. PRO, SP 105/151, fo. 194^r.
37. On whom see particularly Skilliter, *William Harborne and the Trade with Turkey*.
38. BL, Stowe MS 744, fo. 44. At this same time, the company appointed Robert Bargrave company secretary at a salary of six hundred pounds per year. He never assumed his posting, however, for he caught a fever and died in Izmir, where he had first set foot in the Ottoman Empire some dozen years earlier (see Anderson, *An English Consul in Turkey*, pp. 25–26).
39. BL, Stowe MS 744, fos. 42, 48.
40. BL, Stowe MS 744, fo. 52 (4 October 1660).
41. BL, Egerton MS 2542, fo. 439^v.
42. BL, Egerton MS 2542, fo. 439^v.
43. BL, Egerton MS 2537, fos. 19 (Charles II to Bendysh: 28 September 1660), 154–55 (Charles II to Grand Vizier: 25 August 1660), and 156 (Charles II to Sultan: 25 August 1660).
44. Bodleian Library, Rawlinson MS B.516, fos. 42–72.

45. On which see PRO, SP 105/151, fos. 195^{r-v} and 196^v.
46. Bodleian Library, Rawlinson MS B.516, fos. 52–53.
47. *CSP, Venice*, vol. 32, p. 180, no. 194 (Ballarino to Doge and Senate).
48. *CSP, Venice*, vol. 32, p. 192, no. 208 (Giavarina to Doge and Senate: 3 September 1660).
49. *CSP, Venice*, vol. 32, p. 234, no. 259 (Ballarino to Doge and Senate: 3 January 1661).
50. *CSP, Venice*, vol. 32, p. 238, no. 266 (Ballarino to Doge and Senate: 15 January 1661); p. 256, no. 293 (Ballarino to Doge and Senate: 6 March 1661); and p. 278, no. 322 (Capello to Doge and Senate: 16 April 1661).
51. PRO, SP 105/109, fo. 210.
52. PRO, SP 105/175, fos. 38^r–39^v.
53. PRO, SP 105/175, fo. 39^v.
54. PRO, SP 105/175, fo. 44 (19 August 1661).
55. PRO, SP 97/17, fo. 209^r.
56. PRO, SP 105/152, fo. 19^v.
57. PRO, SP 105/152, fo. 19^v.
58. PRO, SP 97/17, fos. 229^v and 234^r. It was rumored that he had been murdered before even departing Izmir (see PRO, SP 105/152, fo. 25^r).
59. PRO, SP 105/152, fo. 73^{r-v}. They were Joseph Edwards, Arnold White, Adam Edwards, Samuel Pentlow, Alexander Myers, Arthur Barnardiston, Jo. Foley, Charles Edwards, Rich. Onslow, Robert Mellish, Geo. Carew, Samuel Boscowen, Thomas Barnardiston Sr., Samuel Reynardson, Charles Brandon, Tho. Lucy Jr., Weymouth Carew, Arthur Jones, Tho. Farington, John Weld, Wm. Fanshaw, Andrew Bendish, Wm. Mellish, Dudley North, Nathaniel Thurston, John Markham, Edward Allen, and Barnard Saltonstall.
60. His letters are preserved in PRO, SP 97/18.
61. PRO, SP 105/113, fo. 4^r (22 January 1663).
62. PRO, SP 105/113, fos. 12^{r-v} (Company to Winchelsea: 10 April 1663) and 13^v (Company to Consul Lannoy at Aleppo: 13 April 1663).
63. On this episode, see Anderson, *An English Consul in Turkey*, pp. 34–36.
64. PRO, SP 105/113, fos. 25^v–27^v (16 September 1663) and 33^r (23 December 1663).
65. PRO, SP 105/113, fos. 39^v–40^r (Company to Winchelsea: 14 March 1664); and PRO, SP 105/152, fo. 117^r (minutes of the company's Court of Assistants: 11 October 1664).
66. Bodleian Library, Clarendon MS 73, fos. 4^r–5^r.
67. Ollard, *Image of the King*, pp. 129–38.

68. Bodleian Library, Tanner MS 41, fo. 23.
69. PRO, SP 105/152, fo. 18^r.
70. PRO, SP 105/152, fos. 31^v–32^r (5 May 1662). This was the same gentleman who had shared Bargrave's misadventures in Istanbul and Izmir (see chapter 9).
71. PRO, SP 105/152, fos. 39^r and 51^{r-v}.
72. PRO, SP 105/152, fo. 51^{r-v}.
73. PRO, SP 105/152, fos. 94^v–96^r. Or was this his other son, John? Wood (*History of the Levant Company*, pp. 79 and 124) refers to him simply as "the younger Bendysh." A third son, it will be recalled, drowned in 1647.
74. PRO, SP 105/152, fos. 94^v–96^r.
75. BL, Additional MS 40,711, fo. 34^v.
76. BL, Additional MS 40,711, fo. 34^v.
77. BL, Additional MS 40,700, fo. 135.

13 / DOMESTIC POLITICS AND WORLDS OVERSEAS

1. Nagai Kafu, "Twilight in the Mediterranean," in *Modern Asia and Africa*, eds. William H. McNeill and Mitsuko Iriye (New York: Oxford University Press, 1971), p. 169.
2. See, for example, Pocock, "British History," pp. 601–28; Bailyn and Morgan, *Strangers within the Realm;* and, from a colonial perspective, Merrell, *The Indians' New World*, and White, *Middle Ground*.
3. For examples, see the works not only of such British writers as E. M. Forster, Graham Green, and Joseph Conrad but also of such postcolonialists as R. K. Narayan, V. S. Naipaul, and Chinua Achebe. For a comparison of these writers, see M. M. Mahood, *The Colonial Encounter: A Reading of Six Novels* (Totowa, New Jersey: Rowman and Littlefield, 1977), especially pp. 166–91. Also striking for their polycultural insights are immigrant writers. Particularly striking in contemporary America are the works of authors such as Maxine Hong Kingston and Bharati Mukherjee. The very field of postcolonial studies is defined in terms of such encounters, on which see Bill Ashcroft, Gareth Griffiths, and Helen Tiffin, *The Empire Writes Back: Theory and Practice in Post-Colonial Literatures* (London: Routledge, 1989); and Vijay Mishra and Bob Hodge, "What is Post(-)colonialism?" in *Colonial Discourse and Post-Colonial Theory: A Reader*, eds. Patrick Williams and Laura Chrisman (New York: Columbia University Press, 1994), pp. 276–90. On its limitations and deceptions, at least in the field of literature, see D. A. Shankar's short and

provocative piece, "The Absence of Caste in R. K. Narayan and Its Implications for Indian Writing in English," in *R. K. Narayan: Contemporary Critical Perspectives,* ed. Geoffrey Kain (East Lansing: Michigan State University Press, 1993), pp. 49–70; and Salman Rushdie's prescient "'Commonwealth Literature' Does Not Exist," in *Imaginary Homelands: Essays and Criticism 1981–1991* (New York: Penguin Books, 1991), pp. 61–70.

4. In his *The Samurai,* trans. Van C. Gessel (New York: Random House, 1982), p. 233. Endo's character compares Spain and Japan as follows: "'The buildings of Nueva España and España were all brightly lit by the sun. They weren't anything like this castle. Everybody smiled when they talked. But here we can't talk as we want or smile as we want. We don't even know where His Lordship is.' Nishi gave a deep sigh. 'So long as we are alive, there is no escaping this darkness.'"

5. George Orwell, "Shooting an Elephant," in *Shooting an Elephant and Other Essays* (New York: Harcourt, Brace, 1945), pp. 3–12.

6. See Paul Theroux, *The Old Patagonian Express* (Boston: Houghton Mifflin, 1978); and V. S. Naipaul, *Among the Believers: An Islamic Journey* (New York: Knopf, 1981). An important analysis of how such literature has reinvented the world for its readers is that of Mary Louise Pratt, *Imperial Eyes: Travel Writing and Transculturation* (London: Routledge, 1992). Her discussion of Theroux's *Old Patagonian Express* is on pp. 216–21.

7. See his and Edwin Van Kley's multivolume and encyclopedic *Asia in the Making of Europe* (Chicago: University of Chicago Press, 1965–93). A recent study of the impact of the Americas upon the European mind, much in the same mold, is that of Karen Ordahl Kupperman (ed.), *America in European Consciousness, 1493–1750* (Chapel Hill: University of North Carolina Press, 1995).

8. See, for example, Haynes, *Humanist as Traveler,* and Ralph Hattox's review of Haynes's book in *Turkish Studies Association Bulletin* 13 (1989): 117–22; and Brandon H. Beck, *From the Rising of the Sun: English Images of the Ottoman Empire to 1715* (New York: Peter Lang, 1987), along with Rhoads Murphey's review of that and other books, "Bigots or Informed Observers? A Periodization of Pre-Colonial English and European Writing on the Middle East," *Journal of the American Oriental Society* 110 (1990): 291–303.

9. On the early East India Company, see K. N. Chaudhuri, *The English East India Company: The Study of an Early Joint-Stock Company 1600–1640* (London: Frank Cass and Company, 1965). On its contextual role in the Indian Ocean, see his *Trade and Civilisation in the Indian Ocean: An Economic*

History from the Rise of Islam to 1750 (Cambridge: Cambridge University Press, 1985).

10. K. N. Chaudhuri, "The World-System East of Longitude 20°: The European Role in Asia, 1500–1750," *Review* 5 (1981): 219–45.
11. See Morrill, *Reactions to the English Civil War.*
12. Bodleian Library, Clarendon MS 46, fos. 73^r–74^r.
13. Bodleian Library, Clarendon MS 46, fo. 73^r. Presumably the Book of Common Prayer, which parliament had banned as part of its anti-Anglican campaign.
14. Bodleian Library, Clarendon MS 46, fo. 73^v.
15. Bodleian Library, Clarendon MS 46, fo. 74^r.
16. See, for example, BOA, ED 13/1, p. 114, no. 1; and ED 14/2, pp. 144–45, 145–46, and 146, no. 1.
17. BOA, ED 26, pp. 38, no. 1; and 59, no. 1. In a curious episode, the Ottoman government also tried to frustrate the export to western Europe of Christian artifacts when, in 1656, the Greek Patriarch accused "Frankish monks" of stealing statuary from the home of the Virgin Mary in Jerusalem and carrying it off to Europe (see BOA, ED 26, p. 88, no. 1).
18. Bodleian Library, Clarendon MS 63, fo. 231^{r-v}.
19. BOA, ED 13/1, p. 14, no. 1.
20. BOA, ED 13/1, p. 16, no. 2.
21. BL, Additional MS 32,094, fo. 210 (18 February 1667); and fo. 214 (19 August 1668).
22. Anonymous, *The History of his Sacred Majesty Charles the II. King of England, Scotland, France and Ireland, Defender of the Faith, &c. (by a Person of Quality)* (London, 1660), p. 88. On the events leading to Hyde's beheading, see Fissel and Goffman, "Viewing the Scaffold."

Glossary

I have tried to minimize the use of Ottoman terms in this book. Although the few that seemed unavoidable are defined contextually, this glossary provides an additional guide. As much as possible, the terms are defined according to their seventeenth-century meanings rather than their current ones.

Seventeenth-century English spellings, even of English words, were variable. The orthography of unfamiliar words can be nightmarish, and Ottoman terms occur in many forms, sometimes tortuous, in the passages quoted in this book (for example, kadi appears as "cadee," "caddee," and "caddie"). In order to impose some order, both in the text (when it seemed necessary) and in this glossary I have provided the modern Turkish orthography of such terms, as spelled in the *New Redhouse Turkish-English Dictionary* (Istanbul: Redhouse Press, 1968), where Ottoman spellings in the Arabic alphabet also are shown.

ağa. Honorific title given to officers, often janissaries.
ahdname. A letter of agreement, of which the capitulations are a specific example; the English used theirs as a principal statement of position in the Ottoman Empire.
akçe. A silver coin, also known as an asper; the basic monetary unit in the Ottoman Empire; notoriously unstable in the seventeenth century.
arz. A petition; used to appeal to the Sublime Porte in grievances.
ayan. Important persons in a town or community; notables.
avania. A fine imposed by the Ottomans upon foreigners or foreign trading companies. Foreigners considered the fine extortionary.

bacdarlık. Position of collector of tolls.
balukbaşı. In this context, synonymous with *çavuş* (q.v.).
berat. Title of privilege or certificate of appointment.
beylerbeyi. Governor of the largest administrative unit in the Ottoman Empire.
bostancı. Member of the imperial guards, powerful particularly in the city of Istanbul.
çavuş. Imperial messenger; often granted extraordinary authority on a particular issue.
defterdarbaşı. Chief of the ministry of finance; sat on the imperial divan.
emin. A head in the Ottoman bureaucracy; often refers to the collector of customs with whom an English factory dealt.
fetva. A written opinion issued by the *şeyhülislam* (q.v).
gavur. A non-Muslim, often a Christian; an epithet similar perhaps to "infidel swine."
gümrük emini. An official who collected customs, particularly on goods loaded unto ships.
hamal. Porter; day laborer.
hatt-i şerif. Also known as a *hattı hümayun;* an imperial decree.
hisar ağası. Commander of an Ottoman castle or fortress.
hüccet-i şerif. A certificate or title-deed.
kadiasker (kazasker). Second most important religious functionary in the Ottoman Empire; in the seventeenth century, there were two: one for the European provinces and a second for the Anatolian provinces; they held seats in the imperial divan.
kapıcıbaşı. The head of the *kapıcı*s, high Ottoman functionaries who, among other duties, served as the conduits between the public and private worlds of the imperial residence.
kapudanpaşa. Commander of the Ottoman fleet; member of the imperial divan.
kayık. A boat similar but not identical to the rowboat found on European vessels; often used to ferry people within Ottoman cities and to place contraband aboard ships.
kaymakam. Often a substitute for or representative of an Ottoman official.
mahalle. Quarter or district in a town or city.

millet. A non-Muslim community in the Ottoman Empire; before the nineteenth century, there were three: Armenian, Greek Orthodox, and Jewish.
müste'min. A foreigner residing in an Islamic state; all members of the English nation in the Ottoman Empire held this status.
naib. Assistant to a kadi; often traveled to towns and villages lacking their own kadis.
okka. A weight of approximately 2.8 pounds.
serdar. Military chief.
şeyhülislam. Highest religious functionary in the Ottoman state; a political position whose possessor enjoyed a seat in the divan.
tezkere. Receipt; it was essential that a merchant possess one to prove that he had paid his duty.
ulema. Masters of Islamic jurisprudence.
valide sultan. Mother of the Ottoman sultan; often a towering political figure in the late sixteenth and seventeenth centuries.
voyvoda. A replacement for an Ottoman official.
voyvodalık. Station of a *voyvoda* (q.v.); often paid for in return for the power and authority of the post.
yasakçı. A guard for an ambassador or consul; a janissary appointed to personal service.

Bibliography

ARCHIVAL SOURCES CONSULTED

Başbakanlık Osmanlı Arşivi (Ottoman National Archives), Istanbul, Turkey
  Bab-i Asafi Dosyaları (Dossiers from the Bab-i Asafi), A.DVN 79–85
  Ecnebi Defterleri (Registers of Foreign Matters) 13/1, 14/1, 16/4, 26/1
  Kamil Kepeci Defterleri (Registers compiled by Kamil Kepeci) 72–73
  Maliyeden Müdevver Defterleri (Registers transferred from Finances) 6004, 23,308
  Mühimme Defterleri (Registers of Important Matters) 88–93
  Mühimme Zeyli Defterleri (Supplemental Registers of Important Matters) 10
  Şikayet Defterleri (Registers of Complaints) 1–4
Bodleian Library, Oxford, England
  Clarendon State Papers 29–31, 39, 45–46, 52–53, 57, 63, 73, 76–77, 81–83, 97, 105–8
  MS.Eng.hist.c.312
  MS.Eng.let.d.195
  MS.Eng.misc.e.218
  Rawlinson Manuscripts A.12, A.30–32, A.35, A.37–38, A.42–43, A.47, A.61–62, A.189, A.255–56, A.261, B.516, C.799 (Bargrave, Robert, *A Relation of Sundry Voyages & Journeys made by mee*), D.60, D.961, D.1483
  Tanner Manuscripts 41, 52, 60, 103, 285–86
British Library, London, England
  Additional Manuscripts 6115; 15,750; 15,759; 15,856; 22,910; 23,120; 28,942; 32,094; 40,700; 40,711
  Egerton Manuscripts 2533, 2537, 2541–42, 2647
  Sloan Manuscripts 867

Stowe Manuscripts 744
Public Record Office, London, England
State Papers 97/13–21; 105/109, 113, 143, 150–52, 174–75, 334; 110/54–55, 111

BOOKS AND ARTICLES CONSULTED

Abbott, George F. *Turkey, Greece and the Great Powers: A Study in Friendship and Hate.* New York: Robert M. McBride and Company, 1917.

Abu-El-Haj, Rifa'at Ali. *Formation of the Modern State: The Ottoman Empire, Sixteenth to Eighteenth Centuries.* Albany: State University of New York Press, 1992.

Achebe, Chinua. *No Longer at Ease.* New York: Random House, 1960.

Ahrweiler, Helene. "Istanbul, Carrefour des routes continentales et maritimes aux XVe–XIXe siècles." In *Istanbul à la jonction des cultures balkaniques, méditerranéennes, slaves et orientales, aux XVIe–XIXe siècles,* pp. 9–26. Bucharest: Association Internationale d'Etudes du Sud-est Européen, 1977.

Alberi, Eugenio, ed. *Relazione degli ambasciatori Veneti al Senato,* 3d ser., vol. 3. Florence: Società Editrice Fiorentine, 1838–63.

Ambrose, Gwylim. "English Traders at Aleppo (1658–1753)." *Economic History Review,* o.s. 3 (1931–32): 246–67.

Anderson, Benedict. *Imagined Communities: Reflections on the Origin and Spread of Nationalism.* London: Verso, 1983.

Anderson, Roger Charles. *Naval Wars in the Levant, 1559–1853.* Liverpool: University Press, 1952.

——— . "The First Dutch War in the Mediterranean." *Mariner's Mirror* 49 (1963): 242–65.

——— . *List of English Naval Captains, 1642–1660.* London: Society for Nautical Research, 1964.

Anderson, Sonia. *An English Consul in Turkey: Paul Rycaut at Smyrna, 1667–1678.* Oxford: Clarendon Press, 1989.

Andrews, Kenneth R. *Trade, Plunder and Settlement: Maritime Enterprise and the Genesis of the British Empire, 1480–1630.* Cambridge: Cambridge University Press, 1984.

Ankori, Zvi. "From Zudecha to Yahudi Mahallesi: The Jewish Quarter of Candia in the Seventeenth Century (A Chapter in the History of Cretan Jewry under Muslim Rule)." In *Salo Wittmayer Baron Jubilee Volume,* vol. 1, pp. 63–127. New York: Columbia University Press, 1975.

Anonymous. *The History of his Sacred Majesty Charles the II. King of England, Scotland, France and Ireland, Defender of the Faith, &c. (by a Person of Quality)*. London, 1660.

Arbel, Benjamin. *Trading Nations: Jews and Venetians in the Early Modern Eastern Mediterranean*. Leiden: E. J. Brill, 1995.

Arvieux, *Mémoires du Chevalier d', Envoyé Extraordinaire du Roy, etc*. Edited by J. B. Labat. Paris, 1735.

Ashcroft, Bill, Gareth Griffiths, and Helen Tiffin. *The Empire Writes Back: Theory and Practice in Post-Colonial Literatures*. London: Routledge, 1989.

Ashton, Robert. *Counter-Revolution: The Second Civil War and Its Origins, 1646–1648*. New Haven, Connecticut: Yale University Press, 1994.

Atay, M. Çınar. *Tarih içinde İzmir*. Izmir: Tifset Basım ve Yayın Sanayii, 1978.

Aymard, Maurice. "XVI. yüzyılın sonunda Akdeniz'de korsanlık ve Venedik." *İstanbul Üniversitesi İktisat Fakültesi Mecmuası* 23 (1962–63): 219–38.

Bağış, Ali İhsan. *Osmanlı ticaretinde gayri müslimler, kapitülasyonlar-beratlı tüccarlar, avrupa ve hayriye tüccarları (1750–1839)*. Ankara: Turhan Kitabı, 1983.

Bailyn, Bernard, and Philip D. Morgan, eds. *Strangers within the Realm: Cultural Margins of the First British Empire*. Chapel Hill: University of North Carolina Press, 1991.

Barkan, Ömer-Lûtfi. "Quelques observations sur l'organisation économique et sociale des villes Ottomanes des XVIe et XVIIe siècles." *Recueils de la Société Jean Bodin* 7 (1955): 289–310.

Barkey, Karen. "Rebellious Alliances: The State and Peasant Unrest in Early Seventeenth-Century France and the Ottoman Empire." *American Sociological Review* 56 (1991): 699–715.

———. *Bandits and Bureaucrats: The Ottoman Route to State Centralization*. Ithaca: Cornell University Press, 1994.

Başbakanlık osmanlı arşivi rehberi. Ankara: T. C. Başbakanlık Devlet Arşivileri Genel Müdürlüğü Osmanlı Arşivi Daire Başkanlığı, 1992.

Bashan, Eliezer. "Contacts between Jews in Smyrna and the Levant Company of London in the Seventeenth and Eighteenth Centuries." *Transactions of the Jewish Historical Society of England* 29 (1988): 53–73.

Baykara, Tuncer. *İzmir şehri ve tarihi*. Istanbul: Ege Üniversitesi Matbaası, 1974.

Beck, Brandon H. *From the Rising of the Sun: English Images of the Ottoman Empire to 1715*. New York: Peter Lang, 1987.

Bostan, İdris. *Osmanlı bahriye teşkilâtı: XVII. yüzyılda tersâne-i âmire.* Ankara: Türk Kurumu Basımevi, 1992.

Bracewell, Catherine Wendy. *The Uskoks of Senj: Piracy, Banditry, and Holy War in the Sixteenth-Century Adriatic.* Ithaca: Cornell University Press, 1992.

Braude, Benjamin. "International Competition and Domestic Cloth in the Ottoman Empire, 1500–1650: A Study in Undevelopment." *Review* 1 (1979): 437–54.

———. "Foundation Myths of the *Millet* System." In *Christians and Jews in the Ottoman Empire: The Functioning of a Plural Society,* vol. 1: *The Central Lands.* Edited by Benjamin Braude and Bernard Lewis, pp. 69–88. New York: Holmes and Meier, 1982.

Braudel, Fernand. *The Mediterranean and the Mediterranean World in the Age of Philip II.* Translated by Siân Reynolds. 2 vols. New York: Harper and Row, 1972.

———. *The Wheels of Commerce.* Vol. 2 of *Civilization and Capitalism, 15th–18th Century.* Translated by Siân Reynolds. New York: Harper and Row, 1982–84.

———. *The Perspective of the World.* Vol. 3 of *Civilization and Capitalism, 15th–18th Century.* Translated by Siân Reynolds. New York: Harper and Row, 1982–84.

Braudel, Fernand, and Ruggiero Romano. *Navires et marchandises à l'entrée du port de Livourne, 1547–1611.* Paris: A. Conlin, 1951.

Brenner, Robert. "The Civil War Politics of London's Merchant Community." *Past and Present* 58 (1973): 53–107.

———. *Merchants and Revolution: Commercial Change, Political Conflict, and London's Overseas Traders, 1550–1653.* Princeton, New Jersey: Princeton University Press, 1993.

A Brief Narrative and Vindication of Sir T. Bendish Knight and Baronet, Ambassador with the Grand Seigneur; in defence of himself, in the matter concerning Sr. Henry Hyde, for the said Embassy, who arrived at Constantinople the 9th of May, and departed for England about the end of August 1650. London: n.p., 1660.

A Brief of the State of the Case of Walter Elfords Complaint against Sr. Sackvile Crow, which is to be reported to the Parliament. Broadsheet, London, December 1649?

Brown, L. Carl, ed. *Imperial Legacy: The Ottoman Imprint on the Balkans and the Middle East.* New York: Columbia University Press, 1996.

Brummett, Palmira. *Ottoman Seapower and Levantine Diplomacy in the Age of Discovery.* Albany: State University of New York Press, 1994.
Buchan, John. *Greenmantle.* London: Holder and Stoughton, 1916.
Burke, John. *A Genealogical and Heraldic History of the Extinct and Dormant Baronetcies of England.* London, 1844.
Calendar of State Papers, Domestic (the Commonwealth). Edited by M. A. E. Green. London: Longman, 1875–86.
Calendar of State Papers, Domestic Series, of the Reign of Charles I, 1625–1649. Edited by John Bruce. London: Longman, 1858–97.
Calendar of State Papers and Manuscripts Relating to English Affairs Existing in the Archives and Collections of Venice, and in Other Libraries of Northern Italy. Edited by Rawdon Brown. London: Longman, 1864–1947.
Capp, Bernard. *Cromwell's Navy: The Fleet and the English Revolution, 1648–1660.* Oxford: Clarendon Press, 1989.
Carlton, Charles. *Charles I: The Personal Monarch.* 2d ed. London: Routledge, 1995.
Çetin, Atilla. *Başbakanlık arşivi kılavuzu.* Istanbul: Enderun Kitabevi, 1979.
Chaudhuri, K. N. *The English East India Company: The Study of an Early Joint-Stock Company, 1600–1640.* London: Frank Cass and Company, 1965.
———. "The World-System East of Longitude 20°: The European Role in Asia, 1500–1750." *Review* 5 (1981): 219–45.
———. *Trade and Civilisation in the Indian Ocean: An Economic History from the Rise of Islam to 1750.* Cambridge: Cambridge University Press, 1985.
Chew, S. C. *The Crescent and the Rose: Islam and England during the Renaissance.* Oxford: Oxford University Press, 1937.
Chowdhury, Neel. "Indian Camp." *Far Eastern Economic Review* 26 (May 1994): 47.
Çizakça, Murat. "Price History and the Bursa Silk Industry: A Study in Ottoman Industrial Decline, 1550–1650." *Journal of Economic History* 40 (1980): 533–50.
Cohen, Amnon. *Jewish Life under Islam: Jerusalem in the Sixteenth Century.* Cambridge, Massachusetts: Harvard University Press, 1984.
Cunningham, Allan. "Dragomania: The Dragomans of the British Embassy in Turkey." *St. Antony's Papers* 11 (1961): 81–100.
Curtin, Philip. *Cross-Cultural Trade in World History.* Cambridge: Cambridge University Press, 1984.
Dalsar, Fahri. *Türk sanayi ve ticaret tarihinde Bursa'da ipekçilik.* Istanbul: Sermet Matbaası, 1960.

Danışmend, İsmail Hami. *İzahlı osmanlı tarih kronolojisi.* 2d ed., 5 vols. Istanbul: Türkiye Yayınevi, 1971.

Dankoff, Robert, trans. and comm. *The Intimate Life of an Ottoman Statesman: Melek Ahmed Pasha (1588–1662) as Portrayed in Evliya Çelebi's Book of Travels.* Historical introduction by Rhoads Murphey. Albany: State University of New York Press, 1991.

Darkot, Besim, et al. "İstanbul." In *İslâm Ansiklopedisi.* Istanbul: Milli Eğitim Basımevi, 1967.

Darling, Linda. "Ottoman Politics through British Eyes: Paul Rycaut's *The Present State of the Ottoman Empire.*" *Journal of World History* 5 (1994): 71–97.

Davis, Ralph. "England and the Mediterranean, 1570–1670." In *Essays in the Economic and Social History of Tudor and Stuart England in Honour of R. H. Tawney.* Edited by Frederick Jack Fisher, pp. 117–37. Cambridge: Cambridge University Press, 1961.

———. *Aleppo and Devonshire Square: English Traders in the Levant in the Eighteenth Century.* London: Macmillan, 1967.

———. "English Imports from the Middle East, 1580–1780." In *Studies in the Economic History of the Middle East from the Rise of Islam to the Present Day.* Edited by Michael A. Cook, pp. 193–206. London: Oxford University Press, 1970.

Deringil, Selim. "Legitimacy Structures in the Ottoman State: The Reign of Abdülhamid II (1876–1909)." *International Journal of Middle East Studies* 23 (1991): 345–59.

Dinçer, Kaya, Daniel Goffman, and Doğan Kuban. *Visions from a Vanishing Past: Architectural Drawings from Izmir and Western Anatolia.* Izmir: Çimentaş, 1994.

Dirlik, Arif. "The Post-Colonial Aura: Third World Criticism in the Age of Global Capitalism." *Critical Enquiry* 20 (1994): 328–57.

Eldem, Edhem. "Istanbul: From Imperial to Peripheral Capital." In *Three Ottoman Cities: Aleppo, Izmir, and Istanbul.* Edited by Edhem Eldem, Daniel Goffman, and Bruce Masters. Forthcoming.

Eldem, Edhem, Daniel Goffman, and Bruce Masters. *Three Ottoman Cities: Istanbul, Izmir, and Aleppo.* Forthcoming.

Encyclopaedia of Islam. New ed. Leiden: E. J. Brill, 1960–.

Endo, Shusako. *The Samurai.* Translated by Van C. Gessel. New York: Random House, 1982.

Epstein, Mortimer. *The English Levant Company: Its Foundation and Its History to 1640.* London: Routledge, 1908.

Ergenç, Özer. "Osmanlı klâsik dönemindeki 'Eşraf ve Â'yan' üzerine bazı bilgiler." *Journal of Ottoman Studies* 3 (1982): 105–13.

Evans, Simpson, ed. *Life of Robert Frampton, Bishop of Gloucester.* n.p., 1876.

Evliya Çelebi. *Seyahatnamesi.* 9 vols. Istanbul: Devlet Matbaası, 1935.

Faroqhi, Suraiya. "Notes on the Production of Cotton and Cotton Cloth in Sixteenth and Seventeenth Century Anatolia." *Journal of European Economic History* 8 (1972): 405–17.

———. "İstanbul'un iasesi ve Tekirdağ-Rodoscuk limanı (16.–17. yüzyıllar)." *ODTÜ Gelişme Dergisi / METU Studies in Development,* special issue 2 (1979–80): 139–54.

———. "Camels, Wagons, and the Ottoman State in the Sixteenth and Seventeenth Centuries." *International Journal of Middle East Studies* 14 (1982): 523–39.

———. *Towns and Townsmen of Ottoman Anatolia: Trade, Crafts and Food Production in an Urban Setting, 1520–1650.* Cambridge: Cambridge University Press, 1984.

———. "Political Initiatives 'From the Bottom Up' in the Sixteenth- and Seventeenth-Century Ottoman Empire: Some Evidence for Their Existence." In *Sonderdruck aus Osmanistische Studien zur Wirtschafts- und Sozialgeschichte in memoriam Vančo Boškov.* Edited by Hans Georg Majer, pp. 24–33. Wiesbaden: Otto Harrassowitz, 1986.

———. "Crisis and Change, 1590–1699." In *An Economic and Social History of the Ottoman Empire, 1300–1914.* Edited by Halil İnalcık with Donald Quataert, pp. 411–636. Cambridge: Cambridge University Press, 1994.

Ferrier, R. W. "The Armenians and the East India Company in Persia in the Seventeenth and Early Eighteenth Centuries." *Economic History Review,* 2d ser., 26 (1973): 38–62.

Fissel, Mark Charles. "Law and Authority in the Collection of the Strangers' Consulage, 1621–47." In *Law and Authority in Tudor and Stuart England.* Edited by Buchanan Sharp and Mark Charles Fissel. Forthcoming.

Fissel, Mark Charles, and Daniel Goffman. "Viewing the Scaffold from Istanbul: The Bendysh-Hyde Affair, 1647–51." *Albion* 23:3 (1990): 421–48.

Fleischer, Cornell. *Bureaucrat and Intellectual in the Ottoman Empire: The Historian Mustafa Âli (1541–1600).* Princeton, New Jersey: Princeton University Press, 1986.

Fraser, Antonia. *Cromwell: The Lord Protector.* New York: Donald I. Fine, 1973.

Frazee, Charles A. *Catholics and Sultans: The Church and the Ottoman Empire, 1453–1923.* London: Cambridge University Press, 1983.

Gardiner, Samuel R. *History of the Commonwealth and Protectorate, 1649–1656,* new ed., 4 vols. London: Longmans, Green, and Co., 1903.

Gerber, Haim. "Jewish Tax-Farmers in the Ottoman Empire in the Sixteenth and Seventeenth Centuries." *Journal of Turkish Studies* 10 (1986): 143–54.

Glazebrook, Nathan. *Journey to Kars: A Modern Traveller in the Ottoman Lands.* New York: Holt, Rinehart, and Winston, 1982.

Goffman, Daniel. "Izmir as a Commercial Center: The Impact of Western Trade on an Ottoman Port, 1570–1650." Ph.D. dissertation: University of Chicago, 1985.

———. "The Capitulations and the Question of Authority in Levantine Trade." *Journal of Turkish Studies* 10 (1986): 81–90.

———. *Izmir and the Levantine World, 1550–1650.* Seattle: University of Washington Press, 1990.

———. "The Ottoman Role in Patterns of Commerce in Aleppo, Chios, Dubrovnik and Istanbul (1620–1650)." In *Decision Making and Change in the Ottoman Empire.* Edited by Caesar Farah, pp. 139–48. Kirksville, Missouri: Thomas Jefferson University Press, 1993.

———. "The Quincentennial of 1492 and Ottoman-Jewish Studies: A Review Essay." *Shofar: An Interdisciplinary Journal of Jewish Studies* 11 (1994): 57–67.

———. "Ottoman *Millet*s in the Early Seventeenth Century." *New Perspectives on Turkey* 11:2 (1994): 135–58.

———. "Demise of a Trading Center: Chios after the Ottoman Conquest." *Mediterranean History Review.* Forthcoming.

———. "Izmir: From Village to Colonial Port City," In *Three Ottoman Cities: Aleppo, Izmir, and Istanbul.* Edited by Edhem Eldem, Daniel Goffman, and Bruce Masters. Forthcoming.

Greenfeld, Liah. *Nationalism: Five Roads to Modernity.* Cambridge, Massachusetts: Harvard University Press, 1992.

Groot, A. H. de. "The Dutch Nation in Istanbul, 1600–1985: A Contribution to the Social History of Beyoğlu." *Anatolica* 14 (1987): 131–50.

Güçer, Lütfi. "Le problème de l'approvisionnement d'Istanbul en céréales vers le milieu du XVIIème siècle." *İstanbul Üniversitesi İktisat Fakültesi Mecmuası* 11 (1949–50): 79–98.

Hacker, Joseph R. "The Impact of the 'Sürgün'-System on Jewish Society in the Ottoman Empire in the Fifteenth through the Seventeenth Centuries." Paper presented at the Fourth International Congress for the Economic and Social History of Turkey (1071–1922). Munich, 4–8 August 1986.

———. "Jewish Autonomy in the Ottoman Empire: Its Scope and Limits. Jewish Courts from the Sixteenth to the Eighteenth Centuries." In *The Jews of the Ottoman Empire*. Edited with an introduction by Avigdor Levy, pp. 153–202. Princeton, New Jersey: Darwin Press, 1994.

Hakluyt, Richard. *The Principal Navigations, Voyages, Traffiques and Discoveries of the English Nation*. 12 vols. Glasgow: James MacLehose, 1904.

Hammer-Purgstall, Joseph von. *Geschichte des Osmanischen Reiches*, 10 vols. Pest: C. A. Hartleben's Verlage, 1827–29.

Hattox, Ralph. Review of Jonathan Haynes's *The Humanist as Traveler: George Sandys's "Relation of a Journey begun An: Dom: 1610." Turkish Studies Association Bulletin* 13 (1989): 117–22.

Haynes, Jonathan. *The Humanist as Traveler: George Sandys's "Relation of a Journey begun An: Dom: 1610."* Rutherford, New Jersey: Farleigh Dickinson University Press, 1986.

Heyd, Uriel. "The Jewish Communities of Istanbul in the Seventeenth Century." *Oriens* 6 (1953): 299–314.

Heywood, Colin. "Sir Paul Rycaut, a Seventeenth-Century Observer of the Ottoman State: Notes for a Study." In E. Kural Shaw and C. J. Heywood, *English and Continental Views of the Ottoman Empire, 1500–1800*, pp. 31–59. Los Angeles: William Andrews Clark Memorial Library, 1972.

———. "Between Historical Myth and 'Mythohistory': The Limits of Ottoman History." *Byzantine and Modern Greek Studies* 12 (1988): 315–45.

Hill, Christopher. *The World Turned Upside Down: Radical Ideas during the English Revolution*. London: Penguin Books, 1974.

Hinde, John. *A True Copy of Sir Henry Hide's Speech on the Scaffold Immediately before his Execution before the Exchange, on the 4th of March, 1650. Taken in Short-hand from his mouth*. London: Peter Cole, 1651.

Hirst, Derek. "The English Republic and the Meaning of Britain." *Journal of Modern History* 66 (1994): 451–86.

Hobsbawm, E. J. *Nations and Nationalism since 1780: Programmes, Myth, Reality*. Cambridge: Cambridge University Press, 1990.

Homsy, Basile. *Les capitulations et la protection des chrétiens au Proche-Orient aux XVIe, XVIIe et XVIIIe siècles*. Paris: Harissa, 1956.

Horniker, Arther Leon. "Anglo-French Rivalry in the Levant from 1583 to 1612." *Journal of Modern History* 18 (1946): 289–305.

Howard, Douglas A. "Ottoman Historiography and the Literature of 'Decline' of the Sixteenth and Seventeenth Centuries." *Journal of Asian History* 22 (1988): 52–77.

Hutton, Ronald. *Charles the Second, King of England, Scotland, and Ireland.* Oxford: Clarendon Press, 1989.

İnalcık, Halil. "Ottoman Methods of Conquest." *Studia Islamica* 2 (1954): 112–22.

———. "Bursa and the Commerce of the Levant." *Journal of the Economic and Social History of the Orient* 3 (1960): 131–47.

———. "Capital Formation in the Ottoman Empire." *Journal of Economic History* 19 (1969): 97–140.

———. "The Policy of Mehmed II toward the Greek Population of Istanbul and the Byzantine Buildings of the City." *Dumbarton Oaks Papers* 23–24 (1969–70): 231–49.

———. "The Ottoman Economic Mind and Aspects of the Ottoman Economy." In *Studies in the Economic History of the Ottoman Empire from the Rise of Islam to the Present Day.* Edited by Michael A. Cook, pp. 207–18. London: Oxford University Press, 1970.

———. *The Ottoman Empire: The Classical Age, 1300–1600.* Translated by Norman Itzkowitz and Colin Imber. London: Weidenfeld and Nicolson, 1973.

———. "Centralization and Decentralization in Ottoman Administration." In *Studies in Eighteenth-Century Islamic History.* Edited by Thomas Naff and Roger Owens, pp. 27–52. Carbondale: Southern Illinois University Press, 1977.

———. "Osmanlı pamuklu pazarı, Hindistan ve İngiltere: Pazar rekabetinde emek maliyetinin rolü." *ODTÜ Gelişme Dergisi/METU Studies in Development,* special issue 2 (1979–80): 1–65.

———. "Military and Fiscal Transformation in the Ottoman Empire, 1600–1700." *Archivum Ottomanicum* 6 (1980): 283–337.

———. "The Rise of the Turcoman Maritime Principalities in Anatolia, Byzantium, and the Crusades." *Byzantinische Forschungen, Internationale Zeitschrift für Byzantinistik* 9 (1985): 179–217. Reprinted in Halil İnalcık, *The Middle East and the Balkans under the Ottoman Empire: Essays on Economy and Society,* pp. 309–41. Bloomington: Indiana University Turkish Studies, 1993.

———. "Tax Collection, Embezzlement and Bribery in Ottoman Finances." *Turkish Studies Association Bulletin* 15 (1991): 327–46.

———. "The Shaykh's Story Told by Himself." In *Paths to the Middle East: Ten Scholars Look Back.* Edited and compiled by Thomas Naff, pp. 105–42. Albany: State University of New York Press, 1993.

———. *The Middle East and the Balkans under the Ottoman Empire: Essays on Economy and Society.* Bloomington: Indiana University Turkish Studies, 1993.

———. "The Ottoman State: Economy and Society, 1300–1600." In *An Economic and Social History of the Ottoman Empire, 1300–1914.* Edited by Halil İnalcık with Donald Quataert, pp. 9–409. Cambridge: Cambridge University Press, 1994.

———. "Imtiyazat." *Encyclopaedia of Islam.* New ed. Leiden: E. J. Brill, 1960–.

———. "Istanbul." *Encyclopaedia of Islam.* New ed. Leiden: E. J. Brill, 1960–.

İslâm Ansiklopedisi. Istanbul: Milli Eğitim Basımevi, 1967.

Israel, Jonathan. *European Jewry in the Age of Mercantilism, 1550–1750.* Oxford: Clarendon Press, 1985.

———. *Dutch Supremacy in World Trade, 1585–1740.* Oxford: Clarendon Press, 1989.

Jennings, Ronald C. "Kadi, Court and Legal Procedure in Seventeenth-Century Ottoman Kayseri." *Studia Islamica* 48 (1978): 133–72.

———. "Limitations of the Judicial Powers of the Kadi in Seventeenth-Century Kayseri." *Studia Islamica* 50 (1979): 151–84.

———. *Christians and Muslims in Ottoman Cyprus and the Mediterranean World, 1571–1640.* New York: New York University Press, 1993.

Kafadar, Cemal. "A Death In Venice (1575): Anatolian Muslim Merchants Trading in the Serenissima." *Journal of Turkish Studies* 10 (1986): 191–218.

———. "Self and Others: The Diary of a Dervish in Seventeenth Century Istanbul and First-Person Narratives in Ottoman Literature." *Studia Islamica* 69 (1989): 121–150.

———. "On the Purity and Corruption of the Janissaries." *Turkish Studies Association Bulletin* 15 (1991): 273–80.

———. "Mütereddit bir mutasavif üsküplü asiye hatunun rüya defteri, 1641–43." *Topkapı Sarayı Yıllığı* 5 (1991): 168–222.

———. "Les troubles monétaires de la fin du XVIe siècle et la prise de conscience ottomane du déclin." *Annales, Economies Sociétés Civilisations* (1991), pp. 381–400.

———. *Between Two Worlds: The Construction of the Ottoman State.* Berkeley: University of California Press, 1995.

Kafu, Nagai. "Twilight in the Mediterranean." In *Modern Asia and Africa.* Edited by William H. McNeill and Mitsuko Iriye, pp. 167–69. New York: Oxford University Press, 1971.

Kahane, Henry R., and Renée and Andreas Tietze. *The Lingua Franca in the Levant.* Urbana: University of Illinois Press, 1958.

Kampman, Arie Abraham. "XVII. ve XVIII. yüzyıllarda Osmanlı imparatorluğunda Hollandalılar." *Belleten* 23 (1959): 513–23.

Katib Çelebi. *The Balance of Truth.* Translated by G. L. Lewis. London: George Allen and Unwin, 1957.

Katz, Jacob. *Exclusiveness and Toleration: Jewish-Gentile Relations in Medieval and Modern Times.* Oxford: Oxford University Press, 1961.

———. *Tradition and Crisis: Jewish Society at the End of the Middle Ages.* New York: Schocken Books, 1971.

Kevonian, Keram. "Marchands arméniens au XVIIe siècle: A propos d'un livre arménien publié à Amsterdam en 1699." *Cahiers du Monde russe et Soviétique* 16 (1975): 199–244.

Kennedy, D. E. "Naval Captains at the Outbreak of the English Civil War." *Mariner's Mirror* 46 (1960): 181–98.

———. "The Establishment and Settlement of Parliament's Admiralty, 1642–1648." *Mariner's Mirror* 48 (1962): 276–91.

Kunt, Metin. *The Sultan's Servants: The Transformation of Ottoman Provincial Government, 1550–1650.* New York: Columbia University Press, 1983.

Kupperman, Karen Ordahl. *Settling with the Indians: The Meeting of English and Indian Cultures in America, 1580–1640.* Totowa, New Jersey: Rowman and Littlefield, 1980.

———. *Roanoke: The Abandoned Colony.* Savage, Maryland: Rowman and Littlefield, 1984.

———. "Errand to the Indies: Puritan Colonization of Providence Island through the Western Design." *William and Mary Quarterly* 45 (1988): 70–99.

———. *Providence Island, 1630–1641: The Other Puritan Colony.* Cambridge: Cambridge University Press, 1993.

Kupperman, Karen Ordahl, ed. *America in European Consciousness, 1493–1750*. Chapel Hill: University of North Carolina Press, 1995.

Kütükoğlu, Mübahat S. *Osmanlı-ingiliz iktisâdî münâsebetleri, I (1580–1838)*. Ankara: Türk Kültürünü Araştırma Enstitüsü, 1974.

Lach, Donald, and Edwin Van Kley. *Asia in the Making of Europe*. Chicago: University of Chicago Press, 1965–93.

Lane, Frederic C. "Economic Consequences of Organized Violence." *Journal of Economic History* 18 (1958): 401–17.

——— . *Venice: A Maritime Republic*. Baltimore: Johns Hopkins University Press, 1973.

Levy, Avigdor. *The Sephardim in the Ottoman Empire*. Princeton, New Jersey: Darwin Press, 1992.

Lewis, Bernard. *The Jews of Islam*. Princeton, New Jersey: Princeton University Press, 1984.

——— . *The Political Language of Islam*. Chicago: University of Chicago Press, 1988.

Lewis, Geoffrey. "Turks and Britons over Four Hundred Years." In *Four Centuries of Turco-British Relations: Studies in Diplomatic, Economic and Cultural Affairs*. Edited by William Hale and Ali İhsan Bağış. Beverley, North Humberside: Eothen Press, 1984.

——— . "English Writers on the Turkish Language, 1670–1832." *Journal of Ottoman Studies* 7–8 (1988): 71–82.

Lewis, W. H. *Levantine Adventurer: The Travels and Missions of the Chevalier d'Arvieux, 1653–1697*. New York: Harcourt, Brace and World, 1962.

Mahood, Molly M. *The Colonial Encounter: A Reading of Six Novels*. Totowa, New Jersey: Rowman and Littlefield, 1977.

Mantran, Robert. *Istanbul dans la second moitié du XVIIe siècle*. Paris: Librairie d'Amerique et d'Orient Adrien Maisonneuve, 1962.

——— . "Foreign Merchants and the Minorities in Istanbul during the Sixteenth and Seventeenth Centuries." In *Christians and Jews in the Ottoman Empire: The Functioning of a Plural Society*, vol. 1: *The Central Lands*. Edited by Benjamin Braude and Bernard Lewis, pp. 127–37. New York: Holmes and Meier, 1982.

——— . "L'état ottoman au XVIIe siècle: stabilisation ou déclin?" In *Histoire de l'empire ottoman*. Edited by Robert Mantran, pp. 227–64. Paris: Librarie Artheme Fayard, 1989.

Marcus, Abraham. *The Middle East on the Eve of Modernity: Aleppo in the Eighteenth Century*. New York: Columbia University Press, 1989.

Masson, Paul. *Histoire du commerce français dans le Levant au XVIIe*. Paris: Hachette, 1911.

Masters, Bruce. "Trading Diasporas and 'Nations': The Genesis of National Identities in Ottoman Aleppo." *International History Review* 9 (1987): 345–67.

———. *The Origins of Western Economic Dominance in the Middle East: Mercantilism and the Islamic Economy of Aleppo, 1600–1750*. New York: New York University Press, 1988.

———. "The Sultan's Entrepreneurs: The *Avrupa Tüccarı*s and the *Hayriye Tüccarı*s in Syria." *International Journal of Middle East Studies* 24 (1992): 579–97.

———. "Aleppo: The Ottoman Empire's Caravan City." In *Three Ottoman Cities: Aleppo, Izmir, and Istanbul*. Edited by Edhem Eldem, Daniel Goffman, and Bruce Masters. Forthcoming.

McGowan, Bruce. "The Age of the *Ayans*." In *An Economic and Social History of the Ottoman Empire, 1300–1914*. Edited by Halil İnalcık with Donald Quataert, pp. 639–758. Cambridge: Cambridge University Press, 1994.

Melman, Billie. *Women's Orients: English Women and the Middle East, 1718–1918 (Sexuality, Religion and Work)*. 2d ed. Ann Arbor: University of Michigan Press, 1995.

Ménage, V. L. "The English Capitulation of 1580: A Review Article." *International Journal of Middle East Studies* 12 (1980): 373–83.

Merrell, James H. *The Indians' New World: Catawbas and Their Neighbors from European Contact through the Era of Removal*. Chapel Hill: University of North Carolina Press, 1989.

Minchinton, Walter Edward, ed. *The Growth of English Overseas Trade in the Seventeenth Century*. London: Newton, 1969.

Mishra, Vijay, and Bob Hodge. "What is Post(-)colonialism?" In *Colonial Discourse and Post-Colonial Theory: A Reader*. Edited by Patrick Williams and Laura Chrisman, pp. 276–90. New York: Columbia University Press, 1994.

Morrill, John, ed. *Reactions to the English Civil War, 1642–1649*. New York: St. Martin's Press, 1982.

Mukherjee, Bharati. *The Holder of the World*. New York: Ballantine, 1993.

Murphey, Rhoads. "Functioning of the Ottoman Army under Murad IV (1623–1639/1032–1049): Key to the Understanding of the Relationship between Center and Periphery in Seventeenth-Century Turkey." Ph.D. dissertation, University of Chicago, 1979.

———. "Provisioning Istanbul: The State and Subsistence in the Early Modern Middle East." *Food and Foodways* 2 (1988): 217–63.

———. "Bigots or Informed Observers? A Periodization of Pre-Colonial English and European Writing on the Middle East." *Journal of the American Oriental Society* 110 (1990): 291–303.

———. "Communal Living in Ottoman Istanbul: Searching for the Foundations of an Urban Tradition." *Journal of Urban History* 16 (1990): 115–31.

———. "The Ottoman Resurgence in the Seventeenth-Century Mediterranean: The Gamble and Its Results." *Mediterranean Historical Review* 8 (1993): 186–200.

Naima, Mustafa. *Tarih-i Naima*. 6 vols. Istanbul: n.p., 1864–66.

Naipaul, V. S. *Among the Believers: An Islamic Journey.* New York: Knopf, 1981.

Narayan, R. K. *The Vendor of Sweets.* London: Penguin Books, 1967.

———. *The Bachelor of Arts.* Chicago: University of Chicago Press, 1984.

Newes from Turkie or, A true Relation of the passages of the Right honourable Sir Tho. Bendish, Lord Ambassadour with the Grand Signieur at Constantinople. London: n.p., 1648.

Ollard, Richard. *The Image of the King: Charles I and Charles II.* London: Hodder and Stoughton, 1979.

Orhonlu, Cengiz. "İstanbul'da kayıkçılık ve kayık işletmeciliği." *Tarih Dergisi* 21 (1966): 109–34. Reprinted in *Osmanlı imparatorluğunda şehircilik ve ulaşı üzerine araştırmalar.* Edited by Salih Özbaran, pp. 83–103. Izmir: Ticaret Matbaacılık TAŞ, 1984.

Orwell, George. *Shooting an Elephant and Other Essays.* New York: Harcourt, Brace, 1945.

Pakalın, Mehmet Zeki. *Osmanlı tarih ve terimleri sözlüğü.* 3 vols. Istanbul: Milli Eğitim Basımevi, 1971.

Peirce, Leslie P. *The Imperial Harem: Women and Sovereignty in the Ottoman Empire.* New York: Oxford University Press, 1993.

Pincus, Steve. "England and the World in the 1650s." In *Revolution and Restoration: England in the 1650s.* Edited by John Morrill, pp. 129–47. London: Collins and Brown, 1992.

Pitcher, Donald Edgar. *An Historical Geography of the Ottoman Empire from Earliest Times to the End of the Sixteenth Century.* Leiden: E. J. Brill, 1972.

Pocock. J. G. A. "British History: A Plea for a New Subject." *Journal of Modern History* 4 (1975): 601–24.

———. "The Limits and Divisions of British History: In Search of the Unknown Subject." *American Historical Review* (1982): 311–36.

Pratt, Mary Louise. *Imperial Eyes: Travel Writing and Transculturation.* London: Routledge, 1992.
Purchas, Samuel. *Hakluytus Posthumus or Purchas His Pilgrimes.* 20 vols. Glasgow: MacLehose, 1905.
Rafeq, Abdul Karim. "Changes in the Relationship between the Ottoman Central Administration and the Syrian Provinces from the Sixteenth to the Eighteenth Centuries." In *Studies in Eighteenth Century Islamic History.* Edited by Thomas Naff and Roger Owen, pp. 53–73. Carbondale: Southern Illinois University Press, 1977.
Rapp, Richard T. "The Unmaking of the Mediterranean Trade Hegemony." *Journal of Economic History* 35 (1975): 499–525.
Riemersma, Jelle C. "Government Influence on Company Organization in Holland and England (1550–1650)." *Journal of Economic History,* supplement, 10 (1950): 31–39.
Roberts, Lewes. *The Merchants Mappe of Commerce: Wherein, the Universall Manner and Matter of Trade, Is Compendiously Handled.* London: Ralph Mabb, 1638.
Rodrigue, Aron. "Difference and Tolerance in the Ottoman Empire." Interview by Nancy Reynolds. *Stanford Humanities Review* 5 (1995): 80–90.
Rouillard, Clarence Dana. *The Turk in French History, Thought, and Literature (1520–1660).* Paris: Boivin, 1941.
Rudé, George. *The Crowd in the French Revolution.* Oxford: Clarendon Press, 1959.
Runciman, Steven. *The Fall of Constantinople.* Cambridge: Cambridge University Press, 1965.
Rushdie, Salman. *Imaginary Homelands: Essays and Criticism 1981–1991.* New York: Penguin Books, 1991.
Russell, Conrad. *The Causes of the English Civil War.* Oxford: Clarendon Press, 1990.
Rycaut, Paul. *Present State of the Ottoman Empire.* London: John Starkey and Henry Brome, 1668. Reprint, Westmead, England: Gregg International Publishers, 1972.
———. *History of the Turkish Empire from the Year 1623 to the Year 1677.* London: John Starkey, 1680.
Said, Edward. *Orientalism.* New York: Vintage Books, 1978.
Schama, Simon. *Dead Certainties (Unwarranted Speculations).* New York: Vintage Books, 1991.
Seaward, Paul. *The Restoration, 1660–1688.* London: Macmillan, 1991.

Sella, Domenico. "Les mouvements longs de l'industrie lainière à Venise aux XVIe et XVIIe siècles." *Annales* 12 (1957): 29–45.

Shankar, D. A. "The Absence of Caste in R. K. Narayan and Its Implications for Indian Writing in English." In *R. K. Narayan: Contemporary Critical Perspectives*. Edited by Geoffrey Kain, pp. 49–70. East Lansing: Michigan State University Press, 1993.

Shmuelevitz, Aryeh. *The Jews of the Ottoman Empire in the Late Fifteenth and Sixteenth Centuries: Administrative, Economic, Legal and Social Relations as Reflected in the Responsa*. Leiden: E. J. Brill, 1984.

Skilliter, Susan A. *William Harborne and the Trade with Turkey, 1578–1582: A Documentary Study of the First Anglo-Ottoman Relations*. London: Oxford University Press, 1977.

———. "William Harborne, The First English Ambassador 1583–1588." In *Four Centuries of Turco-British Relations: Studies in Diplomatic, Economic and Cultural Affairs*. Edited by William Hale and Ali İhsan Bağış. Beverly, North Humberside: Eothen Press, 1984.

The Speech and Confession, of Sr Henry Hide (Embassador for the King of Scotland, to the emperour of Turkie). London: n.p., 1651.

Spence, Jonathan. *The Death of Woman Wang*. New York: Viking Press, 1978.

Sr. Sackvile Crow's Case as it now stands with his request to the Parliament 1 July 1652. London: n.p., 1652.

Steensgaard, Neils. "Consuls and Nations in the Levant from 1570 to 1650." *Scandinavian Economic History Review* 15 (1967): 13–55.

———. *The Asian Trade Revolution of the Seventeenth Century*. Chicago: University of Chicago Press, 1974.

———. "Violence and the Rise of Capitalism: Frederic C. Lane's Theory of Protection and Tribute." *Review* 5 (1981): 247–73.

Subtilty and Cruelty: or a true relation of Sr Sackvile Crow, His Design of seizing and possessing himselfe of all the Estate of the English in Turky. With the Progresse he made, and the Meanes he used in the execution thereof. London: n.p., 1647.

Tenenti, Alberto. *Piracy and the Decline of Venice, 1580–1615*. Translated by Janet and Brian Pullan. Berkeley: University of California Press, 1967.

Theroux, Paul. *The Old Patagonian Express*. Boston: Houghton Mifflin, 1978.

Thomas, Lewis V. *A Study of Naima*. Edited by Norman Itzkowitz. New York: New York University Press, 1972.

Thurloe, John. *A Collection of the State Papers of John Thurloe*. London: n.p., 1742.

Todorova, Maria. "The Balkans: From Discovery to Invention." *Slavic Review* 53 (1994): 453–82.

———. "The Ottoman Legacy in the Balkans." In *Imperial Legacy: The Ottoman Imprint on the Balkans and the Middle East.* Edited by L. Carl Brown, pp. 45–77. New York: Columbia University Press, 1996.

Tulum, Mertol, et al., eds. *Mühimme defteri 90.* Istanbul: Türk Dünyası Araştırmaları Vakfı, 1993.

Ülker, Necmi. "The Rise of Izmir, 1688–1740," Ph.D. dissertation, University of Michigan, 1974.

———. "Batılı gözlemcilere göre XVII. yüzyılın ikinci yarısında İzmir şehri ve ticari sorunları." *Tarih Enstitüsü Dergisi* 12 (1981–82): 317–54.

———. "XVII. ve XVIII. Yüzyıllar ipek ticaretinde İzmir'in rolü ve önemi." *Prof. Dr. Bekir Kütükoğlu'na Armağan.* Istanbul: Edebiyat Fakültesi Basımevi, 1991.

———. "XVII. Yüzyılın ikinci yarısında İzmir'deki İngiliz tüccarına dair ticari problemlerle ilgili belgeler." *Belgeler* 14 (1989–92): 261–321.

Ursinus, Michael. "Millet." *Encyclopaedia of Islam.* new ed. Leiden: E. J. Brill, 1960–.

Uzunçarşılı, İsmail Hakkı. *Osmanlı tarihi,* vol. 3, part 1. Ankara: Türk Tarih Kurumu Basımevi, 1951.

———. *Osmanlı devlet erkani.* Istanbul: n.p., 1971.

Vaughan, Dorothy M. *Europe and the Turk: A Pattern of Alliances, 1350–1700.* Liverpool: University Press, 1954.

Veeser, H. Aram, ed. *The New Historicism.* London: Routledge, 1989.

Veinstein, Gilles. "'Ayan' de la région d'Izmir et commerce du Levant (deuxième moitié du XVIIIe siècle)." *Etudes Balkaniques* 12 (1976): 71–83.

Wallerstein, Immanuel. *The Modern World-System: Capitalist Agriculture and the Origins of the European World-Economy in the Sixteenth Century.* New York: Academic Press, 1974.

Warner, George F., ed. *The Nicholas Papers. Correspondence of Sir Edward Nicholas, Secretary of State.* Camden Society, 2d series, vol. 40 (1886).

White, Richard. *The Middle Ground: Indians, Empires, and Republics in the Great Lakes Region, 1650–1815.* Cambridge: Cambridge University Press, 1991.

Williams, Patrick, and Laura Chrisman, eds. and intros. *Colonial Discourse and Post-Colonial Theory: A Reader.* New York: Columbia University Press, 1994.

Wood, Alfred. *A History of the English Levant Company.* Oxford: Oxford University Press, 1935.

Woodhead, Christine. " 'The Present Terrour of the World'? Contemporary Views of the Ottoman Empire c. 1600." *History* 72 (1987): 20–37.

Zilfi, Madeline. *The Politics of Piety: The Ottoman Ulema in the Postclassical Age (1600–1800).* Minneapolis, Minnesota: Biblioteca Islamica, 1988.

Index

Abbott, Edward, 46
Abbott, George F., 247*n68*
Abbott, Morris, 46
Abdülaziz Efendi, 182
Abdurrahim Efendi, Haci, 155
Abisutt Effendi, 56, 62
Abney, John, 136, 166–67, 183
Achaia, Metropolitan of, 215
Achebe, Chinua, 265*n3*
Achmett, Hoggia, 48
Acre, 217
Admiral, Ottoman: jurisdiction of, 40, 112, 156; and administration, 86, 118, 193; actions of, 147, 149, 152, 154, 196
Admiralty, Committee for the, English, 170, 178–79
Adrianople. *See* Edirne
Aegean Sea: commerce in, 32, 37, 119, 147, 170; and Veneto-Ottoman war, 147, 155
Africa, 7
Ahdname. See Capitulations
Ahmed I (1603–17), 34
Ahmed Pasha, Hezar-pare, 95, 114, 117–18, 119, 133, 147
Ahmed Pasha, Melek, 142, 165, 171, 172, 248*n77*
Ahmed Pasha, Side, 195

Ahmed Pasha, Voynuk, 151, 154
Aleppo: commerce in, 5, 32, 37, 38, 39, 43, 45, 187, 196; English in, 8, 14, 17, 21, 24, 26, 28, 46–47, 81, 98, 107, 138, 215–18; English consul at, 29, 90, 158, 169; development of, 29–31, 230*n4*; factories in, 35, 41–42, 49, 125, 137, 140–41, 145, 185, 208, 216; Jews in, 39; and Crow, 87; Ottoman officials at, 99, 195–96; and Istanbul, 162–63
Alexander, Jeremiah, 90
Alexandretta: caravans in, 21, 27, 217; mariners in, 41–42; ships at, 81, 196–97
Alexandria, 29, 32, 37, 39, 126, 197
Algiers, 29, 155, 156
Ali Ağa, 81
Alicante, 121
Alluffe, Joseph, 129
Ambassador. *See* Diplomats
Americas, 5, 7, 8, 214, 223*n14*
Amon, Aaron, 133
Amsterdam: as commercial center, 38
Anatolia: produce of, 25, 52; and central government, 30, 31, 38; and Istanbul, 31, 170; Ottoman

rule in, 36–37; travel in, 105–6, 216
Anderson, Sonia, 9
Andrea, 133
Andrews, Kenneth, 9, 224n18
Anglicanism, 215–18
Ankara, 29
An Persy (ship), 197
Antalya, 39
Antioch, Patriarch of, 215
Antoine, 76
Arabs: cities of, 41, 230n4; merchants of, 45, 144; language of, 215, 216; historiography of, 225n22
Arbel, Benjamin, 11
Armenians: as Ottoman subjects, 16, 19; laws of, 18, 50, 138; intercommunal disputes of, 20, 130; in Istanbul, 21, 32, 35; English attitudes toward, 23, 24, 144, 215–16; commerce of, 32–33, 47–51, 80, 126–31, 230n9; in Izmir, 38, 46–49, 76, 77, 81, 176, 181–82; in Aleppo, 45, 162
Arsenal, Ottoman, 152, 179
Arvieux, Chevalier d', 27
Arz. See Petitions
Ashburneham, Jo., 69–70
Ashley, William, 121, 148, 150
Ashton, Robert, 6
Asia, 214–15, 221, 223n13
Atlantiç ocean, 13, 16; seaboard, 18, 214
*Avania*s, 55, 56, 103, 113, 130, 141, 149, 154, 208, 210, 251n18
Ayan. See Notables
Ayasoluğ, 36
Aydınoğlus, 36, 231n17

Bacdar, 52, 63–64, 233n13

Bagire, Isaac, 215–18
Bailo: as envoy, 73, 105; and Bendysh, 111, 114, 115, 117, 120, 151, 154, 155, 157, 162, 177; and Ottomans, 116, 147, 148, 152, 182, 244n24; and Hyde, 160, 161
Bailyn, Bernard, 6, 7
Bairan, 151
Baker, Richard, 205–7
Balkans: divines in, 20, 216; role of, in Ottoman Empire, 30, 31, 193; and Istanbul, 33, 37; historiography of, 225n22
Ball, Gyles, 51–67, 75, 85, 100, 121, 218
Ball, Nicholas, 63
Ballarino, Mr., 200
*Baltacı*s, 135
Balukbaşı, 4, 258n58. *See also Çavuş*
Barbary Coast, 143, 150, 153, 155, 156, 190, 210
Bargrave, Robert: in sources, 12; observations of, 24–26, 101, 109–10, 113–14, 115, 117, 118, 154, 165, 179, 184; and Hyde, 66, 159, 164; adventures of, 102, 172–76, 181, 234n14, 263n38; as a source, 229n23, 243n13, 255n16, 258n58
Barington, Thomas, 99
Barnard, Edward, 90, 92, 169
Barnardiston, Nathaniel, 121, 206
Barnardiston, Samuel, 74, 79, 82, 108, 138–39, 166–67, 206
Barnes, Hen., 198
Barton, Edward, 72
Battulations, 50, 128, 129, 130, 131–35, 144, 163, 164, 207, 251n18
Beale, Edward, 133
Bedford, Arthur, 134
Bedouins, 218
Bektaş Ağa, 173

Belgrade: English in, 26, 183
Bell, John, 74
Bendysh, Andrew, 207, 210–11, 260–61*n*36
Bendysh, John, 185, 260–61*n*36
Bendysh, Thomas: as chameleon, 5, 101–2, 111, 177, 179–80, 194–96, 204–5; as ambassador, 9–10, 15, 24–25, 113–14, 119, 125–45, 173, 195–96, 199–201, 213, 215, 216, 219–21, 246*n*52, 248*n*77, 251*n*18; in sources, 12; and English factories, 43, 145, 156–57, 162–63, 180; and Hyde, 66, 158–71, 247; appointment of, as ambassador, 90–97, 122; letters from, 97, 102, 109, 167, 180, 188–89, 194–96, 197, 199, 210–11, 247*n*71; travels of, 98–103, 109–10; instructions from English Levant Company to, 99–101, 127, 188; relations with Charles I, 103, 107, 112, 125; and Izmir, 103–9, 140–43, 257*n*32; and Crow, 104–5, 111–24, 145, 219, 241*n*25, 246*n*42, 246*n*49; salary and expenses of, 141–42, 208–10; responsibilities of, 143–45; and Sublime Porte, 146–57, 176, 181–84, 198–99; and Cretan war, 147–53, 153–56, 193; family of, 162, 200, 226*n*25, 255*n*16; and income, 166–67, 183; and commonwealth, 177–93; authority of, 181–84; recall of, 184–90, 191, 205, 209–11
*Berat*s, 39, 58, 59
Berkeley, John, 161
Bertoni, 76
Bethlehem, 217
Bevenias, Mayer, 47
*Beylerbeyi*s. *See* Governors

Birkley, Thomas, 131–35, 136
Black Sea, 33, 37, 151, 182
Blake, Robert, 9
Bodleian Library, 12
Bogus, 78, 79–80
Bond, John, 67, 90
Borderlands. *See* Frontiers
Bosphorus Straits, 34, 148
*Bostancı*s, 120
Bosteale, Mr., 166
Breda, 168
Brenner, Robert, 9, 224*n*21, 240*n*4
Brent, Dixwell, 74, 79, 106–7, 135
Bretton, Spencer, 142, 174–76, 177, 181–82
Brigands: in western Anatolia, 38; English dealings with, 57
British Empire: first vs. second, 4, 6, 8, 10, 212–13; compared to Ottoman Empire, 4, 24, 35; collapse of, 5; borders of, 7, 9; relations with Ottoman Empire, 14, 29, 88, 197, 201, 205; authority of, 21. *See also* Empires; England
British Library, 12
Britons, 3–4, 7, 118–19, 197–99, 218–21; overseas, 4, 8, 9, 12, 13, 15, 16, 22, 23, 30, 86–87, 134, 140, 213–21, 227*n*6; and English Civil War, 5, 67–71, 102; relating to Ottoman subjects, 16–28, 39, 46–66, 125–31, 143–45; in Ottoman vs. English worlds, 23–24, 26–28, 45, 52–53; in Izmir, 31, 40–41; commercial diaspora of, 43–44; disputes between, 45–67, 125–45; estates of, 112; and Veneto-Ottoman war, 150–57. *See also* Nations
Browne, Richard, 92, 94, 95, 215–16

Index

Browne, Zachary, 123
Buchan, John, 3, 5
Bull, Mr., 108
Bunington, Master, 54
Buonaventura (ship), 148
Burma, 213
Bursa: commerce in, 32, 37; silk in, 38; descriptions of, 110
Byzantine Empire: Ottoman conquests of, 31; Izmir in, 36; frontier of, 223*n*9

Cairo, 197, 210
Canada, 7
Candia, 49, 61, 75, 119, 151–52, 153–54, 169, 196, 200
Capitulations: English, 15, 51, 61, 86, 93, 99, 113, 134–35, 166, 178, 180, 185, 189; Ottoman policy on, 22, 33; as reflection of Ottoman society, 49–50; French, 51
Captain General at Sea, Venetian, 154
Capuchin Priests, 216
Caravans: in Aleppo, 21, 26, 41, 217; networks of, 38; in Anatolia, 110, 140
Cargashan, Isaak, 130
Carisbrooke Castle, 97
Castles: on the Dardanelles, 75, 105, 150, 198; at Izmir, 79, 174–76, 178, 232*n*29, 249*n*83, 258*n*58; and ships, 153, 186, 244–45*n*29; at Istanbul, 178; on Black Sea, 182
Castro, Abraham, 126
Catholics, 6; English policy toward, 18, 109, 192, 217; as Ottoman subjects, 19, 143, 215, 216; intercommunal disputes of, 20; in Istanbul, 34; as merchants, 37

Cavalleria Rusticana, 212
Cave, George, 108
Caversham, 244*n*20
Çavuş: described, 11, 17; activities of, 18, 40, 65, 74, 77–80, 83, 111, 117, 120, 121, 139, 142, 148, 152–53, 154, 171, 172, 173–76, 248*n*72
Cephalonia, 52
Çeşme, 39
Chamlet, Samuel, 183
Chappell, William, 162
Charles I (1625–49): fiscal difficulties of, 15, 68–71; execution of, 43, 71, 145, 146, 153, 156, 158, 159, 162, 165, 168, 171, 191, 201, 218, 219, 241*n*25, 257*n*32; letters from, 53, 56, 57, 67, 71–72, 74, 88, 90, 92, 94, 95, 96, 101, 103, 105, 107, 111, 114–15, 164; authority of, 59, 65, 66–67, 84, 108, 113, 120, 122, 215; letters to, 66, 112, 125; during Civil Wars, 68–72, 134, 179–80, 236*n*2, 247*n*71, 259*n*6; and English Levant Company, 72–73, 106, 186, 214, 243–44*n*20; conspiracies by, 71–87, 92–94, 98, 117, 160, 219, 224*n*21, 246*n*50; and appointment of ambassador, 88–97, 102, 190, 194; and pleas for intelligence, 102–3; family of, 110, 178
Charles II (1649–85): and seizure of Company goods, 4–5, 6, 214; as Prince of Wales, 70; conspiracies by, 73, 224*n*21; and Hyde, 121, 158–61, 162, 170; in power, 123, 201–5, 206–7, 208–11, 220, 240*n*44; during English interregnum, 146, 150, 157, 159, 168, 178, 182, 188, 217, 255*n*7;

Charles II *(continued)*
    and Bendysh, 160, 163, 176, 177, 180; letters from, 161, 164, 166, 203; supporters of, 169, 170
Charleton, Richard, 136, 138, 169, 170, 171
Chew, S. C., 9
Chinese, 230n9
Chios: English consul at, 29; Greeks from, 39
Christianity: civilization of, 4, 143, 156, 158–59, 174, 182; and Islam, 13, 143–44, 191–93, 203, 218; in Ottoman Empire, 19–20, 30, 51, 199–200, 217; heretical forms of, 23, 109, 126, 156–57; and commerce, 39, 196–97; as refuge, 154
Churches: in Izmir, 39, 41, 232n28; in Aleppo, 41; and diplomats, 53, 163
Civil Wars, English: domestic dimension of, 4, 45, 202–3; international dimension of, 5, 6, 9, 16, 21, 29, 53, 66–67, 88–97, 115, 138, 204, 214, 215, 218, 221, 224n21, 236n2; first vs. second, 6, 43, 101, 219; Charles I's defeat in, 66, 98, 122, 159; and Charles I's Levantine policy, 68–73, 87; mirrored in Levant, 73, 108–9, 123–24, 145, 200; and Bendysh, 99, 110, 156–57, 185, 220
Cizye. See Head tax, Ottoman
Clarendon, Earl of. *See* Hyde, Edward
Clarke, Francis, 198
Clobery, Oliver, 121
Coen, Braani, 128–29
Coen, David, 128–29
Coen, Isaac, 128–29
Coen, Moseh, 128–29
Cokayne, William, 54, 89
Coleman, Thomas, 54–55, 56, 62, 164, 167, 169
Collyer, John, 121
Colonel Joe, 115
Colonialism, 3, 7, 214
Colonies. *See* Factories
Commerce: organization of, 11; innovations in, 13–14; English, 24, 75, 91, 95, 100, 102, 104, 109, 122, 124, 129, 137–38, 148, 152, 155, 162, 179, 186, 187, 188, 194, 198, 200, 203, 219, 224n21; in Istanbul, 26, 149, 151; international, 32, 37, 43–44, 145; in Izmir, 36–41, 82, 142; Muslims in, 39–40; in the Morea, 51–67; on Mediterranean, 119, 178, 204. *See also* English Levant Company; Networks
Commissions: Bendysh's, 94, 96, 99–101, 102, 112, 127, 131, 178, 179, 185, 196, 201–2; from the king, 105, 160, 164, 220; Crow's, 114; for ships, 148, 149, 197; from parliament, 188; Winchelsea's, 203–4, 206
Commodities: traded, 37, 45–46, 54–55, 64; stored, 41, 56, 74, 77, 83, 131–32, 140, 187; confiscated, 71–72, 82–83, 92, 114, 117, 130, 135, 165, 174, 177–78, 186, 197–99, 203, 214, 219, 225n24, 237n9, 244n24; surcharges on, 78, 80, 104, 106, 107, 205–6; prices of, 83, 85. *See also* Commerce
Commonwealth, 9, 45, 146, 170, 177–93, 194–96, 220
Concubines, 26
Conrad, Joseph, 265n3

Constantinople. *See* Istanbul
Consulage: collection of, 15, 52, 54, 61, 163, 204, 205–6, 207, 214; from strangers, 42, 67, 72–73, 79, 90, 93, 95, 97, 106, 123, 139, 140, 160, 191; payment of, 63, 106–7, 108
Consuls: and subordinates, 14, 16, 108; stature of, 15, 24, 42; appointment of, 15, 29, 89, 93, 210; and Ottoman authorities, 17, 27, 41, 45, 104, 126; in Izmir, 21, 39, 42, 46, 48–49, 50, 74–81, 83, 137, 138, 139, 141, 142, 149, 160, 167, 169, 170–72, 173–76, 177, 179, 181–83, 205–7, 219, 259n58; in Aleppo, 46, 90, 137, 158, 217; responsibilities of, 47, 51, 86, 131, 141, 208; in the Morea, 52–67, 124, 159, 163–64, 218, 234n14, 247n64; income of, 99, 106, 107–8, 203
Contarini, Nadalin, 126
Convention Parliament, English, 201
Convoys, 186–87, 198, 199
Copes, Signor, 84, 92, 111
Coptics, Church of, 216
Corbin, Robert, 62–63
Corinth, Gulf of, 52
Cornhill, 170
Corsairs. *See* Piracy
Corte, Thomas, 198
Cottington, Lord, 69
Council of State, English: actions of, 158, 170, 184–87, 191; petitions to, 186, 206–7
Courts of Law. *See* Law
Covel, John, 27
Covenant, Scottish, 68, 91, 113, 159

Cress, Simsonn, 47–48
Crete: war over, 75, 76, 77, 79, 104, 118–19, 147, 148–52, 153–54, 155, 184, 192; food from, 105
Cromwell, Oliver: and Bendysh, 5, 184–85, 189, 190–93, 194–96, 199, 207, 210, 220; as imperialist, 6, 9, 110, 192–93, 214; and Levant Company, 91, 123; protectorate of, 145, 165, 188, 195, 197, 200, 202; as general, 168; letters from, 190, 198
Crow, Lady, 120–21
Crow, Sackvile: as royalist, 5, 65–67, 70–87, 98, 103, 106, 111–13, 132, 138, 190, 201, 237n8, 239n45, 241n11; as ambassador, 9–10, 15, 120, 133, 135–36, 140, 213, 244n28; in sources, 12, 225n24; employing Ottoman officials, 27, 124; and English factories, 43, 108–9, 131, 134, 141, 150, 160, 162, 166, 218–19, 251n18; and English factory at Izmir, 46, 48–49, 107, 139, 238n29; and English factory at Patras, 51–67; rulings by, 51, 61–65, 80; petitions to, 55, 56, 58–59, 60; salary of, 78; removal from office of, 88–93, 102, 115–17, 125, 137, 147, 181, 185, 187, 204, 248n74; and Bendysh, 104, 114–17, 145, 188, 195, 241n25, 246n42, 246n44, 246n49, 247n71; in London, 120–23, 157; after recall, 191, 196, 200, 208–9, 210
Crusades: in Izmir, 36; expenses of, 53
Currants, 52–56, 60, 62, 63, 64, 65, 233n12, 234n15
Curtin, Philip, 43–44

Customs collectors, Ottoman: described, 17, 78, 126; in Aleppo, 21, 162; in Istanbul, 22, 81, 151, 177–78; and Britons, 27; in Izmir, 38, 39, 76, 79–80, 174, 175–76; Hyde as, 52–53, 151; in the Morea, 55, 56, 60, 63; as administrators, 86, 99; alleged abuses of, 103–4, 117, 147–48, 150, 199, 244*n*24. *See also* Tax-farming

Cyprus, 196–97

Damascus, 30, 216
Danube River, 31
Dardanelles Straits: blockade of, 76, 105, 118, 119, 147–53, 155, 169, 196, 199; battles at, 193; inspections at, 198. *See also* Venice; Warfare
Davies, Jonathan, 136
Davis, Gyles, 136, 165, 169, 177
Davy, Henry, 74
Dawes, Jonathan, 142, 167, 172–76, 177–78, 181, 183, 197–98, 209, 258*n*58
Day, Thomas, 62–63
Decentralization, Ottoman: influence on provinces of, 31, 37, 42, 85, 86, 137, 169, 219; influence on commerce of, 43–44, 195, 207
Decrees: sultanic, 18, 20, 58–59, 60, 74–77, 82–86, 105, 120, 139, 141, 150, 162–63, 171, 172, 219, 225*n*24; English, 84
Defence (ship), 54, 57, 60, 61–62, 63, 64
Defterdarbaşı, 112, 118
Denmark, 159
Dering, Edward, 202
Diaspora: trading, 14

Diplomats: in Istanbul, 14, 15, 21, 34–35, 42, 116, 147; appointments of, 16; demeanors of, 23, 201–11; and Ottoman officials, 27, 40–41, 45; and English Levant Company, 29, 209–10; and factories, 43; growing importance of, 72; English community of, 98, 193, 215, 220–21, 247*n*68
Districts. *See Mahalle*s
Divan, Imperial: members of, 17, 115, 155; negotiations with, 162, 163, 165–67, 168, 169. *See also* Sublime Porte
Dodington, Mr., 180
Doge, 69, 70, 155
Dorchester, Lord, 127
Downes, Lord, 157
The Downs, 101
Dragomans: as interpreters, 16–17, 42, 57, 62, 74–85 passim, 96, 147, 181; taxes on, 22; appointments of, 39, 200; responsibilities of, 49, 105–6, 111, 113, 128, 227*n*8; salaries of, 54, 108, 210; in Izmir, 77, 78, 82, 84–85; censure of, 130–31, 163, 167
Draperis, Giorgio, 85–86, 130–31, 163, 167, 200
Drapers Hall, 202
Dubrovnik, 32, 216
Dupuy, Jean, 78, 83, 167, 171–72, 173, 175
Dutch. *See* Netherlands
Dutch Levant Company, 13

East India Company, English, 214, 224*n*21, 240*n*4
Eastland-merchant (ship), 197
Edirne, 32, 208, 210
Edward (ship), 60–63, 65, 75

Edwards, Daniel, 74, 79
Edwards, Mr., 27
Egypt: conquest of, 20; food from, 119, 147, 197; travel to, 216
Eldem, Edhem, 227n8
Elford, Walter, 67, 121
Elizabeth (ship), 140
Elizabeth I (1558–1603), 15, 138, 202
Ell, William, 197–99
Emins. *See* Customs collectors
Emirates, Turkoman, 36
Empires: Muslim, 4, 192, 215; religion in, 18–20, 192, 228n11. *See also* British Empire; Ottoman Empire
Endo, Shusako, 213, 266n4
Engagement, Oath of, 178, 259n6
England: imperialism of, 3, 37, 143, 178–79, 191–93, 214–15; civil wars in, 6, 88, 93, 103, 108–9, 110, 115, 122, 145, 146, 158, 161, 166, 168, 177, 259n6; commerce of, 13–15, 38, 107, 114, 138, 202; religion in, 18–19, 23–24, 68, 100, 170–71; society of, 28, 113, 126, 213, 217, 218, 227n6; and exile, 56, 60, 61, 65, 94, 100–101, 121, 123, 131, 137, 157, 159, 168, 169, 170–71, 175, 188, 189, 190, 203–11 passim; Talbot in, 68–71; and Venetians, 68–71, 76, 150, 176, 184–85; estates in, 79, 83–84, 99, 140, 202–3; and ambassadors, 124, 181, 183, 194, 198; during interregnum, 180, 191, 194–96, 200–201; and Dutch, 185. *See also* British Empire; Britons; Civil Wars, English
England, Church of, 108
Englesby, John, 74
Englishman. *See* Britons

Erisey, John, 26–27, 167
Erizzo, Francisco, 69
Essex, 99
Ethnicity, 18–20
Eunuchs, 26
Europe, southeastern. *See* Balkans
Evans, Maurice, 131–34, 136
Evans, Morris, 84
Evliya Çelebi, 248n77
Executions, 43, 118

Factors: defined, 14, 26–27, 227n6; trade of, 17, 43–44, 149, 200, 215; authority of, 21, 122, 180; effectiveness of, 24, 31, 144, 165, 186; in Aleppo, 29, 41–42, 45–47, 162, 217–18; and wine, 35; in Izmir, 46–51, 74, 76–83, 104–9, 169, 170–71, 205–7, 210, 225n24; responsibilities of, 46, 86, 99, 100, 198, 203; in the Morea, 55; as parliamentarians, 72–73, 84, 90, 98, 219; and Bendysh, 101–9, 111, 127, 130, 131–35, 146, 147, 152, 156–57, 162, 164, 167, 168–69, 181, 210; and Ottoman authorities, 104, 116, 128; squabbles between, 137–43, 150, 173–76, 183, 208, 214, 237n9, 251n18
Factories: defined, 14; rivalries between, 31, 15, 73, 125–26, 137–38, 162–63, 164, 185; in Izmir, 21, 42–43, 48–49, 66, 76–85, 89, 103–9, 120, 138–39, 152, 166, 167, 169–76 passim, 187, 205–7, 219; autonomy of, 22, 40–41, 74, 85, 116, 138, 144; in Istanbul, 25, 35, 83–87, 98, 111, 115, 116, 117, 127–35 passim, 147–48, 149, 150, 151, 154, 156–57, 158, 163–64; established, 29; in Aleppo, 30,

Factories *(continued)*
  162–63, 208, 215–16, 217–18;
  of various nations, 30, 216–17;
  compared, 41; disputes within,
  46–49; and Bendysh, 137, 189.
  See also Nations
Fairfax, Thomas, 70
Fethergall, 143–44
*fetva*s, 77
Finch, John, 27
Firmans. *See* Decrees
Fisher, Jeremy, 62–63
Fissel, Mark Charles, x
Fleming, Oliver, 185
Florence, 205
Foça, 36, 39, 154
Food: types of, in Ottoman Empire, 25; for Istanbul, 37, 196–99; scarcity of, 40–41; smuggling of, 60–61, 77
Foreign Affairs, Committee of, English, 185
Forster, E. M., 265*n*3
Forster, Richard, 72
Foulke, William, 234*n*14
Fowke, Roger, 152–53, 153–54, 162
Frampton, Richard, 217
Frampton, Robert, 84, 136, 162, 165, 169, 177, 239–40*n*46
France: consuls of, 14–15, 79, 83, 167, 169; presence of, in Istanbul, 15, 21, 22, 35, 73, 105, 110, 111, 115, 130, 132, 147, 150, 157, 163, 165, 166, 171, 172, 177, 181, 183–84, 195; in Levant, 16, 22, 38, 102, 126, 151, 152, 162, 198, 200, 218, 244*n*24; and Ottoman society, 30, 50, 104, 127, 129; presence of in Izmir, 39, 40, 152, 170–70; and Britons, 51, 62, 63, 77, 84, 92, 94, 98, 106, 173, 204; Britons in, 159–61, 175, 220; travels in, 212; language of, 216. *See also* Haye, de la
Francis, Michael, 132
Franks, Street of the, 38, 40–41, 43, 49–50. *See also* Izmir
Frontiers: as societies, x, 7, 205, 223*n*9, 223*n*14; encounters on, 12; diplomats in, 14; cultural, 23–26, 219; commercial, 31, 201; ideological, 36, 218; Ottoman, 51–53, 123–24, 221, 226*n*25

Galata: foreigners in, 14, 22, 80, 85, 86, 114, 115, 117, 149, 172; Genoese in, 33; as part of Istanbul, 34–35; taverns in, 35; English factory at, 132, 133, 136–45 passim, 147, 152, 154, 156, 162–62, 164, 168–69. *See also* Pera
Gallipoli: Ottoman armies in, 31; officials at, 150, 245*n*29
Garway, Robert, 121
Garway, William, 121, 190
Genoese: commerce of, 13, 37; in Istanbul, 21, 33; on Chios, 39
George (ship), 155–56, 190
Giavarina, 205
Gibbs, William, 129
Gibraltar, Straits of, 13, 102, 186
Giocomo Point, 175
Glorious Revolution, 9
Gloucester, Bishopric of, 240*n*46
Glover, Thomas, 78
Golden Fleece (ship), 92
Golden Horn, 14, 33, 34, 147, 152, 172
Golden Lyon (ship), 82–83
Goodlade, Richard, 54, 101
Gotbed, Mr., 101
Goulden Faulcon (ship), 54, 56

Governors: in Anatolia, 40
Granada, 102
Grand Vizier. *See* Viziers
Great Game, 223*n13*
Greece, 164
Greek Orthodox. *See* Greeks
Greeks: as Ottoman subjects, 16, 19, 92, 129, 216; laws of, 18, 50, 138; intercommunal disputes of, 20; in Istanbul, 21, 33; English attitudes toward, 23, 24, 27, 144, 217; negotiations of Britons with, 27, 51, 57, 62, 63, 67, 126–31, 218; commerce of, 32; in Izmir, 38–39, 77, 83, 176; as dragomans, 74–85 passim, 127; language of, 215
Green, Graham, 265*n3*
Greere, William, 133
Gunpowder, 15

Habsburg Empire, 32
Haggatt, Paul, 139, 166, 167, 170, 191, 257*n32*
The Hague, 158
Hamilton, Mr., 180
*Hammal*s, 83
Hangar, George, 74, 79, 139–40
Harborne, William, 72, 202
Harems. *See* Households
Harman, Thomas, 56
Hasan, 105
Hasan Ağa, 177–78, 199
Hasan Çelebi, 81
Hashimizade, 181–82
Hatchooke, 130
Hatt-i şerif. See Decrees
Haye, de la, 110, 120, 121, 150, 171, 176, 177, 183–84. *See also* France
Head tax, Ottoman, 22
Hekem, Abraham, 130

Henrietta Maria, 110, 161
Hetherington, John, 74–85, 98, 101, 103, 121, 241*n11*
Hirst, Derek, 6
Hisar Ağası, 174–75
Historiography: Anglo-Ottoman, ix–x, 6–12, 212–13, 223*n14*; cross-cultural, ix–x; Little England School of, 7; Ottoman, 19–20, 224–25*n22*. *See also* Sources
Hodges, Witt., 149
Holdenby Hall, 96
Holmuch, 53, 58, 62, 64
Holy Sepulchre, Church of the, 215–16, 217
Honiero, George, 108
Hopefull Imployment (ship), 198
Hopewell (ship), 82, 144
Households: Ottoman, 25, 26, 33, 145, 195; of Charles II, 209
Howe, Roger, 127, 168, 169, 177, 258*n58*
Hunt, Henry, 54, 89
Hurt, John, 127
Hüseyin Ahmed Ağa, 83
Hyde, Edward: during Civil Wars, 69–70, 94, 96, 110, 113; during interregnum, 159, 161, 168, 209, 255*n7*
Hyde, Henry: execution of, x, 54, 66, 67, 170–71; as royalist, 4–5, 73, 81, 98, 120, 201; in sources, 12, 220; in the Morea, 51–67, 85, 123–24, 218–19, 233*n12*, 233–34*n13*, 247*n64*; exile to England of, 101, 121, 177, 204; and Bendysh, 159, 161–71, 178, 188, 195, 205, 237*n9*, 247*n68*, 248*n72*, 255*n7*; in Istanbul, 160, 161–69; in Izmir, 169–71; aftermath of involvement in the Levant,

Hyde, Henry *(continued)*
172–76, 180, 181, 183; and English Levant Company, 187; and Ottoman world, 213

İbrahim, 43
İbrahim (1640–48), 72, 93, 94, 95, 113, 118, 145, 148, 165, 195, 241n25
Imperialism: English, 3–4, 6, 7–8, 15, 37, 215, 221, 222n2, 222n3, 226n25; modern, 5; over time, 24. *See also* Commerce
India, 3, 8, 210–11, 215, 222n2
Indian Ocean, 32
Indies, 143
Inquisition, Spanish, 121
Interregnum: influence of English, overseas, 21, 29, 220; in England, 28, 123; Byzantine, 36; Ottoman, 37
Ireland, 6, 7, 161, 168, 214
Isaackson, Mr., 180
Isaacson, Anthony, 206–7
Isiodoro, 143
Iskenderun. *See* Alexandretta
Islam: civilization of, 4, 21, 22, 213; and Christianity, 13, 39, 109, 143–44, 191–93, 217–18; and factories, 41, 219; and attitude toward non-Muslims, 41; laws of, 51
Istanbul: as market, 5, 15, 37, 130–31, 133, 187, 230n12; Crow at, 5, 46, 62–65, 70–87, 94, 104, 201; English in, 8, 14, 17, 21–26, 28, 29, 71–72, 98, 100, 134, 136, 142, 145, 150, 156, 172–73, 198, 216, 218, 219, 243n13; factories in, 15, 50, 73, 74, 105, 107, 125–35; conquest of, 20, 31, 32–33, 36; English factory at, 29, 30, 31, 43–44, 78, 81–85, 105, 127–135, 137, 141, 146, 158, 180, 183, 185, 237n9; as commercial and political center, 29, 31, 37, 42, 45, 116, 120, 124, 138, 144, 230n6; as Ottoman capital, 31–35, 149, 152, 192, 200; history of, 31–35; as part of Constantinople, 34–35; Jews in, 39, 132; merchants in, 39; politics in, 43, 92, 140, 157, 193; and Ottoman frontiers, 52, 206; Britons brought to, 65, 85; ships at, 76, 115, 140, 147, 149, 151, 155, 179, 189, 197–99, 205, 245n32; Bendysh at, 97, 176, 182, 184, 193, 195, 199–202, 220–21, 226n25; Ottoman officials at, 99, 130, 148, 177–78; Bendysh and Crow together at, 109–12; unrest in, 118, 119, 154, 165, 199–200; Bendysh and Hyde together at, 121, 159–71, 172; replacements for Bendysh at, 186, 187–90, 201–5
Italy, 32, 103, 192, 215
Ivate, George, 89
Izmir: as port city, x, 182; as market, 5, 244n24; English in, 8, 14, 21, 23, 24, 28, 98, 99, 100, 124, 128, 135, 136, 138, 156, 178, 181, 210, 218, 243n13, 263n38; structure of, 18; English factory at, 29, 30, 35, 48–49, 50, 73–83, 91, 103–9, 110, 125, 132, 140, 146, 152, 166, 167, 173–76, 180, 183, 185, 187, 205–7, 219; Ottoman officials at, 31, 74–85, 117, 121, 154; development of, 36–43, 232n28; commerce in, 43, 45, 187; and Istanbul, 46, 84–85, 86, 116, 150, 166–67, 173; English consul in, 47, 89, 149, 158,

160, 164, 177; ships at, 63, 75, 76, 120, 123, 139, 147, 148, 151, 152–55, 169, 172, 174, 175, 179, 186, 189, 199, 205, 245*n*32; and English ambassadors, 66, 112, 137, 140–43, 169, 220, 257*n*32; seizures of goods in, 82–83, 225*n*24; Hyde at, 169–72
Izmir, Gulf of, 39, 40, 106, 115, 120, 140, 147, 172, 232*n*29

James I (1603–25), 15, 203
Janissaries: as guards, 17, 22, 23, 57, 64, 81, 83, 106, 107, 113, 173; salary of, 54; power of, 59, 61–62, 63, 81–82, 118, 181, 244 *n*24; in Izmir, 77, 79, 174–76; in Istanbul, 80, 172; *ağa* of, 153, 182
Jannie, Jacob, 129
Jannie, Samaria, 129
Jantoph, 128
Japan, 212–13, 266*n*4
Jerick, Captain, 121
Jersey, 161
Jerusalem: role of, in Ottoman Empire, 30, 267*n*17; pilgrimage to, 162, 215, 216, 217
Jews: as Ottoman subjects, 16, 19, 114, 223*n*1; laws of, 18, 50, 51, 138; in Istanbul, 21, 33, 35, 133, 134, 168; English attitudes toward, 23, 24, 84, 126–30, 144, 163, 216, 217, 250*n*9; negotiations of Britons with, 27, 51, 53, 67, 75, 100, 126–31, 132, 180, 218; commerce of, 32, 39, 45, 47–51, 140; in Izmir, 38–39, 46–49, 77, 80, 81, 82–83, 176; as English assistants, 62, 78, 107, 135; in Aleppo, 162
John (ship), 148

John Bonaventure (ship), 183
Jonas (ship), 81
Jordon, Captain, 121
Juatt, George, 48

*Kadiasker*s, 25, 86, 130
Kadis: authority of described, 17–18, 59; in Izmir, 40, 42, 74–83 passim, 84, 85, 86, 108, 117, 121, 167, 169, 171–72, 174–76, 181, 219; in Patras, 51, 55, 56, 58–60, 61, 63, 65, 67, 117; in Istanbul, 127, 130; in Ottoman empire, 150, 245*n*29
Kafadar, Cemal, 223*n*9
Kafu, Nagai, 212–13
Kapıcı, 217–18
Kapıcıbaşı, 105–6
Kapudanpaşa. *See* Admiral, Ottoman
Karlowitz, Treaty of, 20
Kayık, 34, 41, 116
Kaymakam, 51, 182
Keble, Robert, 121
Keeble, Jeffrey, 156–57
Keeble, Joseph, 107
Kent, 203
Khan, 41, 49
Killigrew, Peter, 84, 239*n*45
Killigrew, William, 90, 94, 95
Kingston, Maxine Hong, 265*n*3
Koran, 19, 30
Kuşadası, 39

Lach, Donald, 213
Lake, Richard, 26, 46–47
Lancelot, John, 48, 74, 79, 80, 89, 90, 91, 92, 93, 97, 98, 111, 112
Latins. *See* Catholics
Laurell (ship), 131, 148–49, 151
Lawrence, Joanna, 190

Lawrence, Richard, 46–51, 67, 128, 135–36, 137, 187–90, 191, 196, 220

Laws: types of, 17–18, 50, 53, 181, 233*n1*; disputes in Ottoman courts over, 18, 27, 42, 50–51, 56–60, 61, 65, 129, 181–82; English, 18–19, 42, 65, 71, 121–23, 127, 132, 139, 219; Western, 22; sumptuary, 35; extraterritorial, 51, 86; Ottoman, 58, 67, 73, 77, 86, 111, 113, 127, 131, 134–35, 142, 144, 204

Leghorn, 90, 102, 103, 128, 131, 133, 136, 186, 187, 193, 197, 205, 234*n15*

Lello, Henry, 15, 72

Lepanto: commerce at, 52, 54, 55, 58, 62; Ottoman officials at, 61

Levant: English presence in, 5, 9, 15, 29, 37, 46–49, 72, 73, 88, 98, 99, 107, 113, 117, 120, 123–24, 138, 142, 152, 162, 178–81, 188, 192, 200, 219; Britons in, 9, 13–14, 66, 75, 84, 87, 109, 145, 160, 165, 170, 187, 204, 213, 215–18; Venetians in, 16; port cities in, 22, 46; culture of, 144; Dutch in, 185. *See also* Mediterranean Sea

Levant Company, English: factors of, 4, 9, 26–27, 63–64, 108–9, 116, 134, 183; ideology of, 10, 15, 67, 100, 123, 224*n21*, 240*n4*; structure of, 13, 59, 166; goods marketed by, 15, 52–56, 60, 150; development of, 15, 29, 116, 137–38, 202–3, 214; settlement in Istanbul of, 34, 86, 149; appointees of, 47, 65, 72, 78, 102, 143, 186, 189–90, 207, 218; directors of, 54, 124, 126, 170, 181, 220, 237*n9*; disputes with, 55–67, 121, 130, 162, 163, 170–71, 180; correspondence with, 55, 56, 57, 111, 137, 180, 227*n6*; clashes with monarchy of, 72–73, 79, 83–84, 87–98 passim, 121–23, 160, 161, 190–91, 208; and Bendysh, 99, 103, 117, 120, 135, 146, 153, 172, 177, 181, 184, 188, 194, 200, 209–10; ships of, 104, 119, 126, 132; income and expenses of, 106–7, 113, 131, 185, 187, 205–6, 210; and slaves, 156, 198–99; and commonwealth, 158, 178, 179, 197; and Charles II, 201–5

Levant Merchant (ship), 186

Levi, Moise, 62

Leviations: demanded by Crow, 66, 78–79, 80, 81, 89, 162, 251*n18*; description of, 75; as income, 99, 160; demanded by Bendysh, 140–41, 142

Lewis (ship), 133, 170

Literature, travel, 213

Little Lewis (ship), 197–99

Lomby, Martin, 99

London, City of, 10; as commercial center, 14, 29, 30, 38, 41, 86, 103, 159, 220, 224*n21*; religion in, 24, 100, 101, 109; politics in, 43, 68, 88, 110, 177, 178, 180, 184, 201, 205, 207, 209, 214, 220; merchants in, 45, 46–47, 60, 71–72, 89–93, 96, 124, 197; ships to and from, 54, 66, 121, 170, 171, 172; diplomats in, 69, 153, 191, 208, 209–11, 219

London (ship), 98, 101, 105, 106

London Dragon (ship), 170–71

Longland, Charles, 193, 196–97, 198

Lowe, Mr., 243–44*n20*

Lura, Oslan, 108
Lura, Signor, 108
Luvizo, Signor, 233–34*n13*

Madrid, 159
*Mahalle*s: in Istanbul, 34; structure of, 49–50
Mahmud, kadi of Patras, 51, 55, 56, 58–60, 61, 63, 65
Mahmut Efendi, 25
Mahmut Pasha, 59
Majorca, 102, 197
Malaya, 8
Malta, 63, 143
Man, Nathaniel, 127
Manchu Empire, 8
Manisa, 37
Manley, Robert, 197
Manzarat, Monsieur, 175–76
Maplesden, Edward, 131, 148–49
Margaret (ship), 120, 121, 123
Marmara, 37
Marmara, Sea of, 34, 110, 173
Marseilles, 16
Marston Moor, Battle of, 69
Mary (ship), 186
Massey, Edward, 69
Masters, Bruce, 230*n4*
Mawola, 140
May, Thomas, 198
Mayne, Bermet, 149
Mecca, 30
Medina, 30
Mediterranean Sea: as a borderland, x, 5, 10, 115, 119, 179, 186, 191–92, 193, 196–97; commerce in, 13–14, 18, 29, 33, 43–44, 46, 102, 116, 117, 140, 160, 196–97, 198, 204, 214; states bordering, 16, 52, 70, 126, 155, 214; peoples of, 23, 143–45. *See also* Levant

Mehemet Agra, 56, 62
Mehmed II (1444–46, 1451–81): and Istanbul, 32–33; mosque complex of, 34; as prince, 37
Mehmed IV (1648–87), 188, 190, 197, 199
Mehmed Ağa, 135
Mehmed Efendi, Bahai, 181–82
Mehmed Pasha, Ammar-zade, 147, 149, 151
Mehmed Pasha, Derviş, 188
Mehmed Pasha, Gürcü, 183–84
Mehmed Pasha, Haydar-Ağa-zade, 156
Mehmed Pasha, Köprülü, 165, 194, 200
Mehmed Pasha, Sofu, 149
Menemen, 37
Mervin, John, 148
Messina, 103, 133
Middle East, 215
Midleton, Roger, 172
Millets: discussed, 19–20, 232–33*n1*; and foreigners, 20, 22–23, 125–31, 134; disputes within, 45–51; autonomy of, 49–51
Mills, Joh., 198
Milward, Thomas, 48
Mithwold, Mr., 185
Modon, 64
Modona, 155
Modyford, James, 84, 129, 150, 164–66, 167, 172, 173, 176
Montania, 110
Morea, 4; English consul in, 29, 159, 163–64, 166, 218, 247*n64*; English disputes at, 51–67, 85, 237*n9*; currants from, 52–56; stopovers at, 103, 215
Morell, Mosse, 47, 48
Morgan, Philip D., 6, 7

Morian, Joseph, 47, 48
Morosini, Michele, 161, 184
Mosques, 34, 35
Moyer, James, 74, 79
Mughal Empire, 4, 8
Muhammed, Prophet, 19, 30
Mukherjee, Bharati, 3, 222*n*2, 265*n*3
Murad II (1420–44, 1446–51), 37
Murad IV (1623–40), 118
Murad Pasha, Kara, 151, 153, 165, 166, 168, 169, 171, 172
Murat, Hoggia, 47
Musa Pasha, Kara, 118
Muslims: as Ottoman officials, 17, 127, 143; in Istanbul, 21, 33, 35; English attitudes toward, 23, 24, 27, 126, 144, 192, 216, 217; negotiations of Britons with, 27, 51, 57, 58, 67; commerce of, 32, 48, 55–56, 80, 196; in Izmir, 38–40, 46–49, 77, 176; laws of, 50, 138
Mustafa Çavuş, 168, 169
Mustafa Naima, 182
Mustafa Pasha, Kara, 118, 162
Müste'min, 22
Myers, Alexander, 132

*Naib*s, 77, 81–83, 150, 174
Naipaul, V. S., 213, 265*n*3
Narayan, R. K., 265*n*3
Nathalico Road, 62
Nations: as communities of merchants, 16, 25, 29, 42, 46, 50–51, 84, 91, 115, 126, 136, 138, 141, 174, 227*n*6, 232*n*28; English example, 19, 27–28, 43, 48–49, 54, 55, 60, 62, 63, 75, 76, 83, 85, 94, 99, 106–9, 111, 120, 122–24, 128–29, 132, 133, 137, 139, 142–45, 147, 149, 152, 154, 159, 160, 162, 167, 170, 183, 185, 187, 198, 217, 219; vs. empires, 20, 227*n*10; privileges of in Pera, 33; disputes within, 85–87, 121; English, 187, 204; Turks as, 192. *See also* Britons; Factories
Navy, Committee for the, 121–22
Netherlands, 6; innovations of, 13; English rivalry with, 15, 68, 106, 179, 184–85, 186, 189, 191, 192, 198, 234*n*15; presence of, in Istanbul, 21, 35, 84, 92, 105, 111, 147, 183, 190, 195; in Ottoman port cities, 22, 30, 39, 40, 126; commerce of, 38, 187; and Ottoman society, 50, 127; ships of, 152, 155
Networks: commercial, 30, 32, 38, 43–45, 50, 126, 159, 204, 214, 221, 230*n*9; provisioning, 37–38, 119
New Model Army, English, 189
Newcastle, 93, 95, 103
Newcastle Propositions, 91
Newsam, Thomas, 141, 167–68, 169
Nicaea, 36
Nicholas, Edward, 69–70, 202, 205, 206–7, 255*n*7
Nif, 37
Northamptonshire, 96
Northumberland (ship), 168–69
Notables: in Aleppo, 21, 31, 137, 195; in Izmir, 31, 38, 40, 81, 121, 137, 176, 219; in Istanbul, 77

Oceania, 5
Orient, 212–13
Orientalism, ix, 7–8, 11–12, 25, 212–13, 222*n*2, 265–66*n*3
Orwell, George, 213
Osborne, William, 128, 129–30, 131, 133, 134, 136

Ottoman Empire: Britons in, 4, 13, 16–28 passim, 53–67, 94, 102, 108, 124, 139, 163, 181, 189, 198, 206–7, 215–21, 227n6; compared to British Empire, 4, 7, 8, 9, 20, 24, 35, 88; government of, 5, 15, 21, 86, 165, 175, 199–201, 208, 210, 214; historiography of, 10, 38; commerce of, 13, 32, 43–44, 45–46, 76; English trade in, 14, 93, 109, 125; relations with British of, 14, 17, 29, 68, 72, 92, 98, 103, 129, 131, 137, 138, 143, 150–52, 155, 159, 179, 184, 190, 194, 197–99, 205, 220–21; officials in, 16–18, 21, 172–76, 218; society of, 18–23, 27–28, 49–51, 129, 143–44, 173, 204, 213, 218, 223n9, 224n18; non-Muslim subjects of, 19–20, 23, 127, 128–29, 135, 144, 216–17; provinces of, 21, 36–38, 42, 61, 207, 218–19; foreigners in, 22–23, 27–28, 45, 103–4; food in, 25, 151; expansion of, 32–33; authority of, 42; frontiers of, 51–67, 119, 123–24, 130, 230n4; considered as infidel, 73, 191–93; identity in, 134; military of, 148, 152–54, 192–93. *See also* Empires; Sublime Porte

Oxford, 66, 68–71, 72, 94, 164

Oxinden, George, 210–11

Padua, 216

Paris: compared to Istanbul, 34; as commercial and political center, 38, 184; role of, in English Civil Wars, 72, 94, 112, 159, 161, 165, 171

Parliament: and king, 5, 14, 68–69, 88–97, 98, 108, 110, 113, 134, 138, 146, 150, 159, 168, 169, 179, 214, 219; authority of, 59, 65, 66–67, 83, 87, 122, 145, 190–91, 240n4; legitimacy of, 88–89, 158; ideology of, 101, 123, 224n21; letters from, 105, 111, 187–88; during interregnum, 153, 157, 173, 178–81, 186; Scottish, 168; and Bendysh, 177, 184–87

Parliament, Houses of, 90–91, 96, 99

Pashas: described, 17; in the Morea, 51, 59, 61, 63, 65, 67; and Sublime Porte, 126; in Cairo, 197. *See also* Sublime Porte; Viziers

Patras: English at, 8, 51, 65; English consul at, 29, 51, 52, 56; Ottoman officials at, 54, 57, 59, 60, 61, 67, 117; commerce at, 62–64

Patras Road, 54

Paulucci, 184–85, 191

Pearle, William, 127–28, 130, 162

Peloponnesus. *See* Morea

Pennington, Isaac, 54, 88, 89

Pera: diplomats in, 25, 27, 43, 157, 167; as foreign enclave, 34–35, 40–41, 50; commodities at, 131–32. *See also* Galata

Perists, Benjamin, 127

Persia: commerce in, 32, 37, 38

Petitions: to imperial divan, 18, 58, 61, 78, 81, 84–85, 164; from kadis, 59, 65, 167; to English king, 66; to and from Levant Company, 91, 93, 121, 178, 200, 202; to ambassadors, 131–33, 136–37, 162, 206

Philorito, Saphiere, 62

Phocaea. *See* Foça

Pickett, Marmaduke, 131, 169
Pickett, Richard, 136, 165, 169
Piggot, Thomas, 84
Pilgrims, Christian, 23, 217–18
Pincus, Steve, 6
Piracy: as commerce, 13–14, 155; on Mediterranean sea, 101–2, 116, 119–20, 196–97, 199, 245*n32*; and Barbaries, 143–44, 155–56, 210
Pitches, Lambert, 56
Pitler, Mr., 80
Pixley, John, 79, 132, 180
Plague, 132
Plummer, John, 144, 166
Plymouth (ship), 205
Pocock, J. G. A., 6–7
Poland, 32
Poole, Mr., 101
Population: in Istanbul, 32–33, 35, 147; in Izmir, 38–40
Port Cities: typology of, x, 41; English in, 8, 15, 160; in the Levant, 22, 49–50, 126; Ottoman, 29–44, 50; Venice as, 33; Izmir as, 36; Leghorn as one, 102
Porter, Captain, 76
Portuguese, 230*n9*
Postcolonialism. *See* Orientalism
Presbyterianism, 113, 218, 259*n6*
Prichett, Thomas, 64
Protestantism, 6, 102, 191, 192, 203, 216–18
Public Record Office, 12
Puritanism, 215, 218, 224*n21*

Quarles, William, 90, 92

Ragusa. *See* Dubrovnik
Read, Morgan, 157
Reade, Frances, 46–51, 67, 128, 131–33, 135–36, 148

Religion: in the Ottoman Empire, 18–20; in England, 23–24; English controls over, 99, 108. *See also* Christianity; Islam
Renegades: as pirates, 15, 26, 61, 119, 143–44; as fugitives, 134, 151; and Ottomans, 151, 152, 179, 199
Resolution (ship), 54, 196–97, 210
Restoration, English: influence of overseas, 21, 201; living with, 28, 45, 71, 123, 204, 208–11, 217
Reyner, Dr., 101, 162
Rhodes, 156, 190
Rich, Mary, 46–47
Rich, Tho., 46–47
Roberts, Lewise, 46–47
Robinson, John, 121
Roe, Sir Thomas, 9, 78
Roman Empire. *See* Byzantine Empire
Roundheads, 5
Royalism, 5, 6
Rumeli, 25, 59
Rupert, Prince, 179
Russia, 32
Rycaut, Paul, 9, 27, 208
Rydley, John, 128, 129, 131–33, 134, 136

Şaban Çavuş, 172
Sagredo, 184
Saguen, 128, 129
Said, Edward, ix
St. Martin in the Fields, 99
Sainthill, Robert, 90, 92, 102–3
Salih Pasha, 76
Salla, 62
Salmon, Robert, 149
Salonica, 32
Salvetti, Amerigo, 153, 184
Salway, Richard, 185–86, 187, 191

Sampson (ship), 148, 149–50, 151, 186
San Stefano, 116
Scamander River, 110
Scotland: and English Civil Wars, 3, 6, 7, 214; and Charles I, 72, 73, 96, 259*n*6; and Charles II, 159, 161, 168, 178, 180
Seal: Great, of English monarch, 93, 110, 112, 169, 247*n*64; of parliament, 158
Senate, Venetian: English relations with, 69–71, 150, 151, 153, 155, 161, 192–93
Seraglio Point, 147, 178
Serbia, 20, 216
Serdar, 59, 62
Sermony, 128, 129
Sermony, Isaac, 128
Seydee Mohi, Yedee, 143
Şeyhülislam, 112, 118, 154, 181–82, 183, 193, 247*n*68
Shariah. *See* Laws
Ships: innovations in, 13–14; in Mediterranean, 15, 29, 185, 217; at Izmir, 40, 41, 63, 81, 120, 152–55, 169, 172, 174, 175, 179; and goods shipped and smuggled, 56, 62–63, 76, 79, 92, 106, 138–40, 149, 150, 151, 197–99; and piracy, 61, 63, 75, 119, 144, 210; detained, 74–76, 80, 82, 91, 104, 105, 106–7, 109, 114, 131, 149, 155–56, 196–97; and parliament, 96; and storms, 101; skirmishes between, 101–2, 162, 186, 196–97; in Venetian and Ottoman service, 103, 104, 115, 119–20, 152, 153–54, 157, 166, 169, 176, 178, 180, 182, 183, 184, 192–93; supplies for, 104, 152; Ottoman, 116, 143, 152–53; and English policy, 145, 147–48, 186–87, 189, 190, 203, 214, 245*n*32
Shushin, Jacob Aben, 135
Sicily, 215
Silk: as commodity, 32, 37, 133–34, 186, 214; in Izmir, 38; in Aleppo, 45. *See also* Commerce
Simonds, Thomas, 133
Sio, 143
*Sipahi*s, 234*n*15
Slaves: redemption of, 54, 108, 144, 148, 156, 197–98; English, 61, 63, 180; as fugitives, 198
Smith, Captain, 89
Smith, John, 89
Smuggling: during Cretan war, 75; of grains, 79; in Izmir, 80, 106; punishments for, 107, 139
Smyrna. *See* Izmir
Soranzo, 111, 151, 152, 154, 162
Soreson, David, 129
Soreson, Isaac, 129
Sources: English and Ottoman compared, 10–12, 225*n*24; nature of, 39; Ottoman, 85, 226*n*26, 244*n*24; English, 136–37, 145, 148; Venetian, 148. *See also* Historiography
South, John, 134, 136, 150–52, 165, 169, 177, 181, 183–84, 258*n*58
Spahee (ship), 53
Spain, 6, 126, 159, 179, 192, 195, 197, 204, 255*n*7, 266*n*4
Spices: routes, 21, 37; investments in, 47, 214. *See also* Commerce; Commodities
Steeple Bumpstead, 99
Stevens, John, 101
Stevens, Taylor, 173, 174, 175–76, 258*n*58

Stow-on-the-Wold, 71
Stringer, Edward, 46, 48
Stuart, House of, 14, 24. *See also* James I; Charles I; Charles II
Sublime Porte: role of, in seizure of goods, 5, 74–77, 81, 109, 267*n*17; and English ambassadors, 9, 62, 90, 91, 93, 98, 115, 123, 189; and provinces, 11, 20, 21, 30–31, 40, 42–44, 59, 81, 107, 124, 126, 137, 138, 139, 174; definition of aliens by, 22; and consumption of alcohol, 35; failures of, 38; appointments by, 39; petitions to, 58, 78, 121, 167; and smuggling, 60–61; and alleged corruption, 85, 104, 167; and Bendysh, 99, 110–11, 114, 116, 124, 137, 142–43, 145–47, 156, 160, 180, 181, 185, 191–93; and ships, 104, 105, 147, 148–49, 150–55, 156, 157, 180, 183; policy of, 120, 150, 172, 178, 184, 197, 199; and Ottoman subjects, 126, 127, 216–17. *See also* Istanbul; Ottoman Empire; Viziers
Successor States, Ottoman, 11, 19, 225*n*22
Suda, Castle of, 154
Süleyman I (1520–66), 34
Surat, 210
Sweden, 101–2
Swift, John, 121
Syria: conquest of, 20; travels in, 23, 216; and central government, 31
Syrian Tripoli, 21, 29

Talbot, George, 68–71, 74
Talbot, Richard, 117
Tallent (ship), 56, 162

Tarakee, 128
Taverns: in Galata, 35; in Izmir, 39, 82; English in, 143–44, 145
Taxes: on goods, 17, 63, 64, 99, 105, 106–7, 153, 191, 197; Ottoman corporate, 19; for anchorage, 27; relief from, 33, 160, 184; as fines, 107, 140–41, 177, 208, 217–18; English, 186–87
Taxfarming, 78, 108. *See also* Customs collectors
Terrick, Nicolas, 82, 83, 144
Textiles: and English trade, 15, 107, 197; as commodity, 32, 45, 47, 131–32; surcharges on, 75
*Tezkere*s, 80
Theroux, Paul, 213
Thomas (ship), 143
Thomas and William (ship), 151, 155
Thorntone, Lazaro, 133
Thirty Years War, 68
Thurloe, John, 188, 194, 195–96, 197, 199, 201, 207
Thwaytes, Richard, 99
Timone, Domenico, 85–86, 92, 101
Tin, 15
Tiverton, 70
Toma, Hoggia, 47–51
Topkapı Palace, 113–14, 165–66
Tower of London, 66, 67, 99, 121, 123, 157, 164
Trabzon, 29, 32
Trade. *See* Commerce
Transliteration, xiv
Transylvania, 217
Treasurer, English, 107–8
Trednocks, William, 144
Trenchfield, Captain, 168–69
Tripoli, 155, 196, 233–34*n*13
Tristan und Isolde, 212
Trumbull, Lord, 245*n*32

Tunis, 144, 155, 156
Turkey. *See* Ottoman Empire
Turkish/Ottoman language, 84, 86, 96, 127, 166, 195, 216
Turks, 39, 40, 54, 55, 58, 61, 62, 75, 81, 83, 103, 118, 134, 135, 144, 174, 180, 191–93, 203, 216, 218, 224*n*18. *See also* Muslims
Tuscany: Grand Duke of, 184, 186, 198; coasts of, 204

Ulema, 25
Unicorn (ship), 54, 101, 105, 106
United States, 212
Useph, Isaak, 130
Üsküdar, 34

Valide Sultan, 165
Vaughan, Dorothy M., 9
Venice: relations with Ottoman government of, 11, 15, 21, 52, 69, 73, 105, 114, 115, 117, 244*n*24; commerce of, 13, 16, 24, 37, 52; consuls of, 14–15; relations with Ottoman subjects of, 20, 50, 104, 127, 129, 144; and Ottoman port cities, 22, 30, 38, 40, 232*n*28; subjects of, in Galata, 22, 33, 35; and Cretan War, 49, 61, 75–76, 77, 79, 104, 112, 118–20, 140, 147–57 passim, 169, 172, 176, 178, 180, 182, 183, 184, 192, 193, 196, 197, 199, 200; Senate of, 52; negotiations with England of, 68–70, 153, 155, 160, 161, 184–85, 191–93, 201, 204, 205; and Britons, 98, 111, 116, 126, 131, 162, 177, 195, 216; sources from, 148
Vernon, Francis, 92
Vernon, George, 96, 105, 112,
244*n*28
Vestizza, 62
Vienna, 193, 200
Villeroy, Nicolo, 62
Virgin Mary, Church of the, 217
Vivyan, Roger, 121
Viziers: described, 17, 118, 119, 246*n*57; and Britons, 27, 61, 84, 92, 188, 191, 203, 219, 244*n*28; commands from, 58–59; role in seizure of goods and people, 72, 74–78, 80, 114, 116, 133, 172–73; as administrators, 86; gifts to, 99, 117, 127–28, 162; and Bendysh, 109, 111, 115, 138–39, 141, 147–48, 149–50, 151, 154, 156, 168–69, 176, 178, 182, 189, 198, 246*n*52; and French, 110, 183–84; depositions of, 112, 153, 165, 172, 183, 193; appointments of, 142, 200; and Hyde, 161, 164, 166, 169, 172. *See also* Pashas
Voyvoda, 4, 22, 52, 63–64, 150, 167, 218, 234*n*13, 245*n*29
Vuedall, William, 48

Wachill, Abraham, 132
Warfare: between Ottomans and Venetians, 15, 37, 61, 75, 104, 112, 118–19, 140, 148–50, 150–53, 193, 197; between English and Dutch, 184, 186–87, 189, 191–92, 198, 234*n*15; Ottoman, 208
Warren, Samuel, 198
West: influence of, 22; characteristics of, 28, 212–13
Western Design, 192, 262*n*65
West Indies, 7, 192
Whitcomb, Benjamin, 89
White, William, 155–56, 190
Wight, Isle of, 97

William and Thomas (ship), 77, 79
Williams, Philip, 102
Winchelsea, Heneage Finch, Earl of, 201–8, 210, 217–18, 243*n*13
Wine: as commodity, 32; consumption of, 35, 47
Wolfe, John, 75
Women: in Ottoman Empire, 26, 27, 120–21, 144–45, 192; sultanate of, 195; on frontiers, 226*n*25, 238*n*29
Wood, Alfred, 9
Worcester, 168
World War II, 5
Wyche, James, 121, 131
Wyche, Peter, 15, 42, 72–73, 78, 126–27
Wylde, John, 74, 79, 89, 136, 137, 138–40, 149, 161, 169, 170–71

Yachiel the Cape, 128
Yami, Abram, 129
Yarmouth, 99
Yasakçı, 17
Yemamo, Isaak, 128
York, Duke of, 157

Zagreb, 32
Zante, 52, 53, 205, 215, 216, 234*n*15
Zia, 153
Zuma, 74–85